MARCUS AURELIUS

MARCUS AURELIUS

A BIOGRAPHY

ANTHONY BIRLEY

BARNES
&NOBLE
BOOKS

NEW YORK

First published in 1966. Expanded, updated, and reillustrated
edition published in 1987.

This edition published by Barnes & Noble, Inc.,
by arrangement with Routledge

1999 Barnes & Noble Books

ISBN: 0-7607-1186-0

Printed and bound in the United States of America

05 06 07 M 10 9 8 7 6 5 4 3 2

BVG

Contents

The Illustrations

Preface

MARCUS AURELIUS is one of the best recorded individuals from antiquity. Even his face became more than usually familiar: the imperial coinage displayed his portrait for over forty years, from the clean-shaven young heir of Antoninus to the war-weary, heavily bearded ruler who died at his post in his late fifties. For his childhood and early youth we depend largely on anecdote and reconstruction. Then in the correspondence of his tutor Fronto, spanning nearly three decades, we have a series of vivid and revealing glimpses into the family life and preoccupations of Marcus and the court. But what made Marcus Aurelius a household name was the private notebook that he kept in his last ten years, the *Meditations*. The 'philosopher in the purple' has never lacked admirers, ancient or modern. Critics are hard to find – although the author of the *Historia Augusta* was able to invent a notable one, in his fictional life of Avidius Cassius. Gibbon (in 1783) paid sober tribute to a man 'severe to himself, indulgent to the imperfection of others, just and beneficent to all mankind.' Eighty years later, Matthew Arnold – inspired by reading a new English version of the *Meditations* – was unrestrained: 'The acquaintance of a man like Marcus Aurelius is an imperishable benefit'. Marcus was 'perhaps the most beautiful figure in history. . . . Besides him, history presents one or two other sovereigns eminent for their goodness, such as Saint Louis or Alfred. But Marcus Aurelius has, for us moderns, this great superiority in interest over Saint Louis or Alfred, that he lived and acted in a state of society modern by its essential characteristics, in an epoch akin to our own, in a brilliant centre of civilisation. . . . By its accents of emotion . . . the morality of Marcus Aurelius acquires a special character . . . [his] sentences find their way to the soul . . . it is this very admixture of sweetness with his dignity which makes him so beautiful a moralist. It enables him to carry even into his observation of nature a delicate penetration, a sympathetic tenderness, worthy of Wordsworth.' Walter Pater made the hero of his 'novel' *Marius the Epicurean* (1885) – who became the emperor's secretary – a peg on which to hang a set elaborate essays on Antonine Rome, in which the serene Aurelius figures prominently. Meanwhile, Ernest Renan devoted the eighth and last volume of his *Histoire des Origines du Christianisme* to Marcus – 'and the end of the ancient world'. Christianity receives much more attention than the emperor in his pages; and he was at pains to defend the reputation of the beautiful and fertile Faustina and to discuss the paradox of Marcus' degenerate heir Commodus. Gibbon could not use Fronto's letters, Arnold was interested almost solely in the *Meditations*. But Gibbon, Pater and Renan alike – it is unfortunate – swallowed whole the fictional parts of the *Historia Augusta*. The unmasking of the author of that curious work was to begin with Hermann Dessau in 1889 and the task of decontaminating the source continues – spurious items, notably from the *Aelius* and *Avidius Cassius*, still infect serious scholarship.

My own approach to Marcus began with the Marcomannic wars, under the guidance of Sir Ronald Syme, whose first advice to me was to read Dessau's fundamental study of the *HA*. If Marcus seemed modern to a mid-Victorian, he might seem less so now. Yet the wars – which were the catalyst for the *Meditations* – shattered that charmed, golden, civilised Antonine tranquillity. The invasions of Italy and Greece by northern 'barbarians' marked the end of an era: Marcus' wars in central Europe recall 1914–18, it may be claimed. And, whatever the intentions of the artists who portrayed the campaigns on the Aurelian column, the horror and pathos they evoke match the mood of the *Meditations*, in which war is scarcely mentioned.

I first published a book on Marcus twenty years ago (*Marcus Aurelius*: Eyre & Spottiswoode, London; Little Brown, Boston, 1966), now long out of print. Readers will wish to know its relationship to the present work. I have retained the structure and much of the text. The appendices, notes, bibliography and illustrations are entirely new; considerable parts of each chapter have been amended and enlarged. I have benefited a great deal from the work of others (registered in the Notes and in Appendix 1). The complex web of family connections which formed the Antonine dynasty is now much better understood (although there is room for debate); and the order of birth of the numerous children of Marcus and Faustina – at least fourteen – is now better known (these details are summarised in Appendix 2 and the six stemmata). I have taken into account recent research on the Greek intellectual renaissance, on Fronto, and on the emerging Christians (Appendix 4). There has been some welcome new epigraphic evidence for the wars (Appendix 3). But I must stress that this is a biography, not a 'life and times'. I have seen my task as the simple one of recording Marcus' life as accurately as possible, setting him in his context, and allowing him to speak for himself – especially in Chapter 10. If this helps readers of the *Meditations* to understand their author better I shall be content.

No one can write a book of this kind without incurring a multitude of debts. I hope that what I owe to published work is properly registered in the notes and bibliography; but I should like to pay special tribute to C.R. Haines and A.S.L. Farquharson. Four of those whose help I gratefully acknowledged twenty years back are now gone, but not forgotten: Donald Dudley, John Morris, Hans-Georg Pflaum, Erich Swoboda. I continue to benefit from the advice and encouragement of Géza Alföldy, Eric Birley, Jaroslav Šašel, Armin Stylow and Ronald Syme.

ANTHONY BIRLEY
Manchester
10 June 1986

NOTE TO PAPERBACK IMPRESSION

I have taken the opportunity afforded by a reprint to add a list of recent publications (p. 296), with brief comment on their relevance in most cases.

ANTHONY BIRLEY
Friedberg
8 January 1993

· I ·

THE AGE OF
THE ANTONINES

'IF A MAN were called to fix the period in the history of the world during which the condition of the human race was most happy and prosperous, he would, without hesitation, name that which elapsed from the death of Domitian to the accession of Commodus.'

So wrote Edward Gibbon of the 'happy period of more than four-score years,' from AD 96–180, during which the Roman empire was ruled by the 'Five Good Emperors' – Nerva, Trajan, Hadrian, Antoninus Pius and Marcus Aurelius. Marcus' own life (121–80) spanned almost three-quarters of this epoch while his reign (161–80) occupied its last nineteen years. It was in describing Marcus' death, and the accession of his son Commodus, that Cassius Dio, born soon after Marcus' accession, wrote: 'My history now descends from a kingdom of gold to a kingdom of iron and rust, as affairs did for the Romans at that time.'[1]

The 'five good emperors' were individuals of widely differing character and training. One factor linked them: none was the son of his predecessor. Hence it seemed to some contemporary observers and to many subsequent commentators, including Gibbon, that a new principle was then governing the imperial succession: 'the adoption of the best man'. In fact there was no principle or conscious policy at work. All but Marcus had no son to succeed him, and in any case kinship linked Trajan and Hadrian, Pius and Marcus.

In his first work, the biography of his father-in-law Agricola, written at the outset of the new era, Tacitus voices the relief of the senate that their time of servitude was over: 'Now at last our spirits revive.' Nerva had succeeded Domitian, assassinated in 96, and had achieved the impossible: the principate and liberty could co-exist. Tacitus' contemporary, Pliny, expatiated at far greater length, a few years later, on the change which had begun that year. It was no longer necessary to flatter the ruler as though he were a god; he contrasted the humanity, frugality, clemency, generosity, kindness, self-restraint, industriousness and bravery of Trajan, who followed Nerva in 98, with the pride, luxury, cruelty, spitefulness, lust, inactivity and cowardice of Domitian. Tacitus and Pliny were speaking for the senate. To the provincial bourgeoisie and peasantry, on the other hand, the personality of the emperor did not perhaps matter very much. The wayward general Petillius Cerialis is made by Tacitus to remind an assembly of Gallic rebels in AD 70: *saevi proximis ingruunt*, savage emperors vent their spleen on those closest to them – the senators at Rome – and the average inhabitant of the provinces does not suffer. Besides, bad emperors often had good advisers (as Trajan is once supposed to have remarked).

The favourable verdict of history on 'the Golden Century of the Antonines' depends largely on the fact that senators felt more secure when the emperor was 'one of us', as Pliny put it, and behaved as a fellow-senator. This was a kind of safeguard. At any rate, since most Roman historians and biographers were members of the senate or linked with that order in their sympathies, the dominant theme of Roman imperial historical writing was the relationship between the emperor and the senate.[2]

To understand more clearly why this was so, it is worth looking back at the origins of the imperial system. Rome had been dominated by one man before, at various stages in the history of the republic, but autocracy began with the victory of Octavian at Actium in 31 BC. Octavian cunningly and wisely concealed his powers, or at least did not flaunt them. This disarmed opposition and allowed his opponents to preserve a semblance of self-respect. After years of civil war men were anxious for stability. His remarkable talent for survival (forty-four years' sole rule) allowed the innovations which he had introduced gradually, at every stage appealing to ancient precedent and feeling his way, to harden.

By Augustus' death, Rome was in effect an empire, however much his successor Tiberius tried to disguise it. Exactly when the republic had ceased and the empire had begun was not so obvious. Writing during Tiberius' reign, Velleius Paterculus, one of the 'new men' favoured by the new system, felt able to say complacently that Augustus had merely 'recalled to existence the pristine and ancient constitution of the republic'. Augustus wanted to appear as no more than *primus inter pares*. But the man who began life as plain C. Octavius was much more than that.

He had first changed his name to C. Julius Caesar Octavianus when posthumously adopted by the assassinated dictator Julius Caesar. Through the efforts of Antony and others, Caesar was proclaimed a god, or something very like one, and this enabled Caesar's heir to draw attention to his unique ancestry – 'Imperator Caesar divi filius' (son of the deified). *Imperator*, once a title for all Roman commanders, had become a special title of honour, used after their names by generals whose soldiers had thus hailed them at a victory. Octavian abusively turned the title into a kind of name, giving up Gaius – and Julius too, for Caesar now became his family name. In 27 BC the senate granted him a further name by which he became generally known: Imperator Caesar divi filius *Augustus*. In 23 BC Augustus received the 'tribunician power', which gave him wide powers of interference in a multitude of spheres. Other powers and honours followed at various stages in his long life.[3]

Augustus recognized that he could not survive unless he allowed the senate, once the supreme arbiter of Roman destinies, to participate in his rule – indeed, he could not do without senators. The old magistracies of the republic continued. He himself held the consulship thirteen times, and one or two of his close associates whom he wished to mark out with special honour also became consul more than once. To satisfy the aspirations of ordinary senators, whose ambition remained the tenure of the *fasces*, he regularized the institution of the suffect consulship, established originally to replace consuls who had died or been removed from office. The *consules ordinarii*, who gave their names to the year, now resigned before completing their year of office to make way for *suffecti*. This practice greatly increased in subsequent years.

Entry into the senate (a body nominally 600 strong) was hereditary, but suitable persons with the requisite property qualification of one million sesterces could apply for the *latus clavus*, the broad stripe of the senator's toga. This allowed them to enter the senate through election as quaestor at the age of twenty-four or twenty-five, after preliminary service in minor magistracies (and with the army). Thereafter they could climb the ladder of the senatorial *cursus*, becoming aedile or tribune of the people, praetor, and, finally, consul. Patricians, the hereditary aristocracy (enlarged by Augustus and some of his successors), could move direct from quaestor to praetor and could become consul at thirty-two, ten years earlier than the rest. The patricians had more chance of becoming consul *ordinarius*. But very few were consul more than once.

Alongside the old magistracies a new career developed. If they chose, senators could ignore the emperor's existence, serve only as magistrates at Rome and as proconsuls of provinces administered in the old republican way. But Augustus and his successors governed a vast *provincia*, virtually all the provinces which had armies and many others besides, and could also interfere in the 'senatorial' provinces. The imperial provinces and armies were administered and commanded by the emperor's deputies, *legati*, and a career in the emperor's service formed the real basis of the senatorial hierarchy, with the ancient republican magistracies merely stepping-stones, formal stages of qualification for further advancement. Some provinces were not given to senators to administer, for various reasons, but to knights, members of the next highest order in the state, who had the title of procurator or prefect. Other new offices grew up in Rome – for example, prefectures of the treasuries, and of the city of Rome, for senators: of the corn-supply, the city-police and the praetorian guard for knights.[4]

At Rome, Augustus had to keep up 'republican' appearances. In the provinces, he was worshipped as king and god, and his family were sacred. 'It is not necessary to praise political success or to idealize the men who win

31 BC	*September* 2: Octavian, great-nephew of Julius Caesar, gains sole power after defeat of Antony at Actium
27 BC	Octavian given name AUGUSTUS
23 BC	Augustus given *tribunicia potestas*
AD 4	Augustus adopts stepson Tiberius Claudius Nero, who becomes Tiberius Julius Caesar
14	TIBERIUS succeeds to Augustus' position on latter's death
37	GAIUS ('CALIGULA'), great-nephew of Tiberius, great-grandson of Augustus, succeeds Tiberius on latter's death
41	Murder of Caligula. His uncle CLAUDIUS proclaimed emperor
54	NERO, stepson of Claudius, nephew of Caligula, great-great-grandson of Augustus, succeeds Claudius on latter's death
68	*June* 6: Suicide of Nero after revolts in western provinces. GALBA recognized as emperor
69	*January* 2–3: VITELLIUS proclaimed emperor by Rhine armies
	January 15: OTHO instigates murder of Galba and is proclaimed emperor at Rome
	April 15: Vitellius' army defeats that of Otho in N. Italy
	July 1–3: VESPASIAN proclaimed emperor by eastern armies
	October 27–28: Defeat of Vitellius' forces in N. Italy
	December 20: Vitellius killed at Rome
79	Death of Vespasian, succeeded by elder son TITUS
81	Death of Titus, succeeded by younger brother DOMITIAN
96	*September* 18: Murder of Domitian at Rome. NERVA made emperor
97	*October*: Nerva adopts Trajan as his son
98	*January* 28: TRAJAN succeeds on death of Nerva
117	HADRIAN, after ostensible death-bed adoption, succeeds his cousin Trajan
136	*Spring or early summer*: Hadrian adopts L. Ceionius Commodus, who becomes L. Aelius Caesar
138	*January* 1: Death of L. Aelius Caesar
	February 25: Hadrian adopts T. Aurelius Antoninus, who becomes T. Aelius Hadrianus Antoninus and adopts Marcus and L. Commodus junior
	July 10: ANTONINUS succeeds on Hadrian's death
161	*March* 7: MARCUS succeeds on death of Antoninus (Pius), jointly with L. Commodus junior who becomes L. VERUS
169	*January*: Death of L. Verus
177	Marcus' only surviving son COMMODUS made joint emperor
180	*March* 17: Death of Marcus, COMMODUS sole emperor
192	*December* 31: Commodus murdered
193	*January* 1: PERTINAX proclaimed emperor
	March 28: Pertinax murdered, DIDIUS JULIANUS proclaimed emperor (Rome)
	April 9: SEPTIMIUS SEVERUS proclaimed emperor (Danube)
	June 1: Julianus killed at Rome
197	*February* 19: Defeat of Severus' last rival, at Lyon
211	*February* 4: Death of Severus at York

TABLE 1 Roman Emperors from Augustus to Severus

wealth and honours through civil war.'[5] At his death in AD 14 almost everyone did – a few through fear, but most inhabitants of the empire from a sense of awe, admiration and gratitude for the stability which he had created, or allowed to form. Augustus was deified by decree of the senate. So had Julius Caesar been. But although Augustus had at first used the 'deified Julius' to further his own plans, the memory of the murdered dictator had not been unduly emphasised at a later stage. 'Divus Augustus', with his college of priests, his temple and the festivals to commemorate significant days in his earthly life, played a profound role in the subsequent history of the Roman Empire: his successors were assessed in large measure in comparison with him. All his successors (except Tiberius and Vitellius) used his three names, Imperator Caesar Augustus, as part of their official style, and with some modifications their powers were those which he had gradually built up during his long decades of ascendancy.[6]

Tiberius, thanks to his stepfather Augustus' grudging and unwilling use of him, was by far the most distinguished Roman of his day at his accession: he had been consul more often, had commanded more armies and provinces than his peers, and was son by adoption of Augustus, sharing enough of his special powers to make the succession inevitable. He lacked Augustus' pliable qualities (the qualities of a chameleon, the emperor Julian was to call them), and was never popular with the senate, indeed by the time of his death in 37 he was generally feared and hated; and he was not deified. His successor was his grand-nephew, Augustus' great-grandson, Gaius 'Caligula'. Caligula had no other claim to be *Princeps* except his Julian blood: he was only twenty-four and had no higher rank than that of quaestor. This made the autocracy obvious; and Caligula went on to exaggerate even further the concept of 'divine kingship'.

When Caligula was murdered in 41, there was an abortive attempt to restore the republic, but the imperial bodyguard discovered another member of the 'divine family', Claudius, uncle of Caligula, who was a laughing-stock to the aristocracy through his personal failings and dominated by his wives and freed slaves. Under him the autocracy and the bureaucracy increased their powers. Claudius was succeeded in 54 by his sixteen-year-old stepson Nero, who began his rule with professions of deference to the senate, sedulously instilled into him by his tutor and minister Seneca. But soon his behaviour became intolerable to the senate – *saevi proximis ingruunt*. Eventually Nero took fright at a rebellion in Gaul, and, deserted by the praetorian guards, committed suicide in the summer of 68.[7]

There was no attempt to restore the republic now, some ninety-eight years after the battle of Actium. The aim of all parties in the civil war of 68–69 seems to have been (in principle at least) to return to the harmonious state of affairs that had prevailed under Augustus. In 69, the year of the four emperors, the premium on birth fell sharply with successive occupants of the throne – and the secret had already been revealed 'that emperors could be made elsewhere than at Rome'. Vespasian, the eventual victor, was a parvenu. Paradoxically, his having two sons was regarded by some of his supporters as a point in his favour: he could found a dynasty which would, it was thought, stabilize the succession. Opposition from senators influenced by the ideals of Stoic philosophy was stifled. Vespasian refused to allow his powers to be limited and was determined that his sons should succeed him. He was duly succeeded by Titus at his death in 79, and Titus two years later by his younger brother Domitian. Vespasian and Titus had been efficient and popular emperors, and they had cultivated the support of the senate. Domitian, who had been a youth in his late teens at his father's accession, had a suspicious and sensitive personality. As he had never been a normal member of the senate, he had little sympathy with senatorial feeling. He was competent, even talented, as a ruler or administrator, but opposition was provoked by his behaviour (for instance, his insistence on being addressed as 'Lord and God', and his holding the consulship ten times as emperor out of a maximum possible of fifteen). His rule ended with a reign of terror, and he was murdered in September 96.[8]

His successor, Nerva, had not had a very creditable past – he had been an agent of Nero, and then had been honoured by Vespasian and Domitian, for no very obvious reason, except that he was well-connected and, surely, a useful counsellor of the Flavian emperors. In 97 opposition to Nerva became open and his position in grave danger. The situation was saved when he adopted as his son and heir the governor of Upper Germany, M. Ulpius Traianus, who became emperor in his own right on Nerva's death early in 98.

Trajan, a provincial, had been made a patrician as a young man by Vespasian in recognition of his father's services to the new dynasty. He had served Domitian loyally, as had others of his class like Agricola, also a neo-patrician of provincial extraction, whose biography Tacitus had written to demonstrate that good men could exist and perform worthy deeds even under bad emperors. At the death of Domitian a good deal of cant had been talked about opposition to the tyranny: there had in fact been the Stoic group of senators who had suffered 'martyrdom' under Nero and the Flavians. But most of the senate had knuckled under. Trajan became a hero to virtually everyone – a conqueror abroad, he respected senators at home (for example, he was consul only four times in his reign of twenty years, which was but one of the many studied contrasts to Domitian). The senate gave him the title *Optimus* – best of emperors. His name became a proverb for centuries, for he seemed to fulfil everyone's ideals.

Hadrian, a cousin of Trajan and married to his grand-niece, was the natural choice to succeed, but the succession was not made obvious. Trajan died in the east in August 117 and Hadrian, commanding the Syrian army, had no difficulty whatever in gaining the adherence of the troops. But he did not have time to wait for the senate's approval, and within a short time of his accession a number of leading senators, including some of Trajan's closest collaborators, were put to death. On his arrival in Rome Hadrian clearly had met some suspicion and hostility, and although he tried hard to regain the senate's favour, the manner in which his reign opened was never forgotten or forgiven.[9]

Hadrian was a tremendous organizer and systematizer. Trajan's final conquests (in the east) were abandoned, and he reverted to the ultimate policy of Augustus of avoiding further expansion. He was outside Italy for most of his reign, visiting the provinces and armies and reorganizing the frontier defences of the new empire, one of the most celebrated results of which is the wall that bears his name in Britain.[10]

Hadrian's reign gave the empire a breathing-space. Efficiency was increased. By now the imperial household which had administered so many important departments of state had given way to a regular equestrian 'civil service' in which knights could have as varied and important a career as senators continued to have in their own sphere. For a knight, the summit was still – as it had been for a hundred years – the prefecture of the praetorian guard. Below this were the other great prefectures – of Egypt, of the city-police (the *vigiles*), and of the corn-supply (*annona*), the financial department (*a rationibus*), the Secretariat (*ab epistulis*) and similar offices in Rome itself, and appointments as financial procurator throughout the empire and as presidial procurator (i.e. governor) in a number of provinces. Entry into the service was controlled solely by the emperor, but there seem to have been various standard means of starting on the ladder. Some men obtained commissions as regimental commanders of auxiliary units, others began as praetorian guardsmen, obtained a centurion's commission, and then after further military service became procurators; a few, such as the writer Suetonius (who was *ab epistulis* early in Hadrian's reign), seem to have entered the higher grade directly without prior military service.[11]

The major strength of the army lay in the legions, and these were all commanded by senators, with the exception of the two in Egypt. At any one moment some twenty-eight senators would be legionary legates. Most would be men in their thirties, and some of these would be governing a province simultaneously. In provinces where there was more than one legion, the governor was an ex-consul, hence generally in his forties or older. A few key provinces had as many as three legions – Britain, Syria, Upper Pannonia and Lower Moesia. The British and Syrian commands, in more isolated positions than were the Danubian armies, required a correspondingly greater degree of responsibility. Hence the governors of Britain and Syria were usually the two outstanding generals of their day.[12]

But the military senators – the *viri militares* – were not the only figures of influence. Indeed, as they were away from the centre of affairs for long

① GERMANIA INFERIOR
② GERMANIA SUPERIOR
③ LYCIA et PAMPHYLIA
④ MOESIA INFERIOR
⑤ PANNONIA INFERIOR
⑥ PANNONIA SUPERIOR
⑦ SYRIA PALAESTINA

——— Frontier
‑ ‑ ‑ Provincial boundary

0

0

The Roman Empire During the Lifetime of Marcus Aurelius

getusa
Danube
④
RACIA
HIBERI
Phasis
Artaxata
ca
Byzantium
Chalcedon
Nicaea
PONTUS et
BITHYNIA
ARMENIA
Cyzicus
ASIA
GALATIA
CAPPADOCIA
Smyrna
Edessa
Ephesus
③
CILICIA
Cyrrhus
P A R T H I A
hens
Antioch
Tigris
Euphrates
SYRIA
Ctesiphon
Seleucia
CYPRUS
Palmyra
⑦
Alexandria
ARABIA
ENE
AEGYPTUS
Nile
500 Miles
300 Km

periods their voice was often not of much weight in imperial councils. For although the emperor of Rome was still – even increasingly – an autocrat, importance was attached to the opinions of the senate and, by the reign of Hadrian, even more to the emperor's Privy Council – the *consilium principis*. This had grown up gradually (like most Roman institutions) from the time of Augustus, and its members – the emperor's friends, *amici Caesaris* – must have played an important role in influencing policy decisions. Unfortunately, as more than one ancient writer complained, from the end of the republic policy was decided in secret and few significant details are preserved of the discussions where the real business of policy-making was carried on.[13]

The emperor's power rested ultimately on his control of the armies. He also controlled the finances of the state, whatever legal fictions there might have been to assert the senate's share in this. He was the source of rewards both titular and financial. Legates and procurators, legionaries and auxiliaries, were all paid by him. A legionary in the reign of Augustus received 225 denarii a year (it had risen to 300 by Hadrian's day). The senator's property-qualification was more than one thousand times as great as this (one million sesterces or 250,000 denarii). In fact, a procurator eager and able to obtain entry to the senate could soon accumulate the required wealth many times over. The lowest grade of procurators were paid 60,000 sesterces a year, and higher grades were paid at 100,000, 200,000, and – eventually – 300,000. Senatorial salaries in imperial service were higher (and there were many ways of increasing one's earnings). To translate this into modern terms would be meaningless. But the legionaries, on their retirement from the service, were reckoned among the better-off members of society.[14]

The empire ruled by Hadrian was a cosmopolitan world-state, with a varied polyglot population. But there were only two official languages, Latin in the west and Greek in the east. The highest orders in the state were bilingual, and educated Romans of Latin-speaking descent looked increasingly to Greek language and culture. Theorists liked to see the empire as a confederation of city-states, fulfilling the aspirations of the great age of Greek history. This was a myth; but the civilization of the empire was basically urban. The communities of the empire were granted considerable autonomy in local government, although by the second century AD this was coming to be regarded as a burden by the town bourgeoisie and provincial landed gentry who had to reach into their own pockets to support their home towns. In the west city-life was something new, but under Hadrian townbuilding was flourishing even in Britain, and Gaul had for some while been very Romanized. Spain was one of Rome's oldest provinces and, as the home of Trajan and Hadrian, was, not surprisingly, well up to the level of Italy in its social and economic development. The North African provinces had a brilliant city-life along the coast. Morocco was less civilized and the mountains in the south of Mauretania were the home of brigands who constantly disturbed the peace of both Mauretania and Spain. Nevertheless, both the Iberian peninsula and North Africa were deemed sufficiently protected by the presence of one legion each, stationed in Tarraconensis and Numidia respectively. This garrison was, of course, supplemented by the presence of non-citizen auxiliary regiments in substantial numbers. The Gallic provinces also were undefended by legions. But there were three legions in Britain and four in the two Rhineland provinces of Upper and Lower Germany. In Numidia, Upper Germany and Britain abundant traces of Hadrian's activity as a renovator of imperial frontier-defences have been discovered.

The hinge which bound the western and eastern parts of the empire together was the area north of the Alps, notably the provinces of Upper and Lower Pannonia, with three legions and one legion respectively. The two Moesian provinces formed a military zone right along the Danube to the Black Sea; and from the time of Trajan's conquests the Dacian provinces formed a great bastion to the north of the river. Dalmatia was a province of contrasts: the Adriatic coast, opposite Italy, had a brilliant city-life; inland the country was mountainous and wild. The rest of the empire was Greek in language and culture, but as with Latin in the Celtic, Iberian and Berber lands, this was in many areas merely a superficial veneer. Nevertheless, Achaea and Macedonia and the province of Asia were thoroughly Hellenic, with cities that had flourished when Rome was a village. Thrace and Bithynia, Pontus, Lycia-Pamphylia, Cilicia, Galatia, Cappadocia, Syria, Palestine, Arabia, all had benefited in some degree from the presence, before Rome absorbed them, of Greek and Hellenistic settlers. Egypt was in a special category. Only Alexandria was a true city – the next after Rome itself in size – but it was denied local autonomy, and it and the province of Egypt were ruled as the emperor's personal fief through his Viceroy, the Prefect, and a civil service which followed closely the bureaucratic pattern laid down by the Ptolemies.[15]

The empire had enemies of various kinds. Britain, Spain and Morocco were disturbed by brigands, but the damage they inflicted was essentially local. The long river-frontier in the north was more vulnerable: the 'cordon-system' of frontier control is unsatisfactory in many ways, as Napoleon and others have pointed out.[16] The Teutonic tribes of northern and central Europe were often restless, as were their eastern neighbours, of whom the Sarmatians are the best-known, particularly the Jazyges of the Hungarian Plain. Trajan's creation of a province of Dacia had helped to solve the problem of frontier control in the Lower Danube region, but it had created tensions as well. Rome aimed to stifle possible threats by exercising a protectorate over the peoples which bordered her frontiers. The system of 'client-states' in treaty-relationship with the emperor provided Rome with 'invisible frontiers' which stretched far beyond the tangible barriers of the empire.

In the east, the problem was different. In the Parthian Empire Rome had a potential adversary of apparently much higher calibre than the disunited tribes to her north. The Parthians too were loosely-knit, but the conquests of Alexander had extended Hellenic civilization far beyond the Tigris, and in any case the Parthian kings were the inheritors of a Mesopotamian civilization stretching back for several millennia. The main bone of contention between Rome and Parthia was the kingdom of Armenia which each wished to dominate. But Mesopotamia too was sometimes coveted by Rome. The client-state system was used extensively on the eastern frontiers: Rome found it profitable to have allies as far away as the Caucasus; and the Black Sea was virtually a Roman preserve, for the Greek cities of its coasts were under careful supervision.[17]

Augustus had apparently expanded the empire to its natural limits. A number of additions had been made by his successors, but Hadrian gave up Trajan's eastern conquests – Armenia, Mesopotamia, Assyria – and concentrated on making the empire a viable, secure and flourishing concern. In this he evidently succeeded, for he was reaping the harvest sown in the first century. The Hellenized provinces of the east, after long decades of civil peace, were richer than ever before. The rougher west, even distant Britain, now began to enjoy the fruits of the Roman peace. The whole world could lay down its arms as if at festival time, the fulsome young East Greek orator Aelius Aristides could proclaim, six years after Hadrian's death. The cities of the empire had no other concern, he said, but to adorn themselves with public buildings – gymnasia, fountains, arches, temples, workshops, schools. They gleamed with radiance and grace. The earth was now indeed the common mother of all men. An encamped army ringed the world like a rampart, from the inhabited part of Ethiopia in the south to the Phasis in the north, from the Euphrates in the east 'to the great outermost island towards the west'. He might equally have said, with more precision, that from the Upper Nile to the Don, from the Euphrates to the Clyde, from the Sahara to the Rhine, the Danube and Transylvania, the Roman law and the Roman peace prevailed. War was a thing of the past. Rome alone of great empires had ruled such a vast area, and she alone ruled with equity and restraint.[18]

Not everyone profited. Aristides spoke for the upper classes. And the economic system was based on slavery. Many, even the better-off, sought escape from a somewhat soulless materialism in exotic new cults. The cultivated Pliny, on his arrival in Pontus-Bithynia, found that the temples of the ancestral gods were becoming deserted and neglected. The reason soon appeared. There was a sect called Christians – sober, decent people, he found, in spite of the monstrous allegations against them – who preferred their own private cult. Trajan told the governor that these people had to be punished, if, after proceedings had been initiated, they were found to be Christians – punished with death. This was not a new ruling. After the great fire at Rome, under Nero, it had probably become imperial policy that to be a confessed Christian was a capital offence. But Trajan told Pliny that these people should not be searched out. They should be left alone. If they were accused, confessed and refused to recant, the law had to take its course. This is remarkable judicial practice. But it seemed to work.

There were other exotic cults also, Egyptian and Oriental for the most part. Hadrian himself had been initiated into the ancient (and respectably classical) cult of the Mysteries of Eleusis. Others sought consolation in philosophy. What had once been a dangerous and expensive eccentricity or fad – even a deeply believed inner defence against despotism – could now be practised with decorum, publicly. Also, there arose crowds of bogus philosophers.[19]

In the fields of architecture and the plastic arts there was genuine achievement. The gleam of the cities has left its traces. The Hadrianic and Antonine architects and sculptors produced works of considerable grace and beauty, and left a permanent mark on the face of the empire, not least of Rome itself.

There is an air of the eighteenth century about the Antonine Empire. The aristocracy which had been ennobled in the struggles of the previous century wanted now to relax and enjoy their dignity and wealth. The provincial élite and the Italian municipal families had come to the top. Their worth was solid, and their possessions satisfyingly secure. The old aristocracy had almost disappeared. 'Freedom' had long been a catchword under the early principate. It never really denoted what the younger Cato had meant by it. 'Freedom' meant order, stability, regularity. An emperor was a necessity. If he preserved social distinctions and allowed the senate an honoured place in the state, all would be well. The new Roman aristocracy had no disturbing memories of ancient glories under the free republic. But they did prefer an enlightened autocracy to the grim, uneasy and suspicious days of Domitian. The Annii Veri, the Ceionii, the Vettuleni, and their peers, with their riches and their assured place in public life, gained by faithful service even under bad emperors, had come into their own. The virtues which Tacitus had praised in the *Agricola* had gained their reward. Also, it was now safe and fashionable to admire the valiant few who had dared to speak out against tyranny in the past, Thrasea Paetus, Helvidius Priscus – the Stoics. Tacitus had in fact preferred the example of the unrebellious but still untarnished Agricola. But both types could now be admired simultaneously.[20]

The society revealed by the letters of Pliny is contented and industrious, conscious of its own virtues. These men and women, and their imitators in the provinces, provided the gleam of the age of the Antonines. They were, many of them, of provincial origin, as were Trajan and Hadrian. But they did not see themselves as Spaniards or Gauls or Africans, except as an occasional affectation. They were Romans, and the leading Romans of their day. Greek culture was once more on the upsurge. But things Hellenic were permissible, in fact essential (in moderation) to an educated Roman. Hadrian, the restless cosmopolitan, went a little to extremes, in this as in other respects. One may register, for example, the fact that he sported a beard, thereby causing Roman men to abandon razors for the best part of a century. It was, there can be no doubt, a gesture by which he proclaimed his Hellenic allegiance, showed himself to be an intellectual. Meanwhile, wealthy men from the Greek provinces were themselves entering the senate in increasing numbers, in any case, adapting themselves with varying success or enthusiasm to the manners of Rome.[21]

Some of the friends and correspondents of Pliny undertook arduous work in the service of the emperor, governing his provinces and commanding his armies. Others lived in sedate but cultivated retirement. Others still could confine their public as well as their private life almost entirely to Rome and Italy. Those, in particular, who had the rank of patrician, did not need to do more, for patricians were assured of access at an early age to the ancient magistracies of Rome, which remained the principal aspiration of the upper class. Pliny obviously did not know personally (to his regret, perhaps) all the leading figures of his time. But his correspondence gives a remarkable picture of Roman high society in the last decade of the first and the first decade of the second centuries AD. Its self-satisfied and urbane atmosphere mirrors, more accurately than the sombre pages of Cornelius Tacitus, the world into which Marcus Aurelius was born.

The effect of the new stability on the literary world was not entirely happy. The early second century saw the genius of two of the greatest figures of Latin literature, Tacitus and Juvenal. They were also two of the last great Latin writers, and both were dead before Hadrian. There was also Suetonius, the young friend of Pliny. Pliny and Suetonius wrote unexceptionable prose, and are still widely read. But tastes were changing. There was a move back to the past, back to the days before Caesar Augustus had established his New Order. The emperor Hadrian's own tastes accorded well with this. In Greek literature he preferred Antimachus (of whom scarcely anyone had heard) to Homer. There were writers of some distinction in both Greek and Latin in the age of the Antonines – notably Apuleius and Lucian. Of the rest, what has survived is perhaps judged by unfair standards, but much is incredibly tedious.[22]

A by-product of the literary sterility of the age is that little historical writing has survived on which the modern historian can draw. Certainly there is nothing comparable with Tacitus' account of the Julio-Claudians and of the upheaval which followed them, or with Suetonius' portrayal of the first *Twelve Caesars*. The 'kingdom of rust and iron' which followed the age of the Antonines, was equally barren, in fact more so. Conditions were too disturbed to favour great writing or to ensure the survival of much of what was written. The prime source is the historian Cassius Dio, born in 163 or 164, a native of the Greek city of Nicaea in the province of Bithynia, who followed his father into the senate early in the reign of Commodus. Dio wrote in Greek a complete history of Rome in eighty books, from the earliest origins to his own day – his account ends with some sombre reflections on the middle years of Severus Alexander, the late 220s. Dio's work is preserved in various forms. Some of the original work survives, but for the life and reign of Marcus Aurelius there are only epitomes and excerpts; and the entire account of the twenty-three years of Antoninus Pius (138–61) is lost. Cassius Dio, like most of his class, idealized Marcus Aurelius and hated Commodus. His outlook is biased therefore; but he does not appear to distort the facts unduly and provides an invaluable chronological framework.

Marcus Aurelius' own writings naturally offer a unique insight into the man. There are the letters to his tutor Fronto which cover his life between the ages of about seventeen and forty-five, with varying completeness. The letters are difficult to date exactly in many cases, but enough clues are provided to give an approximate indication. The *Meditations* were written late in life, and only the first book dwells in any detail on named persons. This provides an invaluable series of character-sketches of his friends and family. Here and there in the later books casual references are historically illuminating. But the *Meditations* as a whole are informative about the inner life of Marcus, rather than his actions.

Marcus' correspondence with Fronto was re-discovered in the early nineteenth century. Cornelius Fronto had been known of as Marcus' tutor; but he had also been spoken of by writers of late antiquity as the second glory of Roman oratory after Cicero, and this judgement was accepted without question – until his letters to Marcus and others were recovered. Then there was amazement and scorn. The letters were full of small-talk and gossip, vignettes of the unpretentious family life of the Antonines, and therefore they disappointed historians who had hoped for light on matters of greater moment. Students of literature were unimpressed with the artificial style. Fronto, a native of Cirta (Constantine) in Numidia and a member of the senate, had been credited with the revitalizing of Latin. From the letters he is seen merely to have been making a self-conscious effort to get away from the purist dictatorship exercised by writers such as Cicero and Seneca, and to enrich or revive the literary language by drawing on authors earlier than Rome's Golden Age of literature and on the language of daily life. The intention was good, though the result seems a little half-baked. But his speeches, which have not survived, were supposedly renowned for the splendour and seriousness of their style, and it is obviously unfair to judge Fronto by his 'off-the-cuff' productions.

In view of the limitations of Dio, Marcus himself and Fronto, much reliance has inevitably to be placed on another work, the mysterious

THE AGE OF THE ANTONINES

'Augustan History'. This is a set of biographies of the emperors from Hadrian to Carinus (117–284), with a gap in the third century. It was ostensibly composed in the late third and early fourth centuries, by six authors. A peculiarity is that biographies are included not only of emperors but of usurpers and Caesars (in effect, heirs to the throne). It has long been recognized that these latter 'minor lives' are worthless and, in particular, that the 'documents' which they and the later lives contain – supposedly original letters, speeches, and the like – are bogus, the work of the authorship rather than of those to whom they are assigned. There is more to the mystery than that, however. It seems clear that the 'authors' – 'Aelius Spartianus', 'Julius Capitolinus', 'Aelius Lampridius', 'Vulcacius Gallicanus', 'Trebellius Pollio' and 'Flavius Vopiscus' – never existed, and that whoever was responsible for the Augustan History was writing later than he pretends. Quite when, why and who remains a mystery. Many attempts have been made to identify the hand behind it, but none has convinced for long. In the present context no attempt need be made. But it is relevant to ask how the work was composed, in other words, from what materials. The work gives every appearance of having been put together in haste – by a hoaxer perhaps, in the late fourth or early fifth century AD, as a literary 'spoof'. But although the 'minor lives' of second-century characters are virtually worthless, and the lives of the third-century figures contain over fifty per cent fiction, the 'major lives' of second-century figures – the emperors from Hadrian to Severus, at least – are full of factual material, put together haphazardly in many cases, but providing irreplaceable information. This must be derived from a sound source, either an unknown biographer or from Marius Maximus, cited occasionally by the Augustan History. Maximus evidently wrote a second *Twelve Caesars* on the model of Suetonius, probably in direct continuation of him, and he is undoubtedly identical with L. Marius Maximus Perpetuus Aurelianus, a contemporary of Cassius Dio, a leading general in the civil wars of Septimius Severus and a very prominent figure in the reigns of Caracalla, Macrinus, and of Severus Alexander, when the opportunity for composing a second *Twelve Caesars* first arose. The lives of all the emperors from Hadrian to Severus, including those of Marcus himself and of Lucius, contain much valuable material, which has to be used, with caution. But items on offer in the second-century 'minor lives', which have been incautiously accepted in some modern studies of Marcus and other second-century figures, are another matter. Almost all must be rejected.

After that, there is little left. Herodian, a mediocre eastern Greek litterateur who was a younger contemporary of Dio and Maximus, wrote a history of the period 180–238. He opened with the death of Marcus, and his account has nothing of value to add (and on some points is demonstrably false). In this context he is of interest solely as representative of the viewpoint of the third century on the passing of the golden age of the second. Much more useful are contemporary non-historical writers who provide background information and occasional historical facts. Aulus Gellius, an earnest hanger-on of the literary circles in the reign of Pius, provides a number of entertaining accounts of the philological discussions at the salons presided over by Fronto. Philostratus, a Greek intellectual who was a contemporary of Cassius Dio and a protégé of the empress Julia Domna, has left in his *Lives of the Sophists* excellent information on the literary and intellectual life of the age of the Antonines, particularly in his life of Herodes Atticus, one of Marcus' tutors. Other writers such as Lucian, a Greek from Samosata, and Apuleius, a Latin-speaking native of Roman North Africa, are sometimes helpful; and Galen, the great physician who served Marcus Aurelius, mentions in one or two places episodes in the life of Marcus or his family.

Later historians are flimsy. Ammianus Marcellinus began his History with the accession of Nerva, but his account of the late first, second and third centuries is totally lost, and only in occasional flashbacks does he provide information of any value to the study of Marcus Aurelius. The other 'historians' of the fourth century and after are no better than terse chroniclers, often confused and ignorant. Some Christian writers from the second century onwards throw light on the course of events, but their prime interest was naturally the history of the Christian Church and the vicissitudes of individual Christians. The legal sources are in a separate category. Roman jurisprudence was reaching its apogee during Marcus' lifetime, and the compilations of law of the late empire preserve a large number of decisions made by him which illuminate his personality and are informative on social conditions of the age.

Finally there is the evidence of coins, inscriptions and papyri, and of archaeology (including the historical reliefs). Coins can provide a chronological framework, and they can also reveal imperial policy: they certainly expressed in their legends and design imperial attitudes. Inscriptions too are vital for dating purposes. They also reveal the entire careers of individuals otherwise entirely or almost entirely unknown but who played an important historical role. This was a by-product of the Roman love of self-advertisement. Archaeology rarely reveals facts which alter the historical picture at one stroke, but the collation of the results of excavations scattered throughout the empire can and does produce significant changes of outlook. The historical reliefs, notably those on the column of Marcus Aurelius, are tantalizing, as it seems to be impossible to understand the details which they show and to construct a valid narrative history from them. But they do help in our understanding of Marcus and his age by their graphic portrayal of the emperor and his army on campaign.[23]

Thus the sources for the life and reign of Marcus Aurelius are varied and incomplete. But whatever the loopholes in the history of the period, the personality of Marcus himself comes to life more vividly perhaps than that of any other single emperor.

· 2 ·

FAMILY AND EARLY
YEARS

THE *gens Annia*, INTO WHICH Marcus was born, was not particularly celebrated in the annals of Rome. It had produced two consuls in the second century BC; but the only Annius to have achieved fame – or notoriety – was Milo, the unscrupulous politician whose use of violence helped to destroy the free republic. In fact, Annii were widespread, in the provinces as well as in Italy, and Marcus' family, when it first emerges in the mid-first century AD, was settled in the southern Spanish province of Baetica. Their home was the small town of Ucubi, a few miles south-east of Córdoba. The earliest record of an Annius in this region derives from the period of the civil war between Caesar and the Pompeians. A man called Annius Scapula, 'of the highest rank and influence in the province', was involved in a plot to murder Caesar's governor, the hated Q. Cassius Longinus, and was put to death. About a century later Marcus' great-grandfather, Annius Verus, became a senator. During the reigns of Claudius and Nero the colonial élites of the west, especially from the provinces of Baetica, Tarraconensis and Narbonensis, began to achieve prominence. The influence of Seneca, a native of Córdoba, and Burrus, from Vaison, undoubtedly assisted in their rise. The first Annius Verus may have been a beneficiary. He may be assumed to have been a wealthy man; and the likely source of his wealth would be olive oil. In the Augustan History he is said to have been 'made a praetorian senator', that is, to have been given the rank of ex-praetor. Presumably this was a reward for services rendered in the civil war of 68–70. The second Annius Verus, grandfather of Marcus, was made a patrician by Vespasian and Titus in their censorship, 73–74. Both promotions may have come at the same time.[1]

It was the start of an extraordinary career, yet most of it is hidden from view. The fact remains that Marcus' year of birth, 121, was to be known in Roman records as the year when his grandfather was consul for the second time. The young neo-patrician had married well, into a family of considerable standing. His bride was Rupilia Faustina, daughter of Libo Rupilius Frugi. No other Rupilii of this period are known, but the names Libo and Frugi must mean that he was a descendant of Crassus Frugi the

28

consul of 27 and his wife Scribonia, and through them of Pompey, the Calpurnii Pisones, and other houses of the republican nobility. His daughter's name Faustina may even indicate descent from the dictator Sulla. Libo Frugi's wife, the mother of Rupilia Faustina, was no doubt also a woman of standing. Her name is unknown, but it has been conjectured that she was Matidia, mother, by another husband, of the empress Vibia Sabina. If Annius Verus had shared a mother-in-law with Hadrian, this might help to explain his great influence. Matidia died in 119, and the surviving portions of Hadrian's funerary address reveal that he was greatly attached to her.[2]

How Annius Verus had occupied himself under Domitian is unknown. He emerges in the troubled year 97, when an unusually large number of carefully selected persons held office as consul. Annius Verus, now presumably in his early thirties, was of the company. His colleague was the jurist L. Neratius Priscus, from a south Italian family newly prominent under the Flavians. Their tenure of office was remarkable for one item only, a decree of the senate forbidding the castration of slaves. Also consul in 97 was one Arrius Antoninus, holding office for the second time with, as his colleague, L. Vibius Sabinus, the husband of Trajan's niece Matidia. Antoninus had been consul for the first time in another troubled year, 69, the year of the four emperors. He would not congratulate his friend Nerva, when the latter was made emperor in September 96: he congratulated the senate, the people, the provinces, but not the man unlucky enough to be chosen emperor. The younger Pliny was a friend and admirer of this cultivated person, whose grandson was the future emperor Antoninus Pius.[3]

Annius Verus and Rupilia Faustina had three children, two sons, Verus and Libo, and a daughter, Annia Galeria Faustina. The elder son married Domitia Lucilla, daughter of another patrician, P. Calvisius Tullus Ruso, and of the elder Domitia Lucilla. Lucilla the elder had inherited an enormous fortune, the wealth mainly of her maternal grandfather, Curtilius Mancia, and of her paternal grandfather by adoption, the orator Cn. Domitius Afer. The inheritance is described at length in one of Pliny's letters.

The circumstances were that Curtilius Mancia (consul in 55, at the beginning of the reign of Nero) had taken a violent dislike to his son-in-law, Domitius Lucanus. In his will he left Lucilla his fortune, but only on condition that she was released from paternal control – he did not want Lucanus to touch a penny of it. Lucanus complied. But the girl was at once adopted by Lucanus' brother, Tullus. The brothers held their possessions in common, 'and thus the purpose of the will was defeated', Pliny explained. He adds interesting details about the two Domitii brothers, prominent members of the new aristocracy. They had been adopted themselves by Domitius Afer, who had taken steps to ruin their real father, Curvius. The occasion for Pliny's letter was the death of Tullus; 'crippled and deformed in every limb he could only enjoy his wealth by looking at it, and he could not even turn round in his bed without help. He even – a squalid and miserable detail – had to have his teeth cleaned and brushed for him.' The immense wealth of this decrepit old man had attracted a host of fortune-hunters. As it turned out, 'in death he showed up better than in life', for his family were the principal beneficiaries after all, the main heiress being his adopted daughter Lucilla. Pliny supplies a good deal of the complicated and embarassing family history. 'You now have all the city gossip – for all the gossip is about Tullus.'[4]

It seems that the dispositions of this famous will were inscribed on an imposing marble monument on the Appian Way. The testator, who had drawn up his will in the summer of the year 108, is not named on the portions of the inscription that still survive. From the mention, apparently, of his family, he was assumed to have been called 'Dasumius'. The discovery of a new fragment, and further study, showed that, while a lady called Dasumia Polla was one of the beneficiaries, she was not the testator's daughter, listed as first of four main inheritors. Dasumia may be the widow of Tullus. Lacking a son, the testator asked that 'his very special friend' should bear his name. This man, the second inheritor to be mentioned, may be identified as Lucilla's husband, Tullus' son-in-law, henceforward known as P. Calvisius *Tullus* Ruso. Another close friend mentioned in the document is Julius Servianus, brother-in-law of Hadrian. Servianus was to superintend the funeral, and his freedmen were to carry the bier.

Old Tullus' connections with the Dasumii may explain his instruction that a monument be erected at Córdoba. Half-a-dozen members of this family are recorded in Baetica, at Córdoba itself, at Seville, and nearby Ilipa, and at Cadiz. Marcus himself must have had Dasumii in his ancestry, since the biographer reports the legend that he was descended from 'the Sallentine king Malemmius, son of *Dasummus*, who founded Lupiae'. This is the kind of fictitious origin which Romans loved to concoct on the basis of some family name. Furthermore, Hadrian too had links with the Dasumii: a man called L. Dasumius Hadrianus, suffect consul in 93, may be assumed to have been his cousin. These links help to explain the important role in the testament of Julius Servianus, husband of Hadrian's sister. But, above all, Pliny's letter and the great inscription combine to explain the social eminence and vast wealth of the maternal grandmother of Marcus, the elder Domitia Lucilla.[5]

Lucilla had other children besides the daughter with her own name. But it was the younger Lucilla who acquired much of her fortune, including vast brickworks on the outskirts of Rome. This source of wealth had been founded by Domitius Afer, and since there had been an almost continuous building boom at Rome since the great fire under Nero, it is easy to understand how the family's wealth had increased.[6]

The younger Lucilla and her husband Verus had two children, Marcus, born in 121, and his younger sister, Annia Cornificia Faustina, born probably within the next two years. Marcus' father died young, during his praetorship. As a patrician he should have become consul at thirty-two, the minimum age, two years after his praetorship. His younger brother Annius Libo was consul in 128 and can hardly have been praetor later than 126. Verus must have been praetor earlier than this and 124 is the likeliest year of his death. Thus Marcus can scarcely have known his father, but he was later to say of him: 'From my father's reputation and from my memory of him [I learned] modesty and manliness.' Similar qualities were in fact ascribed to Marcus by the biographer. Lucilla was faithful to her husband's memory and did not remarry. The younger Verus, had he lived, would have been assured of achieving a distinguished place in Roman public life.[7]

In the year 126 Marcus' grandfather Verus was consul again, for the third time, an enormous mark of honour, for Hadrian himself did not hold the office more than three times. Verus was the first man given such a distinction by Hadrian. Yet there were others who had held their second consulship earlier than Verus. One was Catilius Severus, who had held it the year before him. But the emperor's brother-in-law Julius Servianus had been consul for the second time as early as the year 102. Now the well-connected Verus had overtaken him. A curious poem is preserved on an inscription, in which a man called Ursus describes himself as the leading player in 'the glass ball game'. But he concludes by confessing that 'I myself was beaten by the thrice consul Verus, my patron, not once but often'. It was originally supposed that this Ursus was a professional sportsman. But the ingenious explanation has been advanced that the ball-player is none other than Julius Servianus – who had taken the name Ursus many years before. Better still, 'the glass ball game' – otherwise unknown, and, it must be said, implausible as a vigorous sport, although it might conceivably describe a game like marbles – is interpreted as a joking way of referring to the game of politics.[8]

The reasons for the political success of Annius Verus must remain obscure. Neither the prestige of his wife Rupilia Faustina's ancestry, nor the links of his daughter-in-law Lucilla with the Dasumii, seem sufficient. Perhaps the Annii Veri too had some kinship with the Aelii. Cassius Dio evidently believed that Hadrian favoured Marcus because of his 'kinship'. Later he states that Marcus 'while still a boy so pleased all his many powerful and wealthy relations that they all loved him', and that 'Hadrian adopted him chiefly for this reason'.[9]

Marcus was brought up as a boy in his parents' house on the Caelian, one of the seven hills of Rome, which he was later to call, with affection, 'my Caelian'. Under the empire the Caelian was the fashionable district of Rome for the leading families. It had few public buildings, but many splendid aristocratic mansions, of which the most imposing was the Lateran

Palace, once the possession, by confiscation, of Nero, and thenceforward imperial property, on the site where the Basilica of San Giovanni Laterano now stands. In Roman times it was next to the barracks of the Imperial Horse Guards, the *equites singulares*. Also next to the Lateran was the palace of Marcus' grandfather, where Marcus spent much of his childhood. The Caelian was on the southern edge of Rome. From it, to the north, one could look across to the Circus Maximus, to the Palatine with its imperial palaces, the Forum, the Colosseum and the Baths of Trajan. In the foreground was the massive temple of the Divine Claudius, and, straddling the area between the Lateran and the heart of Rome, the great aqueduct which brought the *Aqua Claudia* and part of the *Aqua Marcia* into the city.[10]

If Marcus' parents followed the traditional practice, his father would have had to acknowledge the child as his by lifting him up from the hearth at his feet. On the ninth day after this came the ceremony of purification, at which the child was named. It was then that the *praenomen* Marcus was given him, the only one of his names which he bore for the rest of his life. The child would be given presents at this ceremony, a rattle formed of a string with tinkling objects attached to it (*crepundia*) and an amulet of gold (*bulla*), a charm against the evil eye which he would wear round his neck until he assumed the *toga virilis*, the dress of manhood – in Marcus' case this was to be at the age of 14.[11]

After the birth, Lucilla probably had little to do with her son for some time. The historian Tacitus, who may have been still living when Marcus was born, had written with some bitterness in his *Dialogue on Orators* of the changed habits of the nobility in the upbringing of children: 'In the old days, each Roman child born in wedlock was not brought up in the back-bedroom of some slave-girl nurse, but in its mother's bosom and lap. The mother's especial glory was to keep her house and serve her children. . . . Thus we read how Cornelia the mother of the Gracchi and Aurelia the mother of Julius Caesar were in charge of the upbringing of their sons and brought them up to be leaders. . . . Now the new-born infant is handed over to some little Greek serving-maid, who has the help of some other slave chosen from the rest of the household, usually the most worthless and totally unfitted for an important task. The child's green and untaught mind is filled with their stories and mistakes. No one in the whole household thinks it of any importance what is said and done in the presence of the young master.'[12]

It is recorded that Marcus was in the care of 'nurses'. This would certainly have included, at first, a wet-nurse, who would have had the duty of feeding the new-born child. This impression is confirmed by a mention of his nurse in the *Meditations*: 'I follow the way of nature until I lie down and rest, breathing my last breath in the air from which I now breathe, lying down on the earth from which may father drew his vital seed, my mother her blood and my nurse her milk.' The fact that the nurses were usually

Greek was no accident. It was essential for an educated Roman to master Greek, and if the child's nurse spoke Greek, this would be a great help – although there was a slight danger that the child would then speak Latin with a foreign accent.[13]

Not everyone approved of the practice of using wet-nurses, but it was deep-rooted. Aulus Gellius records how he accompanied the philosopher Favorinus to visit one of the latter's pupils, a senator of noble family. The wife had just had a son, and Favorinus wished to bring his congratulations: 'When he had been told how long the birth had taken, and how difficult the labour had been, and that the girl, worn out with her efforts and lack of sleep was now sleeping, he began to talk at some length. "No doubt," he said, "she will feed her son with her own milk?" But the girl's mother said that she had to be spared this, and that wet-nurses had to be provided, so that the tiring and difficult task of breast-feeding need not be added to the pains which she had suffered in labour.' This produced an outburst from Favorinus – '"Do you think that nature provided women with nipples as a kind of beauty-spot",' and so on, for some time. The arguments he used were a little fallacious, for he claimed that '"if she whom you provide to give milk is a slave or of servile background, and, as usually happens, of foreign and barbarous origin, if she is dishonest, ugly, immodest, a drunkard,"' some of her unfortunate qualities would be transferred to the child she fed, through her milk. Modern authorities might agree in principle, although the effect that they would postulate would be psychological rather than physiological. Favorinus, a Hellenized Gaul from Arles, said credibly to have been a hermaphrodite, was a philosopher prominent in the reign of Hadrian and the early part of the reign of Antoninus Pius. He was an intimate of the same circles as the family and friends of Marcus, and the young mother whose conduct occasioned his outburst could well have been Domitia Lucilla. Aulus Gellius gives no names.[14]

At his father's death Marcus was adopted by his grandfather Verus. But in his early years another man played an important role in supervising his upbringing – L. Catilius Severus. Indeed, Marcus bore the names 'Catilius Severus' for some years in addition to his original 'Marcus Annius Verus'. Severus is described as his 'maternal great-grandfather'. It looks as if he had married the widow of old Domitius Tullus, thus becoming the stepfather of the elder Lucilla. Such an alliance would have been valuable to Catilius Severus, a talented man, but with no other known ties to the aristocracy old or new. He was evidently from an Italian family settled in Bithynia. After a slow start to his career he achieved prominence late in Trajan's reign, and had been a key supporter of Hadrian at his stormy accession, when Catilius was commanding one of the eastern armies.[15]

Not much is known about Marcus' uncle Annius Libo, except that he was consul in 128, as junior colleague to one of the old aristocracy. He had a son, also named Libo, who was probably born in about 130, and a daughter named Annia Fundania Faustina. The daughter's second name is a valuable clue to the identity of Libo's wife, who may be assumed to have been a Fundania, daughter of L. Fundanius Lamia Aelianus, consul in 116. Marcus' aunt Annia Galeria Faustina is naturally much better known, for she was married to the future emperor Antoninus Pius, by his full names, at this time, T. Aurelius Fulvus Boionius Arrius Antoninus. Antoninus had been junior colleague to Catilius Severus in the consulship of 120. The existence of another aunt of Marcus, a fourth child of old Annius Verus and Rupilia Faustina, has recently been deduced. She was, it is argued, the wife of C. Ummidius Quadratus, consul suffect in 118, and governor of Moesia Inferior early in Hadrian's reign. Quadratus was a member of an Italian family, from Casinum, near Naples, now to be reckoned among the nobility, for its fortunes had been founded in the time of Augustus and Tiberius. Quadratus had been, as a young man, a friend of Pliny, who was delighted with his promise as a barrister. In a characteristically sententious letter Pliny expressed satisfaction that young Quadratus managed 'to spend his youth and early manhood untouched by scandal', in spite of living with his grandmother, a riotous old lady noted for the troupe of dancers she kept at her house. He had married before he was twenty-four, but had not yet had children in the year 107, when Pliny wrote about him. His son by the daughter of Verus was probably born in about 113 or 114.[16]

The brides and grooms acquired by Verus for his sons and daughters were thus an impressive group. The connections of Domitia Lucilla have already been explored. Fundania's father, as the names 'Lamia Aelianus' indicate, was descended from a family ennobled under Augustus. Furthermore, her aunt Plautia, who had married three times, was at the centre of a powerful aristocratic nexus. Quadratus, husband of one daughter of Verus, was not only noble but a friend of Hadrian. As for Antoninus, he was from a provincial family, which had its origin at Nemausus (Nîmes) in Gallia Narbonensis. The founder of its fortunes had been his grandfather, T. Aurelius Fulvus, whose career had first shown brilliance when he was a legionary legate under the great Corbulo in Nero's reign. He had gone from strength to strength under the Flavians, becoming prefect of the city and holding a second consulship. His son, Antoninus' father, had died when Antoninus was a boy, and his mother Arria Fadilla, daughter of the celebrated Arrius Antoninus, had remarried, to Julius Lupus, a distant connection of the Flavian dynasty. Antoninus was born in 86, and had probably married Annia Faustina in about 110, some years before Marcus was born. They had four children, two sons and two daughters. Three died young, the two boys and the elder daughter Aurelia Fadilla. But Fadilla survived long enough to be married to Lamia Silvanus, son of the consul of 116 and brother of Fundania. She evidently died in 134. Her younger sister, named Faustina after her mother, was probably born in about 130, since she

34

married Marcus, her cousin, in 145 and was still able to bear children as late as 170.[17]

A few glimpses of Marcus' boyhood with his grandfather emerge from the *Meditations*. He places him at the head of the list of those from whom he had benefited: 'From my grandfather Verus; good character and avoidance of bad temper.' On the other hand, some time after the death of his wife Rupilia Faustina, the old man took a mistress, with whom he lived openly. Marcus was grateful in later years that the course of events prevented him from being brought up in the same household as this lady any longer than he was: evidently something about her or her entourage might have placed temptation in his path. The comment recalls the remark of the biographer, that Marcus was 'a solemn child from his earliest infancy'.

Marcus' mother played a large role in his life, even if she did not feed him in infancy herself. The qualities in her which he remembered as influencing him were 'religious piety, generosity, not only refraining from wrongdoing but even from thoughts of it, simplicity in diet, and to be far removed from the ways of the rich'. The last perhaps a particularly surprising tribute, considering the exceptional wealth inherited by Lucilla. Marcus in middle age was grateful that 'although my mother was fated to die young, yet she spent her last years with me'. His correspondence with Fronto is full of natural and affectionate references to her. She was a lady of some talent and education, well-versed in Greek. The great Athenian orator Herodes Atticus, who was to be the instructor of her son, had been brought up in her father's house for a time – presumably to learn Latin – and this no doubt played a part in giving her a fondness for Hellenic culture.[18]

When Marcus reached the age of seven in 128, the time had come when a Roman boy began his elementary education, although he had probably, following Quintilian's principles, already been taught to read. It may have been then that the question arose whether he should be sent to school or should be taught at home by tutors. Formerly the most conscientious fathers instructed their sons in the most elementary subjects in person, as was the case with the great Cato, nearly 300 years before the birth of Marcus, who 'as soon as his son showed signs of sufficient intelligence, took personal charge of him and taught him to read, even though he had an accomplished slave who was a schoolmaster. . . . He thought that it was wrong that his son should be scolded and have his ears pinched by a slave for being slow at his lessons – still less that he should owe to a slave such a priceless benefit as education. He took on himself the task of being his son's reading-master, law-tutor and physical training instructor . . . he even wrote out in his own hand, in large letters, a *History of Rome* for the boy.' Still, Cato was exceptional, even in his own time. His wife not only fed her babies herself, but sometimes provided milk for her slaves' babies, which was going to the opposite extreme. In any case, Marcus had no father by the time he was old enough to begin reading. And even Pliny, who was in favour of boys attending a school when it was run by a man like his friend Julius Genitor, applied this only to secondary education: 'Up to the present your son has been too young to leave your side,' he wrote to Corellia Hispulla, recommending Genitor's school for her son, 'and has had teachers at home, where there is little or no opportunity for going astray.'[19]

There was obviously some discussion among the family as to what should be done, although the discussion may not have arisen until Marcus was ready for his secondary education. The deciding voice was that of Catilius Severus, whom Marcus later remembered gratefully for this: 'From my great-grandfather: not to have attended public places of teaching but to have enjoyed good teachers at home; and to have learned that it is a duty to spend liberally on such things.'

The basis of Roman education, after the elementary lessons in reading, writing and arithmetic, was to teach a boy Greek language and literature, which the Romans regarded as essential for a civilized person. His first teachers were called Euphorio and Geminus. Euphorio was, to judge from his name, Greek, and was presumably responsible for elementary instruction in that language. Geminus, whose name is Latin, is described as an actor, and his task may therefore have been to supervise the boy's Latin pronunciation and elocution in general. Both Euphorio and Geminus, who are otherwise unknown, would undoubtedly have been family slaves or freedmen of the Annii Veri. A third teacher was in general charge of Marcus, as his *educator* (τροφεύς in Greek), to watch over his moral welfare and general development. His name is unknown, but Marcus speaks of him with gratitude in the *Meditations*: 'From my tutor: not to be a supporter of the Greens or the Blues at the races, nor of the Thracian or Samnite gladiators; to bear pain and be content with little; to work with my own hands, to mind my own business, to be slow to listen to slander.'[20]

In 127, at the age of six, probably a year before he began his education, he was enrolled in the order of the *equites* by the nomination of Hadrian himself. This gave him the right to wear a gold ring and a tunic with a narrow border. The honour was not completely exceptional – other cases are known where boys of very tender years were appointed – but Marcus was unusually young. The following year, when he was seven, he was enrolled by Hadrian into the priestly college of the Salii. The qualification for membership was to be of patrician birth and to have both parents living. In Marcus' case the second qualification was lacking, since his father was dead, but perhaps the adoption by his grandfather met the legal requirements; although the fact that he was enrolled by Hadrian, rather than co-opted in the normal way, suggests that there was an irregularity and special favour from the emperor.

The name Salii came from the word *salire*, to leap or dance, which indicates the nature of the ceremonies which they performed: ritual dances. These priests were found in various towns of Italy from earliest times. At

Rome itself they were associated with the worship of Mars, the god of war. There were two companies, each with twelve members, called the Collini and Palatini. Their priestly costume was the old Italian war-uniform, the *tunica picta*, with a breast-plate covered by a short military cloak, and a felt hat of conical shape. They wore a sword and on their left arm they carried *ancilia*, shields of figure of eight shape, which were supposed to be copies of an original which fell from heaven, as a gift from the god Jupiter to Rome's second king Numa Pompilius. They carried a spear or staff in their right hand. Twice a year they played a prominent part in religious ceremonies which marked the opening and close of the campaigning season, at the Quinquatrus on 19 March, and the Armilustrium on 19 October. On some other days in these two months they went in procession through the city carrying their shields. At intervals they halted to perform their complicated ritual dances, beating their shields with their staffs and singing their hymn, the Carmen Saliare, an obscure religious chant in archaic Latin, the words of which were by this time almost unintelligible. In the evening they feasted.

Marcus took his duties as a member of the Salii very seriously. He fulfilled various of the offices in the priesthood in turn, being the leader of the dance, the *vates* (prophet), and the master of the order. In his last function it was his task to initiate new members and formally to dismiss those who left the order. He learned the archaic formulas by heart, so that it was never necessary in his case for them to be read out for him to repeat. While Marcus was a Salian priest an omen occurred, which was remembered (long after, no doubt) as signifying his future rule. When the members of the college were casting their crowns on the banqueting couch of the god, as was the custom, Marcus' crown fell on the brow of the god Mars, as if he had placed it there, whereas the others fell in random places.[21]

No further details of his earliest years of education are recorded. When he approached his twelfth year, he would be ready for secondary education, under *grammatici*. In his case, two other teachers are also recorded. The first, Andro, was 'a geometrician and musician'. His instruction in mathematics probably did not begin until Marcus was eleven. The music teaching may have been mainly in singing. At about the same time he was given another teacher, the painting-master Diognetus. Diognetus was more than a painting-master to Marcus, however. It seems to have been he who first showed Marcus the attractions of philosophy – as a way of life, at least. Marcus remembered in his *Meditations* the lessons he had learned from this man: 'From Diognetus: to avoid passing enthusiasms; to distrust the stories of miracle-workers and impostors about incantations and exorcism of spirits and such things; not to go cock-fighting or to get excited about such sports; to put up with outspokenness; and to become familiar with philosophy; to hear first the lectures of Baccheius, then of Tandasis and Marcianus; to write philosophical dialogues in my boyhood;

to aspire to the camp-bed and the skin coverlet and the other things which belong to the Greek training.' It was when he entered his twelfth year (in April 132) that Marcus was first fired with eagerness to follow the austere way of life of the philosopher, the biographer records. 'He adopted the dress, and a little later the habits of endurance, of the philospher. He followed his studies clad in a rough Greek cloak. He slept on the ground, and it was only at his mother's insistence that he consented, with reluctance, to sleep on a little bed strewn with skins.'[22]

Magicians and miracle-workers of all kinds were flourishing as never before at this time, and were to flourish even more. Marcus as emperor was to come across a charlatan of this kind on the grand scale – Alexander of Abonutichus. The philosophic way of life that the eleven-year-old Marcus adopted sounds from its description like an attempt to imitate the Cynics, who were the most obvious practising philosophers of the time, to the average person, for they made a cult of the simple life to the point of aggressiveness. The sardonic essayist Lucian portrayed one of the leading practitioners of the Cynic philosophy, Peregrinus, in terms almost as scathing as he used to tear in shreds the bogus claims of Alexander, the false prophet and miracle-worker.[23]

The boy's solemn and serious devotion to his studies made an impression on Hadrian, who took a close interest in his upbringing from an early stage. The emperor, playing on his name Verus ('true', 'truthful', or 'genuine'), nicknamed him Verissimus, 'truest'. The name stuck, and has even been found on coins and on an inscription. It is clear however, that Hadrian cannot have seen much of Marcus during these boyhood years. In 121, when Marcus was born, he was in Gaul and on the Rhine. In 122 he was in Britain, he passed through Spain in 123 on his way to the east, and conferred with the Parthian king on the frontier. The years 124 and 125 were spent in the Greek-speaking lands – in fact Hadrian may not have returned to Rome until 127. In 128 he was away again, on a visit to Africa, and after a brief return to Rome left for Athens, the eastern provinces and Egypt. He was back in Rome in 131, but the Jewish war which broke out in 132 and lasted for four years demanded his attention. On his visit to Egypt Hadrian had lost his favourite, the beautiful Bithynian youth, Antinous. He was inconsolable for a time, and the dead youth was deified – a subject for considerable gossip among the aristocracy. Hadrian was no longer as fit as he had been, although in 132 he was only fifty-six years old. The question of the succession began to loom up. In 134 Hadrian made his brother-in-law, the aged Servianus, now nearly ninety, consul for the third time. The belated distinction may have led Servianus to hope for more – even though Annius Verus, Marcus' grandfather, had received a like honour. But Servianus had a grandson, Pedanius Fuscus Salinator, now a young man. As Hadrian's grand-nephew, Fuscus should have been the heir apparent.[24]

Hadrian's last years were spent at his country palace at Tivoli on the edge of the Sabine hills, twenty miles east of Rome. This vast complex of halls, baths, theatres, lakes, porticoes, temples and ornamental gardens was Hadrian's pride and joy. It covered over a hundred acres, with a circumference of several miles. Hadrian had built it himself – and had no doubt taken a personal hand in the architectural design. He filled it with originals or copies of works of art from all the places he had visited in his travels, or copies of buildings – from Thessaly, Athens, Alexandria.

Hadrian began in 135 to build himself a mausoleum as well, for the imperial vaults built by Augustus on the Campus Martius were now full. Hadrian's tomb was to be erected opposite the new bridge he had given Rome, the Pons Aelius. Bridge and tomb have since become more famous as the Ponte and Castel Sant' Angelo. It may have been in these years at Tivoli that Hadrian came to know and acquire a liking for Lucius Ceionius Commodus, now married to the daughter of Avidius Nigrinus, one of the men Hadrian had disposed of at the beginning of his reign.[25] Ceionius Commodus was a young man of taste who may have appealed to Hadrian. His family was one of those that had risen to the peak of social eminence on the foundation of meritorious service under the Flavian dynasty. His grandfather had been consul in the second last year of Vespasian, one of only four men who had the honour of the ordinary consulship in the reign of Vespasian, who were not from the imperial family (the other sixteen places were filled regularly by Vespasian and his sons). He had then been governor of Syria. This distinction was sufficient to allow succeeding generations to settle down to a life of confident and opulent ease, enjoying as a hereditary right the traditional honours of the Roman state, without the need to work as soldier and administrator in the service of the emperors. The second Ceionius Commodus was consul in 106, and this Commodus, the third, was to be consul in 136. His colleague was his step-brother, Sextus Vettulenus Civica Pompeianus – their fathers had been colleagues in 106. The grandfather of Civica Pompeianus, like the grandfather of Commodus, had commanded legions – and had met a violent end through the jealousy of Domitian. These days were done with now. Commodus' mother must have been a remarkable woman. Only her name, Plautia, is known, no details of her personality, but she had three husbands, of whom Commodus' father was only the first. Following his death she married Avidius Nigrinus, so that Commodus' wife, Avidia, had been for a time his step-sister. Finally, after the unfortunate end of Nigrinus, she married Civica Cerialis, the father of Pompeianus, by whom she had another son, Civica Barbarus, born probably about 124. Ceionius Commodus had a son, born in December 130, and two daughters, Ceionia Fabia and Ceionia Plautia. It was to one of these daughters, Fabia, that Hadrian was to arrange the betrothal of Marcus in 136.[26]

But the introduction of Lucius Commodus and his family at this stage is anticipating, very slightly, the known details in the life of Marcus. As already mentioned, it was normal for a boy at about eleven or twelve to pass from the care of the *litterator* to that of the *grammaticus*. This was perhaps the time when the question seriously arose whether Marcus should be taught at home or should go to school. In the event, more tutors were chosen, one Greek, Alexander of Cotiaeum, and two Latin, Trosius Aper, from Pola, in the extreme north-east of Italy, and Tuticius Proculus, from Sicca Veneria in the province of Africa. They must have taken over Marcus' education in about 132 or 133. The task of the *grammaticus* was to instil into his pupil a knowledge of literature. The students had to read aloud and learn by heart passages from classical authors, and the teacher commented on matters of style and inculcated the moral or philosophical lessons to be found in them. Little is known of the two Latin masters. Trosius Aper is only a name, but Tuticius Proculus was later rewarded by Marcus with senatorial rank, and a proconsulship.[27]

Alexander of Cotiaeum, on the other hand, the Greek master, was a well-known literary figure of the early second century, the leading authority on Homer. He was also the teacher of the orator Aelius Aristides, who wrote an elaborate obituary of him, in the form of a speech addressed to the people of Cotiaeum, a Phrygian city in the province of Asia. Marcus had favourable memories of Alexander when he wrote his *Meditations*: 'From Alexander the *grammaticus*: to avoid finding fault and not to criticise in a carping spirit those who use outlandish expressions, solecisms or an awkward style; but to use the right phrase oneself, neatly and precisely, by way of answer or confirmation or handling of the actual subject in question, not its description in words, or by some equally happy reminder.' Something of this training by Alexander – the emphasis on matter rather than elaborate style, the careful choice of language, the occasional use of Homeric expressions – has been detected in the Greek of Marcus' own *Meditations*.[28]

When Marcus was fourteen he assumed the *toga virilis*, the garment of manhood. He would discard the gold amulet and striped toga of his childhood, and assume the plain white toga of a man. He was now a full citizen, ready for a part in public life. But his education had to go on – it was in fact to continue for many years more, by necessity of the station in which he was to find himself, and by his own inclination. Shortly after this, Hadrian expressed the wish that the betrothal should take place of Marcus and the daughter of Ceionius Commodus. Marcus' fourteenth birthday was in April 135, but it is not known whether he became engaged to Ceionia Fabia in 135 or 136. It was probably 136, for the ceremony of the assumption of the *toga virilis* customarily took place at the festival of the Liberalia, on March 17 – hence 135 would be impossible.[29] An additional reason is that soon after the betrothal he was given a new honour, that of being prefect of the city during the *feriae Latinae*. This 'Latin festival' was held every year at Albano, in April, at a date appointed by the consuls, who had to be present in person at the ceremonies. Since this meant that they had to be absent from the city they appointed a prefect of the city to carry on the administration in their place. After the institution of a full-time prefect by Augustus this archaic office had lost any real significance, but it was retained and was customarily held by young members of the aristocracy or imperial family. As it was the consuls who made the appointment, it seems probable that it was Ceionius Commodus who appointed his intended son-in-law. According to the biographer Marcus 'conducted himself very brilliantly when acting on behalf of the magistrates and at the banquets of the emperor Hadrian'.[30]

The entry into the family circle of the Ceionii Commodi had another important effect on the life of Marcus. He met a Stoic philosopher, Apollonius of Chalcedon, who had taught Commodus. Stoicism was by now the fashionable school of philosophy and Apollonius one of its leading expounders. There is no question but that Marcus was enormously influenced by this man whom he names, with two others only, as one of those whom he thanks the gods for having met. He was later to study regularly with Apollonius.[31]

Another family event must have taken place at about this time – the marriage of Marcus' younger sister, Annia Cornificia, to Ummidius Quadratus, who was, it appears, her first cousin. It was presumably at the time of this wedding that Domitia Lucilla asked Marcus if he would give his sister part of the inheritance left him by his father. Marcus replied that he would give it all. He was content with his grandfather's fortune (although his grandfather was still alive), and he added that his mother could leave all her own estate to his sister, so that she might not be poorer than her husband.[32]

In late 136 an event occurred which shook the leading circles at Rome. Hadrian had been ill – he had almost died from a haemorrhage. The uncertainty about the future which the state of his health occasioned gave rise to speculation about his successor. While Hadrian was bedridden in the early stages of his illness he thought first of Servianus, his ninety-year-old brother-in-law, whom he had, after all, recently appointed consul for the third time. Men remembered how Hadrian had once asked his friends at a banquet to name him ten men who were competent to become emperor, and had then added – 'No, I need to know only nine, for one I have already, Servianus.' But then he had the haemorrhage at Tivoli, and in his illness certain actions of Servianus were construed by him as suspicious – 'he had given a feast to the imperial slaves, had sat in a royal chair close to his bed, and although nearly ninety used to get up and go forward to meet the praetorian guardsmen when on duty'. Meanwhile Hadrian also heard reports that Servianus' grandson, Pedanius Fuscus Salinator, had been spurred on by certain prophecies and omens to hope for the imperial power. But Hadrian had another man in view, and Servianus could not conceal his displeasure. The unfortunate pair were forced to commit suicide. Servianus, offering incense to the gods just before his death, affirmed his innocence and cursed Hadrian: 'May he long for death but be unable to die.' Many others, according to Hadrian's biographer, were put to death at this time, either openly or by treachery: and when the empress Sabina died, perhaps also in 136, it was rumoured that Hadrian had poisoned her.[33]

At last Hadrian publicly announced his choice of heir. He adopted Ceionius Commodus as his son. According to the biographer his sole recommendation was his beauty. Hadrian's tastes in this matter, after the affair of Antinous, were only too well known, and the reason suggested is only too obvious – and unlikely.[34]

The adoption might have been an act of conscience on Hadrian's part, to make amends for what had been done to Avidius Nigrinus, the father-in-law of Ceionius Commodus. Nigrinus had even – it was said – been intended as Hadrian's successor in the opening months of the reign, until he was executed in 118 for 'plotting against the emperor's life'. On the other hand, it might have been sheer perversity – Hadrian's desire to infuriate other aspirants. The adoption certainly did have this effect. It was done *invitis omnibus* – 'against the wishes of everyone'. Combined with this might have been the desire not unknown in great men to be succeeded by someone of lesser stature, so that their own reputation might be enhanced by the comparison in the eyes of history. Some believed that Hadrian had sworn some oath to adopt Ceionius Commodus; when, and for what reason, is not recorded.[35] But none of these motives seem plausible. It makes better sense to suppose that Commodus was adopted because of his background and connections. The prospective relationship with Marcus, which Hadrian himself had brought about, was an important part of this nexus. But there were already other links – Marcus' uncle Libo married to Commodus' cousin Fundania, Marcus' cousin Aurelia Fadilla married to Commodus' cousin Lamia Silvanus. The great favour shown by Hadrian to Annius Verus, and the probability that, through the Dasumii, and perhaps through Matidia also, Hadrian was himself linked to the Annii, suggest that Verus' grandson Marcus was part of Hadrian's dynastic plan from the start. Commodus had a young son, but he was at most only five years old at the time of Commodus' adoption. Hence the fifteen-year-old Marcus must have appeared the likely long-term successor. The biographer in the Augustan History claims that Hadrian knew, from Commodus' horoscope, that he would be short-lived; and his health was certainly poor. Hadrian's intentions remain shrouded in mystery, which a modern scholar attempted to dispel by the claim that Commodus was Hadrian's illegitimate son. But proof is lacking.[36]

The adoption was the culmination of Hadrian's growing unpopularity with the senate. The death of Servianus and his grandson had made a deep impression. Cultured circles in the capital perhaps recalled a letter of Pliny: 'I am pleased to hear that your daughter has been betrothed to Fuscus Salinator and I congratulate you. The family is patrician, his father a most honourable man, his mother equally praiseworthy; he himself is scholarly, well-read, something of an orator. He combines a childlike simplicity and youthful charm with the seriousness of a man of mature years . . . I can assure you that he will be a son-in-law who will prove better than your fondest hopes. It remains for him to give you grandchildren like himself as soon as possible. . . .'[37]

The adoption was celebrated publicly with games in the Circus Maximus and with a distribution of bounty to the people of Rome and the soldiers. Commodus took the name Lucius Aelius Caesar, and was designated consul for a second time, for the year 137; at the end of 136 he was also given the tribunician power – the *summi fastigii vocabulum*, 'the name for the highest dignity', as Tacitus, a few years before, had described this creation of Augustus. Hadrian decided that the new Caesar must go to the armies. He had not made a good impression at the beginning of his new duties – he had been unable, through illness, to appear in the senate to make his speech of thanks to Hadrian for his adoption. Hadrian no doubt felt that a tour of military duty might have a beneficial effect. Aelius was sent to the Danube, to Carnuntum, with proconsular power over the two Pannonian provinces. There was some unrest among the German tribes in Slovakia. The presence of a member of the imperial family would be calculated to restore the tribes beyond the Danube to their allegiance, in particular the Quadi, a powerful Suebian tribe that the Roman emperors did their best to keep under a protectorate. The Quadi were settled in the valley of the River March or Morava, which flows into the Danube about a mile downstream from the fortress of the legion XIV Gemina at Carnuntum. The governor of Upper Pannonia had his residence in the town outside the fortress, and it was here that Aelius Caesar had his headquarters. The valley of the March was part of an important north–south trade route between the Baltic and the Adriatic, the Amber Road. Carnuntum, and its province of Upper Pannonia astride this trade-route, was the hinge which bound the western and eastern parts of the empire together.[39]

In the winter of 137 Aelius Caesar returned to Rome. He was to deliver an important speech in the senate on the first day of the year 138. But in the night he fell ill. The medicine which he was given made his condition worse, and he died the same day. It sounds, from the references to his coughing blood even before his adoption, and from his death being caused by a haemorrhage, as if he was tubercular. Hadrian forbade public mourning, which would have prevented the important ceremonial taking of New Year vows on behalf of the state.[40]

The curse of Servianus was now apparently having its effect. Hadrian

AD 121   *April* 26: Birth of Marcus (Rome); his grandfather Verus consul for second time and prefect of the city

c. 122   Birth of Marcus' sister Cornificia

c. 124   Death of Marcus' father while praetor

126   Marcus' grandfather consul for third time

127   Marcus enrolled in order of *equites*, aged 6

128   Marcus made *salius Palatinus*, aged 7. His elementary education begins

132   Marcus first attracted by 'philosophy', aged 11

133   His secondary education begins

135   Hadrian begins to live at Tivoli

136   Marcus assumes *toga virilis*, aged 14 (perhaps on 17 March). He is made honorary prefect of the city during the Latin festival

After his fifteenth birthday, he is betrothed to Ceionia Fabia, daughter of L. Commodus, consul that year. He meets Apollonius the Stoic

L. Commodus, adopted by Hadrian, becomes L. Aelius Caesar. Marcus' sister Cornificia marries Ummidius Quadratus

Suicide of Hadrian's brother-in-law Servianus and Servianus' grandson Fuscus Salinator

137   L. Aelius Caesar in Pannonia

138   *January* 1: Death of L. Aelius Caesar

February 25: Marcus' maternal uncle T. Aurelius Antoninus adopted by Hadrian. Marcus, aged 16, and L. Commodus junior (Lucius), adopted by Antoninus. Faustina, daughter of Antoninus, betrothed to L. Commodus junior. Marcus moves to Hadrian's house in Rome. Marcus designated quaestor for 139. Antoninus designated consul for 139

July 10: Death of Hadrian (Baiae), accession of Antoninus. Marcus' betrothal to Ceionia Fabia and Lucius' betrothal to Faustina cancelled

Marcus betrothed to Faustina. Hadrian deified. Antoninus given name Pius

139   Pius consul, Marcus quaestor (aged 17). Marcus designated consul for 140. Marcus acts as a *sevir turmarum equitum Romanorum*; becomes *princeps inventutis*; is given the name Caesar; and is co-opted into the major colleges of priests. He moves into the palace. His higher education has by now begun, his best-known teacher being M. Cornelius Fronto

140   Marcus, aged 18, consul for first time, with Pius. Marcus studies with Fronto and attends imperial councils

143   Marcus' tutors Herodes Atticus and Fronto hold consulship (January and July)

145   Marcus consul for second time, with Pius

Late spring: Marcus, aged 24, marries Faustina

146–7   Marcus turns wholeheartedly to philosophy

147   *November* 30: Faustina bears Marcus a daughter (Domitia Faustina)

December 1: Marcus receives *tribunicia potestas*, Faustina called Augusta

148   900th anniversary of founding of Rome

149   Faustina bears twin sons; both die within a year

150   *March* 7: Faustina bears a second daughter (Lucilla)

152   Death of Marcus' sister Cornificia. Lucius designated quaestor

153   Lucius quaestor

TABLE II Events of the lifetime of Marcus Aurelius

AD 154 Lucius consul

155 Marcus' friend Victorinus, son-in-law of Fronto, consul

151–60 More children born to Marcus and Faustina

155–61 Marcus' mother Domitia Lucilla dies

161 Marcus consul for third time, with Lucius

March 7: Death of Antoninus Pius. Marcus, aged 39, becomes emperor as Imperator Caesar M. Aurelius Antoninus Augustus, with Lucius, who becomes Imperator Caesar Lucius Aurelius Verus Augustus

August 31: Birth of twin sons (Antoninus and Commodus) to Faustina

Military crisis in the east. Flooding and famine at Rome

162 Lucius sent to the east

Birth of son to Faustina (Annius Verus)

163 Roman victories in Armenia

164 Lucius marries Lucilla (at Ephesus)

165–6 Death of Marcus' son Antoninus

Roman victories against Parthia

166 Return of Lucius to Italy

October: Triumph for eastern victories celebrated

c. 166 Death of Fronto

167 Plague rampant at Rome

Military threat on northern frontiers

168 Marcus and Lucius set off for the north. They winter at Aquileia

169 *January*: Death of Lucius, aged 39

Marcus (now aged 47) returns to Rome. Lucilla marries Pompeianus

Death of Marcus' son Annius Verus, aged 7

Autumn: Marcus returns to northern armies

c. 170 Birth of Marcus' youngest child (Sabina)

170–1 Defeat of Roman offensive. Greece and Italy invaded

172 Marcus defeats invaders. Roman offensive begins. Marcus based at Carnuntum

173 Marcus based at Carnuntum

174 Marcus at Sirmium, is joined by Faustina and Sabina

175 Rebellion of Cassius in the east. Marcus makes armistice with Sarmatians. Commodus summoned from Rome. Marcus and court go to east

Death of Faustina, aged about 45

176 *Late autumn*: Marcus and Commodus return to Rome

December 23: Marcus and Commodus hold triumph

177 *January* 1: Commodus made co-emperor, aged 15, and is consul with his brother-in-law Quintillus

178 Commodus, aged 16, marries Crispina

August 3: Marcus and Commodus go to northern front

179 Roman victory over northern tribes

180 *March* 17: Death of Marcus (near Sirmium), aged 58

was weary of life and was suffering from dropsy; he wished to die but could not. Already in the month of January 138 the observant and superstitious noticed premonitions of his death (or claimed afterwards that they had done so). On the day before his birthday, 23 January, someone came into the senate wailing. The emperor was visibly disturbed. He appeared to be talking of his own death, but his words were unintelligible. Then he made a slip of the tongue. He meant to say 'after my son's death' (Aelius Caesar), but said 'after my death'. He had disquieting dreams as well, evidently. He dreamed that he had asked his father for a sleeping draught; and that he had been overcome by a lion. The next day, his sixty-second birthday, 24 January, he ended the speculation about his successor. He called a meeting at his house of the most prominent and respected senators, in other words, a meeting of his *consilium*. Lying on his couch he made a short speech to them, the gist of which is recorded by Cassius Dio: 'Nature has not permitted me to have a son, my friends, but you have made it possible through law. There is this difference between the two sorts of son: a son that one has begotten turns out to be whatever sort of man heaven pleases; an adopted son is one that a man takes to himself as the result of deliberate choice. A son that is born may be mentally defective or a cripple. One that is chosen will certainly be of sound body and mind. For this reason I formerly selected Lucius [Ceionius Commodus] from all others – a person such as I could never have expected any son of mine to have become. But since heaven has taken him from me, I have found as emperor for you in his place the man I now give to you, one who is noble, mild, tractable and prudent, who is not young enough to do anything rash or old enough to be neglectful, one who has been brought up according to the laws and who has exercised authority in accordance with our ancestral customs, so that he is not ignorant of any matters which concern the exercise of imperial power but can deal with them all well. I am speaking of Aurelius Antoninus here. I know that he is not the least inclined to be involved in affairs and is far from desiring such power, but still I do not think that he will deliberately disregard either me or you, but will accept the rule even against his will.' Thus were Hadrian's intentions announced, and he formally commended Antoninus to the gods.[41]

Afterwards several of those who had been present must have retailed various anecdotes about the occasion. One story in particular records the effect which the entry of Antoninus to a meeting of the senate had produced, some time in that January. He had entered supporting the steps of his venerable father-in-law, Marcus Annius Verus. This Hadrian found such a moving scene that he decided to adopt Antoninus. But the same story is also given as a reason why Antoninus later received the name of Pius. Others recorded that when Hadrian was commending Antoninus to the gods his bordered toga slipped for no apparent reason, baring his head which he had covered to pray after the Roman custom. And his signet-ring, on which a portrait of himself was carved, suddenly slid off his finger.

Both omens of his approaching end, men said.[42]

The motive for the choice of Antoninus as heir was not a sudden impulse. The biographer gives a sufficiently detailed description of his personality for other ostensible reasons to emerge. He was very rich. He was of a calm and benevolent nature. He was cultured and a good speaker. He was thrifty and a conscientious landlord. All these qualities he possessed in their proper proportion and without ostentation. His public service had not, however, given him very wide experience. Apart from the quaestorship, praetorship, and consulship in Rome, he had had only two appointments: as one of the four consulars appointed by Hadrian to administer justice in Italy: and as proconsul of Asia, for one year, probably the summer of 135 to the summer of 136. The consulars assigned to Italy were an innovation of Hadrian's which the senate had resented – it was an infringement of the senatorial prerogative (to administer Italy through the urban magistrates), and it hinted that Italy was on the way to being regarded as just a province. Antoninus was assigned to the area 'in which most of his own possessions lay', hence, probably, Etruria and Umbria. It was later retailed that an omen of his future rule occurred during his term of office. When he ascended the tribunal to give judgment, someone cried out: 'the gods preserve you, Augustus' – i.e. the imperial name, instead of his own name. His proconsulship of Asia was likewise marked by an omen. The priestess at Tralles greeted him with the expression 'Hail, emperor', instead of 'Hail, proconsul', her normal greeting at what were apparently regular visits by proconsuls. At Cyzicus, another city in the province of Asia, a crown was inadvertently transferred to a statue of Antoninus from the statue of a god. Still earlier omens could be adduced to please the credulous. After his service as consul, in 120, a marble bull was found in his garden, hanging by its horns from a tree. His house was struck by lightning from a clear sky – but was not damaged. Certain large jars that had been buried in the ground, in Etruria, reappeared above the surface. Swarms of bees settled on his statues throughout Etruria. Finally, he was frequently warned in dreams that he should include a statue of Hadrian among his household gods.[43]

The omens aside, Antoninus was an amiable and wealthy man, who had played an honourable but not remarkable part in public life. It would seem in fact that he had only spent the year of his proconsulship outside Italy. For the rest, he had not seen the provinces, let alone the armies – for no military service is recorded for him, and, indeed, none was likely. A man of his standing, whose grandfathers had both been consul twice, did not need to prove himself in this way if he had not the inclination. Antoninus did not: he was a man of peace. This was probably a not unimportant factor in Hadrian's choice, for the whole policy of the reign had been one of peace with security. Hadrian would not have been eager to see as his successor a man with lurking military ambitions.

Thus far the personality and qualifications of Antoninus himself. But there was another factor. A condition of his adoption was that he in turn should adopt the young surviving son of Lucius Aelius Caesar, now aged seven – and his own nephew, Marcus. The adoption of Antoninus caused ill-feeling, as had the adoption of Ceionius Commodus. 'All were opposed' to the adoption of Commodus. The adoption of Antoninus 'caused pain to many' – not least to the prefect of the city of Rome, L. Catilius Severus, Antoninus' colleague in the consulship in 120 (but this senior colleague, for Severus was then consul for the second time). Catilius Severus was evidently making plans to secure the throne for himself. His plans, or at any rate his reaction to the choice of Hadrian, were discovered. He was removed from office, to be succeeded by an undistinguished aristocrat with the noble names of Servius Cornelius Scipio Orfitus.[44]

The behaviour of Catilius Severus is another indication that Hadrian's intention all along had been to secure the succession for Marcus, his favourite 'Verissimus' – and that these intentions were known about, or suspected, in the ruling circles in Rome. Catilius Severus was the young man's 'great-grandfather', and Marcus as a boy had included the names 'Catilius Severus' in his nomenclature. It is in the highest degree plausible that Catilius Severus regarded himself as a more suitable candidate than Marcus' uncle, Antoninus, to become the boy's place-holder. From the point of view of seniority and administrative experience he was justified. Consul twice and city prefect, Severus had also been proconsul of Africa, and before that had had a remarkable civil and military career. He had commanded one of the German legions, had served in no less than three junior prefectures at Rome, had governed Cappadocia and then Armenia in the Parthian war (he was the only man ever to govern Armenia, a new province given up by Hadrian in 117) and had been decorated by Trajan. Hadrian, at the critical time of his accession, had transferred him to the Syrian army, a position of the highest importance.[45]

Catilius Severus may have had allies in his bid for power. The disfavour incurred by Ummidius Quadratus, probably another uncle of Marcus, and father-in-law of Marcus' sister, is linked with the disgrace of Catilius, together with a third name, that of the former praetorian prefect Q. Marcius Turbo. A young member of Turbo's family had been selected to serve as quaestor to L. Aelius Caesar in his consulship in 137; but the role played by the former prefect in these critical months is not known. (He may have been dead some while, and the conjunction of his names with those of Severus and Quadratus mere hazard.)[46]

At any rate, Antoninus was chosen. He asked for time to consider his answer. This confirmed the opinion of Hadrian that he was not ambitious. His grandfather Arrius Antoninus had found no cause for envy or congratulation when his friend Nerva had become emperor in 96. On the other hand, had his answer been negative, his position in any future reign, let alone for the remainder of that of Hadrian, would have been almost intolerable. One who had been pointed to by Hadrian as emperor-to-be, and had spurned the offer, would have been the object of envy and suspicion in the reign of another.[47]

How soon Antoninus accepted the offer is not recorded. But the ceremony of adoption did not come for another four weeks, on 25 February. In accordance with Hadrian's wishes, Antoninus, who now became Imperator T. Aelius Aurelius Caesar Antoninus, adopted in his turn his nephew Marcus and the young Lucius Commodus. These boys now became M. Aelius Aurelius Verus and L. Aelius Aurelius Commodus. Further, at Hadrian's request, the surviving daughter of Antoninus, Faustina, was betrothed to Lucius.

Antoninus received powers and titles consonant with his new dignity. He became Imperator, and could place this title before his name, but not yet Augustus. He received the tribunician power and the proconsular *imperium*.[48]

The night of his adoption Marcus had a dream, that he had shoulders of ivory, and when asked if they were able to bear a burden, he discovered that they were much stronger than before. He had been 'appalled, when he learned that Hadrian had adopted him'. It was with reluctance that he moved from his mother's house on the Caelian to Hadrian's private house (not yet, evidently, to the 'Tiberian House', as the imperial residence on the Palatine was known). 'When members of his household asked him why he was sorry to be adopted into the imperial family, he listed to them the evils that the imperial power contained in itself', the biographer records. He gives an attractive and plausible depiction of Marcus' habits at the time of his adoption: 'he was so complaisant that he allowed himself to be taken, at times, to hunt or the theatre or the spectacles. He loved boxing, wrestling, running and fowling. He played the ball-game well and hunted well too. But the zeal for philosophy led him away from all these pursuits and made him serious and reserved. Still, this did not spoil the friendliness in him which he showed to his household and his friends, and even to those less well known to him. He was austere but not unreasonable, modest but not inactive, reserved but not gloomy.' In another passage he makes a revealing comment on the young Marcus' habits after his adoption: 'he had such a high regard for his reputation, moreover, that even as a boy he always used to warn his procurators – those in charge of his estates and financial affairs – not to do anything in a high-handed fashion. He also often refused legacies that were left him, returning them to the next of kin.'[49] He did not want to take any unfair advantage from his position. There is a portrait bust of Marcus as a young man in the Capitoline Museum. It shows a beardless youth with head turned slightly to his right side and leaning forward a little. The chin is firm, the lips full, slightly parted and serious, even solemn, the eyes are wide apart and deepset. The head is crowned by luxuriant curly hair worn long over the forehead and ears as was then the custom. This is certainly a grave young man.

In the spring the time came for the designation in advance of the magistrates for the following year, 139. Antoninus was to be consul, for the second time. Perhaps Hadrian intended to be his colleague. Hadrian requested in the senate that Marcus should be exempt from the law which barred him from taking office as quaestor before his twenty-fourth birthday, and he was designated to be the quaestor of Antoninus, now by law his father. In April Marcus was seventeen, and in the normal course of events would not have begun public life until the following year, when he could have been appointed to one of the junior posts reserved for future senators, a group of offices known as the vigintivirate. Marcus' family background would undoubtedly have secured for him the office of *triumvir monetalis*, the most highly regarded of the available posts, involving token administration of the state Mint. Thereafter it would have been open to him to serve for a year or more as tribune with a legion, its nominal second-in-command. It is unlikely that Marcus would have chosen to undertake this military service. The intervening years would have been spent in travel and further education. This was not to be. His career from henceforth was to be set apart from that of his contemporaries. Nevertheless, his character was unaffected by the change. 'He still showed the same respect to his relations as he had when he was an ordinary citizen, and he was as thrifty and careful of his possessions as he had been when he lived in a private household; and he was willing to act, speak and think according to the principles of his father' – that is, of Antoninus. Antoninus' own attitude is exemplified by his reply to his wife, the elder Faustina, who had reproved him for not being generous enough to his household in some minor matter, shortly after his adoption: 'Foolish woman, now that we have gained an empire we have lost even what we had before.' He realized that for a man in his position, as a private citizen undoubtedly one of the wealthiest men in the empire, the additional possession of imperial funds was far outweighed by the financial outgoings his new status demanded – for a start, largesse to the people of Rome to celebrate the occasion, and public entertainment.[50]

Hadrian was now filled with disgust for life, the biographer records, and ordered a slave to stab him with a sword. When Antoninus heard this, he came to Hadrian with the prefects and begged him to bear bravely the hard necessity of illness: he himself would be no better than a parricide if he, as Hadrian's adopted son, allowed him to be killed. The betrayal of the secret angered Hadrian, who ordered the slave to be put to death, but Antoninus protected him. Cassius Dio tells the same story in slightly more detail. The slave was a barbarian captive named Mastor, a Jazygian. Hadrian had used him as a huntsman because of his strength and daring. The emperor had planned his own death with some care, drawing a coloured line round a place beneath the nipple as his doctor, Hermogenes, had shown him, so that Mastor could hardly fail to achieve his task. When this attempt failed, he drew up his will, nevertheless continuing to take part in administering the empire. He then tried to stab himself, but the dagger was taken from him.

He became violent and demanded poison from his doctor, but the doctor preferred to commit suicide himself.[51]

Two curious episodes then occurred. A woman appeared, claiming that she had been told in a dream to persuade Hadrian not to kill himself: he was destined to recover. For her failure to do this before, she had gone blind; the order had been repeated; and she was told to kiss the emperor's knees, after which she would recover her sight. She carried out the instructions and recovered her sight after bathing her eyes in water from the temple from which she had come. (It sounds as if she had been taking a 'dream-cure'.) Then a blind old man from Pannonia came to Hadrian when the emperor was feverish; when the old man touched him he regained his sight and Hadrian's fever left him. The cynical Marius Maximus, the biographer's source for these anecdotes, declared that both episodes were hoaxes.[52]

Hadrian finally left for the seaside resort of Baiae on the Campanian coast, leaving Antoninus to carry on the work of government at Rome. But he did not improve and sent for Antoninus. On his death-bed the literary minded emperor wrote the brief, tantalizingly untranslatable poem which might serve as a kind of epitaph to his restless spirit:

> *Animula vagula blandula,*
> *Hospes comesque corporis,*
> *Quae nunc abibis in loca,*
> *Pallidula, rigida, nudula,*
> *Nec ut soles dabis iocos?*

> Little soul, little wanderer, charmer,
> Body's companion and guest,
> What places will you leave for now,
> Little pale thing, stiff, little naked thing
> (And you won't make your usual jokes)?

He had abandoned the diet prescribed by his doctors and was indulging in unsuitable food and drink, according to Dio. At the end, as he lay dying, 'he shouted aloud the well-known saying: "Many doctors have killed a king".' He died in the presence of his adopted son on 10 July 138.[53]

Hadrian was never popular with the senate. The circumstances of his accession, and the executions of senators which had come shortly after, made the establishment of good relations nearly impossible. Hence the ugly affair of Servianus, when Hadrian's illness made him act in a suspicious and overbearing way, even to his old friends – 'although he ruled with the greatest mildness', as Dio admits – merely confirmed the opinions of leading circles in Rome. But this must not obscure the fact that Hadrian's achievement as ruler was colossal. His travels from one end of the empire to the other gave the provinces a new sense of belonging to Rome, and his reorganization of the Roman frontier system gave a solid basis to the defences of the empire. Cassius Dio, writing nearly a century later, was no admirer of Hadrian – his description of the suspicious circumstances of the accession in 117 shows he was not biased in Hadrian's favour – but his verdict on Hadrian's military policy is a remarkable tribute: 'To sum up,' he concludes, 'by his example and by his instructions he trained the armed forces throughout the whole empire, and disciplined them, to such an extent that even today the measures he introduced are the armies' law of campaigning. This is why his reign was one of peace with foreign peoples, since they, for the most part, seeing his state of preparedness and that they were not subject to aggression (but even received financial aid), did not cause trouble. In fact his troops had been so well trained that the Batavian cavalry, as they are called, swam the Danube fully armed. The barbarians observed this state of affairs, and had a healthy respect for the Romans. They turned to their own internal affairs and even employed Hadrian as a mediator in their disputes.'[53]

'Other faults which people found in him,' Dio says in another passage, after describing Hadrian's rows with an architect, 'were his great strictness, his curiosity and his interference in other people's affairs. Yet he balanced and made up for these faults by his careful administration, his prudence, generosity and ability – besides which, he did not stir up any war' – in contrast, it is implied, with the militaristic Trajan – 'and he deprived no one of money unjustly, while he presented many, communities and individuals, including senators and knights, with large sums of money, without waiting to be asked.' Trajan too had been a supporter of Hellenic culture, but under Hadrian – derisively nicknamed 'the little Greek' – the Greek-speaking half of the empire began a great step forward. It was no accident that his grandson by adoption, Marcus, was to write his *Meditations* in Greek.[54]

· 3 ·

AURELIUS CAESAR

AT HADRIAN'S DEATH it was the duty of Antoninus to make the immediate arrangements for the remains. As a temporary measure Hadrian was buried quietly at Puteoli above the Bay of Naples, at the villa once owned by Cicero, for the massive mausoleum on the right bank of the Tiber was not yet completed. The ceremony at Puteoli was in private: Hadrian was buried 'hated by all'.

'Marcus was left in Rome and discharged his (adoptive) grand-father's funeral rites', the biographer records, which may have included the announcement through heralds of the date and arrangements of the public funeral. 'He also gave a gladiatorial spectacle, in his private capacity, although he was quaestor,' the biographer adds – but Marcus was presumably still only quaestor-designate: he would not become quaestor until the end of the year.[1]

Immediately after Hadrian's death, Antoninus approached Marcus through his wife Faustina, Marcus' aunt, and asked if he would be willing to alter his marriage arrangements. They wanted him to dissolve his betrothal to Ceionia Fabia and to become betrothed to their daughter, the younger Faustina, his first cousin. This involved also the dissolution of the betrothal between Faustina and Ceionia's brother Lucius Commodus, now the younger adopted son of Antoninus. Faustina was still far too young to be married – her marriage was in fact not until 145, so in 138 she was probably only eight or nine years old. This meant that Marcus had to wait seven years before he could marry. Ceionia Fabia was probably older than Faustina – she was certainly married several years before 145 – so, if Marcus had been allowed to keep to his original betrothal, he would not have had to wait so long. In spite of the temptations to which, he hints in the *Meditations*, he had been exposed while living in the same house as his grandfather's mistress, Marcus had probably not had sexual experience – and perhaps did not have, until his marriage, for he says: 'I preserved the flower of my manhood and did not make proof of my virility before the right time, but even deferred the time.' In any case, the match with Ceionia Fabia had been arranged by Hadrian; and Lucius and Faustina were fairly clearly ill-matched in ages, certainly by Roman standards – Faustina was probably just a little older than Lucius, at any rate very little younger, whereas Roman custom normally required the bridegroom to be several years older than the bride. Marcus consented without demur to the new arrangements. Betrothal did not, in any case, carry very binding legal obligations and could be dissolved without difficulty.[2]

A record of Marcus participating in public life in 138, under his new names, happens to be preserved. The city of Cyzicus in the province of Asia (on an island in the Propontis) had set up an organization for the young men, a *corpus iuvenum*, in which training for public life was provided. They sent to the senate for their action to be confirmed (a very necessary precaution, as the Roman state regarded clubs and societies of all kinds with suspicion, as breeding-grounds for political opposition). Antoninus presided and a motion was passed in his name after a speech by one of the consuls designate, Appius Annius Gallus. Seven witnesses were required to legalize a motion of this kind (as for all legal documents). At the head of the list came 'Marcus Aelius, son of the emperor Titus Aelius Hadrianus Antoninus, of the Papirian voting district, Aurelius Verus.' The name which followed his has not been completely preserved, but it looks as if that of Marcus' grandfather, M. Annius Verus, may be restored. Fourth on the list stood his paternal uncle, Libo. The family was evidently turning out in strength – but Marcus was now senior in rank to them all, except Antoninus. Marcus was probably entitled to be present in his capacity as quaestor or quaestor-designate. Ironically, the answer to the request of the city of Cyzicus is not known, as the stone is broken after the beginning of the decree of the senate. But as the stone which records it was set up in Cyzicus, presumably it was in the affirmative.[3]

The events of the rest of the year 138 did not greatly concern Marcus personally. But Antoninus was involved from the outset in a struggle with the senate. The unpopularity of Hadrian, and Antoninus' own 'democratic' demeanour and easy-going personality, emboldened some members to make a stand against him. Antoninus felt in duty bound to have the memory of Hadrian officially consecrated; he was to be Divus Hadrianus, the Deified Hadrian. The senate was unwilling to consent. Not only that, it was proposed that Hadrian's acts should be annulled. Antoninus resisted: if Hadrian's acts were annulled, his own adoption would automatically become void also. This he could not, of course, allow. He also felt that he owed it to Hadrian to have him deified. Otherwise he would fall into the same category as Tiberius, Caligula, Nero and Domitian: all the other emperors (excluding the ephemeral rulers of 68 and 69, Galba, Otho and Vitellius) had become Divus – Julius Caesar as well. Hadrian might not compare with Augustus – who could? But he deserved consecration as much as, for example, Titus and Nerva – except that, from the senators' point of view, these two rulers were especially distinguished for their benign attitude to the senate itself. That was the crux. Antoninus forced the measure through, 'against universal opposition'.[4]

Thus Hadrian was to be worshipped as a god. Quinquennial games were to be held in his honour. A temple was to be built for him in Rome – and elsewhere, for example at Puteoli, where his body was first buried. A priesthood bearing his name was formed from senators, the *sodales Hadrianales*, with a *flamen* to minister to the cult. When the Mausoleum was ready, the body was transferred to the Garden of Domitia in which it stood, for the official funeral ceremony and *consecratio*, which no doubt followed the by now traditional lines. After the ceremony the ashes were placed in the massive tomb, accompanied by the remains of L. Aelius Caesar and of Antoninus' three older children who had died before his adoption. In spite of Antoninus' rigidity over the official honouring of Hadrian's memory, he demonstrated the change of atmosphere of his own administration by releasing political prisoners and recalling exiles, and by commuting sentences of death imposed by Hadrian in his final months of tortured existence. He had in any case taken steps before Hadrian's death to prevent sentences being carried out.[5]

Antoninus' dignified stand, coupled with his favourable attitude to the senate, won a warm response. He was asked to accept a new name, Pius, and from henceforward was generally known as Antoninus Pius, or, briefly, as Pius. Various versions have survived which purport to explain the origin of this name. It had in fact been borne by a senator named Aurelius mentioned in Tacitus' *Annals*, who could well have been an ancestor of (Aurelius) Antoninus. In other words, Pius may have been a family name, which Antoninus felt entitled to revive for himself. (But none of the sources refer to this.) The most popular version refers to the occasion shortly before the adoption of Antoninus, when he entered a meeting of senators, supporting his aged father-in-law, Annius Verus: this evoked to men's minds, fairly obviously, the legendary founder of the Roman race, Aeneas the Trojan, 'pius Aeneas' as Virgil describes him constantly, who earned the epithet – meaning 'dutiful' – not least by his action in rescuing his aged father Anchises from the flames of Troy and carrying him out of the burning city on his back. There was an antiquarian revival in Rome at this time, and the comparison of Antoninus to Aeneas would have come readily to men's minds. Certainly representations of Aeneas carrying Anchises occur on coins and medallions of Antoninus. Perhaps such an episode prompted someone, for example, to exclaim 'Pius Antoninus' (and the episode was clearly misunderstood: it is even asserted that Hadrian's choice of Antoninus as heir in the first place was prompted by his pleasure at this incident, which is absurd.) But this was not sufficient reason in itself for a Roman emperor to take a new official name. Other considerations were relevant: Antoninus' own deep religious convictions; his dutiful respect to the memory of his adopted father Hadrian; his efforts to prevent Hadrian from killing himself; his success in protecting senators against Hadrian; and his general 'clemency' or mildness (*clementia*).[6]

On 1 January, 139, Pius was consul for the second time. His colleague was C. Bruttius Praesens, also consul for the second time. Praesens was a man who had been a friend of Hadrian for many years and owed his career to him. His family was eventually to become connected with the Antonine dynasty, for his granddaughter Crispina married Marcus' son Commodus – but this was nearly forty years later. However, Praesens and his son were influential figures throughout the reigns of Pius and Marcus.[7]

Pius made few initial changes in the administration. He did not replace any of Hadrian's nominees, according to the biographer. This accession of Pius, indeed, in spite of the initial embarrassments over the treatment of Hadrian's memory, was peaceful and stable. Even so, there were a few changes. Scipio Orfitus, the prefect of the city, 'asked permission' to resign, says the biographer, giving no dates or details. He did not receive the honour of a second consulship, which prefects usually acquired at some stage, and it is possible that the request was a cloak for a swift dismissal. He may have been replaced by Bruttius Praesens. Another change was in the powerful province of Britain (with Syria one of the two senior appointments of this kind for a senator), where a new governor was appointed by Pius in 139. His name was Quintus Lollius Urbicus, African in origin, younger son of a knight and the first of his family to enter the senate. He had been prominent in the Jewish war of 132–135, after which Hadrian had made him consul and then governor of Lower Germany. It was common for governors of Lower Germany to be promoted to Britain, and the appointment of Urbicus by Pius is not therefore unusual; and his predecessor may have been due for replacement in any case. But as Urbicus was soon to take action which reversed an important and very expensive policy decision of Hadrian, his arrival in Britain seems a significant move.

Urbicus may have been recommended by the leading general of the day, Sextus Julius Severus, his commander-in-chief in the Jewish war of Hadrian. Severus had previously governed Britain himself and may well have found the frontier system established by Hadrian and Platorius Nepos difficult to operate. Another move of Pius which reversed Hadrianic policy was his abolition of the four consulars who carried out judicial functions in Italy (Pius himself had served as one). The removal of imperial 'interference' in Italy may have been taken kindly by the senate.[8]

In 139 Pius took further steps to enhance the dignity of his nephew and elder adopted son. Marcus was designated consul for 140 and Pius was to be his colleague. Further honours included the appointment as one of the *seviri* at the annual parade of the knights on 15 July. As heir apparent Marcus was head of the equestrian order, *princeps iuventutis*. He now received the name Caesar and from this time until Pius' death he was officially styled Marcus Aelius Aurelius Verus Caesar. He had no more than the name so far, none of the powers. But it was no ordinary name, as Marcus was well aware. 'See that you do not turn into a Caesar', he told himself in the *Meditations* many years later, 'do not be dipped into the purple dye – for that can happen'.

The implication is clear. But at one of his first official appearances, Cassius Dio records, when as *princeps iuventutis* 'he had become leader of the knights', it created a favourable impression that 'he entered the Forum with the rest, although he was a Caesar'.[9]

At the senate's command Marcus was made a member of the priestly colleges, the four principal ones being the *pontifices*, the *augures*, the *quindecimviri sacris faciundis* and the *septemviri epulonum*. An ordinary senator could not expect to belong to more than one of these, and the majority had to be content with membership of one of the less distinguished bodies – the Arval Brethren, the *fetiales*, and the *sodales* of the imperial cult, to all of which Marcus, as a matter of course, was probably co-opted, although direct evidence is available only in the case of the Arval Brethren.[10]

Pius himself acquired a new distinction in 139: he received the title of *pater patriae*, 'father of the fatherland', one which all emperors sought – but it was deemed proper to defer acceptance for a while. Hadrian had waited eleven years. Pius' assumption of the title after only one year is a little surprising, but it was probably at the pressing request of the senate. 'He refused it at first when the senate offered it, then accepted with an elaborate speech of thanks.'[11]

Pius now required Marcus to take up his residence in the House of Tiberius, the imperial palace on the Palatine hill, and provided him with the outward and visible signs of his new station, the *aulicum fastigium*, the 'pomp of court', in spite of Marcus' objections. The difficulty of living a normal life – or a good life – in a palace is a theme which recurs on several occasions in the *Meditations*: 'where life is possible, then it is possible to live the right life; life is possible in a palace, so it is possible to live the right life in a palace'. In a later passage in the *Meditations* Marcus tells himself: 'let no one, not even yourself, ever hear you abusing court life again'. He must have realised that it was too easy for him to make his position an excuse for not being able to live up to his own high standards. But he must have known the lines of the Stoic poet Lucan:

> Let him leave the palace,
> Who wishes to be pious.

Antoninus Pius helped Marcus 'to strip off all my pride and brought me to realise that one can live in a palace and yet not need bodyguards, embroidered uniforms, candelabra or statues carrying lamps, and things like that, all that goes with pomp and ceremony; but that one may live very nearly as a private citizen, without thereby losing any dignity or being less active in the duties necessary for a prince on behalf of the state'. As quaestor in 139 Marcus' role in the senate was a subordinate one. His main duties, as the emperor's own quaestor, would be to read letters of the emperor to the senate when Pius was not present himself, and in general to act as a kind of parliamentary private secretary. In 140, as consul, he would have more important duties: as one of the two senior representatives of the senate during his period of office he would be required to preside over meetings and perform official and religious ceremonies, and take a leading part in the senate's administrative functions.

He was now to take an important part in his adoptive father's administration, initially by attending meetings of the imperial council to observe how the business of the empire was carried out: 'he had to be prepared to rule the state', as the biographer puts it.[12]

The influence of Pius on the young Marcus was enormous; and of all the tributes in the first book of the *Meditations* to those whose effect on him he remembered with gratitude, the tribute to Antoninus Pius is by far the longest. The picture of the emperor and the man that it presents is so vivid that it deserves to be quoted in full:

'From my father – gentleness and to be unshakeably resolute in judgments made after full investigation; no vain-glory about outward honours; love of work and perseverance; readiness to listen to any who had something to contribute to the good of the state; his practice of rewarding every man impartially according to his deserts; knowing from experience where to tighten the reins, where to relax them.

'He prohibited homosexual practices. He was tactful in his social relations. He excused his friends from attending all his banquets and from accompanying him every time he made a progress outside Rome – but those who could not attend on him because of some necessary engagements of their own always found him the same towards them when they did see him. At meetings of his council he made a careful scrutiny and was persistent – he was not content with first impressions, avoiding further investigations. His practice was to keep the same friends' – the term 'friend' here has an official significance, not only a private one: the members of the imperial council had the title of 'friends of the emperor'[13] – 'and not to tire of them: he was not subject to sudden mad changes of feeling. He was always satisfied and cheerful. He had the foresight to plan well in advance and could deal with the most trivial matters without any theatrical fuss. He restrained applause by the people and all forms of flattery. He always kept a watch on the needs of the empire and was a good steward of its resources. To criticism in everything of this kind he was long-suffering. His attitude to the gods was not superstitious and he did not court the favour of men – he did not try to cultivate people by gifts or flattery, but was temperate in every respect, without any mean behaviour or love of novelty for its own sake.

'As for the material comforts of life, in which fortune had been lavish to him, he used them without ostentation and at the same time without apology – when they were there he enjoyed them, when they were not, he did without. No one could have said of him that he was a sophist, an impostor or a pedant. He was acknowledged to be a mature and complete personality, who was above flattery and competent to deal with his own affairs and those of others. As well as this he had a respect for genuine followers of philosophy, but did not find fault with the other sort – yet was not taken in by them. He was affable and good-humoured, but not excessively so. He took care of his health, in moderation, not in the way that a man does who is attached to life or thinks of his personal appearance. He did not neglect himself, but he rarely needed a doctor, or to take medicine, or to have some external application.

'A particular characteristic was his readiness to give way without ill-feeling to the experts in special fields, whether it was in the use of words, the knowledge of civil law or traditions, or anything else – he even shared in the enthusiasm of the expert so that they could get the credit that their special qualifications deserved. In everything he followed traditional ways, without making a fetish of it. He was not inclined to alter his position or change his mind. He liked to stay settled in the same places and to do the same things. After his sudden attacks of headache he returned to his usual tasks fresh and vigorous. He did not have many secrets, only very few, quite exceptionally, and these only for reasons of state. He was prudent and economical in his provision of shows, in carrying out public building, in largesse to the people and so forth. It was the behaviour of a man who is interested in what has to be done, and not in the reputation that he gets' – this perhaps a recollection by Marcus of his own boyish concern for his good name, a tendency to mind what other people thought of him which he had to fight against for the rest of his life.[14]

'He was not the kind of person who took his bath at odd hours. He did not have a mania for building, did not mind what he ate, did not worry about the colour or material of his clothes, or about the personal beauty of his slaves. His clothes were brought from Lorium, his country house down on the coast. [I remember] his way of life at Lanuvium, and how he treated the tax-collector who apologized at Tusculum, and all his behaviour in that sort of matter. He was in no way harsh, merciless or violent – never carried anything "to fever pitch", as you might say. Everything was examined and divided up carefully, as if he had plenty of leisure. No rush, but complete orderliness, with vigour and consistency. What is recorded of Socrates would fit him exactly – that he could equally well abstain from or enjoy what many are too weak to abstain from and too self-indulgent in enjoying. He was strong enough to bear the one and could be sober in the other – the mark of a man of perfect and invincible spirit, like Maximus in his illness' (a reference to Marcus' friend Claudius Maximus).[15]

High on the list of subjects for discussion at the imperial council meetings in 140 must have been Britain. Because of his military inexperience, Pius relied a good deal on experts, prominent among whom were the two praetorian prefects, M. Petronius Mamertinus and M. Gavius Maximus. The previous career of Mamertinus, a kinsman of Fronto, is little known. One of his grandsons was to marry a daughter of Marcus. Gavius Maximus was of Italian origin, from Firmum in Picenum, near the Adriatic coast. He had been procurator of Mauretania Tingitana some ten years previously and then procurator of the province of Asia. It is not improbable that he had met Pius there when the future emperor was proconsul, and that he had made a favourable enough impression to be selected for the vital task of praetorian prefect without going through the normal stages of promotion beforehand. Maximus was to remain prefect for nearly twenty years – an unparalleled length of tenure. He was not universally liked – 'a man of great severity' – but he must have been competent and was in a position to influence profoundly the military policy of the reign.[16]

Other advisers were available to give their views on Britain. Sextus Julius Severus has already been mentioned. Platorius Nepos, the builder of Hadrian's Wall, may still have been living, but his views were perhaps not much valued. P. Mummius Sisenna had been in Britain as governor only five years before and his son Sisenna Rutilianus was legate of the Sixth Legion there. A young man named Pontius Laelianus, whose military abilities were highly thought of in this reign, had gone to Britain from Lower Germany with Platorius Nepos and the Sixth Legion, as tribune. And there were others who had served there.

In the autumn of 140 Pius and Marcus called on a former governor of Britain. Marcus recalled the occasion in 143: 'Three years ago, I remember, as I was returning from the vintage with my father, we turned aside to the estates of Pompeius Falco. I saw there a tree with many branches which he called *catachanna*. It seemed to me a wonderful new sort of tree, having on one trunk the shoots of practically every kind of tree. . . .' Here the manuscript of the letter breaks off. Even if the complete text had survived there would probably not have been any reference to Britain. But there is little doubt that Pius would have discussed developments there with Falco, as well as admiring his experiments in grafting. Falco had been governor immediately before Platorius Nepos, and perhaps had quite different ideas as to how the truculent north Britons should be treated.[17]

In effect Lollius Urbicus abandoned the expensive permanent stone frontier barrier erected by Nepos for Hadrian, and invaded southern Scotland. There had been, no doubt, provocation, but the reprisal need not have involved the giving up of the frontier wall unless the Roman High Command had begun to find it unsatisfactory. Urbicus won victories, and began the construction of a new frontier, between the Forth and Clyde, only half the length of Hadrian's wall and built of turf not stone, hence much cheaper (but easier to outflank, especially down the west coast).

The success in Britain prompted Pius to accept the acclamation by the victorious troops of the British legions, in 142. The following year the title

'*Imp. II*' appeared on the coinage. It was the only such military title that Pius was to accept throughout his entire reign, a sign of the special importance attached to the British war – and also a sign of the peaceable nature of the reign as a whole. Pius himself was credited by his flatterers with personal direction of operations from Rome: 'Although he committed the conduct of the campaign to others,' said the orator Fronto, 'while remaining in the Palace at Rome, yet like the helmsman at the tiller of a warship, the glory of the whole navigation and voyage belongs to him.'[18]

Although the war in Britain was the only major one, there was also trouble in Dacia. Under Hadrian Dacia had been divided into three provinces, two of which were governed by procurators with no legionary troops under their command. Disturbances of an unknown nature which affected Lower Dacia made it necessary to send in legionary troops, which could normally only be commanded by a senator, with the title *legatus*, to reinforce the procurator's garrison. It was evidently felt impolitic to send a senator to campaign in Lower Dacia, so the procurator was given special powers as *pro legato*. The man in question was a close relative of Hadrian's great praetorian prefect Q. Marcius Turbo, who had himself taken military action in Dacia with special powers in 118. Meanwhile, on the middle Danube there was a diplomatic success. The troublesome Quadi allowed Rome to choose their new ruler, an event announced on the imperial coinage with the legend REX QUADIS DATVS.[19]

There was also diplomatic activity in the east. The Armenians too accepted a Roman nominee to the throne, and the king of the distant Hiberi from the Caucasus, useful allies of Rome in any difficulties with Parthia, came on a state visit to Rome in or soon after 140. He treated Antoninus with great respect – more than he had shown to Hadrian, it was said. Firm action had backed the diplomacy: the Syrian army was reinforced, and war with Parthia was averted.[20]

In addition to these matters of state, Marcus was – 'with great eagerness' – pursuing his studies. The taking of the *toga virilis* was normally the moment for the beginning of the third stage of education, in oratory or rhetoric. Although Marcus was only fourteen in 136 when he took the *toga virilis*, he may well have been advanced enough to begin oratorical training. This meant far more in ancient times than we understand by the term today. The simplest definition of the term *orator* was that given by Cato the Elder several centuries before: 'a good man skilled in speaking'. This emphasises the importance attached to training in morals and character-building, for the aim was not simply to produce a man who could make a good, or even a brilliant speech, although this was then a far more important qualification than it is now. In ancient times to make a speech was the *only* way of communicating with a mass audience, in the absence of printing and broadcasting. To be trained as an orator was to be trained for the whole of public life. On the other hand, this must not be exaggerated – even its leading exponents sometimes admitted, in any case, that the practical aspect of the oratorical training was not always very great. It was nevertheless a humane university education that was offered, covering philology, literature, history and philosophy.

Marcus had three tutors in Greek, Aninius Macer, Caninius Celer and Herodes Atticus, and one in Latin oratory, Cornelius Fronto; although Fronto and Herodes probably did not become his tutors until his adoption by Antoninus. As always, it was felt important that Greek should receive particular attention.

Marcus also had a tutor in law, Lucius Volusius Maecianus. Maecianus was a knight, whom Pius had taken on to his staff at his adoption. He was now holding office as director of the public posting-service (*praefectus vehiculorum*), a job given him so that he could remain in Rome, where he would be available to give advice on legal problems in the council – one of those experts to whom, Marcus relates, Pius was so ready to listen.[21]

The great educationalist of the preceding age, Quintilian, appointed to a state chair of rhetoric by the emperor Vespasian, had held that philosophy could not decently be omitted from the syllabus for a future orator, although there was a traditional rivalry between the orators and the philosophers, as educationalists, stemming back to the days of Isocrates and Plato. But the Roman prejudice against philosophy, which had made the mother of Agricola restrain her son when 'he was drinking in philosophy too deeply for a Roman and a senator' at the university of Marseilles, no longer obtained. Marcus had previously been attending classes given by the Stoic Apollonius. The philosopher was now back in his native Chalcedon, and Pius sent for him. He came, his detractors said, like a Jason after the Golden Fleece, in reverse. On his arrival in Rome he was summoned to the palace to teach Marcus. But his answer was: 'The master ought not to come to the pupil, but the pupil to the master.' Pius made fun of him – 'It was easier for Apollonius to come from Colchis to Rome than from his house in Rome to the Palatine.' But Marcus went to the house of Apollonius, all the same. Pius is reported to have found Apollonius greedy over the matter of his salary. Marcus' own memories of Apollonius in the *Meditations* were quite different. He is mentioned as one of the three people that he was especially grateful to the gods for having come to know. From Apollonius he learned 'the meaning of moral freedom, not to expose myself to the uncertain cast of fortune; to look to nothing else, even briefly, except reason. To be always the same, in sharp attacks of pain, in the loss of a child, in long illnesses. To see clearly from his living example that a man could be at the same time completely serious and yet relaxed. Not to find fault when explaining something. To see a man who obviously regarded his technical accomplishment and his facility in expounding philosophical principles as the least important of his gifts. The lesson how one ought to accept the pretended favours of friends, without either lowering one's self-respect on their account or tactlessly returning them.' This last point is interesting in the light of Pius' opinion: Marcus seems to be thinking of how Apollonius had reacted to presents from him in return for his teaching, presents which as mere material objects could not be compared in value with his lessons.[22]

How much attention Marcus paid to his training in philosophy with Apollonius at this stage is not known; probably the practical Pius insisted that the major emphasis be placed on oratory. Not much is known about two of Marcus' tutors. A chance mention in Philostratus reveals that Caninius Celer was the author of a work entitled *Araspes the Lover of Panthea* – which presumably told the tale of the wife of Abradatus, a Persian king: she fell in love with her Median captor Araspes. Celer also wrote on rhetoric, and 'although he was a good imperial secretary [apparently to Hadrian], he lacked proficiency in declamation'. Aninius Macer is otherwise unknown. Celer is mentioned once, in passing, by Marcus in the *Meditations*, Macer not at all.[23]

Marcus' other two teachers, Herodes Atticus and Cornelius Fronto, were the two most celebrated practitioners of oratory of the age, in Greek and Latin respectively, and many details of their lives are known. Herodes – Tiberius Claudius Atticus Herodes – was a controversial figure. His connection with Marcus' family went back to the period when he had lived for a time as a young man in the house at Rome of Marcus' maternal grandfather, Calvisius Tullus Ruso. Herodes was an Athenian, from an ancient family, and enormously wealthy. 'No man used his wealth better', says his biographer Philostratus. But he could be tactless and hot-headed as well. His father had been consul under Hadrian, so entry into the senate, and ascent to the highest honours in the state, were assured to him. He had been in contact with Antoninus when the latter was proconsul of Asia and he himself was administering some of the communities there as a special commissioner. The versions of their meeting differed: some said the self-assured Greek jostled the proconsul in the street – and no more. Philostratus is forced to admit the authenticity of the story – 'they did shove one another aside, after a fashion, as happens in a rough place and a narrow road; still, they did not break the law by coming to blows'. The episode is curious. Possibly both exalted senators were in carriages and the quarrel was over who had the right of way. The affair did not, however, jeopardize his future when Antoninus became emperor.

Herodes was not merely rich. He was probably the richest man in the eastern half of the empire. But the proud Athenians resented his patronizing manner and from time to time complaints were made, beginning with his father's death, when it was alleged that he had tried to defraud them of a legacy in his deceased parent's will. But he could be generous. One public building which he had built at his own expense at Athens still testifies to this – the Odeum. Cities in other parts of the empire likewise benefited. Herodes was married to Appia Annia Regilla, daughter of an Italian noble house. The marriage was not welcomed by all the members of Regilla's family, and it was to end in tragedy, with unpleasant recriminations.

Herodes' oratorical abilities were lightly acquired – 'no man ever found it easier to learn than he', Philostratus declares. 'He did not neglect hard work, but he used to study while drinking wine, and at night, in periods of sleeplessness. Hence he was called "The Stuffed Orator" – by the lazy and small-minded.' He was a restrained speaker, whose speciality was subtlety rather than vigorous attack, according to Philostratus. 'His language was pleasing and full of metaphors – graceful.'[24]

The second century was the heyday of the sophist – the professional lecturer and teacher, the travelling professor (but some had university chairs endowed by the state). Public men like Herodes and Fronto were the doyens of the profession in a sense, although they would not regard themselves as being in the same category as Favorinus, for example, or even as Caninius Celer. Fronto especially, as a forensic orator, would have justification in looking down on the theorists. The earnest Aulus Gellius was an admirer of both Herodes and Fronto and related in his *Attic Nights* the occasions on which he had had the privilege of hearing the great men hold forth. Two of the stories about Herodes are of occasions when he put so-called philosophers firmly in their place. 'When we were students at Athens,' one story begins, 'Herodes Atticus the consular, of true Greek eloquence, often invited me to his country house near the city, with the senator Servilianus and several other Romans who had come to Greece from Rome in search of culture. At that time, when we were there at his villa called Cephisia, we used to be protected against the unpleasant heat in the summer or the burning autumn sun by the shade of his spacious groves, the long avenues and the cool position of the house. It had elegant baths with abundance of sparkling waters and as a whole was a charming place, with a melodious sound of running water and birdsong.

'There was with us on one occasion a young student of philosophy, "of the Stoic persuasion", as he himself used to put it – intolerably talkative and presumptuous. During the normal after-dinner conversation he used to lecture away at immoderate length about philosophical principles, in a quite inappropriate and ridiculous way, claiming that in comparison with himself all the Greek authorities and all the toga-wearers – all the Latin name in general – were ignorant boors . . .' and so on. But, Gellius concludes, 'Herodes waited for him to finish' and then silenced him by having the first volume of *The Discourses of Epictetus*, edited by Arrian, brought in and having a passage read out, in which the great Stoic had given a simple definition of the distinction between good and evil. The self-confident young man was reduced to embarrassed silence.[25]

On another occasion Herodes dealt with a man who asked him in the street for money to buy bread. 'The man was dressed in a cloak with hair and beard down to his waist' – the normal appearance of a certain type of philosopher. 'Herodes asked him who he was, which annoyed the man. "I am a philosopher," he replied. "Why do you ask what should be obvious?" Herodes said that he could see a beard and a cloak but not a philosopher. "By what evidence do you think I can recognize you as a philosopher?" he asked. Some of those with Herodes told him that the man was a well-known tramp of low character.' Herodes then in munificent manner gave the tramp enough money to buy bread for thirty days, afterwards deploring the practice of men posing as philosophers.

On a third occasion Gellius heard Herodes attacking Stoicism. 'I once heard the consular Herodes Atticus speaking at length, in Greek, in which language he was outstanding among all the men of our time in the seriousness, fluency and elegance of his diction. He was speaking at the time against the "lack of feeling" of the Stoics' – their belief that emotions should be kept in check. The emotional Herodes could not accept this attitude and compared the Stoics with an ignorant barbarian, who having learned that pruning is good, proceeds to chop down all his vines and olives. '"Thus", said Herodes, "these disciplines of the cult of the unemotional, who want to be considered calm, brave and steadfast because they show neither desire nor grief, neither anger nor pleasure, cut out the more active emotions of the spirit and grow old in a torpor, a sluggish, enervated life".'[26]

Marcus was to become a Stoic. As a young man when he was mourning the death of one of his teachers, some of the palace staff restrained him. Pius intervened: 'Let him be human for once – for neither philosophy nor the empire takes away natural feelings.'[27] Perhaps the teachings of Apollonius had been having some effect on Marcus. Little is known about Herodes as Marcus' teacher. They were to come into contact a good deal for the rest of their lives. But Marcus does not refer to Herodes at all in the *Meditations*.

The urbane Marcus Cornelius Fronto rivalled Herodes in popular esteem. Fronto, from Cirta (Constantine) in the Latin-speaking province of Numidia, did not care greatly for his flamboyant rival, although Marcus later managed to bring them on to terms of polite acquaintanceship. As an orator Fronto was highly regarded in ancient times – he was thought to be second only to Cicero, or even to be an alternative choice as 'the glory of Roman eloquence' – a choice which is puzzling now when only fragments of his speeches and some letters and anecdotes survive. One anecdote, not startlingly amusing, but pleasant enough, is found in Cassius Dio. 'Cornelius Fronto, who held first place at the bar among the Romans of those times, one night was returning home from a banquet very late. A man he was to plead for told him that Turbo was already sitting in court. He went to the court as he was, in his banqueting dress, and greeted the prefect with "ὑγίαινε" (good night), instead of "χαῖρε" (good morning).'[28]

But the stories in Aulus Gellius give a better picture of Fronto, the man of letters, and help to show him in the context of the literary society of the time. 'When I was at Rome as a young man, before I left for Athens, when my sessions with my teachers and my attendance at lectures allowed me the spare time, I used to go to Cornelius Fronto, for the pleasure of seeing him and to enjoy his conversation, which was full of useful instruction expressed in the most classical way. Invariably we went away more cultured and better educated than before, after seeing him and listening to him talking – as for instance with that discussion of his on one particular day, on a minor matter certainly, but not irrelevant to the study of the Latin language. For when a certain acquaintance of his, a well-educated man and a well-known poet of the day, said that he had been cured of the dropsy by the application of heated "sands" (*arenae*), Fronto said, in a bantering way:

'"You are cured of your disease, to be sure, but not of corrupt usage of words. For Gaius Caesar the life dictator [Julius Caesar], the father-in-law of Gnaeus Pompeius, from whom the family and name of Caesars are derived, a man of the foremost intellect and distinguished beyond all his contemporaries for the purity of his diction, holds in his work *On Analogy*, dedicated to Marcus Cicero, that 'sands' is an incorrect usage and that sand is never used in the plural any more than sky or wheat. . . ." Fronto went on to give more examples, and his acquaintance argued the other side, quoting from Plautus and Ennius. Fronto produced his copy of Caesar's work, and then was asked by his poet friend to justify the dictator's arguments.' Aulus Gellius took the opportunity of memorizing the opening words of the book by Caesar (of which, presumably, he did not possess a copy). Fronto's exposition ended with a recommendation to look out for 'sands' plural, or other words normally plural only used in the singular – 'not, I presume,' says Gellius 'because he thought they were in fact to be found in any of the classical authors, but so that he could give us practice in reading by our search for rare words'.

Gellius later visited Fronto with his friend Favorinus when the great man had gout, but was nevertheless in full swing at a literary *salon*. The learned men present were discussing the words used to describe colours. Favorinus put forward the view that Greek had more words to describe, for example, shades of red. Fronto was not to be outdone and produced seven Latin words for different varieties of red, in addition to the three which Favorinus had been able to think of – and had maintained to be exact synonyms in any case. Favorinus had only been able to produce four Greek words, and gracefully conceded to Fronto's brilliance in argument.

At another discussion Fronto dealt with a critic who maintained that 'many mortals' was an absurd expression for the historian Claudius Quadrigarius to use, when he could have said simply 'many men' or 'many people'. Fronto firmly explained the subtle distinction of atmosphere that Quadrigarius had intended to convey. Details of this kind were meat and drink to Fronto. 'I remember once that Julius Celsinus, the Numidian, and

I went to see Cornelius Fronto, who was then suffering from gout. When we were shown in, we found him lying on a Greek-style couch, surrounded by many men of eminent learning, noble birth, or wealth. Several architects were present who had been called in to construct a new bath-house, and were showing sketches of various types of baths, drawn on little parchment scrolls. When he had chosen one type and sketch, he asked what the estimate of the cost for completing the work was. The architect said it would be about 300,000 sesterces. "Plus another 50,000, or thereabouts (*praeter propter*)", said one of his friends.' Fronto suddenly put off further discussion of the new baths and began an investigation into the use of the expression *praeter propter*.

A final illustration will give another glimpse into the atmosphere of these literary circles. Fronto was standing in the entrance-hall of the palace, talking with Postumius Festus, another senator from Numidia, and Gellius' own teacher, the great scholar Sulpicius Apollinaris (also the teacher of Pertinax, the future emperor, at that time a young man of low origin and no prospects). 'I was standing near at the same time with the others, eagerly listening in to their conversation on literary topics' – the debate was going on about the alternative Latin words for dwarf. But all was grist to Gellius' mill. In some ways he would have made a perfect Boswell, but perhaps he lacked a single Johnson whose every word he could have recorded. The spirit of Gellius' curious work and of the things which he found interesting is perhaps best conveyed by giving a few of the headings of the short essays in his *Attic Nights*: 'The vigorous assertion by Julius Hyginus that he had read a manuscript of Virgil from the poet's own household, which had the version *et ora tristia temptantum sensus torquebit amaror*, instead of the usual version *sensu torquebit amaro*'; 'Concerning a shameful error of Caesellius Vindex, which we find in his work *Early Words*'; 'A story taken from the works of Tubero about a snake of unprecedented length'; 'In what manner and how severely the philosopher Peregrinus, in my hearing, rebuked a young Roman of equestrian family, who was standing in front of him inattentively yawning all the time'; 'About the strange suicide of the virgins of Miletus'.[29]

This then was the literary world in which Marcus was to immerse himself under the guidance of Fronto. It was above all a world which was trying to look back to the early days of Latin literature for its inspiration. The greatest figures of the golden age, Cicero and Virgil, were still admired and read. But later writers, such as Seneca, Lucan, Martial, Juvenal, Pliny, Suetonius and Tacitus, were ignored. Fronto and his friends went back to Ennius and Cato, Plautus, Terence, Gaius Gracchus and, although he was comparatively modern, to Sallust. The movement back to the early days of Latin literature is reminiscent of the nineteenth-century English literary world, when Keats and Charles Lamb looked for their inspiration to the Elizabethan period rather than to the writers of the eighteenth century. But for orators and historians there was a dilemma. The death-throes of the Roman republic had been the great age of Roman literature, precisely because of the political upheavals. It was difficult to find inspiration under a stable and benevolent autocratic régime, as Tacitus complained. The students of rhetoric or oratory had to go back to the past to find subjects for debate. As Juvenal mockingly pointed out, Hannibal's remarkable career – for example – might have been especially designed to provide debating themes or essay subjects for the schools.[30]

Nevertheless, Fronto had a prince to educate, which meant that his pupil was required to speak in the senate on subjects of high importance during his actual period of instruction, which was, for the times, an enviable state. Quintilian had died before his two imperial pupils, who were in any case much younger than Marcus was in 138, could put his instruction into effect.[31]

· 4 ·
THE EDUCATION OF AN
HEIR APPARENT

BY A FORTUNATE chance the correspondence between Fronto and Marcus
has been preserved. Although few of the letters are precisely dated, they
give a rare insight into the education of a future ruler. In one of the later
letters in the collection, written when Marcus was already emperor, Fronto
recalls the early days of their association. 'Do you remember that speech of
yours which you delivered in the senate when you were scarcely more than
a boy? You used in it the simile of "a leather bottle" to illustrate a point, and
were very anxious in case you had made use of a linguistic image little
suited to the dignity of the place and of a senator. I wrote that first fairly
long letter to you, and in it I said that I inferred from this – quite rightly, in
fact – that it was a sign of great ability to meet the dangers involved in
expressing thoughts of that kind with boldness; but that you would rise to
what was needed, by your own study and with help from me, namely, to
the command of language sufficiently luminous to match such great
thoughts.'[1]

The letter to which he referred has also survived. 'Fronto to my Lord. In
all the arts, I think, complete inexperience and ignorance are better than
half-experience and half-knowledge. For a man who realizes that he knows
nothing of some art will attempt less, and consequently is less likely to
come to grief – in fact, diffidence prevents rashness. But when someone
ostentatiously pretends to have mastered something of which he has merely
a superficial knowledge, he makes mistakes of all kinds because of his false
confidence. They say that it is better never to have touched the teaching of
philosophy, as well, than to have tasted it superficially, with the edge of the
lips, as the saying is – and that those who enter the corridors of some art and
turn aside before they have penetrated within, turn out the most
perfidious.' This reference to philosophy was undoubtedly a direct piece of
advice to Marcus to watch where he was going. Fronto never had much
sympathy for philosophy and philosophers and cannot have viewed
Marcus' sessions with Apollonius and others with great enthusiasm.

In other arts one might be able to get away with it for a time, he went on,
'but in the choice and arrangement of words the ignorant are shown up at
once. . . . Comparatively few of our classical writers gave themselves up to

the laborious and hazardous pursuit of seeking out words with real industry. M. Porcius [Cato] was alone among all the orators, and his constant imitator C. Sallustius; of the poets especially Plautus, and above all, Q. Ennius and his great rival L. Coelius, not to omit Naevius, Lucretius, Accius too and Caecilius, Laberius also. In addition to these you might notice certain writers who are elegant in specialized fields, Novius and Pomponius and that sort in country dialect and facetious or amusing language, Atta in women's talk, Sisenna for erotic language, Lucilius for the technical language of each art and business.

'At this point you will perhaps have been wanting to know for some time in what category I place M. Tullius [Cicero], who is famed as the head and fount of Roman eloquence. He used the most beautiful language on all occasions, I think, and was magnificent – above all other orators – in embellishing what he wished to set forth. However, he seems to me to have been far from disposed to search out words with extra effort, perhaps from his high-mindedness, or to avoid the effort, or because he felt confident that he would always have ready to hand what others find with difficulty after careful search. . . . In all his speeches you will find only very few words that are surprising and unexpected, the kind that can only be hunted out by careful study and watchfulness and by memorizing a lot of classical poetry. By a surprising and unexpected word I mean one which is produced when the listener or reader is not expecting it or thinking of it, yet could not think of any substitute himself or one to express the particular meaning if you took the word out and asked him to find another. So I commend greatly your hard work and industrious application to the task of digging deep for your word and fitting it in to what you mean. . . .' He went on to emphasize the dangers of doing this half-heartedly, and added, 'I may say that I noticed, when you were reading out to me what you had written, and I altered a syllable in one word, that you did not pay attention to it and thought that it did not matter much. So I do not want you to be ignorant of the great difference which one syllable can make' – and he went on to illustrate his point with different words for 'washing' – *colluere* and *pelluere*, *lavare* and *lavere*, *eluere* and *abluere* – and so forth, depending on what was being washed.

'Possibly someone might ask: "Who is to prevent me from saying *vestimenta lavere* rather than *lavare*, *sudorem lavare* rather than *abluere*?" And you, certainly – no one will have the right to interfere with you in this or set up standards for you, you who are a free man, born of free parents, who have more than the knight's property qualification, who are asked for your opinion in the senate. But we who have dedicated ourselves in dutiful service to the ears of the men of learning, we must of necessity study these slender minutiae with the greatest care. . . . It will be better for you, if you are to search out words more expertly, to remember when you have been corrected, and not to reject criticism or slacken your efforts when caught out. For if you give up searching you will not find; if you go on, you will. Finally, you seemed to me even to have made light of it when I changed your word order, to make you say "three-headed" before "Geryon"' – and he explained why the change was necessary – 'then again, when you were pointing out why the Parthians wore rather loose long sleeves, you wrote, I think, to the effect that heat was *suspended* by the gaps in the garment.' Fronto commended Marcus for looking for the right word to express what he intended here, but felt that 'suspended' was an impossible choice in this instance. 'After that I advised you what you should study to prepare yourself for the writing of history, since you requested it. That subject would need rather a long discussion, so I will end here, to avoid extending this letter beyond due limits. If you want me to write to you on that subject as well, you must remind me again and again.'[2]

Not long afterwards Fronto wrote another letter, as a letter from Marcus with some work he had been doing had 'crossed in the post' with his own previous letter. 'To my Lord. Cratia [his wife] returned here last night. But my delight at having her back was no greater than my pleasure at seeing that you have translated your [Greek] sentences so splendidly; the one I received today was almost perfect and could be inserted into a book of Sallust without being out of place or inferior in any way. I am happy, merry, healthy, even young again when you make such progress. What I shall require of you is difficult, but I must ask you to do what I remember was so useful in my own case. . . . If the gods are favourable, when you return to Rome I will exact your daily verses from you again. Greet my Lady your mother.'[3]

Marcus was evidently in the country, probably at one of Pius' two main family estates, at Lorium north of Rome on the *via Aurelia*, or at Lanuvium, near Albano in the hill-country south of the city. Marcus received both these letters by messenger. 'To my master. I have received two letters from you at the same time. In one of them you reprove me and show that I had written a sentence carelessly; but in the other you strove to encourage my work with praise. But I swear to you by my health, by my mother's too and by yours, that the first letter gave me the greater pleasure and that as I read it I exclaimed several times "How lucky I am!" "Are you then so lucky?", someone will say, "to have a teacher who will show you how to write a translation of your Greek maxims more expertly, more clearly, more briefly, more elegantly?" No, that is not my reason for calling myself fortunate. Why then? It is because I learn to speak the truth (*verum dicere*) from you' – there may perhaps have been a play of words here: he was still Marcus Aurelius *Verus*. He was delighted to have a master who was not afraid to criticize him and treated him as a normal person. 'Farewell my good master, best of masters – I am delighted that you have come to be my friend in this way. My Lady [his mother] greets you.'[4]

This exchange of letters may well date from the end of the year 138. In

139, when he received the name or title Caesar, Marcus had a good deal more public speaking and, in particular, had to make a speech of thanks in the senate for the grant of the name. In a letter from somewhere in the country he told Fronto of his anxieties. 'Hail, my best of masters. If any sleep returns to you after the sleepless nights of which you have been complaining, do write to me, and I beg you this first of all, to take some care of your health. Then, as for that axe of Tenes that you are threatening us with [a proverbial expression meaning 'strict justice'] – hide it away somewhere and bury it and do not give up your intention of pleading in court – or let all other mouths be dumb as well. You say you have composed something or other in Greek which pleases you as little else you have written has. Wasn't it you that was giving me a severe reprimand lately for writing in Greek? As a matter of fact I feel the need now more than ever to write in Greek. "Why?" you ask. I want to make an experiment to see if what I haven't learned comes to me easier, seeing that what I *have* learned is failing me. But if you loved me you would have sent me that new piece that you say you like. Still I read you here even if you are unwilling and by this alone do I live and am sustained.

'The theme you have sent me is a bloodthirsty one. I haven't read the extract from Coelius that you sent me yet – and I shan't read it until I can collect my wits together. But my Caesar speech is gripping me with hooked claws. Now I finally realize what a task it is to shape three or five lines and to take time over writing something. Farewell, my soul – should I not burn with love for you, you who have written to me as you have. What shall I do? I cannot resist telling you – last year at this very time and place I was consumed with passionate longing for my mother. This year it is you that inflame my longing. My Lady greets you.'[5]

The piece written in Greek which Marcus mentioned is included in the correspondence. It is a 'Discourse on Love', very much a mannered piece of writing, in which Fronto takes on the role of Socrates to Marcus' Phaedrus. It is the kind of thing which is almost embarrassing to read now. Still, Marcus appreciated it and thanked Fronto in an effusive way; 'This I can swear without rashness: if that Phaedrus of yours ever really existed, if he was ever away from Socrates, Socrates never felt for Phaedrus a greater longing than I have felt for the sight of you all these days – do I say days? I mean months. . . .'[6]

In another letter from this period Marcus mentions that he is working on another literary exercise set him by Fronto. 'To my master. When you rest and do what is good for your health you do me good as well. Have a pleasant time and be lazy. My opinion is that you have done right in taking care to cure your arm. I too have done something today. I have been on my couch from the seventh hour and have finished about ten similes. In the ninth one I must call you in as my ally and adjutant, because my efforts to pin it down haven't been too successful. It is the one about the island of

Aenaria [Ischia] which has a lake in it; in the lake is an island and it too is inhabited, "from which we draw a certain simile". Farewell, sweetest soul. My Lady greets you.' Fronto wrote back to explain the simile. What he had had in mind was that 'your father carries on his shoulders all the troubles and difficulties of the Roman Empire and keeps you safe in his own calm breast, the partner in his rank, glory and all his possessions' – just as the island protected the little island in its lake from the raging of the sea. Marcus was to make use of this simile in his speech of thanks, either for the Caesar-speech in 139 or for his speech on the consulship in 140.[7]

The firm bond between pupil and master is further illustrated by a letter written by Marcus for Fronto's birthday. 'Hail, my best master. I know that on everyone's birthday his friends undertake vows. But I, because I love you as I love myself, want to make today, your birthday, a good prayer for myself. I call on all the gods, therefore, who anywhere among the nations of the world offer their present and ready power to men, who give aid and show their power in dreams or mysteries or cures or oracles, wherever it may be, I call on each and every one of these gods with my vows, and I place myself, according to the nature of each vow, in the place where each god is endowed with that power may hear me the more readily. Therefore I now climb first the citadel of Pergamum and call on Aesculapius to regulate well and protect the health of my master. Then I go to Athens and clasping Minerva around the knees beseech and beg her that if ever I know anything of literature this knowledge may enter my heart above all from the lips of Fronto. Now I return to Rome and implore the gods of the roads and the seas that in every journey of mine you may accompany me and that I may not be worn out by so fierce a longing for you. Lastly I ask all the gods who watch over all peoples, and the very grove whose rustling is heard on the Capitol hill, to grant this to me, that I may keep with you this day on which you were born for me, with you in strength and happiness. Farewell my sweetest and dearest master – I ask of you that you take care of your health so that when I come I shall see you. My Lady greets you.'[8]

Fronto's reply was brief but grateful. 'To my Lord. All is well with me since you wish it so for me, for there is no one who deserves more than you to have his prayers granted by the gods – or rather, when I pray for you, there is no one who better deserves the fulfilment of prayers on his behalf than you do. Farewell, my sweetest Lord. Greet my Lady.' Marcus' prayers for Fronto's health were more than conventional for Fronto was often ill – at times the letters give the impression that he was a constant invalid, suffering from a variety of ailments. 'Hail my best master,' wrote Marcus on another occasion, 'am I to study when you are in pain, especially when it is my fault? Shall I inflict myself of my own accord with every kind of discomfort? I deserve it, by Hercules. For who else was responsible for that pain in your knee which you write was worse last night, who else but

Centumcellae, not to mention myself?' Fronto had evidently been visiting Marcus at Centumcellae (Civitavécchia) on the Etrurian coast, about fifty miles from Rome, where there was an imperial palace built by Trajan. 'What then shall I do, when I cannot see you and am tortured with such anxiety? Add to that the fact that even if I want to study the courts prevent me – they will take up whole days according to those who know. Still I am sending you yesterday's Greek sentence and the day before yesterday's commonplace. We spent the whole day yesterday on the road. Today it is difficult to find time for anything except the evening's Greek sentence. "Do you sleep all night through?" you will say – "Yes, I can do that, for I am a great sleeper, but it is so cold in my bedroom that I can hardly put my hand outside the bedclothes." But as a matter of fact what really puts me off studying is the thought that my excessive love for reading caused you discomfort at the Harbour, as it turned out. So farewell Catos and Ciceros and Sallusts, until *you* are well and I see you in good health even with no books. Farewell my chief delight, sweetest master. My Lady greets you. Send me three Greek sentences and commonplaces.' The 'Harbour' refers to Centumcellae and it sounds as if Fronto had come there with some books for Marcus, or to advise him about his reading, and Marcus blames himself for being the indirect cause of Fronto's knee-trouble, which must have come on there.[9]

Some of the letters give a little more insight into Marcus' other activities, when he describes what else he has been doing. One letter begins tantalizingly with a gap in the manuscript and then the words 'and my wrestling-trainer had me by the throat'. It goes on to describe a day in the country. 'But what was the story, you ask? When my father got home from the vineyards, I as usual mounted my horse and set off along the road and went on a little way. Then I met a lot of sheep crowded together in the middle of the road as usually happens in narrow places, with four dogs and two shepherds – nothing else. Then one shepherd said to the other when he saw our little group of horsemen: "Watch out for those fellows on horseback – they're the ones who usually steal the most." When I heard that I spurred my horse and galloped straight at the sheep. They were terrified, and scattered in all directions, bleating and wandering all over the place. The shepherd hurled his crook at us. It fell on the knight who was following me, and we got away. So the man thought he was going to lose his sheep and lost his crook instead. You think I'm making the story up? It's true and there is more that I could write to you about it, but a messenger is calling me to the bath. Farewell my sweetest master, most honourable and most rare of men, my dearest joy and delight.'[10]

Another occasion in the country which Marcus described to Fronto was a visit to Anagnia. 'After getting into the carriage, when I had said goodbye to you, we did not have too bad a journey although we got a slight soaking from the rain. But before we got to the villa we turned aside to Anagnia, about a mile off the road. Then we looked round the ancient town, which is very tiny, certainly, but has many antiquities and buildings, and a vast number of religious ceremonies. There isn't a corner in the place that doesn't have a sanctuary or shrine or temple. There are many books written on linen too, which has a religious significance. Then as we were going out we saw an inscription on the gate, written twice: *flamen sume samentum*. I asked one of the locals what the last word meant. He said it was Hernician for the sacrificial victim's skin which the priest puts on his peaked cap when he enters the city. We learned quite a lot of other things that we wanted to know – but the only thing that we do not want is your absence. That is our chief concern.

'When you left us did you go to the Aurelia or to Campania? Be sure to write and tell me, and whether you have begun the vintage, and whether you have brought a multitude of books to your villa, and this too – if you are missing me, which is a foolish question, for you will do that of your own accord. Well, if you do miss me and if you love me, send me letters often to console and cheer me. For I would ten times rather sip your letters than wine from all the Massic or Gauran vineyards. For the vines of Signia have too rank clusters and bitter grapes – I'd rather drink wine made from them than the must, though. Besides, it is pleasanter to chew parched grapes than pulpy ones. I would rather tramp pulpy ones with my feet than champ them with my teeth. . . .'[11]

Marcus managed to keep at his books when he was in the country for the vintage. 'Today by a careful arrangement of meal-times I worked from the ninth hour of the night until the second hour of the day. From the second hour until the third I walked about in my slippers outside my bedroom in a happy state of mind. Then I put on my boots and my cloak – for we had been told to come in that dress – and went to greet my Lord. We set off for the hunt and did valiant deeds. We heard that boars had been taken but were not lucky enough to see it. Still, we climbed quite a steep hill, and in the afternoon came home – I to my books. I took off my boots and my clothes and lay on my bed for nearly two hours reading Cato's speech *On the Property of Pulchra*, and another one in which he impeached a tribune. "Ho!" you will cry out to your boy, "go as fast as you can and bring me those speeches from the Libraries of Apollo." It is no use you sending for them, for those volumes as well have followed me here. So you must get round the Palace Librarian – a small bribe will be necessary (which he and I can share when I come back to the city!) Well, when I had read these speeches I wrote out a little miserable stuff which I ought to dedicate to the gods of water and fire. Really I have been unlucky in my writing today – certainly that was one of the hunters' or a vintager's little bit of work, one of those whose songs are resounding through my bedroom – a noise quite as hateful and tiresome as the pleaders in the law-courts. What did I say? No, it's all right, my master is an orator (not just a pleader). I think I must have got a chill, either from walking about in my slippers this morning or from writing badly. I don't know which. Certainly I am usually quite full of rheum anyway and today I am drivelling more than ever. So I will rub some oil on my head and go off to sleep – I'm not going to pour a drop of oil into my lamp tonight. I'm so worn out from my riding and sneezing. Farewell my dearest and sweetest master whom I would rather see than Rome itself, I dare to say!'[12]

In another letter the description continues, 'We are well. I slept rather late because of my slight cold, which seems to have subsided. From the eleventh hour of the night till the third hour of the day I spent part of the time reading Cato's *Agriculture* and part in writing – not quite such miserable stuff as yesterday. Then, after greeting my father, I soothed my throat, rather than gargled (though the word *gargarisso* is found in Naevius and elsewhere I think), by swallowing honeywater as far as the back of my throat and spitting it out again. After seeing to my throat I went off to my father and accompanied him when he made a sacrifice. Then we went to have lunch. What do you think I had to eat? I only had a little bit of bread, while I watched the others tucking into beans, onions and herrings with plenty of roe. Then we worked hard at gathering the grapes, sweating away and merry and, as the poet has it "left some high-hanging survivors of the vintage". After the sixth hour we came home. I studied for a little bit and what I did hadn't much sense in it. Then I had a long gossip with my little mother as she sat on the bed. My conversation was as follows: "What do you think my Fronto is doing now?" Then she said, "And what do you think my Cratia is doing?" Then I said, "And what do you think the little sparrow is doing, our tiny little Cratia?" While we were chattering away and arguing which of us loved one or the other of you two the more, the gong sounded, the signal that my father had gone to the bath-house. So we had supper after we had bathed in the oil-press room – I don't mean we bathed in the oil-press room, but we had supper there after the bath and enjoyed hearing the country people making jokes at each other. Then back here and before I turn on my side and start snoring I am doing my duty and giving an account of the day to my sweetest master – and if I could miss him more I would not mind tormenting myself a little more. Farewell my Fronto, wherever you are, my most sweet love and delight. How is it between you and me? I love you and you are not here.'[13]

The description of the vintage and their other country activities confirms the brief statement in the biography that Pius 'took great delight in fishing and hunting and in walks and conversation with his friends. He used to spend the vintage-time like a private citizen with his friends.' It also records that 'he never performed any sacrifice by proxy except when he was ill', although the one that Marcus mentions would only have been a normal family sacrifice. In the *Meditations* Marcus mentions that his tutor (*tropheus*) had taught him 'to work with my hands', so he must have been used to helping with the vintage from an early age.[14]

The mother and child both called 'Cratia' in the last letter quoted were the wife and daughter of Fronto. Their name is generally transmitted as the Latin 'Gratia', but in one of his Greek letters Fronto spells his wife's name 'Krateia', and the daughter is later recorded on an inscription as 'Cornelia Cratia'. Hence it has been suggested that his wife was of Greek family, perhaps a kinswoman of Claudia Crateia of Ephesus, a lady with senatorial rank of this period. The daughter was still a tiny girl, and was the only one of Fronto's six children to survive infancy. Eventually she was to marry another of Fronto's pupils, Gaius Aufidius Victorinus, who is mentioned in the biography as being one of Marcus' special friends from among his fellow-students, along with another also of senatorial rank, Seius Fuscianus, and two of equestrian family, Baebius Longus and Calenus. Both Victorinus and Fuscianus remained lifelong friends, and Victorinus in particular was an important adviser and leading general in the reign of Marcus. He is referred to several times in the letters.[15]

In late October or early November 140 the empress Faustina died. She received a state funeral and was deified, but there is no clear reference to her in the letters. Her character is little known, but apparently there were a lot of stories about her, because of her 'excessive frankness and levity', an ambiguous expression. However, at her death she was deified and a temple was built for her above the Forum. Both before and after her death the coin issues emphasised the good relations between her husband and herself. The commemoration continued for many years after her death, and there is no doubt that Antoninus wanted it to be known that he remembered her with respect and affection. He took a mistress after her death, one of Faustina's freedwomen, Galeria Lysistrate. It would have been out of place for him to remarry at the age of fifty-two. The fourth-century emperor Julian, in his satire on the *Caesars*, describes Antoninus as 'a wise statesman – not a wise lover'. Perhaps this alludes to Faustina's embarassing outspokenness, perhaps also to Lysistrate's influence in filling key positions. An example is known from the end of the reign.[16]

Fronto, it need hardly be emphasised, had not become the full-time teacher of Marcus. He continued his career as an advocate. One celebrated case in which he appeared created a potentially serious conflict of interest for him.[17] He was retained as defence counsel by a prominent Athenian, Ti. Claudius Demostratus. The chief prosecutor was Herodes Atticus, the richest and most influential Athenian of his day, and a controversial figure in his native city. An obvious strategy for Demostratus' defence lawyers was to attack Herodes. Ample material was available, not least because of the acrimony caused by the way Herodes had prevented the people of Athens from receiving a benefaction in the will of his father Atticus. As the correspondence reveals, Marcus found the prospect of two of his friends appearing in court on opposite sides alarming. 'Aurelius Caesar to his own Fronto, greeting. I know that you have often said to me "What can I do that will please you most?" Now is the time. If my love for you *can* be increased, you can increase it now. The trial is approaching at which men will not only listen favourably to your speech but will also observe with displeasure any expression of indignation. And I don't see anyone who might dare to advise you in this affair. Those who are not your friends would rather see you acting unlike yourself, and those who are more friendly to you are afraid of seeming too friendly to your opponent if they prevent you from levelling accusations at him as you are entitled to do. Then again, if you have composed some particularly neat passage for your speech in this action, they cannot bear to deprive you of the chance of delivering it, by enforcing silence on you. So, even if you think that I am being inconsiderate in giving you advice, or an impertinent little boy, or too favourable to your opponent, I still won't hesitate to give you the advice that I think is right. But why have I said "advice"? It is a favour that I am asking from you and, if you grant it, I promise to lay myself under obligation to you in return. But you will say "What! If I am attacked am I not to repay it in like terms?" But you will win yourself greater praise if you do not reply when you are attacked. Still, if he is the first to attack, it will be pardonable for you to answer as best as you can. But I have asked him not to begin it and I think that I have gained my request. For I love both of you, each for his own merits – and I remember that he was brought up in the house of my grandfather Publius Calvisius, and that I have been educated with you. So for this reason I am most anxious that this most hateful business should be handled as honourably as possible. I hope that you will approve my advice, for you must commend my goodwill. I would certainly rather make a fool of myself by writing than fail in friendship by not saying anything. Farewell, my Fronto, my dearest and most loving friend.'[18]

Fronto's reply was generous, although it was a very awkward situation for him. 'Fronto to my Lord Caesar. I have been right to devote myself to you, I have been right to invest all the gains of my life in you and your father. What could be more like a friend, more pleasant or more true' – *verius*, here again alluding to Marcus' name Verus – 'Away with this "impertinent little boy" and this "inconsiderate in giving advice", I beg you.' Marcus had more good sense than many much older men, Fronto told him, and he agreed that there was no point in making a spectacle out of the business. He said that he had not realized that Marcus counted Herodes as a friend. At first sight the comment is surprising. Perhaps Fronto was being disingenuous. But it is easy to conclude that Marcus had not begun to receive instruction from Herodes at this stage. The date of the lawsuit is uncertain – except that the weight of the evidence as a whole favours a date in or soon after the year 140. Fronto's reply – a letter he must have found taxed his skill as a writer – went on to affirm that the facts of the case were going to make his position difficult. He could not refrain from making use of the material available. 'I have no doubt that I ought not to say anything which might harm Herodes which does not bear on the case itself. But the facts of the case – they are undoubtedly frightful – how am I to deal with them? That is what I *am* in doubt about and I need your advice. An account has to be given of men cruelly beaten and robbed, of one of them even killed. An account must be given of an unfilial son unmindful of the prayers of his father. Cruelty and avarice must be denounced. A man has to be proved to be a murderer in this trial. But if you think I ought to attack and press my opponent in those charges with all my might, inform me, best and sweetest Lord, if that is your advice. But if you think I ought to let him off to some extent in these, I shall consider what you advise to be the best thing to do. At any rate you may take it as certain and definite that I won't say anything about his character and the rest of his life outside the case itself. But if you think that I must serve my own side, I warn you that I won't even use in a disproportionate way the opportunity that I have in my case, for the charges are frightful and must be spoken of as frightful. Those in particular which refer to the beating and robbing I will describe in such a way that they savour of gall and bile. If I happen to call him an uneducated little Greek it will not mean war to the death. Farewell, my Caesar, and see that you love me to the utmost. I even love your handwriting – so when you write to me I would like you to write in your own hand.' Fronto thus revealed, with his closing remark, that he had sensed from the fact that Marcus' letter had been dictated to a secretary, not written by himself, a gentle rebuke, in spite of the sentiments expressed.[19]

Another letter followed straight after. 'Hail, my Lord. I had closed and sealed the previous letter when it occurred to me that those who plead in this case – and it looks as if many will be pleading – may say something quite unkind against Herodes. So be careful not to think that I am the only one involved in the affair. Farewell my Lord and live, that I may be happy. Capreolus, who is away at present, and my friend Marcianus seem likely to plead; also Vilianus.' These three men are otherwise unknown, although Vilianus was perhaps from a Greek-speaking family and Marcianus, whom Fronto describes as his friend, may be the father of P. Julius Geminius Marcianus, later on record as a senator from Fronto's home town of Cirta.[20]

Marcus was relieved at Fronto's reaction. 'Hail, my dearest Fronto. I must render you my thanks at once, dearest Fronto, for not only not rejecting my advice but actually approving of it. As for the points on which you consult me in your most friendly letter, my opinion is this. Everything relevant to the case which you are representing should obviously be put forward. What concerns your own private feelings, although justifiable and provoked, should, all the same, be left unsaid.' In this way, he ended,

Fronto would not lose his self-respect – and the others could say what they liked. In a reply Fronto said that he was satisfied with this – but even so, 'my gaze will be quite piercing and my voice earnest and my words stern, and I must show anger by pointing a finger here and there – and your man ought to be able to put up with that'.[21]

How the trial went is unknown. Fronto's speech *Pro Demostrato* was published at some stage; but this does not necessarily mean that his client was acquitted. Demostratus continued his hostility to Herodes for over thirty years, but the millionaire intellectual retained his dominant position at Athens. He also went on to enjoy public recognition at Rome. His father Atticus had been consul before him. His own position was doubtless strengthened by his marriage to Regilla. At any rate, he took office at the beginning of the year 143 as consul. Fronto also achieved this status in 143, but only as suffect consul, for the months of July and August. As a 'new man', *novus homo*, with no known posts in the emperor's service to his credit, he was in fact remarkably fortunate to gain the consulship. His kinship with the prefect of the guard Petronius Mamertinus may have been a useful asset.[22]

Fronto would probably have been the first to admit that his only qualifications for supreme office were his skill as an orator and the fact that he had been teaching Marcus. In a letter to Marcus written at about this time he asks Marcus, in a joking way, what he had done to deserve such affection – such affection that 'my Lady your mother often says jokingly that she envies me for being loved so much by you'. 'What benefit has your Fronto conferred on you that you have such affection for him? Has he given his life for you or for your parents? Has he undergone dangers in your place? Has he successfully administered some province? Has he commanded an army? None of these things.' The last two of these questions might have been asked by anyone who wondered why Fronto was being made consul. It was left to the fourth-century orator Ausonius, whose pupil the emperor Gratian made him ordinary consul for the year 379, to complain on Fronto's behalf, when he alluded to the consuls in whose consulship Fronto was consul. In fact, Herodes as the son of a consular had a clear claim to priority. At that time it was most exceptional, and would have caused ill-feeling, for a new senator, i.e. a man from a non-senatorial family, to have become *consul ordinarius*. The fact that Fronto became consul in the same year as Herodes, and not later, shows that an effort was made to give him parity.[23]

While Fronto remained in Rome in the summer of 143, Marcus and the imperial family were on the coast at Baiae. Fronto had evidently written Marcus a little essay *In Praise of Sleep*, probably partly to persuade Marcus to sleep longer and not wear himself out by studying late. Marcus took up the challenge. 'Marcus Caesar to Fronto his master, greeting. Accept now a few little points in favour of sleeplessness against sleep – although, I think, I am in collusion with the other side, considering that I'm always in the presence of sleep day and night and don't desert him and he does not desert me, we are such intimates. But I hope that he may be offended by this accusation and leave me for a while and allow me the chance of burning the midnight oil at last. Now for some crafty arguments: of which the first I shall use is this, that if you say I have taken on an easier subject in accusing sleep than you in praising it – for who, you say, cannot easily accuse sleep? – I reply: what is easy to accuse is hard to praise, and what is hard to praise can serve no useful purpose. But I let that pass. Well, as we are staying at Baiae in this long labyrinth of Ulysses, I will take from Ulysses a few little points relevant to this matter. For he surely would not have only finally come "back to his fatherland in the twentieth year", nor would he have wandered about in that lake for so long, nor suffered all the other things which make up the *Odyssey*, "if sweet sleep had not come over him in his weariness".' He went on to quote more from Homer, then from Ennius and Hesiod. 'Enough of this, which I have indulged in more from love of you than from any confidence I have in it.' He ends, 'Now, after a fine accusation of sleep I am off to sleep – for I have spun this out for you in the evening. I hope sleep will not pay me back.'[24]

The chief moment of Fronto's two months' tenure of office in July and August 143 was to be his speech thanking Antoninus Pius for the honour – it was an opportunity for a public man to have his say about the course of events. Pliny's *Panegyricus* is the best-known example of this type of speech. It was difficult for the orator to avoid being banal, repetitious and obsequious. Fronto wrote to Marcus of his plans. 'You asked me in your last letter why I have not delivered my speech in the senate yet. Well, I have to return thanks to my Lord your father by proclamation too, and I am going to issue that at my Circus Games. The beginning of the proclamation will be as follows: "On the day on which by the favour of our great Prince I am exhibiting a spectacle most pleasing to the people and exceedingly popular, I thought it opportune that I should render thanks to him, so that the same day" – followed by some Ciceronian ending. My speech itself I will deliver in the senate on the Ides of August (13 August). Why so late? you may ask. It is because I am never in a hurry to discharge a solemn duty at the first possible opportunity, and in any fashion. But seeing that I ought to deal with you with no disguises, and unambiguously, I will tell you what I have in mind. I often praised your grandfather, the deified Hadrian, in the senate, with considerable effort – and with a ready effort too (and those speeches are still constantly in people's hands). Yet if your family loyalty will pardon me, I wanted to propitiate and please Hadrian in the same way as Mars Gradivus or Father Dis, rather than loved him. Why? Because to love requires some confidence and intimacy. I lacked confidence, hence I dared not love one whom I revered so greatly. Antoninus, however, I love and am devoted to, like the sun and the day and life and breath, and I feel that I am loved by him. I will be ungrateful to you too if I do not praise him in such a way that my praise is not hidden away in the *Acts of the Senate*, but rather so that it comes into the hands and before the eyes of men. As they say that the courier who ran away said: "I have run sixty miles for my master, I'll run a hundred for myself, to escape." So I too, when I praised Hadrian, was running for my master, but today I am running for myself – for myself, I say, and I am writing this speech to please myself. So I will do it at my ease, slowly, in a leisurely, gentle fashion. If you are impatient for it, amuse yourself some other way in the meanwhile. Kiss your father, embrace him, and finally, praise him yourself. But you may certainly expect to hear something on the Ides of August that you will want to hear, expressed in the way you wish. Farewell, Caesar, and be worthy of your father, and if you want to write anything, write slowly.'[25]

With Fronto's assumption of office Marcus could address him in a new way: 'My Fronto, most glorious consul.' In another letter he speaks again in the extravagant half-joking way of their friendship, but added 'Now Cratia will be a rival, and I fear that I cannot defeat her. For, as Plautus says, in her case, "The rain of love has not only soaked her dress with great drops but has rained in to her very marrow." [This was in reply to a letter in which Fronto had reaffirmed his affection.] That other letter of yours, in which you pointed out why you were going to put off making your speech in the senate in praise of my father, pleased me so much that I could not resist – and you must see whether I acted rashly – reading it out to my father himself. I don't need to go into detail about the great pleasure it gave him, because you know his very great good-will towards you and the splendid elegance of your style. But out of this a long conversation arose between us about you, much longer than yours and your quaestor's about me. So I don't doubt that your ears must have been tingling in the Forum at about that time. My Lord approves then, and is sympathetic to the reasons for your putting off the delivery of your speech till later. . . .'[26]

Finally Fronto gave his speech and wrote to describe the occasion to Marcus, but told him that he could hear from 'our friend Aufidius' [Victorinus] about the shouts of applause with which it was greeted. With his letter he sent back to Marcus some verses which he had written by Victorinus as courier. 'I have sewn the paper up carefully and have sealed the thread in such a way that that little mouse will not be able to poke in through a crack anywhere. For he has never shared any information about your hexameters with me, he's such an evil and malicious fellow – he says you always recite them so fast that he cannot memorize any of them. So he is paid back by me, quite fairly – he won't hear a single line. I remember, as well, that you reminded me not to show your verses to anyone.'[27]

Antoninus Pius was pleased with Fronto's speech and wrote to him. 'You have done well to find something new in such a hackneyed and worn-out subject. . . . I will not be guilty of defrauding you of your very well-deserved praise for fear of insolently praising your praise of myself! You have done well then and in a most appropriate fashion, for which – quite apart from the subject matter – you deserve all honour. But as for showing me your mind – it has not done much. For I know well that you interpret *all* my actions and words in the most favourable way. Farewell, my dearest Fronto. That part of your speech which you most kindly gave up to honouring my Faustina seemed to me no less true than eloquent. For the fact is this: I would rather live on Gyara with her than in this palace without her.' The Faustina here is his daughter, his only surviving child and Marcus' betrothed. Gyara was an island to which banished persons were sometimes sent.[28]

Marcus wrote his letter of congratulations as well, of course, in the most glowing terms. 'In future be careful not to tell so many lies about me,' he ended, 'especially in the senate. This speech of yours is horribly . . . well written.' With his last letter Fronto had enclosed one for Domitia Lucilla, written in Greek as a compliment to her high standard of education. The letter is an elaborate literary exercise, in which he apologizes for not having written before with the excuse of having had to make his speech, and says little else, but says it gracefully, ending with an apology for his barbarous Greek, 'for I am a Libyan of the Libyan nomads'.[29]

Marcus was still hard at work. 'You very kindly ask for my hexameters,' he says in another letter, 'and I would have sent them at once if I had them with me. But my secretary – whom you know, I mean Anicetus – did not send any of my writing with me when I set off. He knows my weakness and was afraid that if I got hold of them I should do as usual and put them in the oven. In fact those particular hexameters were in practically no danger. For, to tell my master the truth, I am fond of them. I do my studying at night here because the daytime is spent at the theatre. So I don't do all that much in the evening and I get up sleepy in the morning!' Marcus was missing Fronto and found time passing slowly. The two months of Fronto's consulship seemed like two years.[30]

Another letter of Marcus to Fronto in one of these two months of July and August 143 describes his life at Naples. 'Marcus Aurelius Caesar to his own consul and master, greeting. Since I last wrote to you there has been nothing worth writing about or that you would be particularly pleased to know about. For we have spent more or less whole days in the same activities – the same theatre, the same dislike for it, the same longing for you. What? – do I say the *same*? I mean a longing that is renewed and increased every day, and, as Laberius says about love, in his own fashion and his own special style:

Your love grows as fast as an onion, as firm as a palm.

What he says about love I apply to my longing. I want to write a longer letter to you, but there is nothing to write about.

'But wait, I have thought of something. We have been listening to the official speeches in our honour here. The speakers are Greeks, of course, but amazing creatures, as far removed from Greek literature as my own Caelian hill is from the land of Greece – so much so that I could even rival Theopompus (for I hear that he is the most eloquent of the Greeks), in comparison to them. So these people, whose "ignorance", as Caecilius says, "is assured", have almost driven me, clownish mortal that I am, to write in Greek.

'The weather at Naples is certainly pleasant but violently changeable. Every few minutes it turns colder, or warmer, or wilder. To start with, at midnight it is warm, like Laurentum. At cockcrow it's chilly, like Lanuvium. The first part of the night, the small hours and dawn, till sunrise, is cold, just like Algidus. Then the morning is sunny, as at Tusculum. At midday it is boiling, like at Puteoli. But when the sun has gone off and dipped in the Ocean the temperature at last becomes more reasonable, the sort we have at Tibur. It stays like this for the evening and when you first get off to sleep, until, as Marcus Porcius [Cato] says, "the dead of night flings itself on you". But why am I collecting these bits of Masurius-type nonsense, when I said that I would only write a few words? So farewell most kindly master, most glorious consul, and long for me as you love me.'[31]

Fronto had to stay in Rome for the whole two months of his period as consul, although once he had given his speech he began to want to be away (or said that he did). 'The consul to his own Caesar. Lucky brother of mine to have seen you for those two days. I stick at Rome, bound fast with golden fetters. I am waiting for the Kalends of September as the superstitious do for the star at whose appearance they break their fast. Farewell, Caesar, glory of your country and of the Roman name. Farewell, my Lord.'[32]

The brother mentioned in this letter was Quintus Cornelius Quadratus, who was also to be consul, four years later than Fronto. Cratia was also staying at Naples with the imperial family, to join in the celebration of Domitia Lucilla's birthday. Fronto had to content himself with writing a birthday letter to Lucilla, again in Greek, and again, like his previous letter to her, full of elaborate compliments. 'Women from all over should have come to greet you on your birthday', he wrote, 'those that love their husbands and children and are virtuous, the genuine and truthful, the kind-hearted, friendly, accessible and humble, and many others – since you possess all these virtues.' In the meantime Marcus was not without occupation – listening to lawyers. Presumably he had to sit in judgment as an assessor to his father.[33]

On an occasion not long after Fronto's consulship, it would appear, Fronto had delivered a speech in court which was highly praised. He sent a copy to Marcus, who declaimed passages of it to Pius, then wrote back to

Fronto to tell him that the emperor had greatly admired it. Fronto was delighted: it pleased him more than his consulship, he said, that something of his should be performed by Marcus, so to speak, with Pius as the audience. Marcus quotes a lengthy extract – it involved an inheritance dispute in the provinces. At the end of his letter Marcus mentioned that Herodes Atticus had just suffered a misfortune. His new-born son had died. Marcus asked Fronto to write him a note of condolence, and part of the resulting letter, in Greek, has survived. Herodes was not too old to have other children, and he should follow Fronto's own practice when he had lost one whom he loved, to reflect that others had been preserved. 'If you too love a certain noble youth, distinguished for virtue and education and fortune and prudence, you will not go wrong if you attach yourself to him and set all your assurance of good things on him, for as long as he remains to us – and I confess that I am a rival for his love, I make no secret of it – everything else can easily be remedied and is a long way second in importance.' Clearly Marcus had succeeded in persuading the two men to put aside the strong feelings engendered by the Demostratus case. Another letter explicitly refers to Marcus' qualities as a reconciler. At the beginning of the letter, now missing, Fronto evidently referred both to Herodes and to the legend of Orpheus. 'If anyone ever had power by his character to unite all his friends in mutual love for one another', he goes on, 'you will surely accomplish this much more easily, since you were born to practise all the virtues before you had any training in them. For before you were old enough to begin education you were already perfect and complete in all noble accomplishments, before adolescence "a good man", before manhood 'skilled in speaking''. But of all your virtues this is the most admirable: that you unite all your friends in harmony. I cannot conceal my opinion that this is much more difficult than to tame wild beasts and lions with the lyre.' The letter ends with a reference to another friend. 'I love Julianus – for this conversation started from him – I love all those who love you. I love the gods who watch over you. I love life for your sake. I love literature with you. With your friends I take in deep draughts of love for you.'[34]

In his reply Marcus reveals that the first part of Fronto's letter had described his visit to Julianus when the latter was ill. Marcus was grateful that Fronto, when he was 'so busy with important affairs at home and abroad, nevertheless made a point of going to see Julianus chiefly on my account – I would be ungrateful if I did not realise that.' Then he turns to something else Fronto had mentioned. 'As for Herodes, go on with what you were saying, I beg you; as our Quintus [Ennius] has it, "prevail with pertinacious persistence!". Herodes loves you, and I am doing my best in that direction – in fact, anyone who does not love you neither understands with his heart nor sees with his eyes. I won't say anything about the ears, for the ears of all your listeners have passed under the yoke and are the slaves of your dear voice. To me this day seems and will seem longer than a spring day and the coming night more long drawn out than a winter's night, because I so much want to greet my Fronto, to embrace the writer of this last letter. I have written this in a hurry, because Maecianus was pressing, and it was only fair that your brother should return to you in good time. So if you find any solecism or confused expression or shaky writing here, please put it down to my haste. For although I am so very fond of you as a friend I still ought to remember that I must show as much respect to you as my master as I show you love as my friend.'[35]

The Maecianus who was 'pressing' was Volusius Maecianus, a leading jurist of the day, and law tutor to Marcus. He was possibly another African, like Fronto and like the most distinguished jurist of the time, Salvius Julianus, whom it is tempting to identify with the man visited by Fronto – but Julianus was so common a name that no certainty is possible.[36]

No events of particular importance for the private or public life of Marcus, or indeed in the external history of the empire, are known from the period from the end of 143 until Marcus' marriage in April 145. But it was in the spring or summer of 144 that the young Greek orator Aelius Aristides delivered at Rome his famous speech of praise for the Roman empire, which is the main basis for the favourable verdict of history on the age of the Antonines.

Aristides' speech is imbued with Platonic concepts, and is thoroughly literary in its style and construction. He was also being deliberately flattering, making no attempt to see the darker side of the picture. But the tribute remains remarkable, when all allowances have been made. He speaks of the vastness and universality of Rome's empire, and compares it favourably with those of the past, such as the Persian and the Macedonian. The pre-eminence of Rome lay as much in its perfection as in its great size. The government was carried on in a just and orderly fashion. The emperor was not a despot but a 'great governor', and he ruled free men not slaves. The whole world was now like one city-state. But the emperor protected the weak, which did not happen in a city-state 'democracy'. The Roman constitution embodied the best elements of democracy, aristocracy, oligarchy and monarchy. The greatest single 'work of perfection' in the empire was the army – in its method of recruitment, its conditions of service, its deployment, its training, its discipline. If there happened to be a few peoples who were not in the empire, they could only be pitied. War was a thing of the past, even if there might be a few madmen like the Getae (Dacians), wretches like the Libyans (Moors) or ill-doers like the dwellers on the Red Sea. (Thus he alludes to military operations in Dacia and Mauretania, and, probably, to a minor revolt in Egypt.) There are even some lofty allusions to imperial frontier policy. 'To place walls around the city itself as if you were hiding her or fleeing from your subjects you considered ignoble. Nevertheless you did not forget walls, but these you placed around the empire, not the city. . . . Beyond the outermost ring of the civilised world, you drew a second line. . . . Here you built walls to defend you. . . . An encamped army like a rampart encloses the world in a ring . . . as far as from Ethiopia to the Phasis and from the Euphrates to the great outermost island towards the West; all this one can call a ring and circuit of the Walls. They have not been built with asphalt and baked brick, nor do they stand there gleaming with stucco. Oh, but these ordinary works too exist at their individual places, yes, in very great number, and, as Homer says of the palace wall, "fitted close and accurately with stones, and boundless in size and gleaming more brilliantly than bronze".' Although Aristides goes on to emphasise that the ring of men is much more impressive than the actual Wall, his high-flown description of Rome's frontier barriers may have amused some of the high officers who had been building the Antonine Wall of turf – between Forth and Clyde. Lollius Urbicus may well have been back at Rome, and if he did not attend Aristides' speech, at least one might suppose that A. Claudius Charax, who had commanded the legion II Augusta, was there. He was himself a Greek man of letters, an historian, from Pergamum. Aristides would not prophesy the future of Rome, but he felt convinced that its 'Golden Race' would be there until the end of the world. He concluded with a prayer that the city and the empire should last for ever, and that the 'great governor and his sons' should be preserved and provide good things for men.[37]

A second speech was delivered by Aristides on this visit, addressed to the emperor himself. It has long been regarded, mistakenly, as the work of an unknown later orator, perhaps from the reign of the emperor Philip in the 240s. But a brilliant re-examination has demonstrated that the language and content are entirely authentic. In the first sentence Aristides refers to 'a festival and holiday' and it has been suggested that he may have delivered it at the *Eusebeia* founded by Pius at Puteoli in honour of Hadrian. If so, Pius and the other members of the audience may have felt that Hadrian's memory was not much enhanced by the address. The orator devotes almost the entire speech to praise of the new emperor and scarcely veiled hostile comparisons with his predecessor. Some inherited power or gained it by force; he did not even seek it but at last yielded to persuasion. He had no rivals, whereas previous rulers came to power amid wars and murders, destroying many in high position. 'So purely and virtuously did he begin his charge of affairs that neither while becoming emperor nor when he started to reign did he require the death of anyone . . . the gods took such care that he should come to power purely and piously that they left to others acts of madness and insanity, and reserved for him actions of justice, beneficence and general piety.' He had not punished any who plotted against him. His steadying hand had checked the empire's 'continuous, irrational and violent lunges' (perhaps a reference to Hadrian's erratic conduct at the end of his life). 'These things are a demonstration . . . that the sovereignty is neither shaken by fears, nor panicked by events, nor quick to anger and wrath, but adopts a constant and unmoved disposition towards all.' Like a good pilot, the emperor had settled the empire, 'just as a ship is moored after a great storm'. He goes on to stress the emperor's piety, 'for he began, as is fitting, with piety', alluding to the award of the name Pius soon after the accession; his excellent financial and judicial policy and his great love of the Greeks and support for Greek education, in contrast to what had been happening before. This is a surprise – and led many to suppose the speech could not be by Aristides, nor the emperor Pius: Hadrian was, surely, a fanatical philhellene. Yet at the end of his reign he had turned against a number of Greek intellectuals, just as he had attacked other friends and his own relations: the contrast, if a little exaggerated, was not unjustified.

The compliments and contrasts that follow certainly ring true: the new atmosphere of freedom and confidence, compared with the fear inspired by spies – a clear allusion to Hadrian's conversion of military commissariat soldiers, *frumentarii*, into secret agents; the emperor's gentleness and goodness and approachability; his consistent character – he was the same man as emperor as he had been when a private citizen; his personal morality and self-restraint, unlike certain other emperors; his firm discipline with the troops; his prudence with regard to war and preference for diplomacy, combined with exemplary firmness when needed, as with the Celtic peoples (a reference to the north Britons) and those beyond Euphrates and Tigris. As he neared the end of the speech, Aristides reverted to the emperor's virtues, in which he excelled all his predecessors: wisdom, bravery, piety and good fortune. Then, turning to Marcus, he added a prayer: 'And may you, boy, noble of the noble, follow in your father's footsteps.'[38]

· 5 ·

THE STOIC PRINCE

THE YEARS 145 to 147 were of great importance in the life of Marcus. On 1 January 145, he became consul for the second time, an honour that a private citizen could rarely expect and only at a fairly advanced age, whereas Marcus was twenty-two. His father was his colleague, holding the office for the fourth time. Marcus' tenure of office required another important speech from him, and it may have been at this time that he was unwell and Fronto wrote him a brief note, urging him to have plenty of sleep 'so that you may come into the Senate with a good colour and read your speech with a strong voice'. Marcus' illness may be the one he referred to himself in another letter. 'My present condition, as you can easily judge, is revealed by the shakiness of my handwriting. As far as my strength is concerned, I am beginning to get it back; and there is not race of the pain in my chest. But that ulcer . . . [here the manuscript is uncertain] . . . I am having treatment and taking care not to do anything that interferes with it. For I feel that a long illness can only be made more tolerable by conscientious care and following doctors' orders. Anyway, it would be a bad business if a physical illness should last longer than one's mental determination to regain one's health. Farewell, my most delightful master. My mother greets you.'[1]

Marcus was never very strong physically. Cassius Dio speaks with admiration of his devotion to duty in spite of the handicap of physical weakness. He himself, in a passage already quoted, tells how his teacher in philosophy, Apollonius, had taught him to preserve his equanimity, even in long illnesses. Twenty or more years later, as emperor, he suffered constantly from chest and stomach complaints, and had to take drugs to alleviate them. Speculation about the nature of these is perhaps un-profitable, in view of the small amount of data available. In any case, there is no evidence that the 'pain in the chest' he had as a young man, which had left him when he wrote the letter to Fronto just quoted, was from the same cause as 'the poor condition of his stomach and chest' twenty-five years later.[2]

In 145 there were military problems to deal with once more, and as Pius must have been very busy Marcus would have had to play his part. Serious revolts in Mauretania developed into a full-scale war. Neither of the two Mauretanian provinces had legionary garrisons, and reinforcements had to be brought in on a large scale, not only of legionaries, but of auxiliary units as well. Some reinforcements came from Britain, now relatively tranquil, brought by an officer named Sextus Flavius Quietus. At first, the same man who had dealt with the trouble in Dacia, Flavius Priscus, was made *pro legato*. But the situation soon demanded a senator to take command of the large new army-group concentrated for the war. A certain Uttedius Honoratus was appointed. The praetorian prefect Gavius Maximus would undoubtedly have been able profitably to capitalize on his experience as procurator of Mauretania Tingitana fifteen years previously, when the selection of officers and other matters concerning the war had to be discussed at the imperial council.[3]

It may have been at this period that Marcus wrote to Fronto complaining about the amount of correspondence he had to deal with. 'Hail my sweetest master. At last the courier is setting off, and I can send you at last an account of my doings in the last three days. But I cannot *say* anything – I am so out of breath from dictating nearly thirty letters. For as to the opinion that you recently expressed about the letters, I haven't mentioned it to my father yet. . . .' The word used for letters here (*epistulae*) is that also used for official correspondence, and from the number involved Marcus had obviously been performing official duties. It may be that Fronto had expressed some indignation about this, but that is only guesswork.[4]

It was probably in 145, on 17 March, at the Liberalia, that Marcus' adopted brother Lucius Aurelius Commodus assumed the *toga virilis*, as he would then be fourteen. Pius made the occasion even more festive by dedicating the temple to the deified Hadrian and largesse was given to the people of Rome. Little is heard of Lucius in these early years. In fact he does not emerge into the fullest light until after Pius' death, when some of his correspondence with Fronto is preserved. But having now officially entered the status of manhood he was ready to be taught by Fronto. Hitherto he had received instruction from *grammatici* named Scaurinus in Latin and Telephus, Hephaestio and Harpocratio in Greek. He was now handed over to Caninius Celer and to another Greek rhetorician named Apollonius, and to Herodes Atticus and Fronto. He also had philosophy teaching from Apollonius of Chalcedon and Sextus of Chaeronea (who also taught Marcus). A general eye was kept on his upbringing by a faithful freedman of his (real) father named Nicomedes, whom Antoninus had honoured for his devotion by bestowing on him the rank of knight (normally forbidden to freedmen). Less is related about Lucius' character in these early years than about Marcus, not surprisingly. He is said to have been deeply fond of all his teachers, and to have been loved by them; and to have tried his hand at composing verses as a boy.[5]

Marcus and Faustina were married at last in April 145. As Marcus was by adoption son of Pius, Faustina was his adoptive sister. One or other of them must have been formally released from Pius' paternal authority (*patria potestas*), to allow the ceremony to take place. Pius made it a noteworthy occasion. Coins were struck with the heads of the young couple. The soldiers were given a special bounty to commemorate it. As the couple were both patrician, the ceremony would undoubtedly have been that of *confarreatio*, few details of which are known. Pius, as Pontifex Maximus, would have been required to officiate. At some stage in the ceremony a cake of spelt (*far*) would be used. But there is no need to attempt to describe the occasion. All that is known is that it was 'noteworthy'.[6]

None of the letters refers to the marriage itself, unless Marcus is doing so in an oblique way when he talks about something that was to happen 'in two days time', in a letter that is incompletely preserved. 'I am beginning to be fastidious, as often happens with those who at last have in their grasp what they long for. . . .' But that is guesswork. The only mention of Faustina in the earlier letters had been by Pius when he had said that he would rather live in exile with her than without her in the palace. The first reference to her in the letters after her marriage speaks of her as being ill. Fronto mentions that Victorinus had told him that 'your Lady is more feverish than yesterday. Cratia had reported that everything was getting better'. Fronto too was ill – 'The reason why I have not seen you is because I am weak from a cold.' In his reply Marcus reported that Faustina was still feverish but was a good patient. In another letter from this period he describes a small chapter of accidents in the family. 'This is how I have spent the last few days. My sister was suddenly attacked with such a violent pain in her private parts that her face was dreadful to look at. Then my mother, in her worry, accidentally hit her side on the angle of a wall, which caused a great deal of pain to us as well as to her. As for me, when I went to lie down I found a scorpion in my bed – but I managed to kill it before lying on it. If you are in better health that is a consolation. My mother is now a bit better, thank the gods. Farewell, my best and sweetest master. My Lady greets you.' There are more letters which describe mutual illnesses and convalescences, and some of the later correspondence, as Fronto grew older, seems to have been almost exclusively concerned with the subject of ill-health.[7]

In September 145 a puzzling episode took place. A certain Cornelius Priscianus was condemned by the senate 'for hostile action disturbing the peace of the province of Spain', as the official records describe it. The historians add that Priscianus was attempting to seize the throne and that he committed suicide, but give no more details. He must have been the governor of the province of Hispania Tarraconensis at the time – if he was genuinely seeking to make a *coup d'état*. On the face of it this seems an unlikely place from which to start a rebellion. The governors of Britain, Syria, and above all the strategically placed Upper Pannonia, were better equipped since each was armed with three legions, and within ready reach of possible allies. The Iberian peninsula was isolated, and had only one legion. It is true that a governor of Tarraconensis, Galba, had overthrown Nero in AD 68. But Galba took power when others had done the work for him. It is possible that Priscianus had tried to tamper with the loyalty of troops being sent through Spain, from Britain and the Rhineland, to reinforce Mauretania. One other rebel or conspirator is heard of during Pius' reign, a senator named Atilius Titianus. No dates or details are supplied, but it is conceivable that he might have been an ally of Priscianus, even Priscianus' candidate for the throne. However obscure, this business is at least a reminder that all was not quite so happy in the reign of Pius as the speech of Aelius Aristides quoted earlier might lead one to suppose.[8]

Another death in high places occurred in March of the following year. The prefect of Rome, Sextus Erucius Clarus, expired from natural causes, while enjoying the accolade that normally went with his office, a second consulship. He was a link with a bygone age. The younger Pliny had been his friend and patron, and had obtained entry into the senate for him from Trajan. He had gone on to distinguish himself in the Parthian war, and had become a patron of learning, mentioned by Aulus Gellius as a friend and correspondent of the scholar Sulpicius Apollinaris. Clarus may have been the second prefect appointed by Pius. His predecessor was probably Bruttius Praesens (another protégé of Pliny). It is not certain who succeeded him, but later in the reign this prestigious post was held by Lollius Urbicus, the man who had reconquered southern Scotland. It may be judged a shrewd move on the part of the unmilitary Pius to single out the great general in this way. It was also a further sign that the North African Romans were advancing on all fronts. Urbicus' home, Tiddis in Numidia, was a small town close to Fronto's Cirta.[9]

Meanwhile Marcus' studies with Fronto appear to have been proceeding, perhaps in a slightly desultory fashion. A letter, which seems to be from after his marriage (from the mention of 'my lady' rather than 'my mother') and which carries a hint of discontent, gives a good indication of the position. 'To my master. I will have the whole day free. If you have ever loved me, love me today and send me a rich subject, I beseech and ask, and I request and require and implore. For in that law-court subject I found nothing but exclamations. Farewell, best of masters. My Lady salutes you. I want to write something where there should be shouts of acclamation – humour me and look out a "shouting" subject.'

The letter which seems to be Fronto's reply gives him a subject. 'I have slept late. I have sent you a subject: the case is a serious one. A consul of the Roman people, putting aside his toga, has put on the mail tunic and with the people of Rome looking on, at the feast of Minerva, among the young men, has slain a lion. He is denounced before the censors. Shape it up and develop. Farewell, most sweet Lord. Greet your Lady.'

Marcus' reply showed that he was not completely satisfied. For some reason it has no heading, except the word 'Answer', but that may be chance. 'When did it happen and was it at Rome? You don't really mean that affair that happened under Domitian at his palace at Albano, do you? Besides, with this subject it will take longer to make it seem credible than to get angry about it. It seems to me an improbable subject, and I would definitely have preferred the kind I asked for. Write back by return about the date.'[10]

In a letter written a little later Fronto does provide another subject. 'I am rather late, my Lord, in replying to you, because I delayed to open your letter on my way to the Forum to plead in court. I am feeling better but the sore is deeper. Farewell my sweetest Lord. Greet my Lady. M. Lucilius, a tribune of the people, has forcibly imprisoned a free Roman citizen when his colleagues had ordered him to be released against their decision. For that action he is "marked" by the Censors. First divide the case, then take either side, as prosecution and defence. Farewell, my Lord, the light of all your friends. Greet your Lady mother.'[11]

Marcus' answer is not preserved, but he seems by then to have found this kind of intellectual exercise a rather barren occupation. In a fairly long letter written when he was twenty-five, that is between April 146 and April 147, he displays considerable signs of discontent with his study of jurisprudence as well, and, indeed, a general sense of malaise.

'To my master. Gaius Aufidius [Victorinus] gives himself airs, extols his judgment to the skies, denies that a juster man than himself – I must not exaggerate – ever came from Umbria to Rome. What more do you want? He would rather win praise as a judge than as an orator. When I smile, he is disdainful. It is easy to sit yawning next to a judge, he says, but to *be* a judge is noble work. This is a hit at me. Still, the affair has turned out well. It is all right – I am pleased. Your arrival makes me happy but also anxious. No one would ask why it makes me happy. As to why I am anxious, I will tell you, by heaven: although I have had some free time I haven't given a single little bit of it to the task you set me to write. Aristo's books are treating me well at the moment, but also treating me badly. When they teach me better things then certainly they treat me well. But when they show me how far away from these better things my character is, your pupil blushes again and again, and is angry with himself, because at the age of twenty-five my soul still has not drunk in any draught of noble doctrines and purer principles. So I am doing penance, I am angry, I am sad, I am comparing myself with others, I am not eating. Being completely bound up in this disquiet, I have been putting off the duty of writing every day, until the next day. But now I will think up something, and as some Attic orator once warned an assembly of the Athenians, "the laws must be allowed to sleep sometimes" – so I will propitiate Aristo's books and allow them to rest for a little while, and after reading Cicero's minor speeches I will turn my attention fully to that stage poet of yours. But I can only write on one side or the other, for

Aristo will certainly never allow me to sleep well enough to defend both sides. Farewell best and most honoured master. My Lady salutes you.'[12]

The Aristo whose writings Marcus had been studying has been convincingly identified with the jurist Titius Aristo, a friend of the younger Pliny. In a letter to Catilius Severus, Pliny wrote of his anxiety over Aristo's ill-health. 'His authority, uprightness and learning are unequalled . . . what experience in both civil and constitutional law!' In comparison to the prominent philosophers of the day, Pliny added, Aristo 'is superior in virtue, duty, justice and courage'.[13] Marcus had always had a keen interest in philosophy – since he was eleven years old. He had acquired his first teachers in the subject when he was fourteen, notably the Stoic Apollonius. In what may have been the first letter that Fronto wrote to Marcus there are warnings about dabbling in philosophy. In a later letter Fronto carried the warning further: Marcus had evidently criticized the insincerity of conventional language. Fronto defended the language of oratory. 'I think all speech without these conventions is rough, provincial and uncouth, in fact, unskilful and useless. And I do not think that devices of that kind are any less necessary for philosophers than they are for orators.' Fronto gave the example of Socrates as a philosopher whose command of language was a vital part of his equipment. But at twenty-five Marcus had had enough of taking both sides in imaginary debates.[14]

His formal education was now over. Marcus had enjoyed the best of relations with all his teachers. This would be apparent even without the evidence of his correspondence with Fronto. 'He gave so much honour to his teachers that he kept gold statues of them in his private chapel, and always honoured their tombs by personal visits and offerings of sacrifices and flowers,' the biographer records. His grief at the death of one of his teachers has already been quoted. The biographer adds at this point that 'he devoted so much attention and labour to his studies that it affected his health adversely – the only thing with which fault can be found in his entire boyhood'.[15]

Apollonius had obviously played an important part in introducing him to Stoic philosophy. But the greatest influence on him was probably Quintus Junius Rusticus. Rusticus was at least twenty years older than Marcus, a little older than Fronto, probably. His very name was almost a political philosophy or programme in itself, for he was a descendant, probably the grandson, of one of the martyrs to the tyranny of Domitian. The 'Stoic opposition' to the bad emperors in the first century, especially to Nero and Domitian, was an important force in shaping the character of the Antonine principate. Apollonius, Rusticus, and a third friend, Claudius Maximus, were the three to whom Marcus must have felt he owed most, since it is for coming to know them that he gives particular thanks to the gods. His tribute to Rusticus is a full one. 'From Rusticus: to acquire the impression that there was need for reform and treatment of character; not to be led astray into enthusiasm for rhetoric, for writing on speculative themes, for discoursing on moralizing texts, for parading in fanciful fashion the ascetic or the philanthropist. To avoid oratory, poetry and "fine writing". Not to parade around at home in elaborate clothes or do things like that. To write letters in a simple style, like the one he himself wrote from Sinuessa to my mother. To be accessible and easy to reconcile to those who provoke or offend, as soon as they are willing to meet me. To read books accurately and not to be satisfied with a general superficial impression or to agree quickly with people who talk round a subject. To have come to know the *Discourses* of Epictetus – of which he let me share his own copy.'

Clearly it was Rusticus who attracted Marcus away from oratory – the implied criticisms of Fronto are more than hints: 'enthusiasm for rhetoric'; 'oratory, poetry and "fine writing"'; 'letters in the simple style'. The contrasts are quite plain. Rusticus' letter to Domitia Lucilla written from Sinuessa has not survived. But Fronto's two letters to her could be called anything but simple in their style.[16]

In spite of the implied criticisms of Fronto, some years later, at least, Fronto could speak of the man who had 'wooed Marcus away' from him with respect and affection as 'that friend of mine, the Roman Rusticus, who would gladly give his life for your little finger'. Ironically, however, the occasion for his reference to Rusticus was to mention a disagreement he had had with him over Marcus' natural abilities as an orator. Rusticus gave way, unwillingly and with a frown, when Fronto insisted on the reality of his former pupil's talent.[17]

Fronto himself, years later, put a rather uncharitable interpretation on the conversion to philosophy. 'Then, you seem to me, in the fashion of the young, tired of boring work, to have deserted the pursuit of eloquence and to have turned aside to philosophy, in which there is no introductory section to be carefully elaborated, no account of the facts, bringing them together with concision, clarity and skill. . . .' By contrast, 'you would read a book to your philosopher, listen in silence while your master explained it and nod to show your understanding; would hear again and again: "what is the first premiss? What is the second premiss?" and when the windows were wide open, the point that "If it is day, then it is light" would be laboured. Then you would go away, carefree, with nothing to think over, or to write up at night, nothing to recite to your master, nothing to say by heart, no search for words, no adorning of a single synonym, no translation from Greek to our language.'[18]

Although it was Rusticus who had family connections with the Stoic opposition of previous generations, it was not he but another friend, Claudius Severus, who brought Marcus to a knowledge of what these men had stood for. Severus was probably about eight or nine years older than Marcus. He was from a Greek family of the Paphlagonian city of

Pompeiopolis in Asia Minor, and his father had been the first governor of Trajan's new province of Arabia. He had evidently been born there during his father's administration, for he bore the additional name of Arabianus. He was consul in 146, as colleague of Erucius Clarus. A further witness of his close friendship with Marcus is that his son was to marry one of Marcus' daughters. Claudius Severus was not, apparently, a Stoic. He is described by the biographer as being an adherent of the Peripatetic school, in other words an Aristotelian. Marcus' friendship with him, and the influence that he had over Marcus, illustrate that Marcus was not to become a dogmatic Stoic. 'From Severus' Marcus learned 'love of family, love of truth and love of justice. And through him to have got to know Thrasea, Helvidius, Cato, Dio and Brutus. To form the conception of a balanced constitution, based on equity and freedom of speech and of a monarchy which honours above all else the liberty of the subject. From him too, consistency and uniformity in regard for philosophy. To do good, to be generous to others, to be hopeful. To trust in the love of friends, to be frank and open with those who met with his disapproval, and that his friends did not need to make guesses about his wishes or his dislikes, but he was open with them.' More must be said later about Thrasea and the others whose political ideals Marcus made his own. Even if their application had no long-term effect on the autocratic imperial rule, it was a remarkable thing to find a ruler who professed them and gave every sign of attempting to put them into practice.[19]

The other philosophical friends whose influence Marcus records in the opening book of the *Meditations* are Claudius Maximus, Sextus of Chaeronea, and Cinna Catulus. Claudius Maximus, like Fronto, Rusticus and Claudius Severus, played a part in public life. With Apollonius and Rusticus, he was one of Marcus' three most significant friends in the development of his character. He must have been some years, perhaps twenty years, older than Marcus. He was consul in about 144, and for some five years was governor of the key military province of Upper Pannonia, from 150–4. In 158 he was to go to Africa as proconsul, where he had to sit in judgment in a *cause célèbre*, the trial of Apuleius of Madauros, one of the few original writers of the second century AD. He is thus immortalized by Apuleius, who took good care to propitiate his judge by referring to him in flattering terms. 'You are making a mistake, Aemilianus,' said Apuleius, addressing one of his opponents, who had apparently hoped to gain Maximus' support by reproaching the poverty of Apuleius – just because Maximus 'happens to be the owner of an ample estate'. 'You are ill-acquainted with his views if you estimate him according to how Fortune has treated him and not according to the strict rules of philosophy; if you think that a man of strict philosophical principles and such long military service is not more favourably inclined towards moderation rather than to fastidious opulence; if you suppose that he does not approve of riches only on the same principle that he does of some piece of clothing, rather when it fits the person who wears it than when it is unusually long.' Apuleius continually addresses Maximus in person, and credits him with wisdom and learning, in one passage taking it for granted that he is familiar with Aristotle's works *On the generation of animals, On the anatomy of animals,* and *On the history of animals.*

Apuleius' favourable language about Maximus might have been regarded as mere flattery, but Marcus' tribute to him is unequivocal. 'From Maximus: mastery of self and in nothing to be hesitant. To be cheerful in all circumstances, especially in illness. A character that was a happy blend of mildness and dignity. Readiness to do what has to be done without fuss. To see in every instance that he said what he really thought and did what he did without any malicious intention. His imperturbability and his ability not be shocked, never to hurry or to hang back, never to be at a loss what to do, not to be downcast or fawningly hypocritical, and again, not to be angry or suspicious. To be generous, forgiving and sincere. To give him the impression of being completely straight by nature, not of a forced rectitude. The fact too that no one would ever think that he was looked down on by him but would not venture to regard himself as his superior. And to be agreeable in social life.'[20]

Sextus of Chaeronea was the nephew of the celebrated writer Plutarch. He was a professional philosopher, unlike Maximus, Severus and Rusticus, in the sense that he did not enter on a career in public service, and devoted his life to teaching philosophy. Marcus continued to attend his lectures after becoming emperor, a fact which caused a good deal of surprise and comment. 'From Sextus' Marcus learned 'kindliness, how to behave as head of a family, and the meaning of living according to Nature. Dignity without pretence, special consideration for friends, tolerance for amateurs and men whose opinions have no theoretical basis. Readiness to adapt himself to everyone, so that his company was pleasanter than flattery, at the same time commanding the greatest respect among those around him. His sure grasp and method in discovering and systematizing the principles necessary to human life. Never to give the impression of anger or any other emotion but being at one and the same time unemotional and yet full of natural affection. To praise quietly and to be modest about encyclopaedic learning.' The 'natural affection', which Sextus possessed in spite of his philosophical detachment, was a quality which the Roman upper-classes lacked – in fact, as Fronto pointed out to Lucius, there was no word for it in Latin. Marcus remembered Fronto for this observation too.[21]

Marcus' tribute to Cinna Catulus is briefer. 'From Catulus' Marcus learned 'not to neglect the rebukes of a friend, even if they happen to be unreasonable, but to try to regain his favour. To praise teachers wholeheartedly, as is recorded of Athenodotus and Domitius, and to have a genuine love for children.' Catulus is totally unknown, but his names suggest that he was of western rather than eastern descent; and the mention of Athenodotus makes it clear that he was a Stoic.[22]

Marcus in his *Meditations* was never actually to call himself a Stoic. In certain respects he might be more accurately described as an eclectic, for he was attracted by some elements in other philosophies. In any case, he had little interest in the more technical aspects of Stoicism, logic and physics. But Stoicism, coupled with the best in the traditional Roman outlook, as personified by the character of Antoninus, gave Marcus his philosophy of life. Hence a brief introduction is required.[23] It took its name from the public hall, portico, or *Stoa*, in which Zeno, son of Mnaseas, the founder of the school, gave his teaching at Athens. Zeno was not an Athenian, and it even seems doubtful if he was Greek. He was from Citium in Cyprus, and was certainly of partly Phoenician origin, like many of the inhabitants of his native island. It may be even that he was of completely Semitic descent. He was born in 333/2 BC, the year that Alexander the Great ascended the throne of Macedon. He left his home at the age of twenty-two to go to Athens, and, so far as is known, never returned. He was thus ideally fitted, in both time and place, to found a philosophical school which combined elements of eastern thought with the advanced and disciplined intellectualism of Hellenic culture. He was at first attracted to the teaching of the Cynics, but before long ceased his allegiance to that somewhat perversely eccentric and ascetic sect. He was clearly greatly influenced by the teaching of the Platonic Academy; indeed the life and teaching of Socrates remained an inspiring force throughout the history of Stoicism. After he had begun to work out his own system, the Athenian authorities provided him with rooms in the *Stoa Poikile*, where he began his teaching in 301–300 BC, attracting numerous followers over a long life as a philosophic theorist and director until his death in 262 BC.

Marcus does not refer to Zeno, nor to his successor as head of the Stoa, Cleanthes. A good deal of the credit for the originating of Stoic principles went to the third head of the school, Chrysippus, a prolific writer, who did much to systematize the work of his predecessors. Marcus refers once or twice to Chrysippus, as does Fronto in the correspondence, when he wants to give an example of a Stoic.[24] Only a small proportion of the works of the three great initiators of Stoicism has survived, as is the case with most of their successors, so it is not always easy to distinguish between the teachings of individual Stoics at different periods. More than four hundred years elapsed between the early lectures of Zeno and the birth of Marcus.

There were three main sections into which the Stoic system was divided, logic, physics and ethics. Logic included the theory of knowledge and the study of language, as well as logic in the narrower sense – the study of syllogistic argument and dialectic. Physics included theology and metaphysics as well as all the natural sciences. Ethics, the pursuit of the good life, was the ultimate aim. The relationship between the three branches of the system was illustrated by the Stoics by the use of metaphor. Logic was compared to a wall, physics to the trees protected by the wall, ethics to the fruit borne by the trees. Again, the philosophy as a whole was compared to a body, of which the bones and muscles were logic, the flesh and blood physics, and the soul ethics.

The basis of the Stoics' thought was that knowledge is attainable. They believed the evidence of the senses, and evolved an elaborate explanation of the mode by which the senses and the mind acquire knowledge, which seems now a curiously confused mixture of physiology, psychology and philosophy. Waves of sensation emanate from objects of sense-perception, which strike the sense-organs. This explains the basic acquisition of sense-data. The mind acquires information by the meeting of waves from the mind and waves from the senses. The impact produces a mind-picture – *phantasia*. This was, of course, only the starting-point of their theory of knowledge. The crucial point around which it hinged was the 'criterion' for judging the truth of mind-pictures. On this they cannot be said to have made more progress than most other philosophers before and after. Nevertheless their logical theories, such as they were, provided a groundwork from which they could go on to formulate a theory of the universe and a number of fundamental rules of conduct, or rather, one fundamental rule.

The Stoics viewed the universe as a single, unified body, finite, continuous and of spherical shape, existing in an infinite void. Some Stoics toyed with the notion of the sun being the centre of this universe, but rejected this in favour of the earth – unfortunately for the progress of science. The universe is in itself a rational, living being. All its parts are united in a mysterious unity, which make up this indivisible – and divine – whole. In a sense, God is the soul of the universe. The life-force was conceived by Stoics as having the properties of fire: thus fire, heat and motion were the source of all life. It can be seen from this brief summary that the Stoics were, from one point of view, materialists and from another, pantheists. But this would misrepresent their views. They were not materialists in the modern sense, although they believed that everything was made of the same ultimate 'stuff'; and although their God was not separate from the world, their conception of him is nevertheless different from that of the pantheist.

The central concept of the Stoic teaching was the 'rational principle' – *logos* – which, they believed, animated the universe. The aim of the Stoic philosopher was 'to live in harmony with "nature"', a concept which it is extremely difficult to explain in any other language than Greek. True nature was guided and formed by the *logos*. This was also identified with fate, or divine providence. They believed, with a contradiction which not surprisingly they could never resolve with complete success, both in predestination and in free will. Some Stoics also believed that the universe would come to an end in fire, and that a new universe would then be formed through the action of fire, the life-giving force. But this was subsequently abandoned as being incompatible with the conception of a beneficent providence. The sole good in human life is virtue, the acquisition of which depends on the individual human will. If a man acquires virtue, and lives in harmony with nature, he is thereby freed from dependence on external factors. Desire for external, apparently good things comes only from false judgment, which can be overcome by knowledge. The pursuit of virtue is an end in itself. Nothing else matters. All emotions should be avoided. This may make the doctrine seem cold and selfish. But Stoics also believed in the 'Fatherhood of God and the Brotherhood of Man', and this universalism gives it a more exalted note than the at first sight narrow insistence on *being* virtuous.

By the time of the death of Chrysippus, in the last decade of the third century BC, the Stoa had acquired a recognized place as one of the leading schools of philosophy. Chrysippus, like Zeno, came from a region (Cilicia in his case) where Semitic and Hellenic elements were intermingled. The father of Chrysippus was from Tarsus, the city of Paul. Later prominent figures in the Stoic school were also from the eastern Mediterranean. Many commentators have noted similarities between Jewish religious thought and the philosophy of the Stoa. In fact, it may certainly be said that Stoicism was to become, for its adherents, very much of a religion. In the second century BC the school grew in influence and in the middle of the century spread to Rome, then the leading Mediterranean power. By the last century of the Roman Republic, chiefly through the direct and indirect teaching of Panaetius and later of Posidonius, its effect on the outlook of numerous leading Romans had become profound. The revolutionary Tiberius Gracchus was influenced by a number of Stoic doctrines, for example, as were his brother-in-law and political antagonist Scipio Aemilianus and Scipio's friend the younger Laelius. The circle of these two men gave Stoicism a considerable following among the Roman nobility. But the imprint of its teaching was to be seen most markedly in Julius Caesar's enemy, the younger Cato, and in Cato's nephew Brutus, the assassin of Caesar. In spite, or perhaps partly because of, the political defeat and deaths of Cato and Brutus, the philosophy which had animated their activity continued to flourish after Caesar Augustus had founded his New Order. Stoicism became the refuge and inspiration of those who found the unashamedly despotic rule of the later Julio-Claudian emperors and of Domitian distasteful and oppressive.

Seneca was the leading expounder of Stoicism in the mid-first century AD, and although for a time he was the tutor and then the minister of Nero, he was eventually implicated in the unsuccessful conspiracy of 65 and forced to suicide. But Seneca, although his reputation in his own time and in the Renaissance was enormous, was not thought highly of in the second century AD. Fronto disapproved of his literary style and the leading Stoics clearly felt that his philosophical teaching had been compromised or tainted by his association with Nero. These criticisms also applied to his nephew, the poet Lucan, whose epic the *Pharsalia* was a glorification of Cato:

victrix causa deis placuit, sed victa Catoni –

The winning side was favoured by the gods,
But the losing by Cato.

Lucan's end, at the same time as that of Seneca, had in fact been somewhat inglorious, although his uncle faced death with dignity. The heroes of the second-century Stoics were the political leaders of the Stoic opposition to absolutism, Thrasea Paetus, his son-in-law Helvidius Priscus, and Junius Arulenus Rusticus, probably the grandfather of the 'teacher' of Marcus. These three men lost their lives under Nero, Vespasian and Domitian respectively.[25]

With the assassination of Domitian in September 96, philosophy, and Stoicism in particular, could come out into the open again, and became at first respectable, and, before long, fashionable. Its leading teacher was, at the beginning of the second century, Epictetus, a lame ex-slave of Phrygian origin, who had belonged to a freedman of Nero, Epaphroditus. Ironically, it was Epaphroditus who had been mainly responsible for unmasking and suppressing the conspiracy of 65, in the aftermath of which Seneca, Lucan and Thrasea Paetus lost their lives. Epictetus is said to have been taught by Musonius Rufus. Musonius was no doctrinaire Stoic and the fragments of his teaching and the anecdotes about him that survive give the impression that he remained a typical Roman. His teaching was simple: everyone is capable of goodness; God wants man to be virtuous and superior to pleasure and pain; virtue demands practical training, just like music or medicine – theory is not enough. In his pursuit of the simple, natural life Musonius was a vegetarian, wore simple clothing, did not shave his beard and praised the virtues of working on the land. He insisted on a strict sexual morality – his teaching on marriage, with its emphasis on a true equality and community of minds, and on mutual sharing of possessions, was among the most advanced of ancient times. He did not, however, advocate escapism in any form: he preached good citizenship, involving the giving of whatever help was possible to one's fellow-countrymen and fatherland. In his own case this was an impossible aim, as he was exiled by Domitian. In exile he did not compromise: 'Have you ever seen me humble myself before anyone, because I am an exile?' he would say.[26]

Epictetus too was exiled under Domitian, to Nicopolis on the Adriatic coast of Greece (in modern Albania). After Domitian's murder he was content to remain there, and disciples from many walks of life came to him.

He was, like Musonius, far more concerned with the moral side of Stoicism; and Marcus too was to bother very little about Stoic metaphysical or scientific doctrines. The important thing for the Stoic now was freedom to live as one wanted, genuine inner freedom: to be master of one's own soul. It is perhaps not surprising that one who had been a slave should have more to teach about freedom than any other ancient philosopher. The contrast between physical and moral freedom was all the more telling when it came from the lips of one who had experienced both as something new. The emphasis on inner freedom was, also, particularly appropriate under the empire – for Caesar was the common master of all men. But if Caesar too were a Stoic, thinking along the same lines? Epictetus did not know Marcus. But the irony of the fact that the two last great Stoics should have been a lame Phrygian slave and the ruler of the world empire has struck many. Perhaps it should not be emphasized too much. Epictetus had been, as slaves went, in a relatively high grade – an imperial slave at secondhand, so to speak; and he was given his freedom.[27] Still the essential point about slavery was that the slave was the property of his master. Epictetus made light of the condition of slavery, but he could still remind the masters of slaves that slaves were 'kinsmen, your brothers by nature, the offspring of Zeus'. All men are the children of God, with a spark of the divine fire within them. A master who looks on his slaves as less than that is looking not to the laws of the gods, but 'to the earth, the pit, these wretched laws of ours – the laws of the dead'.

A great deal of Epictetus' teaching has survived, in the form of detailed records of individual periods of teaching with question and answer, longer discourses and short aphorisms. This cannot be summarized briefly, but Arrian, the pupil of Epictetus who recorded his teaching, did make the attempt to do this, and a few key points from that summary may be given here. 'Some things are under our control, others are not. The things under our control are: our mental concepts, choice, desire, aversion, in a word everything that we do. The things not under our control are: our body, property, reputation, public office, in a word everything that is not our own doing. And the things under our control are by nature free, unhindered, unimpeded. The things not under our control are weak, in servitude, subject to hindrance, not our own.' Once this had been recognized, the way was clear. 'Do not seek to have everything happen as you desire, but desire that things happen as they actually do happen, and then you will be well-off.' 'Whoever wants to be free, should not wish for anything or avoid anything that is under the control of others. Otherwise, he has to be a slave.' 'Keep death and exile and all dreadful-seeming things, most of all death, before your eyes day and night; then you will never have any mean thought, or long for something too much.' 'When you have become adjusted to simple living in respect of your body, do not preen yourself about this . . . and if you ever want to train yourself for physical endurance, do it by yourself and not for outsiders.' The summary ends with the famous saying of Socrates, about those responsible for his death: 'Anytus and Meletus can kill me, but they cannot hurt me.' Marcus' Stoic hero Thrasea Paetus, the enemy of Nero, 'used to say: "I would rather be killed today than exiled tomorrow".' But Musonius told him: 'If you choose death as the heavier of the two, what a foolish choice. If as the lighter – who gave you the choice? Are you not willing to practise contentment with what you are given?'

The influence of Epictetus is apparent on every page of the *Meditations*. Their character is different from the *Discourses* of Epictetus, more sombre perhaps. But this is not surprising, considering that they were written in the middle of war and death. Marcus had every reason to take to heart the recommendation 'to keep death . . . before your eyes day and night'. The *Meditations*, of course, were written at the end of his life. But from the age of twenty-five onwards the teaching of Epictetus was one of the mainsprings of Marcus' life.[28] Several of Marcus' philosopher friends evidently set him an example, which in his *Meditations* he was to recall with gratitude, of the right kind of family life – Sextus in 'how to behave as head of a family', Severus 'love of family', Cinna Catulus 'to have a genuine love of children'. Before long Marcus was to become a father. In the year 147 Faustina bore their first child, a girl, who was named Faustina after her mother but also had the names 'Domitia', from the mother of Marcus, and 'Aurelia' from Marcus' official family name. If there had been any anxiety about Faustina's fertility – the first child was not born until 30 November 147, more than eighteen months after the marriage – it cannot have lasted long. She was to bear at least thirteen more children during the next twenty-three years, including two sets of twins. In the *Meditations* Marcus was to thank the gods that his wife was 'so obedient, so warm-hearted, so artless'. She acquired a reputation among posterity for infidelity; Marcus never complained.[29]

The birth of a child was of public importance for Marcus. Pius decided that the time had now come to invest him with some of the imperial powers – in fact the decision must have been taken before the birth, for the powers were proclaimed on the following day, 1 December. Marcus received the tribunician power and the *imperium* – the authority over the armies and provinces of the emperor – and the right to bring one measure before the senate after the four which his father could introduce. Marcus' proper style was now M. Aurelius Caesar, Augusti filius, *trib. pot.* Nine days later, on 10 December, his tribunician power was renewed and he became *trib. pot. II*, for this was the day on which his father also renewed his tribunician power. Meanwhile, on 1 December, Faustina received the title Augusta.[30]

Pius did not consider it necessary after this act of confidence to send Marcus to the provinces and armies, to allow him to gain experience by direct participation. But Pius himself had never had any experience abroad, other than his year as proconsul of the non-military province of Asia; and the reign was a reign of peace. Still, the failure of Pius to give Marcus this experience must be deplored, in the light of future events. Pius himself did not undertake any expeditions in his reign. His expressed reason for this was that 'it was a serious problem for the provincials to support an emperor and his suite, even an economical one'. Marcus was allegedly only absent from Pius for two nights during the entire twenty-three years of the reign.[31]

It is remarkable that Marcus was able to fill the role of virtual co-emperor for thirteen-and-a-half years without ever exciting the suspicion that he was impatient to have sole rule for himself. The acid-tongued Valerius Homullus apparently took the opportunity of insinuating to Pius that Domitia Lucilla was eager for her son to come to the throne without delay. He observed her praying in her garden in front of an image of the god Apollo, and commented to Pius: 'That woman is now praying that you may come to your end and her son may rule.' Pius' reply is not recorded, but Homullus was well known for his barbed tongue. Pius had had to put up with it himself when dining with him. He noticed that his house had some porphyry columns and asked where they had come from – no doubt fully aware that the only source of supply were imperial quarries on the Red Sea. Homullus told him 'When you come to someone else's house, be deaf and dumb.' Pius took the joke well enough, and no doubt took the joke about Lucilla too. In fact Marcus' deference to his father was very striking, the biographer reports – but not surprising, in view of the tribute in the *Meditations*. In turn, Pius accepted his advice very readily, no doubt increasingly as the years went on, 'and did not easily promote anyone without consulting him'.[32]

One possible reason why Marcus was not sent abroad is that in 148 the 900th anniversary of the founding of Rome was celebrated. Pius did not hold Secular Games – too many emperors had already held them, for political reasons, for Pius to stoop to this easy way of gaining popularity. But he did hold magnificent games for the people of Rome, with elephants, giraffes, tigers, rhinoceroses, crocodiles and hippopotami – all to be slaughtered for the pleasure of the Roman populace. The celebrations of 148 had been heralded in advance from the start of the reign with allusions on the coinage to the legendary origins of Rome (one of which, the rescue of Anchises from the flames of Troy by Aeneas, has already been mentioned in connection with the name Pius). These reminders of Rome's past fitted in well with the religious aspirations of the age and with Pius' own deep religious sense, which earned for him the comparison with Numa, Rome's semi-mythical second king, who was supposedly re-sponsible for much of the religious ritual of the state. The year 148 was also the tenth anniversary of Pius' accession, so there was plenty to celebrate.[33] There were, of course, trouble spots. The war in Mauretania was still in progress and in the east a new king had ascended the throne of Parthia. He was later to adopt a threatening posture towards Rome.

It might, perhaps, have been a good thing if Pius had taken decisive military action, for the grievances of the Parthian ruler were merely put into cold storage, until a more favourable opportunity should present itself. The presence of Marcus on either the eastern or the south-western frontiers might well have been profitable for Rome and for the dynasty. But he was not sent.[34]

Marcus kept in close touch with Fronto after his teaching ended, sometimes writing several letters in one day. Fronto was appreciative, but in one letter expressed anxiety in case his own letters and the duty of answering them might have taken up too much of Marcus' time – 'in case I should add to your necessary labours some extra trouble and burden, if in addition to those letters which you write daily, as a necessary duty, to so many people, I too should weary you with having to reply to me'. Thereafter, for some years, the correspondence, as it now survives at least, concerns mainly family news.[35]

Marcus' and Faustina's baby daughter was, it might seem, a sickly infant. At any rate the first mention of her in the correspondence with Fronto is to describe an illness. 'Caesar to Fronto. If the gods are willing we seem to have a hope of recovery. The diarrhoea has stopped, the little attacks of fever have been driven away. But the emaciation is still extreme and there is still quite a bit of coughing. You understand, of course, that I am writing this about our little Faustina, for whose sake we have been pretty occupied. Let me know if your health is improving in accordance with my prayers, my master.' Fronto replied that the way Marcus' letter opened had given him a serious shock. 'Fronto to Caesar. Good heavens, how shocked I was when I read the beginning of your letter. The way it was written made me think some danger to *your* health was meant. Then when you made it clear that the danger which I had taken to be yours at the beginning of the note was to your daughter Faustina, how my apprehension was transformed! In fact not just transformed, but in some way not a little relieved. You may say "Did my daughter's danger seem less important to you than mine. Could it seem so to you, who protest that Faustina is to you a serene light, a festive day, a near hope, a prayer fulfilled, a complete joy, a noble and assured glory?"' He admits that he does love Marcus more than he loves Marcus' daughter, although he says at first that he does not know why danger to Marcus should shock him more than danger to little Faustina. 'You are more likely to know the cause of this, since you have learned more about the nature and feelings of men than I have, and learned it better.' This is a reference to Marcus' studies in philosophy, which would include psychology, for Fronto goes on to mention his own former teacher in philosophy, the Stoic Athenodotus. He then wrote once more of the nature of his love, two illustrations of which deserve quotation. 'I have sometimes criticized you behind your back in quite strong terms, in front of a very few of my intimate friends. This was in the days when you used to go about in public with too serious a face and used to read books at the theatre or at banquets – I still used to go to the theatre and to banquets myself in those days – and it was on occasions like this that I used to call you a hard and unreasonable person, even a hateful character, when I had been roused to anger. But if anyone else found fault with you in my hearing I could not listen with patience. So it was easier for me to say these things about you myself than to allow others to say them – just as I would find it easier to strike my daughter Cratia myself than to see her struck by anyone else. . . .' He adds another interesting sidelight. 'You know that in all the banks, shops, taverns, eaves, colonnades and windows, everywhere, there are portraits of you exposed to public view, badly painted for the most part and modelled or carved in a plain, not to say worthless, artistic style. Still, all the same, your likeness, however unlike you, never meets my eyes when I am out without making me part my lips in a smile and dream of you.' This little detail is instructive. The likenesses of Marcus which now survive are for the most part expensive and lasting effigies in marble or bronze, or the portraits on the official coinage. But portraits of the prince and the other members of the imperial house, the *domus divina*, 'divine family', must have been as widespread as photographs and portraits of kings and rulers in modern countries, if not more so. Fronto ends his letter with a very human touch. He asks Marcus not to tell Faustina that he loves Marcus more than her – 'for there is a danger that your daughter will be upset by this, as she is a serious and old-fashioned lady, and when I ask to kiss her hands and feet, she may take them away, being annoyed about it, or give them grudgingly. And, the good gods be witness, I shall then kiss her tiny hands and plump little feet with more gladness than your royal neck and honest, merry face.'[35]

In 149 Faustina gave birth again, this time to twin sons, duly commemorated on the coinage of the year, with, on the reverse, crossed cornucopiae surmounted by busts of two small boys, and the legend *temporum felicitas*, 'the happiness of the times'. But first one of the infants died, then the second, both before the end of 149. The coinage of Marcus and Faustina depicts a tiny girl – Domitia Faustina – with one boy baby; and then the girl alone. The infants were buried in the Mausoleum of Hadrian, and their simple epitaphs survive. One, called Titus Aurelius Antoninus, is styled 'son of M. Aurelius Caesar, grandson of the emperor Antoninus Augustus Pius, father of his country'. The other, T. Aelius Aurelius, has the same description except for the addition, after 'Aurelius Caesar', of the words 'and of Faustina Augusta'. There is no trace of this loss in the surviving correspondence with Fronto. But on several occasions in the *Meditations* Marcus was to refer to the grief caused by the loss of children. Apollonius had taught him to bear it, but he had to relearn the lesson. 'I see that the child is ill. I see it. But I do not see that he is in danger.

In this way always stick to your first impressions and add nothing of your own from inside yourself.' This seems to be a reminder that he must not panic when one of his children fell ill. 'One man prays: "How I may not lose my little child", but you must pray: "How I may not be afraid to lose him".' 'For one who is imbued with true doctrines even the briefest and most familiar saying is sufficient reminder to dispel sorrow and fear, for example:

> . . . leaves –
> The wind scatters some of them on the ground:
> Such are the children of men.

Yes, your children too are "leaves" . . .' 'Epictetus used to say that as you kissed your child you should say in your heart: "Tomorrow perhaps you will die." "These are ill-omened words." "No," he replied, "nothing that means an act of nature is ill-omened, for otherwise it would be an evil omen to say that the corn has been reaped."' 'Perhaps you will die' here refers to the parent no doubt, rather than to the child.[36]

The next child was born on 7 March 150, another daughter. She was given the names Annia Aurelia Galeria Lucilla, the first and third names being those of Faustina herself, the second being the family name of Marcus, the last, by which she was to be known, the *cognomen* of Marcus' mother. One or two letters refer to Lucilla and her elder sister Domitia Faustina. 'We are experiencing the summer heat still', Marcus writes, 'but our little girls are, I think I may say, in quite good health, so we think we are enjoying spring temperatures.' A letter of Fronto's asks Marcus 'to give your Faustina a message from me and congratulate her. Kiss our little ladies in my name – and, as I always do, kiss their feet and hands as well.' Another letter, of uncertain date, refers to one of Faustina's pregnancies. It was written when Fronto was ill, and Marcus too had anxieties. 'To my master, greeting. You have increased my anxieties, which I hope you will relieve as soon as possible by the subsidence of the pains and swelling in your knee. As for me the weakness of my Lady mother does not allow me to rest. There is too Faustina's approaching confinement. But we must trust the gods. Farewell, my master, most delightful to me. My mother greets you.' Domitia Lucilla was still living in 155, but had died before Marcus' accession to the throne in 161. As he says in the *Meditations* that she did not have a long life, she was presumably dead soon after 155. The pregnancy referred to may have resulted in the birth of Lucilla, because a letter placed a little after the one just quoted, in the manuscript, speaks of Fronto's delight at seeing the child. 'I love you ten times as much – I have seen your daughter: I feel I have seen you and Faustina as babies at the same moment, so much that is good in both your faces is blended in hers.' But it must remain pure guesswork which of the daughters born between 147 and the death of Marcus' mother is intended.[37]

In 151 Faustina probably had another daughter, but in the meantime it seems that the first-born, Domitia, had died. At any rate, the next daughter, born not later than 153, was named Annia Galeria Aurelia Faustina. It may be inferred that her *cognomen* would not have been given her if Domitia Faustina were still alive. Another son was born in 152, named T. Aelius Antoninus. Once again the coinage showed several imperial children, two girls and an infant, and the legend celebrated 'the Augusta's fertility', *fecunditati Augustae*. But this son too did not survive for long. By the year 156 only the two girls were depicted.[38]

Whether or not the son born in 152 died the same year is not known. But Marcus was certainly bereaved of his sister Cornificia in that year. The cause of her death is not known, but she cannot have been more than thirty. She and her husband Quadratus had two children, a son named Marcus Ummidius Quadratus, aged about seventeen in 152, and a daughter, Ummidia Cornificia Faustina.[39]

In the same year, Lucius, who was to be twenty-two on 15 December, was designated quaestor for the next year, before the legal age. In fact as quaestor in his twenty-third year he was only two years under age. Marcus had been quaestor at seventeen. As quaestor in 153 Lucius gave gladiatorial games, sitting in a place of honour between Pius and Marcus. In 154 he was consul, with a member of one of the oldest aristocratic families (far older than his own), T. Sextius Lateranus. Thus he received this honour some nine years earlier than the normal minimum age of thirty-two, and had omitted the praetorship, but again this privilege was not as great as that received by Marcus, consul at eighteen, and for the second time at twenty-three. Lucius received no other marks of distinction, except, of course, that he was 'son of Augustus'. On official journeys, while Marcus travelled with Pius, Lucius was placed alongside the praetorian prefect Gavius Maximus. He showed loyalty to Pius, rather than affection, according to the biographer. His character was markedly different from that of Marcus, although to a certain extent he was moulded by the example of his adoptive brother, encouraged by Pius, who admired 'the frankness of his nature and his unspoiled way of life'. Lucius was a devotee of sports of all kinds, especially hunting and wrestling, and was something of a pleasure-lover, 'rather too carefree, and a good performer, within bounds, at all kinds of sports, games and fun'. He took an unashamed pleasure in the circus-games and the gladiatorial spectacles, unlike Marcus who used to take a book along to alleviate his boredom. Pius did not entirely approve, but he felt that he had to keep him in the family – without, however, giving him any powers.[40] It is puzzling that Lucius did not marry at this stage. But perhaps he was encouraged to wait until one of Marcus' daughters should be old enough. In 154 he was already older than Marcus had been at his marriage in 145; and apparently he was to remain unmarried for a further ten years. Perhaps he married a wife who died young. Alternatively, Pius may have discouraged him from marrying, in case dynastic complications should be produced by the birth of a son.

Now that he was in the senate Lucius' training with Fronto had to be put to practical use. The biographer says that he was quite a good speaker, but uncharitably adds the story that the better passages in his speeches were written by his friends. One of his speeches is mentioned in a brief letter of Fronto to Marcus, which also comments on a speech by Pius. 'To my Lord. Whether the merit of the deed enhanced the speech or the speech managed to equal a most noble act, I am uncertain. But certain it is that these words had the same author as those deeds. But your brother's speech also delighted me, for it was polished and judicious – and I am certain that he had very little time to consider it.' Marcus' reply was in agreement. 'Answer. On returning from my father's banquet I got your note, and gathered that the messenger who brought it had already gone. Therefore I am writing this reply quite late in the evening, so that you may read it tomorrow. It is not surprising that my father's speech seemed to you worthy of its subject, my master. But my brother's speech of thanks is, in my opinion, especially praiseworthy, seeing that he had less time to consider it, as you guess. Farewell, my most delightful master. My mother greets you.' There is no clue as to the subject of either speech, but, as Lucius' was a speech of thanks, it may be that he was speaking after the grant of the quaestorship in 153 or the consulship in 154.[41]

In 155 Marcus' friend Victorinus was consul. He had probably become Fronto's son-in-law by now. Soon after, Fronto became eligible for the ballot which was held every year for the two senior proconsulships, Asia and Africa (the only two held by former consuls, normally, at this period, between twelve and fifteen years after their consulship). At some time in the period 155–8 Fronto was successful in the ballot and was appointed proconsul of Asia. He began to make preparations. Marcus wrote to him to recommend to his protection when he reached his province a certain Themistocles, made known to Marcus by the son of his philosophy teacher Apollonius. 'For you will, I know, be always very ready to show justice and equity to all the Asians, but your counsel, friendship, and whatever honour and conscience allow a proconsul to extend to his friends, so long as no one else is thereby harmed – these I ask you to extend freely to Themistocles. Farewell, my most delightful master. There is no need to reply.'[42]

But all Fronto's preparations were in vain. His state of health did not permit him to make the journey and undertake the task. He wrote to Pius to explain the position. 'Fronto to Antoninus Pius Augustus. Most reverend Emperor, the facts themselves bear witness that I have made every effort and have been exceedingly eager to fulfil the duties of proconsul. As long as the matter was undecided I claimed my right of balloting. When through having more children another had a prior claim, I was as satisfied with the most splendid province which remained to me, as if I had chosen it myself.' Clearly Fronto had hoped to become proconsul of Africa, the province adjacent to his native Numidia (to which, in fact, Numidia still *de iure* belonged, although not, for the past hundred years and more, *de facto*.) Since the time of Augustus, who had legislated with the hope of increasing the birthrate among the upper classes, children were of assistance to senators in increasing the rate of their promotion (and unmarried men older than twenty-four were penalized). Fronto with only one daughter would not be very greatly favoured.

Fronto's preparations had been fairly extensive, and they throw an interesting light on the methods of the Roman administration. 'I made careful preparations to facilitate the transaction of the quantity of business connected with the administration of the province, by enlisting numbers of my friends. I summoned from my home relatives and friends of mine of whose loyalty and integrity I was confident. I wrote to my intimates at Alexandria, instructing them to hurry to Athens, to meet me there, and I handed over the direction of my Greek secretariat to these most learned men. From Cilicia too I urged some distinguished men to come, for having always acted as counsel for the Cilicians in both public and private cases before you, I have a great number of friends in that province. From Mauretania too I summoned to me a man whose love for me is equal to my great affection for him, Julius Senex, in order that I might avail myself not only of his loyalty and diligence, but also of his military effectiveness in the hunting down and keeping in check of brigands.' Fronto's procedure was in fact the normal one for all provincial governors. A governor of a military province would in addition have a number of actual appointments in the armed forces which he could fill by his personal choice. But Fronto was unable to put his plans into practice.[43]

His attack of ill-health may be the one which he describes in a letter to Marcus. 'To my Lord. I have been so seriously afflicted with "cholera" that I lost my voice, gasped and struggled for breath, finally my veins ceased functioning and I lost consciousness and had no apparent pulse. In fact my family gave me up for lost, and I remained insensible for some time. The doctors had no time or chance to revive me with a bath or cold water or food, or of relieving me, except that after nightfall I swallowed a few small pieces of bread soaked in wine. So I was gradually completely resuscitated. For three whole days afterwards I did not recover my voice. But by now, with the help of the gods, I am in pretty comfortable health, I can walk more easily and can speak more clearly. In fact, if the gods will aid me, tomorrow I intend to take a drive. If I find that I can stand up to the flint-paving I will hurry to see you – only when I see you will I live. I will set out from Rome on the seventh day before the Kalends, if the gods will aid me. Farewell, sweetest Lord, most longed for, my best reason for my life. Greet your Lady.' The illness sounds something like a mild stroke, especially as he lost the power of speech for three days. But that is conjecture.[44]

At home there was little of moment. In 156 Lucius' cousin M. Ceionius Silvanus was consul, followed the next year by his uncle, his father's half-brother M. Vettulenus Civica Barbarus. His brother-in-law Plautius Quintillus (probably related in any case to the Ceionii Commodi) was consul in 159. Quintillus was the husband of Ceionia Fabia, once the betrothed of Marcus.[45]

It is not known whether Pius, Marcus and Lucius ever saw a remarkable document which was addressed to them at this period. 'To the Emperor Titus Aelius Hadrianus Antoninus Pius Augustus Caesar and to Verissimus his son, the philosopher, and to Lucius the philosopher, son of Caesar by nature and of Augustus by adoption, a lover of culture, and to the holy senate and the whole Roman people, on behalf of men of all nations who are unjustly hated and reviled, I, Justinus, son of Priscus and grandson of Bacchius, of Flavia Neapolis in Syria Palestina being one of them myself, have drawn up this plea and petition.' It is the *Apology* of the future martyr Justin. It is perhaps surprising that he calls Lucius 'philosopher and lover of culture' – unexpected attributes. But the fact that he was able to give Marcus the name 'Verissimus,' and that he knew Lucius was the son by birth of (L. Aelius) Caesar, suggests that this description deserves some attention. Justin's *Apology*, which was delivered not much later than 154, was not the first of its kind – a certain Quadratus had apparently addressed a similar appeal to Hadrian, of which only a brief fragment is preserved, and, early in the reign of Antoninus, Aristides of Athens, of whose work a few extracts survive, had done the same. Justin was making an appeal for toleration. But he went further and boldly stated the claims of the Christian faith to pre-eminence, refuting, at the same time, allegations that had been made against Christians. He went dangerously far in attacking the morality implicit in the legends of the deities of the Greco-Roman world, in speaking rather scornfully of the deification of emperors and even in making a slightly derisive reference to the deification by Hadrian of his favourite Antinous – 'whom everybody hastened to worship as a god, through fear, although they knew quite well who he was and where he came from'. The *Apology* concludes with an account of the trial before the prefect of Rome Lollius Urbicus of a Christian named Ptolemaeus. He had converted 'a woman married to a man of evil life, in which she too formerly participated'. On her conversion she had sought a divorce, but her aggrieved husband had filed a complaint against her, adding that she was a Christian. The wife successfully petitioned the emperor to be allowed to settle her affairs and then to defend herself. Ptolemaeus had in the meanwhile been arrested and punished on unspecified charges. The husband persuaded the centurion who had arrested him to ask Ptolemaeus if he was a Christian. When he admitted it he was put in chains and eventually brought before Urbicus on this charge. A bystander named Lucius protested, when Ptolemaeus was sentenced to death merely for being a Christian, although not guilty of any crime: 'Your verdict, Urbicus, is unworthy of the emperor Pius or his philosopher son or the holy senate.' Lucius suffered the same fate, as did a third man who came forward in the same way.[46]

One of those who had attacked the morals of the Christians was Fronto. In one speech he told the familiar tale of the 'incestuous banquets' of the Christians, referring to the ceremony of the *agape*, the 'love-feast' which followed the evening Communion rite in the early Church. The fact that it occurred at night, with both sexes and all ages present, in secret, led to the presumption that it was in fact an orgy. 'After a lot of feasting, when the banquet has warmed up and a passion for incestuous lust and drunkenness has flared up, a dog tied to the lamp is incited to jump and leap by throwing a little cake to it beyond the reach of its tether.' When this put the lights out, the guests began their hideous orgies, Fronto proclaimed.[47]

If Fronto had taken up his appointment as proconsul of Asia he would have come across evidence of Christianity of a very different kind. It was probably in early 156, when the proconsul of Asia was L. Statius Quadratus (who had been consul in 142, the year before Fronto) that the aged Polycarp was martyred by being burned and then stabbed to death in the arena at Smyrna. But in any case, there were the martyrdoms at Rome also, in which the sentences of death were issued by Lollius Urbicus, Fronto's fellow-countryman, the victor in Britain. The *Apology* of Justin probably never reached the emperor and his sons. It would have been handed in to one of the imperial secretariats. Nevertheless, Marcus could hardly have remained unaware of Christianity as a young man. During his reign he was to be confronted with the problem which its existence created, and, more important from his point of view, the reaction which it provoked from the common people, on two notable occasions.[48]

In 156 Pius became seventy. He had nearly five more years to live. He was still fit, but being tall found it difficult to keep an upright posture without the use of stays, and he found that he had to nibble some dry bread when he got up, to sustain himself for his morning receptions. As Pius grew older, no doubt Marcus played an increasingly important role. This may have increased with the death, in about the year 156 or 157, of the prefect of the guard Gavius Maximus. He had occupied the post for a record tenure, nearly twenty years, and it seems probable that he played a major part in advising Pius on the running of the empire. His immediate successor C. Tattius Maximus had been Gavius' own protégé, but Tattius did not last long. In 160 he was succeeded by two men, the experienced T. Furius Victorinus and Sex. Cornelius Repentinus. Repentinus was a friend of Fronto's and was evidently from the Numidian town of Simitthu. But he was said to owe his appointment to the influence of Pius' mistress Galeria Lysistrate. Whereas Victorinus had had a long and varied career, combining military service with a great variety of administrative posts, Repentinus was elevated to the guard from being *ab epistulis*, head of the secretariat.[49]

Gavius Maximus had not been universally liked. Fronto had been involved in an embarrassing affair when his friend Censorius Niger died, leaving him heir to five-twelfths of his estate. In his will he had used intemperate language to attack Maximus. Fronto had to write to the emperor, whose friendship Niger had lost before his death, to excuse both his own continued association with the man and the way he had behaved. He also wrote to Maximus himself. 'Grief added to anger disturbed the man's mind. His other virtues were poisoned and ruined by anger.' He claimed that he had often seen Niger weeping from being deprived of Maximus' friendship. He explained the whole position in a letter to Marcus, but briefly. 'I began a long letter to you on the subject, but on thinking everything over I decided not to disturb you or call you away from more important matters.'[50]

At about the same period, in the late 150s, there was an even greater *cause célèbre*, but one which finds no mention in the surviving correspondence of Fronto. It involved Herodes Atticus, whose wife Regilla had died towards the end of a pregnancy. Her brother Bradua accused Herodes of murder. He had doubtless treated his wife harshly, but the charge was excessive. Herodes was acquitted, and mourned his wife with an ostentatious display of grief verging on vulgarity.[51] In the second half of the 150s trouble recurred in Britain. The man chosen to deal with it was Gnaeus Julius Verus, evidently either the son or the nephew of the great Sextus Julius Severus who had governed Britain and suppressed the Jewish revolt under Hadrian. In the middle of the decade references to Britain reappear on the imperial coinage and Pius for a time allowed the title gained by the victory there in 142. '*Imp. II*', to be included with his other titles once more. Julius Verus seems to have found the new frontier of Lollius Urbicus unsatisfactory, and Hadrian's Wall was reoccupied. Thus, for the time being at least, the territory which is now southern Scotland was being abandoned, less than twenty years after the conquests of Urbicus.[52] It might be imagined – although it must be pure speculation – that Urbicus himself, probably still alive and in office as prefect of Rome, regarded the withdrawal with some displeasure. It may not then be coincidence that at about the same time an extension of Roman territory was carried out in southern Germany. The governor of the Upper province, probably a man called C. Popillius Carus Pedo, supervised the construction of a new artificial frontier, with a corresponding advance in the adjacent province of Raetia. The new frontier was a modest fifteen miles further forward, but it had remarkable features: one section runs absolutely straight for some fifty miles.[53] The fact that, at about the same moment, the frontier in northern Britain reverted to the Hadrianic line, while that in Germany was extended, is puzzling. Was Pius trying to conciliate elements at Rome that might regard withdrawal from his Wall in Scotland as a sign of weakness? Or, alternatively, the advance in Germany may have been intended to warn the free Germans that Rome remained strong. The changes might equally be related to the disappearance from the scene of Gavius Maximus. Another slight indication that a change of emphasis was on the way could be inferred from the case of Statius Priscus. This man had served as an equestrian officer in Britain and in the Jewish war of Hadrian, among other appointments, had become a procurator, and then entered the senate. Men like this should have been useful additions to the high command, yet Priscus' progress through the senatorial *cursus honorum* was laborious. Only in the late 150s did he come to the fore, winning some military successes as governor of Upper Dacia, and then achieving the remarkable distinction of becoming consul *ordinarius* in 159. This too may reflect a 'new broom' at work. In 160, as the *Fasti Ostienses* record, the prefect of the city died. It is not known whether this was Lollius Urbicus or a successor. The new prefect was Marcus' Stoic friend and mentor Junius Rusticus.[54]

More children were born to Marcus and Faustina at this period, first a son. Congratulations were despatched from the 'Synod of the temple of Dionysus' at Smyrna in the province of Asia. By the time that Marcus replied, however, writing from Lorium on 28 March 158, the child was dead. He thanked them for their good wishes, 'even though this turned out otherwise'. The name of this son is unknown.[55]

In 159 and 160 Faustina gave birth again, on each occasion to daughters. They were named Fadilla, after a sister of Faustina who had died many years earlier, and Cornificia, after Marcus' sister who had died in 152.[56]

In 160 Pius may have been ill, for Marcus and Lucius were designated as joint consuls for the following year, for the third and second times respectively – perhaps a deliberate precaution. He finally succumbed, after a short illness, on 7 March 161, the year known to the Romans as that when his adoptive sons Marcus and Lucius were consuls together. His end was tranquil, as was his life. His death was 'very sweet, and like the softest sleep', says Dio. The biographer adds details. The old emperor had eaten some Alpine cheese at dinner, rather greedily. During the night he vomited and the next day had a fever. The day after, when he saw that he was becoming worse and that the end of his life was near, in the presence of the praetorian prefects Furius Victorinus and Cornelius Repentinus, and of his friends, members of the imperial council, whom he had summoned, he commended the state and his daughter to Marcus, and Marcus to them, and gave orders that the golden statue of Fortune, which used to be placed in the bedroom of the emperors, should be transferred to the bedroom of Marcus. Then he gave the watchword to the tribune of the guard: 'Equanimity'. He turned over as if to go to sleep, and breathed his last, at Lorium, on his ancestral estate, in his seventy-fifth year. In his fever, when delirious, he had spoken of nothing else besides the state and those foreign monarchs with whom he was angry.[57]

One of Marcus' tributes to Pius has already been quoted – the one which came from the first book of the *Meditations*. There is a briefer tribute, perhaps written earlier, in the sixth book, in which Marcus reminded himself to behave 'in all things like a pupil of Antoninus; his energy in dealing with what had to be done in accordance with reason, his equability everywhere, his piety, the serenity of his face, his sweetness, his disregard for empty glory, and his determination to grasp his work. Also, how he allowed nothing to pass without first looking into it well and understanding it clearly; how he put up with those who found fault with him unjustly, without finding fault with them in return; how he never hurried; how he never listened to slander; what an exact critic he was of men's characters and actions, not given to reproaching, not disturbed by rumours, not suspicious, not pretending to be clever; how he was content with little, in the way of lodging, bed, clothes, food and service; how he loved work and was long-suffering. What a man he was, too, for remaining in his place until the evening, because of sparing diet not needing even to relieve nature except at the normal time. And his constancy and uniformity in his friendships, his tolerance of outspoken opposition to his views and his delight when anyone proposed something better than he did; and how he revered the gods without superstition. May your last hour find you like him, with a conscience as clear as his.'[58]

These recollections are a remarkable tribute. Perhaps the greatest service of Antoninus Pius, and of Marcus too, was that they provided an example of high character on the throne, in admirable conformity with the aspirations of thinking people, such as Dio of Prusa,[59] who had wanted an ideal ruler. There are certainly defects to be found in his administration, most particularly that his military policy seems to have been somewhat neglectful, as was to appear almost at once in the reign of his successor.

· 6 ·

THE FIRST YEARS AS EMPEROR

Marcus was now sole ruler, lacking only the name Augustus and the appellation Imperator. He waited, of course, for the senate to confer his powers and names on him, for the formal election as *pontifex maximus*, and for any other power which he may have lacked. But at the meeting of the senate Marcus refused to be made emperor unless equal powers were conferred simultaneously on his brother Lucius Commodus.

Marcus had made some show of reluctance to assume the burdens of empire; and the biographer says that 'he was compelled by the senate to assume the direction of the state after the death of Pius'. Expressions of unwillingness to rule had not been unknown. Tiberius, like Marcus the sole and obvious successor to the previous ruler, had also made such protestation – undoubtedly both felt genuine reluctance. In Tiberius' case, his complex character was such that men never knew what his true feelings were, but the tradition of his original family was one which found monarchy repugnant and for such a man to be called on to rule openly as a monarch was a moment of unpleasant torment (and his predecessor was the first of all emperors). Marcus, from a family which owed its fortunes to the existence of monarchical government, had a dilemma of a different kind. His natural inclinations were not to public life, but his training for twenty-three years and his Stoic philosophy had made the path of duty plain. He knew that 'the measureless body of empire' required a director, without which it could not stand, as Galba, another ostensibly unwilling ruler, was alleged to have put it. Marcus obviously had a genuine *horror imperii*, but he knew what he had to do. He must have felt that the presence of an imperial partner would, possibly, lighten his task. But, more than that, it would fulfil an obligation to Hadrian, whose intention had been clearly stated, that Marcus and Lucius should rule jointly in succession to Pius. Since Pius had done little to forward these wishes in respect of Lucius, Lucius had 'remained a private citizen in his father's house for twenty-three years'.[1]

Now, however, Lucius became in name and in fact joint emperor. He was granted the tribunician power, the *imperium*, the name Augustus. His own names and those of Marcus were altered. Out of respect for Pius, Marcus assumed the surname Antoninus, becoming Imperator Caesar

Marcus Aurelius Antoninus Augustus. Lucius gave up his name Commodus and took instead the name which Marcus had borne from birth, Verus, becoming Imperator Caesar Lucius Aurelius Verus Augustus. The niceties of these variations may not be entirely clear to us. Certainly they completely confused the author of the Augustan History. In the biographies the alteration of names is recorded. But complication is added by the mistaken belief, which recurs constantly, that 'Verus' was a name which originally belonged to Lucius in any case, and to his father, Hadrian's first adopted son.[2]

Two emperors thus ruled the Roman world for the first time, an innovation, but like most Roman innovations one for which there was ample precedent. It set an example which was followed with increasing frequency. The continuing existence of the ancient twin magistracy of the consulate was one precedent. Previously, too, emperors had had colleagues with powers slightly less wide than their own – as indeed was the case with Marcus and Pius from 147–61. But rulers other than Hadrian had intended that two should succeed them, only to be frustrated. Thus Augustus' grandsons Gaius and Lucius were destined by Augustus to succeed him jointly. Germanicus and Drusus the younger, sons of Tiberius by adoption and birth respectively, appeared likely to succeed him together at one time, as did at the end of his life Gaius Caligula and Tiberius Gemellus, their respective sons. Nero and Britannicus were another pair, intended by the deluded Claudius to have equal rank. These succession arrangements of the ill-starred Julio-Claudian family proved abortive. Later, Domitian apparently felt that Titus, his elder brother, had thwarted him of his birthright when he did not make him co-ruler at the death of Vespasian.[3]

Marcus and Lucius were joint rulers then. But Marcus had more *auctoritas* – that intangible, but measurable factor in Roman public life. He had been consul once more than Lucius. He became *pontifex maximus*, the highest priesthood being indivisible; Lucius was only *pontifex*. Most important, he had shared in the imperial powers of Pius for nearly fourteen years – and he was ten years older than Lucius. There was little doubt in men's minds which emperor was the senior. But they were to work together for the good of the state. The coins of 161 proclaimed the *concordia Augustorum*, the harmony of the emperors.[4]

The first act of the emperors, after the meeting of the senate at which their powers and titles had been granted, was to go to the camp of the praetorian guard on the north-eastern outskirts of the city, beyond the *porta Viminalis*. Here Lucius addressed the troops on behalf of both, and they were hailed as *imperator*, emperor. They promised a bounty, or donative, to the troops of 20,000 sesterces (5,000 denarii) per man, more to officers. This expensive ceremony was now a necessary opening to every reign, as it had been since the stormy and opposed accession of Claudius in 41. The enormous size of the donative – equivalent to several years' pay for the guardsmen – was not perhaps immediately necessary, considering the peaceful circumstances of their accession. It was emperors who desperately needed military support who had to make promises of this kind. But a double accession naturally required exceptional celebration – and this generosity was a useful insurance for the future. In return the soldiers would swear allegiance, binding themselves with a military oath – *sacramentum* – no doubt similar in content to extant examples of oaths of allegiance to other emperors.[5]

The next public action was to arrange for the funeral and deification of Antoninus Pius. No opposition came from the senate, such as Pius himself had experienced in 138. The remains were laid to rest, after elaborate funeral ceremonies, in the massive mausoleum of Hadrian, which now housed the ashes of several prematurely deceased members of the imperial house, for example children of Pius and Marcus, as well as those of its builder.[6]

No detailed account of the funeral ceremonies is preserved, but presumably it followed the lines of other imperial obsequies – a funeral pyre on the Campus Martius, on which the body was burned in the presence of the leading dignitaries of the state. From the pyre an eagle would fly aloft, released when the flames began to burn, symbolizing the translation of the dead emperor's spirit to the abode of the gods whom he was now joining. Marcus and Lucius addressed the people in funeral orations in praise of their father, who now became known as 'Divus Antoninus', and, by the same token, his sons now each became 'Divi Antonini filius'. A *flamen* was appointed to minister to the new deity, and a college of priests was chosen from among the closest friends of the imperial family, whose duty it would be to meet on appointed days to sacrifice and feast in honour of Antoninus – on his birthday, for example, and the other days particularly associated with his memory. The temple which Antoninus had dedicated above the Forum to his own wife, to Diva Faustina, now became the temple of Antoninus and Faustina. It survives as the church of San Lorenzo in Miranda.[7]

At this early stage in the reign came another announcement portending future benefit to the dynasty and the state. Marcus' eldest daughter, Annia Lucilla, now a girl of just eleven, was formally betrothed to Lucius, her uncle by adoption. Lucius was now thirty. Marcus had married at twenty-four, by no means early for a Roman. Perhaps the marriage of Lucius and Lucilla had been long intended. Even so, the situation was slightly paradoxical, for Lucius had once as a boy of seven or eight been betrothed to Faustina, the mother of Lucilla. At any rate the match was arranged, and in public commemoration new provision was made for the support of poor children, on the lines of the institution created by Pius in memory of his wife and earlier imperial foundations.[8]

Faustina had been the chief beneficiary in the will of Pius' private fortune, which had been very large at his accession and was probably not much smaller at his death. Marcus had no need of her wealth, of course – in fact, at his accession he transferred part of his mother's estate to his nephew Ummidius Quadratus, as his sister Cornificia was now dead. Faustina was three months gone in another pregnancy when her husband ascended the throne. During her pregnancy she dreamed that she was giving birth to two serpents, and that one of them was fiercer than the other. On 31 August she gave birth at Lanuvium to twin sons, who received the names of T. Aurelius Fulvus Antoninus and Lucius Aurelius Commodus, in honour of Pius and Lucius. Antoninus was probably the elder twin, to judge from these names. The astrologers cast favourable horoscopes for both of them. The event was appropriately celebrated on the imperial coinage. The omens were favourable – except that their birthday was the same as that of the unbalanced emperor Caligula, assassinated 120 years earlier.[9]

The new emperors were popular with the people of Rome, the normal index of favour. What was especially approved of was their lack of pomp. They conducted themselves *civiliter*. An example of this was the freedom of speech permitted. A writer of comedies named Marullus criticized Marcus and Lucius openly in a new work – and got away with it. In other times, under another emperor, such behaviour would have meant death. But the times were easy. 'No one missed the lenient ways of Pius.'[10]

Fronto was, not surprisingly, overjoyed to see his pupils wearing the purple, and expressed himself in his usual humorous and flattering style. Marcus had told him that he had been re-reading the speech written by Fronto nearly twenty years before, when he became consul, in 143, in which he delivered a eulogy of Antoninus, and at the same time added praises of the youthful heir-apparent. 'That you have been reading with pleasure the praises of your father which were spoken by myself in the senate as consul designate and on entering office, does not surprise me at all. . . . It was not my speech but your father's merits that you admired, not the language of the praiser but the actions of the praised that you found praiseworthy. As for my praises of yourself, delivered in the senate that same day – I want you to think of them in this way. There was then an outstanding natural ability in you; there is now perfected excellence. There was then a crop of growing corn; there is now a ripe, gathered harvest. What I was hoping for them, I have now. The hope has become a reality.'[11]

Lucius too wrote to his former tutor several times soon after his accession. He 'complained seriously' in his first letter – as he phrased it with good humour – that he had not been given the chance of embracing or speaking to Fronto when he visited the palace 'after so long an interval'. (Fronto had been away for four months.) Fronto had called at the palace just as Lucius had gone out. He had talked to Marcus alone and neither Fronto nor Marcus had thought of calling Lucius back. Fronto replied at once, apologizing and letting his pen run grandiloquently as he expressed the measure of his indebtedness to Marcus and Lucius. 'For indeed since you and your brother, placed amid such powerful resources, surrounded by such a multitude of men of all sorts and all ranks, on whom you strew your love, since you bestow on me also some portion of your love, what should I do – whose every hope, and all my fortune, are centred in you alone.'[12]

Fronto had returned to his town house in Rome at dawn on 28 March, exactly three weeks after the death of Pius, from his country estate, after four months' absence. It may be that he had been on a visit to his home town Cirta in Africa, and that he had set off as soon as the news had reached him. On returning to the city he wrote a brief note in Greek to an imperial freedman, Charilas, asking if it would be convenient for him to call on the emperors. He had not dared, he explained later, to write direct to Lucius or Marcus.[13] Fronto never gave, in his letters at least, any indication which of his imperial pupils he preferred. But one might guess from the fact that he and Marcus made no attempt to send for Lucius on that occasion, that Lucius occupied second place. Lucius' interests remained on a lower plane than those of Marcus. At about this time he was writing to Fronto asking him to adjudicate in a dispute he and a friend named Calpurnius had had over the merits of two actors. Marcus by contrast wrote to Fronto of his reading – the classics, Coelius and a little Cicero – and of his family. His daughters were in Rome, staying with their great-great-aunt Matidia, because the evening air in the country, where Marcus was (at Lanuvium) was too cold for them, it was thought. (Perhaps also it was thought advisable to give their mother Faustina a rest from them as her confinement approached.) Marcus added a request for 'some particularly eloquent reading matter, something of your own, or Cato, or Cicero, or Sallust or Gracchus – or some poet, for I need distraction, especially in this kind of way, by reading something that will uplift and diffuse my pressing anxieties'.[14]

We do not know at what precise moment after his accession he wrote that letter. But he soon had plenty of cares. He had begun his reign 'by giving himself wholly to philosophy, and seeking the affection of the citizens'. He continued to attend public lectures, notably those of Sextus of Chaeronea, which he did not regard as now being beneath his dignity. 'If you had both a mother and a stepmother,' he was to write later, 'you would wait upon your stepmother but would still constantly return to your mother. This is now what philosophy and the palace are to you.' But troubles soon came thick and fast to disturb 'that happiness and freedom from care of his', that *felicitas temporum* proclaimed on his coinage in 161.[15]

There was a severe flood of the River Tiber, which destroyed many buildings in the city, drowned a great number of animals and left a serious famine in its wake. This was presumably in the autumn of 161. 'All these disasters Marcus and Lucius dealt with by their personal attention.' Italian communities that had been hit by famine were relieved by use of the city's grain supply. Since the year 15 there had been a Tiber Conservancy Board headed by a senator chosen from the recent consuls, with a staff of permanent officials. Some of the senators may have taken their duties seriously. Pliny had been *curator alvei Tiberis et riparum et cloacarum urbis* ('Curator of the Tiber Bed and Banks and of the City Sewers') some sixty years before, but although one can hardly imagine him not performing the duties of the office with almost excessive conscientiousness, he gives no hint in his letters that it took up much of his time. The *curator* in 161 was A. Platorius Nepos, probably son or grandson of the builder of Hadrian's Wall of the same name, but one cannot particularly blame him for inefficiency. His probable predecessor was M. Statius Priscus, consul in 159. Military men like Statius Priscus perhaps looked on urban appointments, like Tiber Conservator, as not much more than paid leave.[16]

Still, Statius Priscus was probably justified, for he had done more than his fair share of hard work in the frontier provinces, work for which the ordinary consulate of 159 had been very belated recognition. In 160 or 161 he went to Singidunum (Belgrade), to govern Upper Moesia. He can only have been there a few months when he was transferred to Britain, an indication that the trouble with which Gnaeus Julius Verus had had to deal a few years before was still not under control.[17]

But the most disturbing news was from the eastern frontier. The foreign kings with whom Pius had been angry on his deathbed were clearly the king of Parthia and the rulers of the other independent states on Rome's eastern borders. The change of rulers at Rome no doubt emboldened the Parthian king Vologases III to act quickly. He entered the Roman-protected kingdom of Armenia, expelled its ruler and installed his own nominee, Pacorus, a member of the Parthian royal family (the Arsacids). Trouble had obviously been expected by Rome. The senior Roman general in the eastern provinces, the governor of Syria L. Attidius Cornelianus, had been due for replacement by 161. He had been left at his post, no doubt to avoid giving the Parthians the opportunity of catching a new man on the wrong foot.[18] But the responsibility for dealing with trouble in Armenia always lay in the first instance with the governor of Cappadocia. In 161 this was M. Sedatius Severianus, a Gaul. Severianus had had plenty of military experience. But it sounds as though the effect of the Greek East on him was unfortunate. He was taken in by an itinerant vendor of oracles, of high pretensions, Alexander of Abonutichus, a practitioner of mumbo-jumbo on a grandiose scale, with friends in high places – he had become father-in-law of a highly respected senator, P. Mummius Sisenna Rutilianus, who was proconsul of Asia, probably at this very time. Alexander led Severianus to suppose that he could deal easily with the situation and that he would win himself military glory. Severianus took one of his legions into Armenia, clearly hoping to restore the situation himself. But he was trapped by the leading Parthian general, Chosrhoes, at Elegia beyond the frontiers of his province, high up by the headwaters of the Euphrates. After a short attempt to fight back, he realized that further resistance was futile, and committed suicide. His legion was massacred. Various romantic stories were soon in circulation, according to Lucian, concerning the death of Severianus – that 'foolish Celt'. He was said to have fasted to death during a relatively lengthy siege, and a centurion named Afranius Silo was said to have delivered a funeral oration over his tomb in the high tragic manner, and then to have killed himself on the spot. The truth was harsher. The affair had been brought to its ignominious end in about three days.[19]

Meanwhile trouble was brewing on other frontiers. War threatened in Britain, and on another northern frontier of the Chatti of the Taunus mountains had crossed the *limes*, invading Upper Germany and Raetia.[20] Again, enemy peoples had benefited from the change of emperor, hoping to find the new rulers lacking in vigilance. Marcus and Lucius had many rapid decisions to make. But military matters were a sphere for which their previous experience had given them no training. They had never seen an army – other than the praetorian guard – let alone any military action. Antoninus Pius must be held responsible for this serious deficiency in their education. Marcus himself had less experience of war than virtually all his predecessors – but the equally unmilitary Pius perhaps never realized that this mattered. Of all his predecessors, only Nero had never been outside Italy at his accession – even Caligula had lived with the Rhine armies as a boy; Claudius had been born in Gaul; Pius had been proconsul of Asia. Hadrian could hardly have approved, had he foreseen this. He had after all taken immediate steps to give his first choice as heir, the father of Lucius, some experience of armies, frontiers and provincial government, by dispatching him to Pannonia.

One decision had to be made at once. Some improvement was obviously required in the machinery of choosing officers, perhaps even generals and governors. One of the imperial secretaries of state was dismissed, the *ab epistulis* Sextus Caecilius Crescens Volusianus. Volusianus was, no doubt, an amiable figure of literary inclinations (and he was an African, like Fronto). Pius had presumably chosen him as *ab epistulis*, in the way that his predecessors had been chosen, on the basis of his literary talents. The bureau, as its name indicates, handled imperial correspondence. But as the tenth book of Pliny's letters demonstrates, a large proportion of this was with provincial governors; it had to be on the basis of material in the files of this bureau that the talents of officers and administrators were assessed. Marcus replaced Volusianus with T. Varius Clemens, a man from the province of Noricum. Clemens had had a long military career, which included active service in the war in Mauretania; and latterly he had been procurator in five provinces, two of them provinces where the procurator was also the governor and commander in chief, Mauretania Caesariensis and Raetia. Such a man was better suited than Volusianus to advise the emperors on the choice of men to meet a military crisis.[21]

L. Volusius Maecianus was governing Egypt as prefect at the accession, succeeding Furius Victorinus. By 162 he had been recalled, and made a senator. The only further promotion open to him in the equestrian order was the prefecture of the praetorian guard, but this office had just been filled. Maecianus was appointed prefect of the treasury (aerarium Saturni) and soon after designated consul. Thus Marcus was able to keep this eminent lawyer, his former tutor, by his side.[22]

The replacement of the fallen Severianus was crucial. Surprisingly the choice fell on Statius Priscus, at that time as far away from Cappadocia as he could possibly have been, in Britain. It shows that care was taken to find the right man. To Britain in Priscus' place, to meet an active enemy, was sent Sextus Calpurnius Agricola. To deal with the trouble from the Germans, Marcus' friend Aufidius Victorinus, Fronto's son-in-law, was chosen, with the appointment as governor of Upper Germany.[23]

Meanwhile reinforcements for the eastern armies were under way. An African senator, P. Julius Geminius Marcianus, perhaps son of a friend of Fronto, certainly a fellow-Cirtensian, who had been commanding the Tenth legion at Vindobona (Vienna), took detachments of the Danubian legions to Cappadocia. Besides this, three entire legions were ordered to the east, I Minervia from Bonn in Lower Germany, II Adiutrix from Aquincum (Budapest) in Lower Pannonia and V Macedonica from Troesmis on the Danube, in Lower Moesia. The northern frontiers were thus weakened at strategically placed intervals. But the governors of the northern provinces were instructed to avoid hostilities and deal with disturbances by diplomacy wherever possible. Unmistakable signs of future turmoil in central Europe had been noted, but for the time being a solution had to wait on events in the east. Before long further bad news came. Attidius Cornelianus had been defeated and put to flight in an engagement with the Parthian forces. The situation was clearly becoming desperate.[24]

At some stage in the winter of 161–2, when the news from the east was bad, with the Syrians in a rebellious mood, Marcus and Lucius decided that one of them must go to the war in person. The frontier armies had not fought a full-scale war under direct imperial direction for forty-five years, since Trajan's death in 117. It was decided that Lucius should go, 'because he was physically robust and younger than Marcus, and better suited to military activity', Dio says. The senate consented. Marcus himself was to remain at Rome, because affairs in the city demanded the presence of an emperor. This is sufficient explanation of the chosen course of action. In the biography of Lucius play is made with other motives. Marcus sent Lucius to the Parthian war, it is asserted, 'either so that his immorality could not be

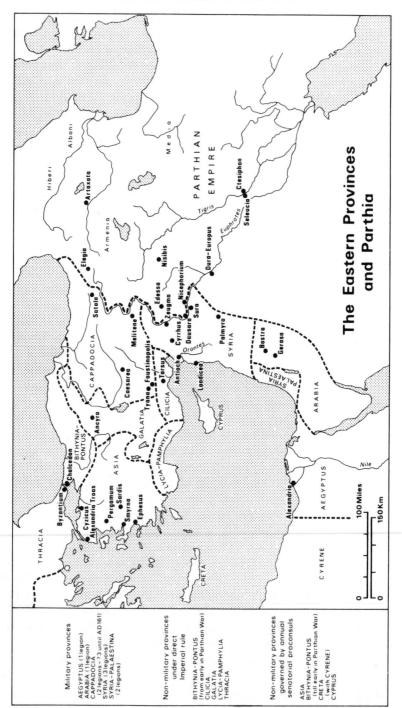

The Eastern Provinces and Parthia

Military provinces

AEGYPTUS (1 legion)
ARABIA (1 legion)
CAPPADOCIA
    (2 legions – 73 until AD 161)
SYRIA (3 legions)
SYRIA-PALAESTINA
    (2 legions)

Non-military provinces
under direct
imperial rule

BITHYNIA-PONTUS
    (from early in Parthian War)
CILICIA
GALATIA
LYCIA-PAMPHYLIA
THRACIA

Non-military provinces
governed by annual
senatorial proconsuls

ASIA
BITHYNIA-PONTUS
    (till early in Parthian War)
CRETA
    (with CYRENE)
CYPRUS

carried on in the city, under the eyes of all, or so that he would learn thriftiness by travel abroad, or so that he would return as a reformed character through the fear inspired by warfare, or so that he might realize that he was an emperor – *imperator*'. There is probably some truth in this, but the biographer has made the spirit behind it seem hard and calculating, when it was probably warm and friendly.[25]

It was realized that Lucius would need a full and experienced staff. One of the praetorian prefects had to go, taking some of the guard. Furius Victorinus was selected. He had served in the eastern provinces before, as procurator of Galatia. Besides this, he had served in Britain, on the Danube, in Spain, as prefect of the Italian fleets and as prefect of Egypt, in addition to occupying various posts in Rome. It was thought advisable to have some senators of wide experience, as well as the prefect. First and foremost they selected M. Pontius Laelianus Larcius Sabinus. He was getting on in years now – his son was to be consul in 163 – but his military experience was unrivalled. He had begun his career as a young man as tribune of the legion VI Victrix in Germany and was transferred with it from Lower Germany to Britain in 122, when Platorius Nepos went to build Hadrian's Wall. He had governed both the Pannonian provinces, and then, nine years before, in 153, he had been governor of Syria. Hence he knew at first hand the major army of the east and the problems of the frontiers. Laelianus was given the honorific rank and title of *comes Augustorum*, 'companion of the Emperors'. Previous emperors had had *comites* with them on travels and campaigns. From now on they seem to have played a more important role; certainly, an exceptional number are recorded in the reign, all of consular rank. Laelianus was described by Fronto a little later as 'a serious man and an old-fashioned disciplinarian'.[26] Meanwhile, M. Iallius Bassus, who had recently been appointed governor of Lower Moesia, was directed to go to the east as another *comes*. To replace L. Attidius Cornelianus as governor of Syria, there was a rather surprising choice, M. Annius Libo, first cousin of Marcus. As Libo had been consul only the previous year, 161, he must have been in his early thirties, and as a patrician must have lacked military experience. It seems that Marcus' intention was to have on the spot a man on whom he could rely. Lucius decided to take his favourite freedmen too, of whom Geminus, Agaclytus, Coedes and Eclectus are named. Another freedman, his old foster-father Nicomedes, now (most exceptionally for a freedman) a procurator and a knight, gave up his duties as head of the posting-service (*praefectus vehiculorum*) in Rome, to take charge of the commissariat for the expeditionary force, retaining his old rank. Thus Lucius could keep his faithful old friend by his side. The Misenum fleet was to convey the emperor and to act as a means of communication and transport.[27]

Lucius set off in the summer of 162, to take ship from Brundisium (Brindisi). Marcus accompanied him as far as Capua. Lucius went on towards the east coast, feasting in the country houses on his route, and hunting in Apulia. At Canusium (Canossa) he fell ill and Marcus hurried south to see him again, after undertaking vows to the gods for his safety in the senate. Three days fasting and a bloodletting apparently cured him. But it might have been a mild stroke. Fronto was most upset to hear the news, but a letter from Lucius describing his treatment and recovery reassured him. In his reply he recommended a quiet convalescence, and urged that 'as suits your outstanding character you should be moderate in all your desires, which are bound to be keener and more importunate than usual after this enforced abstinence'. Lucius finally embarked, and Marcus fulfilled his vows to the gods. The journey east was by way of Corinth and Athens. It was a true royal progress, accompanied by musicians and singers (uncomfortably reminiscent of Nero, whose birthday, and, to a certain extent, tastes, Lucius shared). At Athens he stayed with Herodes Atticus, and was initiated into the Mysteries of Eleusis, as Hadrian had been a generation before. While he was performing a sacrifice a shooting-star or meteor was observed crossing the heavens from west to east. He then took ship across the Aegean and finally arrived at Antioch, the Syrian provincial capital, by way of the coastal towns of Asia, Pamphylia and Cilicia, dallying particularly in those that were renowned as pleasure resorts, the biographer takes care to record. It is not known how long this journey took.[28]

In the meantime Statius Priscus must have arrived to take command in Cappadocia, having probably travelled rapidly up the Rhine and down the Danube, and through Thrace, Bithynia and Galatia. In the course of 163 his vigorous generalship gained success for Roman arms. Priscus became something of a legend – it was rumoured that on one occasion the general's bellowing cry had caused twenty-seven enemy soldiers to drop dead.[29]

Marcus found life full of anxiety at this time. He spent a four-day public holiday at Alsium on the Etrurian coast, a famous holiday resort. But he was unable to relax. Apart from anything else one of his daughters had a fever. He wrote briefly to Fronto, saying that he would not describe his activities at Alsium in detail, because he knew that he would be reprimanded. Fronto replied with good humour: 'What? Do I not know that you went to Alsium with the intention of devoting yourself to games, joking and complete leisure for four whole days?' he wrote ironically. Marcus must relax, he insisted. His ancestors could do it, even though they were occupied with extending the frontiers of the empire. His father, he reminded Marcus, for all his supreme personal qualities, had been keen on exercise in the *palaestra*, and fishing, and had appreciated comedians. He went on to give more examples – 'even your own Chrysippus [the Stoic] used to have his drink every day, they say. . . . Yet, if you have declared war on games, relaxation and pleasure, at least have as much sleep as a free man needs.' He went on to relate an elaborate fable of the appointed boundaries of Morning and Evening. Marcus was evidently devoting much of the night to his judicial business. 'So, Marcus,' Fronto concluded, 'if you need a dream hereafter, I recommend you to sleep freely, until the time comes when your desires are fulfilled, in the way you would wish, in your waking hours.'

Marcus' reply showed that he found the advice difficult. He dictated a hasty acknowledgement: 'I have just received your letter, which I will enjoy properly later. For just now I have duties hanging over me, tasks which cannot be begged off. Meanwhile I will tell you, briefly, as I am busy, what you want to hear, that our little girl is in better health and is running about her room.' Later he continued the letter, while the others were having dinner. He himself had had a light snack. 'That is all the notice you have taken of my advice, you will say,' he wrote after telling this to Fronto. 'But I have taken a lot of notice of it, for I have rested, as your letter suggests, and I will re-read it the oftener, so that I may rest the oftener. But – this devotion to duty! Who knows better than you how demanding it is!' He ends by inquiring solicitously after Fronto's health – he had a pain in his hand. 'Farewell, my best master, man of warm heart.'[30]

The war was proving a strain on Marcus. Some time after it began Fronto wrote a long and carefully composed letter, full of historical analogies, to show Marcus how initial reverses in war could turn into splendid victories. 'Mars has spoken of the Romans often, and in many wars, in this strain. . . . But always and everywhere he has changed our troubles into successes and our terrors into triumphs.' He spoke of reverses under Trajan, Hadrian and Pius. He recalled Herodotus' story of Polycrates of Samos, the man with too much good fortune. 'But you may soon hope for victory, for always in her history has Rome experienced frequent changes of her fortunes.' He had earlier sent Marcus suitable reading matter, including especially a speech of Cicero's, the *pro lege Manilia*, in which Cicero recommended the appointment of Pompey to take supreme command in the war against Mithridates. 'You will find in it many chapters aptly suited to your present counsels, concerning the choice of army commanders, the interests of allies, the protection of provinces, the discipline of the soldiers, the qualifications required for commanders in the field and elsewhere.' The speech emphasized in particular that there was only one man who could lead Rome in the war, only one man that Rome's allies demanded, and so on. This advice may have been a factor in the decision to send Lucius out as supreme commander. The parallel was indeed apt – for Pompey had had to campaign in Armenia.[31]

For all the cares of state and for all his increasing ill-health, Fronto had probably never been happier. 'I have had my fill of life,' he said, replying to Marcus' good wishes for his birthday, 'I see you, Antoninus, as excellent as emperor as I hoped, as just and as free from fault as I guaranteed, as popular and as welcome to the Roman people as I desired, as fond of me as I could wish and as eloquent as your yourself could wish.' The last point naturally gave Fronto enormous pleasure. Marcus, as a result of his increased public duties, now had to put into practice all Fronto's old lessons in public speaking as never before, in a way that he had once thought he would never be able to do with any pleasure. He was 'beginning to feel the wish to be eloquent once more, in spite of having for a time lost interest in eloquence'. Fronto was especially gratified by Marcus' speech in the Senate after an earthquake at Cyzicus in Asia Minor. Marcus had captured the dramatic nature of the event in his language and his audience had been impressed and moved.[32]

Fronto addressed a number of letters to him in which he reminded him at length of the lessons on eloquence inculcated twenty years before. In a telling passage he reminded Marcus of his position. 'Suppose, Caesar, that you can attain to the wisdom of Cleanthes and Zeno, yet, against your will, you must put on the purple imperial cloak, not the philosopher's woollen cape.' He repeated the message of twenty years before, that even philosophers had to command language to express their teaching forcefully: 'Philosophy will tell you what to say, eloquence will tell you how to say it.'[33]

At this time we gain another glimpse into the emperor's family life. One of the twins, Antoninus, had been ill with a cough, but was on the mend. Fronto had not then seen them. When he did so, he was delighted: 'I have seen your little chickens, the most welcome sight in my life. They are just like you in appearance, so much so that nothing could be more alike.' Going to see them was like taking a short cut to Lorium, where Marcus was at the time, he wrote, for 'I saw you not only opposite me but in more places than one, whether I turned to the right or to the left. They have quite a healthy colour, the gods be praised, and strong lungs. One was holding a piece of white bread, like a royal child, the other a piece of black bread – clearly the offspring of a philosopher! . . . So now you must take care that you don't find me somewhat prouder – for I have those that I can love instead of you, not only with my eyes but with my ears.' Marcus was touched by this letter: 'I saw my little sons when you saw them, and I saw you when I was reading your letter. I beg you, my master, love me as you love me, and love me too as you love those little ones of ours. . . . Write often to my lord brother,' he added, 'for he especially wants me to gain this request from you. His desires, indeed, certainly make me unreasonable and violent. Farewell, most delightful of masters. Give my love to your grandson.' In the meantime, Faustina was again pregnant. Before the end of 162 she bore Marcus another son, who was given his father's original names, Marcus Annius Verus.[34]

As Fronto had predicted, the fortunes of war had swung to Rome, with the successes of Statius Priscus, who had stormed and taken the Armenian capital Artaxata in 163. By the end of the year Lucius, as Roman supreme commander, for all that he had not participated actively in the fighting, took the title 'Armeniacus', 'conqueror of the Armenians', and was hailed as *Imperator* by the troops, which allowed him and Marcus to style themselves *Imp. II* in their official titulature. Lucius had stayed at Antioch for the most part, but spent part of the winter at Laodicea and the summer months at Daphne, a resort on the outskirts of Antioch. Critics claimed that he was spending his time in riotous living of various kinds. Certainly he had become fond of gambling with dice and he had sent to Rome for actors. Fronto later justified this on his behalf by allusion to Juvenal's satirical remark that the people needed 'bread and circuses' (*panem et circenses*): 'knowing that two things especially hold fast the Roman people, the corn-dole and public spectacles' (as he somewhat pompously paraphrased it). Lucius' passion for the sporting life had to be assuaged by dispatches from home conveying the latest news about the fortunes of his favourite chariot team, the Greens, and he had with him a golden statue of the Green horse Volucer as a reminder.[35]

In Syria Lucius also acquired a mistress, no ordinary 'low-born girl-friend', as his biographer unkindly described her. The lady in question was named Panthea, portrayed by the normally biting satirist Lucian in the most rapturous terms. She was 'a woman of perfect beauty', from Smyrna, one of the Ionian Greek cities of the coast, more beautiful than any statue by Phidias or Praxiteles. Her voice was 'soft, delicious and winning'. She sang wonderfully well to the lyre, spoke pure Ionic Greek, flavoured with a classical Attic wit, possessed the gifts of all the Muses, had a shrewd understanding of public affairs, and a gracious, loving and modest nature. Lucian wrote this panegyric in the form of a dialogue between two friends. It had a sequel – Panthea read it, and reproached the author for being too flattering, especially in comparing her to the goddesses, which frightened her. She had power over Lucius, who even shaved off his luxurious beard to please her, provoking a lot of comment from the Syrians.[36]

Lucius had plenty of work to do, particularly in the training of troops, for the Syrian army had apparently become slack from long years of peace. The soldiers stationed at Antioch used to spend more time lounging at tables in open-air cafés than with their units. Pontius Laelianus undertook some formidable kit inspections, ordering the troopers' padded saddles to be slit open; and he jumped heavily on gambling and drinking in the camp. Training was stepped up. Lucius was said by Fronto later to have taken things in hand in person, 'marching on foot at the head of his men as often as he rode on horseback, putting up with the blazing sun and choking dust, leaving his head exposed to sun and shower, hail and snow – and missiles, sweating unconcernedly as if playing games. He inspected soldiers in the field and their quarters in camp, including the sick-bay. He observed casually but keenly the dandified Syrians and the unsophisticated Pan-nonians. He took a belated bath after his work was done, and ate simple camp-food, drank local wine. Often he slept on leaves or the turf.' He was nevertheless lenient. 'Through so many provinces, so many open dangers of sieges, battles, citadels, posts and forts stormed, he lavished his care and his advice.' The language is suitably ambiguous, for it is fairly certain that Lucius saw little actual fighting himself. Fronto wrote this at the end of the war. In the early stages he heard little from Lucius directly, and after a long interval received an apology for the silence. 'I was unwilling to describe in detail plans which were liable to be altered daily,' Lucius explained, 'and I did not wish to make you . . . a partner in my anxieties, which have made me completely miserable day and night, and almost made me despair of success.' One reason for Lucius' despondency may have been the failure of his attempt at negotiation with Vologases after the successes in Armenia, an attempt which was obviously regarded as an admission of weakness or cowardice.[37]

The Parthians were clearly in no mood yet to give way. While Statius Priscus was occupying Armenia they evidently deposed Mannus, the pro-Roman ruler of Osrhoene, the principality in north-western Mesopotamia with its capital at Edessa. The initial Roman response was to move forces across the Euphrates further downstream. Dausara and Nicephorium on the northern, Parthian bank were occupied, after an engagement at Sura on the Roman side of the river – suggesting that Parthian forces may still have been in the province of Syria in 163.[38] Before long other Roman forces entered Osrhoene from Armenia, and occupied Anthemusia, south-west of Edessa. This group was led by M. Claudius Fronto, a man of Greek origin from the province of Asia, probably the first senator of his family. Fronto had served under Priscus in Armenia, after conducting the Bonn legion I Minervia to the front, commanding a mixed force of legionaries and auxiliaries. Another general who had served under Priscus was P. Martius Verus, a westerner, perhaps from Tolosa (Toulouse), and a man of winning personality. He had brought the legion V Macedonica to the east from its base on the Lower Danube. But the key role was perhaps already being taken by a young Syrian senator, from Cyrrhus in the north of the province, C. Avidius Cassius. Although Cassius' father Heliodorus had not been a senator, he was, apparently, the descendant of the Seleucid kings, and had enjoyed considerable power and prestige under Hadrian: he was *ab epistulis*, in which capacity he had accompanied Hadrian on some of his travels; and at the end of the reign he had become prefect of Egypt. Cassius himself was now in command of one of the Syrian legions, III Gallica.[39]

Meanwhile Marcus' cousin Libo had died, after quarrelling with Lucius, which also no doubt caused him – and Marcus – distress. Libo had taken a high-handed attitude, holding that he was responsible only to Marcus, and no doubt criticizing Lucius' actions. Perhaps not surprisingly his death was the subject of malicious rumour: Lucius was said to have had him poisoned. He was succeeded as governor of Syria by the experienced Gnaeus Julius

Verus. Later, when back at Rome, Lucius antagonized conservative opinion by marrying off Libo's widow to his own freedman Agaclytus, against the wishes of Marcus, who some years afterwards made such marriages (between persons of senatorial and freedman status) illegal by decree of the senate.[40]

Another marriage was planned for 164, that between Lucius himself and Lucilla. Stories of the incomparable Panthea had possibly decided Marcus to advance the date of the wedding. But Lucilla was now of marriageable age in any case (her fourteenth birthday was on 7 March 164). Marcus escorted her as far as Brundisium from where she took ship, accompanied by the bridegroom's uncle M. Vettulenus Civica Barbarus (the very much younger half-brother of Lucius' father), who was made a *comes Augusti* and was perhaps intended to play the role of a family watchdog on Lucius' behaviour (the task in which Libo had failed). Marcus apparently told the senate that he would conduct his daughter to Syria himself. If this was the case, he must have changed his mind later. At any rate he returned to Rome, having sent despatches to the proconsuls of the provinces on her route not to provide any official reception. Ordinarily, the empress Faustina might have accompanied Lucilla, as mother of the bride, but she had her younger children to look after, the twins, now two-and-a-half, and Annius Verus, just over a year old. Another member of the family did go with Lucilla, as well as Civica Barbarus, a lady described as 'his sister', meaning the sister of Marcus. As Cornificia had been dead for twelve years this must be a slip of the pen, and one cannot say who this person was – it might have been one of Lucius' sisters, Ceionia Fabia and Ceionia Plautia. Lucius travelled west from Syria to meet the bridal party at Ephesus, chief city of the province of Asia, where the wedding was celebrated. On becoming junior empress, Lucilla was granted the title Augusta.[41]

The year 164 saw something of a lull in military operations, and it was mainly to be spent on preparation for the assault on the Parthian homeland – this was probably the reason why the moment was chosen for the wedding, rather than *vice versa*. Armenia was now firmly under Roman control. A new capital was built to replace Artaxata. It was called simply Kaine Polis – 'New City' – and it was sited more strategically some thirty miles closer to the borders of Roman territory. Lucius crowned as king of Armenia a pro-Roman Arsacid prince, Sohaemus – not merely pro-Roman, in fact: he was a senator and had even been made consul, so he must have been in exile with Rome for some time, being held in readiness for just such an occasion as this. The event was celebrated on coinage of the year, which bore the legend *rex Armeniis datus*, and depicted Lucius sitting on a platform surrounded by his officers, while Sohaemus standing in front of him saluted. In this year Marcus was finally persuaded by Lucius to share the title of victory Armeniacus.[42]

The means chosen to persuade him was to include the request in an official despatch to the senate in 164. Fronto was not well enough to be in the senate to hear this, but he read the official record, from which he derived enormous pleasure – especially from the successful 'assault on that fortified and unconquered and impregnable citadel which is planted in your brother's heart against the name *Armeniacus* which he had refused'. He pretended that he rated this achievement higher than anything done in the war, when he wrote to Lucius to congratulate him on the despatch: 'eloquent, as befits an orator's letter, vigorous, as befits a general, dignified, as befits a letter to the senate, not too excessive, as befits a letter on military affairs'. As he found Marcus' official reply wonderfully eloquent also, Fronto's cup was full to overflowing.[43]

Marcus had had a troublesome family matter to deal with. His great-aunt Matidia had died and there was a legal squabble about her will. She had been enormously wealthy and like most rich, childless old women in Rome had attracted a horde of parasites, who at one time had persuaded her to include them in codicils to her will. These had never been confirmed, but as she lay unconscious some of her would-be heirs had taken the opportunity of sealing them up, making them valid. This created a complication, as it meant that more than threequarters of her estate was now willed outside the family – contrary to the provisions of the *lex Falcidia*. Marcus was in an embarrassing position. Fronto urged him to press the claims of the family: 'That famous string of pearls which everyone knows about and the rest of those pieces of jewellery of such value – who will buy them? If your wife buys them, people will say she has pounced on the spoil and snapped them up for a minimal price, to make sure the legatees get as little as possible. But Faustina won't buy them, you say. Who then will buy these pearls – which were, after all, left to your family?' Marcus replied that he had considered the matter carefully and was going to write to his brother and make him give the decision.[44]

Meanwhile Fronto sent an account to his son-in-law Victorinus in Germany: 'I have not been free from apprehension that philosophy might persuade him to some perverse decision', he concluded. Victorinus had his wife with him in Germany and she had borne him a son there whom Fronto had not yet seen. Their other son, also a boy, named Fronto, had stayed behind with his grandparents. The situation in the north was far from reassuring. The Germans had destroyed at least one Roman frontier post in the invasion, and the signs were that all the barbarian peoples of northern and central Europe were in turmoil. It would only be a matter of time before they came into conflict with Rome all along the northern frontier. Another problem that Victorinus had to face was corruption among his officers: a legionary legate who had been taking bribes eventually had to be asked to resign his command.[45] The governors of all the northern provinces had a difficult task. In Upper Pannonia, the key province, L. Dasumius Tullius Tuscus, a distant connection of Hadrian's family, succeeded the experienced M. Nonius Macrinus. Lower Pannonia, with no legion at all in the absence of II Adiutrix, was under the little-known Ti. Haterius Saturninus. Upper Moesia was being governed by M. Servilius Fabianus Maximus, one of Fronto's friends. He had moved from the Lower Moesian province which he had taken over from Iallius Bassus when the latter joined Lucius' staff; and he was followed in Lower Moesia by the son of Pontius Laelianus. The Dacian provinces were still administered in three separate sections, under a senator of praetorian rank and two procurators.[46]

In Rome Marcus had legal business of a more pressing and public nature than had been provided by his great-aunt's will. His attention to the theory and practice of legislation and the administration of justice were intensive, and it is notable that he was described by professional lawyers as 'an emperor most skilled in the law', and (by the great Papinian) as 'a most prudent and conscientiously just emperor'. The badly-informed and muddled chronicler Aurelius Victor, writing in the fourth century, expressed the opinion that under Marcus 'the ambiguities of the law were wonderfully well clarified'.[47] The biography in the Augustan History, in a passage based on a detailed and accurate source, provides a good deal of useful information about Marcus' legal and administrative activity, and this is confirmed and amplified by the citations in legal sources and by inscriptions.

In all the legislation preserved three major interests are apparent. The first is the question of the 'manumission' – liberation – of slaves; the second is the appointment of guardians for orphans and minors; the third is the selection of councillors (*decuriones*) to run the affairs of local communities throughout the provinces. That the liberation of slaves should particularly concern Marcus is not surprising, and the special interest shown in the appointment of trustees and guardians may to some extent be explained by the fact that he had himself lost his father at an early age. The concern with local government is less personal: it was an attempt to combat the growing apathy that was coming over the empire – well-to-do people in the provinces were becoming increasingly anxious to avoid playing their part in local life, partly because this automatically involved them in a heavy financial burden.

The biographer's account of Marcus' administrative and legal activity (which comes after the mention of the marriage of Lucius and Lucilla and before recording the end of the Parthian war) is worth quoting in full here, omitting only the parts which describe activity from later in the reign. 'In the meantime he made safeguards for lawsuits concerning personal freedom, laying down – the first to do so – that every citizen should give names to freeborn children within thirty days of birth and declare them to the prefects of the treasury of Saturn'. This was the senate's treasury. One of its prefects in the early 160s was the lawyer Volusius Maecianus, and he may well have been the originator of the proposal – which was admittedly a step towards increasing the powers of the bureaucracy, but nevertheless ensured that it would be difficult in the future for anyone's status as a free man and a citizen to be called in question. Similar measures were taken for the provinces: 'In the provinces also he established the use of Public Registries, where entries of births were to be made, in the same way as with the prefects of the Treasury of Saturn at Rome, so that if anyone born in the provinces should have to bring an action at law to prove his status as a free man, he could produce this as evidence. He also strengthened the whole of the law dealing with suits to prove freedom; and he enacted other laws to deal with money-lenders and auctions.

'He gave singular attention to the administration of justice: he added a number of court-days to the legal calendar, finally allotting 230 days in the year to the pleading of cases and judgment of suits. He was the first to appoint a *praetor tutelaris* (for previously the appointment of trustees had been the duty of the consuls), so that greater care might be exercised in their appointment. As regards guardians, whereas previously they had only been appointed under the Plaetorian Law, or in cases of prodigality or madness, he decreed that all youths might have them appointed – without specific reasons being given.' By a fortunate chance the first man given the new post of praetor to deal with the appointment of trustees has left epigraphic record of this. He was Gaius Arrius Antoninus (no relative of the imperial family, in spite of his names, but a fellow-countryman and friend of Fronto). It was always difficult to find suitable persons to act as trustees or guardians and most of the references to decisions of Marcus in this connection in the legal codes involve the adjudication of claims to exemption – poverty was one valid excuse, as were state service and the tenure of local magistracies above the office of aedile.

'He made the senate the judge in many judicial enquiries, even in those which belonged to his own jurisdiction. None of the emperors showed such respect to the senate as he did. To do honour to the senate, moreover, he delegated the settling of disputes to many senators of praetorian and consular rank who held no magistracy at the time, so that their prestige might be enhanced through their administration of the law. . . . He granted senators the further privilege that when any of them was to be tried on a capital charge, he would examine the evidence in secret and only afterwards bring the case to a public hearing; and he would not allow members of the equestrian order to attend such investigations. He always attended sessions of the senate when he was in Rome, even if there was no measure to be proposed, and if he wished to make any proposal himself, he even came from Campania in person. Besides this, when elections were being held he often stayed in the Senate House until night, and never left the building until the consul had said: "we detain you no further, Conscript

Fathers". Further, he made the senate the court to hear appeals from the decision of the consuls.' This deference to the highest order in the land may perhaps seem slightly reactionary now, but it was the only basis in the imperial system for the continuance of orderly government. Emperors who despised and ignored the senate had to rely entirely on naked military rule.

'He was careful in his public expenditure and prohibited libellous accusations, placing a mark of public disgrace on false accusers. He treated with scorn accusations that might profit the imperial treasury.' This refers to accusations of treason, which were at many periods the bane of men of standing: a cheap way of gaining profit and advancement was to be a public informer, and under emperors such as Tiberius, Nero and Domitian the informers had been rampant. 'He made many prudent new arrangements for the support of poor children under state care (de alimentis publicis). He appointed supervisors from the senate for many communities, so that he might give wider scope to the exercise of authority by senators. To the Italian communities in time of famine he provided food from the city of Rome, and in general made careful provision for the supply of corn. . . . He maintained the streets of the city and the public highways most diligently. He appointed legal officers for Italy on the example of the consulars that Hadrian had appointed to administer the law.' This last measure was against the policy of Antoninus, and, in contrast to his other actions, might have been unwelcome to the senate. On the other hand it created further civilian posts in the administration, and this may have been well received. The appointment of supervisors for the cities meant, of course, increased centralization of control. But with the unwillingness of well-to-do people to serve on local councils, it was to become increasingly necessary to cope with the resultant inefficiency and corruption by direct governmental interference in local authorities' affairs. At the same time efforts were made to fill the local councils. In reply to an inquiry by Lollianus Avitus, the governor of Bithynia (a province where the local town-councils were notoriously corrupt and inefficient), it was stated that even persons of illegitimate birth could serve on the councils, provided that they were in other respects eligible. Other legislation from the period deals with similar problems.

Summarizing his activity, the biographer says that Marcus 'restored the old laws rather than introduced new ones. He always kept by him prefects, with whose authority and responsibility he framed his laws. He made use of Scaevola also, a particularly skilled lawyer.

'Towards the people he behaved at all times as in a free state. He was at all times extremely reasonable in restraining people from bad actions and urging them to good ones, generous in rewarding, quick to forgive, thus making bad men good, and good men very good, and he even took insults, which he had to put up with from some people, with equanimity. For when a certain Vetrasinus, a man of deplorable reputation, was standing for office and Marcus advised him to stop the public talk about himself, and he replied that many who had fought with him in the arena were now praetors, he took it with good grace. Again, to avoid taking an easy revenge on anyone, instead of making a praetor who had handled some cases very badly resign his office, he merely handed over the man's legal business to his colleague. The imperial treasury never affected his judgment in any lawsuits involving money. Finally, if he was firm, he was also reasonable.'[48]

A number of cases in private law with which Marcus had to deal, during the first eight years of his reign, concerned family affairs. In reply to a lady named Flavia Tertulla, who had evidently been reported to the authorities as having contracted an illegal marriage, the official reply, in the name of both Marcus and Lucius, stated: 'We are moved by the length of time during which you have been married to your uncle in ignorance of the law; and because you were given in marriage by your grandmother; and because of the number of your children; taking all things together, we confirm the status of your children in this marriage, because it was contracted forty years ago, so that they should be regarded just as if they were conceived legitimately.' In another case a dispute between husband and wife reached the highest court. 'It is a new thing that Rutilius Severus seems to desire, that his wife, who is separated from him, and says that she is not pregnant, should be placed under surveillance. Hence no one will be surprised if we for our part suggest a new plan and a new remedy. Therefore, if he persists in the same demand, the most suitable possible house should be chosen, belonging to a thoroughly respectable woman, to which Domitia may come. There, three midwives, approved both for their professional qualifications and for their trustworthiness, who have been chosen by yourself [the magistrate Valerius Priscus, to whom the judgment was addressed], shall inspect her. If all of them, or two out of three, declare that she is pregnant, then the woman must be persuaded to accept being put under surveillance, just as if she had requested it herself. But if she does not in fact have a child, the husband may know that, as far as any odium he incurs and his reputation in general are concerned, he cannot be regarded as having sought this, to do injury to the woman without just cause. But if all, or more than one, declare that she is not pregnant, there will be no reason to have her placed under surveillance.'[49] The background to this glimpse into the social history of the time is unfortunately unknown. But reliable tests for pregnancy are a relatively modern invention, and the action taken in this case must be regarded as reasonable in the circumstances.

Inheritance cases were a continuing source of litigation. Apart from other considerations, the imperial treasury (*fiscus*) had an interest, as death duties had to be paid, and the property of persons who died intestate could go to the treasury. A knotty problem arose when it was not completely clear whether a man had died intestate or not, in other words, whether or not his will was valid. The case is reported by the distinguished jurist Ulpius Marcellus. It belonged to the year 166. 'Recently at the emperor's court, when a certain man had crossed out the names of his heirs and his property, having no owner, was claimed by the imperial treasury, there was for a long time doubt about the legacies, especially about the ones of which the drawing up had been crossed out. For the most part, also, it was thought that the legatees should be excluded, which I certainly thought was the course to be followed, if the man had cancelled all that was written in the will. Some adjudged that what he had crossed out was void by law, all the rest was valid. What then? Can it not also be believed sometimes that a man who had crossed out the names of the heirs should have thought that he had done enough to die the death of an intestate? But in a doubtful case it is not only juster but also safer to follow the more liberal interpretation.' With this preamble Marcellus introduces his account of the proceedings of the imperial council. 'Marcus said: "When Valerius Nepos changed his mind, cut open his will and crossed out the names of his heirs, his inheritance, according to the decision of my Divine Father, does not appear to belong to those whose names had been written down", and he [Marcus] said to the treasury counsel (*advocatus fisci*): "You have your judges." Vibius Zeno said: "I ask, Lord Emperor, that you hear me patiently. What is your decision about the legacies?" Antoninus Caesar [Marcus] said: "Does it seem to you that a man who crossed out the names of the heirs wanted the will to be valid?" Cornelius Priscianus, the counsel for Leon, said: "He only crossed out the names of the heirs." Calpurnius Longinus, the treasury counsel, said: "No will can be valid that does not have an heir." Priscianus said: "He manumitted certain (slaves) as well as giving legacies." Antoninus Caesar dismissed everyone. When he had weighed the matter up, and had ordered them to be admitted again, he said: "The present case seems to admit of the more humane interpretation, so that we may at least consider that Nepos wanted what he had crossed out to be void." He crossed out the name of a slave whom he had ordered to be free. Antoninus in his official reply decided that he should be free none the less. This decision he certainly made from a partiality for freedom.'[50]

This interest in giving any slave the maximum possible chance of attaining his freedom, if there had ever been any question of his master wishing to grant it, was a matter which Marcus was concerned with throughout his reign, and towards the end of it, a decision he made, in a case involving manumission brought to his attention by his friend Aufidius Victorinus, was to be constantly cited by the jurists as the decisive precedent. Not surprisingly, it was a verdict in favour of the slave, as were virtually all his verdicts in cases involving slaves. Two such cases came up at this period of the reign. In one, he was asked by a senator named Voconius Saxa, who was holding some official post, for advice on how to deal with a slave named Primitivus who had gone to remarkable lengths to avoid being sent back to the master from whom he had run away. The slave had confessed to murder. Under torture, to which he was submitted to learn further details about his alleged accomplices, he admitted that the 'confession' was a put-up job, and that no murder had been committed. The imperial reply to Voconius Saxa recommended that the slave should be sold by Saxa's staff, with the condition that he should never be returned to his former master's power. The master should receive the money paid for the slave.

Another case involved the decision whether slaves who had been given their freedom by their master's will were ineligible to receive it if they had been serving a term of imprisonment. The reply to this was that if their sentence had been completed, they could qualify; if they were still serving it, they could not. The position of slaves was gradually being improved throughout the second century. It had been a notable advance when Antoninus Pius had made a master liable to trial for the murder of his own slave, which previously had not been the case, as the slave was simply regarded as a chattel; and Marcus' 'partiality for freedom', noted by Marcellus, operated in their favour.[51]

A case which came up in February 169 illustrates Marcus' continuing concern for slaves. In a will the slaves had been made heirs to an estate, and were described as 'freedmen', although there was no explicit mention of their being set free. Marcus decided that 'the favourable interpretation' should be put on it: they were to be free and to inherit. A number of other cases from the middle period of the reign show Marcus following the same principles. A particular difficulty always arose when no one would accept an inheritance because of the debts that went with it. Marcus did his best to make sure that slaves freed under such wills did in fact achieve their freedom, and added an interesting rider to a judgment in one such case: 'In case the benefit afforded by this rescript is rendered ineffectual in another way, by the imperial treasury (fiscus) laying claim to the property, let it be hereby known to those engaged in our service that the cause of liberty is to be preferred to pecuniary advantage. . . .' The same attitude is expressed in another case involving the award of freedom to a slave who was to be called to present a financial statement of his stewardship: 'It seems fairer that liberty should be awarded to Trophimus on the basis of the testamentary request (fideicommissum), as it was agreed that it was given without the condition of rendering the accounts, and it is not humane that delay should be made in a question of liberty because of a money matter. An arbitrator must, however, be appointed by the praetor, before whom he must render the account which he appears to have administered.' A great many cases illustrate continuing concern over trustees and guardians. One particularly interesting case reveals Marcus' attitude on an important general principle. 'There is extant a decree of the deified Marcus in these words: "The best course for you if you think that you have any legal demand is to bring it to the test of a legal action." Marcianus replied that he had used no violence. The emperor replied: "Do you think that there is no violence except where people are wounded? It is just as much a case of violence whenever a man who thinks that he has a right to something demands to have it given up to him without going to the courts. So if anyone is shown to me to be in possession of or to have taken, recklessly or without judicial authority, anything belonging to his debtor, or money which was owing to him, and so to have laid down the law for himself – he shall lose his rights as a creditor."'[52]

A straightforward case which came before Marcus throws an interesting light on a rather distasteful development in Roman law. A housebreaker who happened to have the rank of knight was punished by being banished from his native province of Africa, from the city of Rome and from Italy, for five years; and it is added here that the penalty for *honestiores* (literally 'the more honourable ones') must not exceed five years' banishment. The term *honestiores* is used for the upper classes, as opposed to the *humiliores* (literally 'more humble ones'). By the second century AD it really had become the case that there was 'one law for the rich and one law for the poor', at least so far as punishment went. Even in capital cases penalties or sentences varied strictly according to the rank of the convicted person – and rank depended in the long run on wealth. These scales of rank were becoming gradually more stratified, and it is in fact just during the reign of Marcus that various titles of rank hitherto used unofficially and informally, such as *vir clarissimus* (meaning roughly 'right honourable') for senators and corresponding titles for various grades of knight, first seem to have become official. Imperial procurators began at this period to describe their rank in terms of the salary which went with it.[53]

A detailed investigation of Marcus' legal pronouncements has identified four chief characteristics: 'a painstaking thoroughness and attention to detail; an overcareful insistence on elaborating obvious or trivial points; purism in the use of both the Greek and Latin languages; an earnestness which produces an attitude to the pretensions of the Greeks far more serious-minded than Pius'.' This contrasts with Pius, who displays humour, 'ranging from harsh sarcasm, through milder irony, to a gentle comment on human weakness'.[54] It is in no way surprising. After all, Marcus had been trained for the imperial role from the age of sixteen, with an unexampled set of tutors. His inclination to philosophy ensured that he would display an almost excessive sense of duty. Furthermore, the times had changed, for the worse. The reign of Pius had been almost uniquely calm, peaceful and prosperous. Marcus was faced with a series of desperate crises.

· 7 ·
TRIUMPH AND CRISIS

IN 165 THE ROMANS thrust forward into Mesopotamia. In the north Edessa was occupied and the pro-Roman ruler Mannus was restored to the principality of Osrhoene. A Roman army pursued the Parthians eastwards to Nisibis, which was also captured. When the retreating enemy reached the Tigris their general Chosrhoes only escaped by swimming the river and taking refuge in a cave. This part of the campaign may have been led by Martius Verus. Meanwhile, Avidius Cassius advanced down the Euphrates, and a major battle took place at Dura-Europus, an originally Greek city refortified by the Parthians, with a flourishing commercial and agricultural life. By the end of the year Cassius had brought his men far to the south and moved across Mesopotamia at its narrowest point to attack the twin cities on the Tigris, Seleucia on the right bank and the Parthian capital, Ctesiphon, on the left.[1] Seleucia welcomed the Romans and opened its gates. The vast city, with a population supposedly as large as 400,000, still retained its Hellenic characteristics. This support must have made it much easier for Cassius to complete the victory over Parthia by capturing Ctesiphon and burning the palace of Vologases. Yet Cassius was to blacken his own reputation and that of Rome by permitting the destruction of Seleucia as well. How this came about is not recorded in detail. Not surprisingly, a Roman version was to claim that 'the Seleuceni had broken faith first'. Whatever the truth, the action marked the end of one of the major outposts of Greek civilisation in the east, not quite five hundred years after its foundation.

Cassius' army was suffering from shortage of supplies and from disease – some men had contracted the plague at Seleucia – but he led the united force back in good order. Laurelled dispatches were sent to Rome announcing the victory. Lucius took the title Parthicus Maximus – 'greatest conqueror of Parthia' – and he and Marcus became *Imperator III*.[2]

A number of changes had, inevitably, taken place in the administration of the eastern provinces as a result of the war. Pontus-Bithynia in the north of Asia Minor was governed at the opening of the reign by annual proconsuls of praetorian rank, chosen by lot from the senate. Its importance as a supply base and line of communications with the west made it essential to place it under direct imperial rule. The people of Pontus, in the north, were wild and somewhat intractable, and a young regimental commander from Upper Pannonia, named Marcus Valerius Maximianus, was placed on the Black Sea coast to supervise difficult areas which might have been susceptible to brigandage and piracy in time of war. The Bithynians were a sophisticated and volatile people. Their rich cities were continually engaged in rivalry over precedence and status, and frequently ran into debt through over-ambitious civic development projects. The joint province was now placed under a governor of consular rank, appointed by, and responsible to, the emperors. The governor in 165 – who may well have been appointed at the opening of the war – was L. Lollianus Avitus, consul twenty years before, in 144. He had already been proconsul of Africa and came from a noble family. The choice of such a distinguished man might perhaps have compensated the provincials for any fancied indignity at being returned to direct governmental rule. But the real reason for the choice of so senior a man was probably the shortage of suitably qualified men nearer the normal age. The resources of the senate were at full stretch with the extra needs created by the war. For this very reason the province of Nearer Spain (Tarraconensis) was also governed by some rather senior men at this time. The younger men were needed in more active roles. In Bithynia-Pontus Lollianus Avitus had some trouble from Alexander the 'prophet', but the influence of Alexander's distinguished son-in-law Rutilianus made it impossible for any action to be taken against him.

One other administrative change may belong to this period. The great trading city of Palmyra on the eastern frontiers of the province of Syria, which still retained a great deal of independence and organized most of the overland trade between Babylonia and Syria, was placed under the administration of a *logistes*, Fulvius Titianus, who could be the same Titianus mentioned by Lucian as one of the men who played a role in the eastern war.[3]

By the end of 165 the war was virtually over. Lucius was jubilant and was making arrangements for Fronto to write the official history. He directed Avidius Cassius and Martius Verus to draw up memoranda for him, which he promised to send to Fronto, and asked whether he should prepare material himself. He showed his vanity plainly when he asked Fronto 'to dwell at length on the causes and the opening stages of the war, and especially on our lack of success in my absence. Take your time to come to my share. Further, I think it necessary to make crystal clear how greatly superior the Parthians were before my arrival, so that the scale of my achievement will be apparent. . . . In conclusion – my achievements are no greater than they actually are. But they can be made to seem as great as you would have them seem'.[4] Statius Priscus is not mentioned in this correspondence, and, indeed, is not heard of again after his successes in Armenia, so it seems likely that he had died, or retired. This would not be surprising, considering that he had seen active service as a young man in the Jewish war of Hadrian. Not every Roman general could be so robust as Pontius Laelianus and Julius Verus.

The bearer of Cassius' 'laurel-crowned despatches' was a young tribune in his legion, III Gallica, Junius Maximus. As an inscription at Ephesus, from the base of a statue in Maximus' honour, reveals, the young officer was rewarded not only with lavish military decorations, but with a special cash bounty. Not since Trajan's successes fifty years before had there been Roman victories of this magnitude. So that the despatches could be read to the senate in person, Maximus was designated to the quaestorship forthwith. Then Maximus went to report to Fronto, as Fronto described in a letter to Cassius. 'Junius Maximus, the tribune who brought the laurelled despatches to Rome, not only discharged his public mission promptly, but also his private obligation to yourself with friendship. He appeared in every sphere a tireless eulogist of your labours, your plans, your effort and your sleepless care. In fact, when he came to see me – when I was far from well – in my country house just outside the city, he did not cease till nightfall from telling tale after tale of your expeditionary marches and the discipline which you had restored and kept up to the ancient standard; then your most strenuous vigour in leading the column and your deliberate care in choosing the right moment for battle. . . . He spoke of you with love and the utmost loyalty', he concluded, 'and he deserves your affection and to profit from your patronage. Whatever you do to enhance the honour of your eulogist will redound to your own glory.'

Maximus was to be sent back east in the course of 166, as quaestor in the province of Asia for a year – hence the statue at Ephesus, where he will have been able to play a part in ensuring that the troops returning to the European provinces when the war ended had a smooth passage.[5] As for Cassius himself, he was to be made consul in May of this year. Two of the other young generals who had made their names in the war had already gained this distinction, Claudius Fronto in 165, Martius Verus immediately before Cassius in spring of 166. But they were a little older than Cassius, who cannot have been more than thirty-five – and he still had one further feat of arms ahead.[6] Meanwhile, the relaxation of urgency in the east allowed the return to other duties in the west of a number of the generals. Julius Verus, the governor of Syria, and Claudius Fronto, the successful army commander, returned to Italy with an urgent mission, the recruitment of two new legions, intended for service in the forthcoming northern campaigns, which Marcus realized could not be delayed much longer. In the past – and in the future – the raising of new legions, which was generally done in Italy itself (although the regular recruitment for existing units was by now mostly done in their province of garrison), was generally a prelude to new conquests, the inclusion of new territory within the empire. The raising of a new Second and Third legion was clearly no exception. Marcus must have had far-reaching plans. Iallius Bassus, *comes* of Lucius, was also released from his duties, and was sent to the Danube with a new assignment, the governorship of the most important province along the whole northern frontier, Upper Pannonia. He had already governed

Lower Pannonia, which was sometimes considered sufficient preliminary training in provincial government for governors of the Upper province. But Bassus had also governed Lower Moesia and had been in the eastern wars. At about the same time, or shortly afterwards, another experienced man, like Avidius Cassius of Syrian origin, was sent to govern Lower Pannonia. This was Tiberius Claudius Pompeianus, son of a knight from Antioch. He was to play an important role in the years to come.[7]

In the autumn or winter of 165 Marcus had suffered a blow in the loss of one of the twins, Antoninus, who died at the age of four. Marcus had learned from Apollonius 'to be always the same, even at the loss of a child', and obviously he will have borne this in accordance with his Stoic creed. It was harder for Faustina, and as Lucilla was pregnant, it was decided to let her go out to the east to be with her daughter, taking some of the other children.[8]

At about the same time Fronto too was bereaved, by the loss of his three-year-old grandson (whom he had never seen), following a few months after the death of his wife, Cratia. The old man was desperately upset, and unlike his Stoic pupil showed his distress openly. Marcus wrote him a brief letter of consolation: 'I have just learnt of your loss. Since I always suffer torment when a single joint of yours is aching, my master, what do you think I feel when it is your heart that is aching? I am so upset that I can only think of asking you to keep safe for me my sweetest of masters, in whom I have greater solace for this life than you can find sorrow from any source. I have not written this with my own hand, because this evening after my bath even my hand is trembling.'

Fronto's letter of reply was full of bitterness at his fate. He had lost five children himself. Each was an only child, so that he never had a child born except while bereaved of another. Yet somehow he had borne these afflictions. Now 'as my Victorinus weeps, I waste and melt away. Often I even make protest to the immortal gods and reproach the fates. For Victorinus, a man of loyalty, gentleness, sincerity and complete innocence of life, a man of conspicuous accomplishments in all the noblest arts, to be thus afflicted by the most cruel death of his son – was this in any sense fair or just?' He questioned the meaning of 'Providence' and 'Fate'. But he could reflect a little further: 'Unless perhaps quite another error misleads us, and through ignorance of the truth we are coveting what is evil as though it were good, turning away from what is good as though it were harmful – and death itself, which seems to everyone a thing of grief, which brings pause to our labours, our anxieties, our troubles, in fact transports us, freed from the miserable chains of the body, to calm and pleasant assemblies of souls, supplied with all good things. That this is the case I would rather believe, than that all human affairs are governed by no providence – or by an unfair one.'

Thus he attempted to console himself. But the presence with him of

143

another grandson, instead of helping him, tormented him more – 'for in his features I see the one that was lost, I imagine I see a copy of his face, I fancy I hear the same sound of his voice in my mind. . . . Not knowing the real appearance of the dead child I torture myself trying to imagine what he was like.' He knew that his daughter would get over the loss. As for himself – 'it would have been more fitting if I had died first myself. . . . But I console myself with the thought that my life is now almost complete and death is near.' He felt that he had lived honourably and well and reflected on his life. At the end of the letter the grief broke in again: 'I have suffered much and seriously from ill-health, my dearest Marcus. Then, afflicted with the most miserable disasters, I have lost my wife, I have lost my grandson in Germany. . . . If I were of iron, I could not write you any more at this time. I have sent you a book which you can take as representing my thoughts.'[9]

Fronto wrote to Lucius as well: 'Worn out as I am with long-drawn-out and more than usually serious ill-health, and afflicted too with the most distressing sorrows which have come almost continuously – for in the space of a very few months I have lost both my dearest wife and my three-year-old grandson – in spite of all these blows, still I confess I am a little restored to know that you are remembering me and have been wanting something of mine.' He sent him a copy of one of his speeches, chosen by Marcus, and added: 'Your brother also earnestly discussed with me the thing that I am still more earnestly anxious to undertake, and as soon as you send me your memoranda I will get down to work with the best will in the world.' He was referring, of course, to the projected history.[10]

In 166 came the final demonstration of Roman might when the Parthian kingdom was invaded again. This time an assault was made across the northern Tigris, into Media, homeland of the ancient rulers of the east. The new victories of Cassius' armies led Lucius to take a further title, Medicus; meanwhile Marcus accepted the title won in 165, Parthicus Maximus, and both became *Imperator IV*. Cassius' victories in the far-off lands beyond the Tigris set people in the east talking. It was rumoured that he had crossed the Indus with one of the Syrian legions, the Third, and some German and Moorish auxiliaries. According to Lucian, one of the many writers who had cashed in on the war by producing histories of it actually included such an episode.

As a matter of fact, in this year, 166, some Romans did penetrate to the east, in fact very much further than to the Indus – to the court of the Celestial Emperor. Chinese annals record that in this year 'ambassadors' from 'Ngan-touen', or 'An-toun', i.e. Marcus Antoninus, ruler of 'T'a-ts'in' (one of the Chinese names for the Roman empire), brought gifts for the emperor: ivory, rhinoceros horn and tortoise shell. They had come by 'Ji-nam', i.e. Annam, not by the northern route. (A gold medallion of Marcus has been found near Saigon.) Clearly the 'ambassadors' were freelance traders, probably from Alexandria, who had acquired their gifts on their journey, rather than official envoys. There is no mention of it in Roman sources.[11]

Fronto wrote to congratulate Lucius: 'although it has for a long time now been wearying and painful for me to go on living, with this ill-health of mine, yet when I see you return with such great glory gained by your own excellence, I will not have lived in vain, and will not be unwilling to live on for as long as life is granted to me. Farewell, my Lord, whom I long for so much.' He added greetings to Faustina, and to the children of both of them. Lucilla must have borne Lucius a child before he returned. As some sixteen years later Lucilla evidently had a son-in-law, it was probably a daughter.[12]

The date of Lucius' return and the exact circumstances of the conclusion of hostilities are not recorded. But the Misenum fleet was still lying off the mouth of the Orontes at the end of May 166, so it was later than this. In any case, Lucius could not well have returned until the Median campaign was over and peace had been made. Rome could now have annexed Mesopotamia. There was certainly some expectation that the empire would be enlarged: an inscription at Ostia calls Lucius *propagator imperii*, 'extender of empire'. Some territory was however acquired, for the province of Syria was increased, to include Dura-Europus. Further, garrisons were left in several strongpoints beyond the frontier, including Kaine Polis in Armenia and Nisibis in northern Mesopotamia.[13]

The return journey probably began before midsummer. The imperial party travelled via Ephesus, where the rich sophist Flavius Damianus, then holding office as Secretary of the city council, provided food for all the troops that passed through the city over a period of thirteen months, while his son-in-law Vedius Antoninus, who was gymnasiarch, furnished olive oil. Lucius himself stayed with Vedius, as he had done in 164 at the time of his wedding.[14] The European legions could now return to their home bases. I Minervia went back to Bonn and II Adiutrix to Budapest, where it came under Claudius Pompeianus. But V Macedonica did not go back to its old base at Troesmis in Lower Moesia. It was sent instead across the Danube to Potaissa in Dacia. The three Dacian provinces were reunited and, as there were now two legions in Dacia (XIII Gemina was at Apulum in the west), it was assigned to a governor of consular rank. The first was evidently Sex. Calpurnius Agricola, fresh from his work on the northern frontier in Britain.[15]

Lucius had evidently left Syria with reluctance. Although the Syrians had made jokes about him at the stage performances which he patronized so avidly, he felt he was leaving his own kingdom when he had to return to Rome. To ensure that the Parthians kept the peace, the man who had gained the major victories in the war was installed as governor of Syria. Compared with almost all his known predecessors in this post, Cassius was unusually young. But Martius Verus, probably not much older, was made governor of Cappadocia at the same time. Both were to be left in these posts for many years.[16]

Lucius and his entourage probably reached Rome in August. By this time Lucilla may have been expecting another child. A minor official at the law-courts dedicated an altar to Juno Lucina, the patroness of childbirth, on 23 August, 'for the health of the house of the emperors', Marcus and his Faustina, Lucius and his Lucilla, and their children.[17] Fronto was awaiting the triumphant hero's return eagerly, and this pleased Lucius: 'why should I not picture to myself your joy, my dearest master. Indeed I seem to myself to see you hugging me tightly and kissing me many times,' he wrote. When he finally arrived, the favour shown to Fronto created a certain amount of ill-feeling, in spite of careful effort to avoid causing anyone jealousy. Everyone was eager to greet the conquering hero. Still, Fronto was gratified: 'this honour which you reserved for me I regard as far outweighing everything. Many a time besides this have I noted the special honour which you have shown me by what you have done and said. I value in the highest possible way the many times you have supported me with your hands, lifted me up when I could hardly walk through my weakness; your ever cheerful and friendly look when you speak to me, your readiness to talk to me and your readiness to continue our conversation so long, your unwillingness to end it. . . . Therefore whatever favours I have had to ask from my Lord your brother I have preferred to ask and obtain through you.'[18] This is the last surviving letter of Fronto to either of his imperial pupils, and he must have died soon after this. There are a few further letters from him, to some of his friends – commending one friend, Sardius Saturninus, to another, Caelius Optatus (then governing Fronto's native province); commending Saturninus' son Lupus to Petronius Mamertinus; a friendly letter to the young man he had met recently, Junius Maximus; a letter to his friend Squilla Gallicanus, congratulating him on the successful oratorical debut of his son, Fronto's pupil. Fronto did not complete his history of the Parthian war. Only a Preface survives. He may not even have survived to see the triumph celebrated.[19]

Fronto and his contemporaries might have been piqued had they suspected the unfavourable modern verdict on his style. But Fronto would perhaps have been content to have been remembered as the imperial tutor, praised by Marcus for his insistence on sincerity and humanity, praised by Lucius who was glad to say that he had learned from his master 'sincerity and the love of truth far before the discipline of polite speaking'. It is not known who was responsible for the preservation and publication of the correspondence, but Fronto's memory and name survived with Victorinus, and some fifty years after his death his grandson, Marcus Aufidius Fronto, commemorating a son who died young, proudly described him as 'great-grandson of Cornelius Fronto, consul, master of the emperors Lucius and Antoninus'. So it was probably the family of Fronto that preserved this record of an attractive friendship, and thus revealed intimate details of the family life of Marcus.[20]

The triumph for the eastern victories was held on 12 October. On this day the young prince Commodus, now aged five, and his brother Annius Verus, aged three, were given the name or title of Caesar at the request of Lucius. They and some of Marcus' daughters rode in the triumphal procession. At the same time Marcus and Lucius were awarded the 'civic crown' of oak leaves, presumably by the senate. This was given 'for saving the lives of fellow-citizens' – in their case, clearly, by their wise conduct of the campaigns. They also each received the title 'pater patriae', 'father of the fatherland', which had been offered to Marcus during the war; but he had deferred acceptance of it until his brother's return. The successful generals and others who had participated in the campaigns were decorated appropriately, according to their rank. Furius Victorinus, the prefect of the guard, received 'three Crowns, four headless spears and four siege standards'. Pontius Laelianus, as a consular, received the same decorations, as did Claudius Fronto.[21]

Rome had not seen a triumphal procession for nearly fifty years, since the slightly bizarre triumph celebrated by Hadrian in honour of the dead Trajan, when Trajan's effigy was paraded through the streets. The arrangements were presumably those by now standard, of which the most celebrated illustration comes from the Arch of Titus in Rome, depicting the destroyer of Jerusalem riding in triumph through the streets of Rome, while the seven-branched candlestick and the table of the shewbread are carried before him with the other spoils. In the procession of Marcus and Lucius, without doubt, the senate and magistrates walked. There would be trumpeters, white oxen to be sacrificed, the spoils taken from the enemy laden on wagons, and perhaps pictures illustrating exciting moments in the war, captives in chains, and lictors, behind which came the chariot of the *triumphatores*, dressed in a special costume, carrying sceptres, with crowns on their heads and their faces painted red. Behind them marched their armies (or representatives of their armies). If tradition were followed, a slave stood immediately behind the *triumphator*, whispering 'remember that thou art a mortal', while the army and the people cried out 'Io, Triumphe!' The route followed by the procession began outside the city, beyond the Vatican, at the Porta Triumphalis, went down the Via Triumphalis and across the Tiber, passed the Circus Flaminius, into the Forum, and along the Sacred Way, where the emperors would descend from their four-horse chariot to deposit the laurels of victory in the lap of the statue of Jupiter on the Capitol.[22]

In spite of the lavish public celebration of the eastern victories, Marcus must have realized that the four-year-long war had been an expensive and ultimately unnecessary interlude. Had it not been for the rash action of

Sedatius Severianus, 'that foolish Celt', diplomacy and a vigorous show of force might have produced the results which had been obtained by bitter and lengthy fighting. Admittedly, Rome's relations with her dangerous but unwieldy eastern neighbour seem always to have followed a consistent pattern, with Rome engaged in serious hostilities at fairly regular intervals to maintain her influence in the vital client-states, of which Armenia was the largest. There may too have been hidden factors, such as the need by Rome to keep trade routes with Central Asia and the Far East free from Parthian interference – such causes are generally not mentioned in Roman sources, but they may have influenced the emperors. The shock to Roman prestige at Elegia had made a war in the east inevitable. As it turned out, it was conducted with some success and it provided officers and men with valuable fighting experience for what was to come in the north. But it delayed Rome's response to the situation building up in central Europe for a shade too long.

After the triumph, more entertainment was provided for the urban populace at Rome, in the shape of games in the Circus. Marcus had perhaps mastered his boredom and dislike of these occasions. The biographer records that 'among other illustrations of his consideration for others this too must be mentioned: after a boy tight-rope walker had fallen, he ordered that safety mattresses should be spread out – this is the reason why safety nets are stretched out today'. Dio also records something of Marcus' attitude to public spectacles. 'So averse was he to bloodshed that he even used to watch the gladiators at Rome contend, like athletes, without endangering their lives – for he never gave any of them a sharp weapon, but they all fought with blunted weapons, like buttoned foils. And so far from allowing bloodshed was he that although he did give orders, at the request of the people, that a certain lion, which had been trained to eat people, should be brought on, he did not look at it and would not give the trainer his freedom, in spite of the persistent demands of the spectators. Instead he ordered a proclamation to be made that the man had not done anything which deserved to win him his freedom.'[23]

When the festivities were over there was pressing public business to attend to. The situation in the north was finally reaching the predicted breaking point. The tribes bordering the empire were being subjected to unbearable pressure from their wilder neighbours in the far north. Big movements of population had begun, including, probably, that which was to take the Goths from Scandinavia to southern Russia. The tribes immediately beyond the Rhine and Danube had been subjected to a Roman protectorate for a century and a half. There had been moments when it had broken down, and on occasion serious warfare, but for the most part the system worked well. An illustration of its smooth operation had been seen early in the reign of Pius, that master of Roman diplomacy. To a certain extent this had forced on these barbarian peoples a degree of peaceful behaviour to which they were ill adapted. Their population had clearly expanded beyond the means of their primitive agricultural techniques. Now the pressure from beyond was forcing them out of their own lands. They were ready to invade – and they wanted land. They wanted to settle, not merely to raid and plunder.

Some time in late 166 or early 167 the first invasion came. Six thousand Langobardi and Obii burst into Pannonia. A rapid Roman combined operation, under a young cavalry officer named Macrinius Avitus Catonius Vindex and an infantry force under a certain Candidus, swept them out again. Eleven tribes sent envoys to Iallius Bassus, governor of Upper Pannonia, suing for peace, choosing as their spokesman the king of the Marcomanni, Ballomarius. The envoys made peace, which they ratified with oaths, and returned home. The situation was apparently in hand. The victorious troops had hailed Marcus and Lucius as Imperator for the fifth time, it would seem, but the title *Imp. V* did not appear regularly in their official titulature until 168. Possibly there was hesitation at accepting it for a comparatively minor success; perhaps subsequent reverses were to make it seem, at first, a hollow victory.[24]

Without doubt Marcus intended to set off for the north in person in 167. But he was prevented from doing so by a new and particularly pressing threat – the plague. This had been caught first by the army in Mesopotamia, and the returning troops spread it all over the empire. 'It was his fate', the biographer says of Lucius, 'to bring the plague with him to those provinces through which he made his return journey, right up to Rome.' Wild stories circulated about the pestilence as its effect was felt further and further afield. It was believed that a soldier had accidentally cut open a golden casket containing the dread vapour in the temple of Apollo at Seleucia. Cassius too was blamed: he had sacked Seleucia in violation of an agreement, after the city had received the Roman soldiers as friends. The plague was a punishment sent by the city's protecting deity. Alexander the 'prophet' cashed in again on the public anxiety, selling magic apotropaic charms to pin to doorposts – 'guaranteed to keep out the plague'. But they had no effect. 'From the frontiers of the Persians as far as to the Rhine and Gaul,' wrote Ammianus Marcellinus two centuries later, 'the foul touch of plague polluted everything with contagion and death.' Orosius, the fifth-century cataloguer of pagan misfortunes (perhaps disposed to exaggerate a little), is even more graphic: 'such great pestilence devastated all Italy that everywhere estates, fields, and towns were left deserted, without culti-vators or inhabitants, and relapsed into ruins and woodland.'[25]

The effect and scale of this epidemic are a matter of dispute; and it is not even known for certain what disease it was – smallpox, exanthematous typhus, and bubonic plague have been suggested in modern times. Certainly the sources are unanimous in describing it as exceptionally destructive of human life. One of those sources is the great doctor Galen, who was in Rome in 166, and left soon to return to his native Pergamum, to avoid the plague. But it has been modern scholars who have concluded that it was the most serious plague in the whole of antiquity, and a major factor in the decline of Rome. This view is probably exaggerated. But the effect of the plague was startling and severe, especially in the capital, by far the most densely populated place in the empire, and on the army, which, living in barracks, was particularly susceptible. The loss of life there was very serious. Marcus was later able to look more calmly on the plague: 'the corruption of the mind is a pestilence, much more indeed than any such corruption and change of the air which surrounds us. For this corruption [i.e. the plague] is a pestilence of animals in so far as they are animals; corruption of the mind is a pestilence to men as human beings,' he wrote in his *Meditations*. But the plague was troubling him on his deathbed thirteen years later, and in Rome in 167 it must have been his foremost consideration.[26]

The biographer gives a confused but graphic description of the situation in the city at the time. 'The dead were carried away on carts and wagons. At this time, moreover, the emperors enacted the most stringent laws on burying the dead and on tombs; no one was permitted to build a tomb at his country villa (a law still in force today). And indeed the plague carried off many thousands, including many prominent figures. Antoninus erected statues to the most eminent of these. Such too was his kindliness of heart that he ordered funeral ceremonies for the common people to be carried on, even at public expense. There was one foolish person who, with a number of accomplices, was trying to create the opportunity for wholesale burglary. He stood by the wild fig-tree in the Campus Martius, making speeches all the time to the effect that fire was going to come down from heaven and the end of the world would come if he were to fall down from the tree and turn into a stork. Of course at the appointed time he fell down and let a stork out from a fold in his clothes. He was hauled off to the emperor, and confessed to the whole business. But the emperor pardoned him.'

Naturally a good deal of the legal activity of this time was concerned with the plague and its effect. It was normally prohibited to carry a body through towns. When Marcus was asked to adjudicate in a case where this had been infringed, he replied that 'those who have transported the body of a man who died on a journey through villages or a town do not deserve punishment, although such things ought not to be done without the permission of the relevant authorities'. The cemeteries were obviously becoming overcrowded. Marcus and Lucius had to issue an edict to prevent unlawful appropriation of other people's graves: 'a body which had been delivered to a lawful sepulchre, that is, has been covered with earth, must not be disturbed'. In a rescript Marcus declared that 'the heir who prohibits the man chosen by the testator to conduct the funeral from doing so, is not acting rightly'. But he added that there was no statutory penalty for this. Quite what was involved is not clear. But it is possible that the price of funerals and tombs had enormously increased and that those who had been left money preferred to make their own arrangements to deal with the remains of their benefactors, realizing that the carrying out of the full testamentary instructions would greatly diminish the value of the bequest. Another rescript of Marcus and Lucius illustrates the shortage of burial space. It was illegal to buy and sell sepulchres, but it was ruled that 'if the monument has not yet been used (i.e. for burial), anyone may sell it or give it away; or if it is a cenotaph it can be sold, for this is not religiously consecrated'. This was contrary to a previous ruling. Another by-product of the increased death-rate was a rescript excusing those who were attending funeral ceremonies from answering a summons to court.[27]

The man who made his ridiculous speech of warning in the Campus Martius for his own ends had rightly gauged the hysterical temper of the urban populace; and wild stories had, of course, been circulating about the plague being some form of retribution from the gods. To satisfy this feeling in the obvious way Marcus 'summoned priests from all sides', the biographer records, 'performed foreign religious rites and purified the city in every way. The Roman ceremony of the feast of the gods' – the *lectisternium*, an ancient ceremony at which statues of the gods were placed on banqueting-couches in public places and offerings were placed on a table before them – 'was celebrated for seven days'. The religious ceremonies of 167 necessitated the presence of the emperor, who was, apart from anything else, the *pontifex maximus*. Also, his presence was an important factor in maintaining public morale. But the measures necessary in 166 and 167 delayed Marcus' departure for the northern front. An *expeditio Germanica* had been prepared, but the *profectio* of the emperors had to be postponed.[28]

The pressure had shifted a little in the north in 167. During the summer the gold mines in western Dacia (Rosia Montana in Transylvania) were attacked. Local records cease there with a document of 29 May. Calpurnius Agricola clearly had fighting to do. V Macedonica saw action under his command and so, no doubt, did XIII Gemina, the legion nearer to the disturbances. Meanwhile in Pannonia the situation had eased. On 5 May Claudius Pompeianus was able to discharge time-expired veterans of some of the auxiliary units under his command. One of the *diplomata* issued then has survived, and on it Marcus and Lucius bear for the first recorded time the new title *Imp. V.* The situation was sufficiently well in hand for legionaries of the newly returned II Adiutrix to be able to concentrate on road-repair projects.[29]

Lucius had opened the year 167 as consul for the third time, an honour which made him equal in one respect to Marcus. His colleague was M. Ummidius Quadratus, Marcus' nephew. But his official duties only occupied him for a few months of the winter at the most. After his return from the war he was eager to relax, and 'behaved with less regard for his brother', according to the biographer, 'for he indulged his freedmen in a rather shameful manner and settled many matters without consulting his brother'. His behaviour left a great deal to be desired – to judge from the biographer's account: 'He brought home actors out of Syria as proudly as if he were bringing foreign monarchs to his triumph. The chief of these was Maximinus, on whom he bestowed the name of Paris' – the name of a favourite actor of Nero. 'Besides this he built a villa on the *via Clodia*, where he indulged with enormous extravagance in orgies for many days, in company with his freedmen and friends of inferior rank in whose presence he felt no shame. In fact he even invited Marcus, who came, to show his brother his own way of life as worthy of respect and imitation. He stayed for five days in that same villa and devoted himself for the entire time to judicial business, while his brother was either banqueting or getting ready for a banquet. Lucius had brought home with him another actor, Agrippus, surnamed Memphius, like a trophy of the Parthian war, to whom he gave the name Apolaustus' – which means 'Enjoyable'; he was manumitted by Lucius, took the names L. Aelius Aurelius Apolaustus Memphius, and had a successful and prosperous career for many years before meeting a sticky end in 190. Lucius 'had also brought with him harpists and flautists, actors and jesters from the mime-shows, jugglers and all types of slaves whose entertainment Syria and Alexandria feeds on – all in such numbers that he seemed to have won a war not against the Parthians but against the stage profession'. Marcus had to cope with the anxiety of the people of Rome single-handed.[30]

One reflection of public feeling at Rome among a population suddenly affected by the plague was hostility towards the Christians. The 'atheists', notorious for their 'hatred of the human race' and expecting the end of the world, were a natural target. Their failure to honour and propitiate the gods, particularly at a time when special religious rites were being carried out, would make them more than usually conspicuous. It was easy for any who hated them to have them arrested and sentenced to death: the very name was a capital offence. Among the Christians martyred at this time was Justin. What appears to be a verbatim record of his trial survives, in three versions, the first of which, the shortest, is clearly authentic. (In the sequel this account was elaborated for the edification of the faithful.)[31]

The church historian Eusebius of Caesarea, writing well over a century later, records that it was a Cynic philosopher named Crescens, smarting under the impact of frequent – and public – dialectical defeats at the hands of Justin, who instigated his arrest. Eusebius relied on Justin's pupil Tatian, whom he misquotes as reporting that Crescens 'counselled others to despise death but himself was so afraid of it that he intrigued to inflict death on

Justin, as though it were a great evil, because Justin, by preaching the truth, convicted the philosophers as gluttons and impostors'. Crescens' advice 'to despise death' accords well with the circumstances of the year 167, and the identity of the presiding prefect also fits this date. It was Marcus' friend Junius Rusticus, his principal guide to Stoicism. There is an irony about this confrontation. Justin was deeply imbued with Greek philosophy, towards which he displays a 'generous and optimistic approach'. As his last work, the *Dialogue with Trypho*, records, he had studied first with a Stoic tutor, in his quest for the truth, passing on to an Aristotelian, a Pythagorean and a Platonist before his conversion – but it was a conversion which did not lead him to renounce what he had learned from the Greeks, especially Plato.[32]

'In the time of the lawless decrees of idolatry', the account begins; perhaps this is a reference to the *lectisternium* and other emergency rituals. 'After they were led in, the prefect said to Justin:

"What kind of life do you lead?"
"Blameless and uncondemned by all men," said Justin.
"What doctrines do you practise?" said Rusticus the prefect.
"I have tried to learn all doctrines", said Justin, "but I have committed myself to the true doctrines of the Christians, even if they do not please those with false beliefs."
"Those then are the doctrines that please you?", said Rusticus the prefect.
"Yes, since I follow them with belief."
"What sort of belief?"
"Our worship of the God of the Christians, who alone we think was the maker of all the universe from the beginning, and the Son of God Jesus Christ, who was also foretold by the prophets, that he would come down to mankind as a herald of salvation and a teacher of good knowledge. But I think my words are insignificant in comparison with his divinity, acknowledging the power of prophecy, in that it was proclaimed about him who I said just now is Son of God. For you know that in the past the prophets foretold his presence among men."
"Where do you meet?" said the prefect Rusticus.
"Wherever each prefers or is able. Besides, do you think we can all meet in the same place?" said Justin.
"Tell me where you meet – or in what place?"
"I have been living above the Baths of Myrtinus during all the time that I have been staying at Rome (and this is my second stay). I know no other meeting-place but there; and if anyone wanted to come to me I shared the words of truth with him," said Justin.
"So you are a Christian?" said Rusticus.
"Yes, I am a Christian," Justin replied.'

Rusticus then turned to question five others, one woman, Charito, and four men, Euelpistus, Hierax, Paeon and Liberianus. He established that Euelpistus was born in Cappadocia and that Hierax was from Phrygia. In the longer versions of the trial Euelpistus is described as an imperial slave, perhaps an authentic detail. Converts in the imperial household are attested in the lifetime of Paul. Euelpistus and Hierax both came from eastern provinces, as did Justin himself, and Charito and Paeon also have Greek names. The church at Rome was still Greek, as it was to be for another century.

Rusticus concluded the trial with a few more questions to Justin.

"If you are scourged and beheaded, do you believe that you will ascend to heaven?"
"I hope for it if I am steadfast in my perseverance. But I know that for those who live in the right way there awaits the divine gift even to the consummation", said Justin.
"So you guess this, that you will ascend," said the prefect Rusticus.
"I do not guess, I am completely convinced," said Justin.
"If you do not obey, you will be punished," said the prefect Rusticus.
"We are confident that if we are punished we shall be saved," said Justin.
The prefect Rusticus pronounced:
"Those unwilling to sacrifice to the gods, after being scourged are to be executed in accordance with the laws."

The holy martyrs, glorifying God, went out to the customary place and accomplished their witness (martyrion) in the confession of our Saviour.'

There is a faint trace in this account of the intellectual curiosity of the prefect; but he did not hesitate to pass sentence. If Christians were accused, they had a remarkable privilege: a free pardon if they recanted. No other crime was so treated. Marcus was presumably aware of these proceedings. It may have been at the time of the condemnation of Justin that he began to form the only opinion about the Christians that he expresses in the Meditations: 'How wonderful is that soul which is ready, if it must be at this very moment released from the body, either to be extinguished, or to be scattered, or to survive. This readiness must come from a specific decision, and not out of sheer parataxis like the Christians.' The word parataxis is one that is used elsewhere to describe the drawing up of troops in battle and the marshalling of a political party. This describes something a little different from the mera obstinatio, 'sheer obstinacy', that others imputed to Christians. It implies rather that Marcus felt that they were not expressing an individual choice by their willingness to suffer death by martyrdom, but were expressing a choice that had been instilled into them: that they were trained to die. This would then be a view of the Christians rather similar to that of Epictetus – and it will be remembered that Rusticus had allowed Marcus to share his copy of the Discourses. 'The Galilaeans', Epictetus taught

— surely referring to the Christians — were fearless 'by habit'.[33]

Rusticus cannot have survived long after the trial of Justin. His successor as ‿prefect was Sergius Paullus, from the Roman colony of Antioch-towards-Pisidia. He might have had especial familiarity with Christianity, for a namesake, probably his great-grandfather, had met the apostle Paul at Paphos on Cyprus. The proconsul, 'a man of understanding', had invited Paul and Barnabas to appear before him 'and sought to hear the word of God'; impressed by Paul's blinding of the sorcerer Elymas, 'he believed, being astonished at the teaching of the Lord'. Paul had gone on from Cyprus to Perge and then to Pisidian Antioch itself. The new prefect had intellectual interests. He had attended demonstrations in anatomy by the brilliant young doctor Galen, along with Flavius Boethus, Civica Barbarus, the uncle of Lucius, and Claudius Severus, son of Marcus' philosopher friend, by now probably married to Marcus' second oldest daughter, Annia Faustina.[34]

Meanwhile, Marcus had even more pressing preoccupations than the plague and the hysteria of the people of Rome – the danger to the northern frontiers of the empire. On 6 January 168, Marcus went to the barracks of the praetorian guard, where he addressed the men. No doubt the principal subject of his speech was the forthcoming campaign. All that has survived is concerned with another matter. Veterans of the praetorian guard had evidently been having some difficulty in finding wives for themselves (perhaps another by-product of the plague – the praetorians might have become unpopular, as responsible for bringing it back from the east). To assist their task as suitors Marcus announced that prospective fathers-in-law of veteran guardsmen would gain the same privileges from the birth of a grandson that they would receive at the birth of a son of their own.[35]

When the emperors finally 'departed, clad in the military cloak', in the spring of 168, for the north, they were accompanied by an experienced general, Furius Victorinus, who may have been sole prefect. A number of *comites* were attached to the general staff, including Aufidius Victorinus, Vitrasius Pollio (husband of Marcus' cousin Fundania Faustina), along with the redoubtable Pontius Laelianus and Dasumius Tullius Tuscus. The experience of these two former governors of Upper Pannonia would be invaluable. Lucius chose as *comes* his former subordinate Claudius Fronto. The reports from the north were discouraging. The Marcomanni and another tribe called Victuali were creating trouble on the frontier, together with other tribes who had been driven on by the more distant peoples to the north. They threatened to invade unless they were peaceably admitted. Nevertheless, negotiation produced some success and several tribes sent ambassadors to the governors of the frontier provinces asking pardon for their treaty-breaking. Lucius felt that this was enough and had been unwilling to set off. By the time the imperial party reached Aquileia (the ancient predecessor of Venice) the situation seemed well under control. The Quadi, always one of the most important peoples, had been defeated. Their king lost his life and they were anxious that Rome should approve the choice of successor, as in the old days. Other peoples retreated and their kings put to death the tribesmen responsible for the incidents.[36]

Lucius now felt, again, that the personal participation of himself and Marcus was unnecessary, a feeling heightened by a new development. 'The prefect Furius Victorinus was lost and part of the army had perished.' No details are given to elucidate this cryptic statement in the biography of Marcus. As a result it has been often assumed that the prefect and the troops had been killed in battle. But the context of the biographer's information gives no indication that any fighting which involved the guard had taken place at this juncture. On the other hand the other sources paint a consistent picture of enormous losses from plague among the armies of Rome: 'whole Roman armies perished', says Eutropius; 'the Roman army was destroyed, almost annihilated' by it, according to Jerome, who is followed by Orosius; and the biography itself, already quoted earlier as describing the thousands wiped out by the plague, in a later passage is more explicit, speaking of 'many thousands of civilians and soldiers'.[37]

Victorinus was replaced by M. Bassaeus Rufus, a tough soldier who had risen from humble Italian peasant origins. Rufus had not long before been appointed prefect of the city police, the *vigiles* – he was still in office on 10 March 168 – not a usual position for a man of his strictly army background to fill, and a sign that Marcus had been determined to keep the situation in the city under firm control in the difficult period after the triumph. But in the spring of 168 Rufus had been sent out as prefect of Egypt and was there when news of his further promotion reached him. His urgent recall indicates that it was still thought worth while to wait for the right man for the job. Before long it was going to be increasingly difficult to find the right men at all. Rufus was soon given a colleague, M. Macrinius Vindex, perhaps the father of the dashing cavalry officer whose action in Pannonia had stemmed the first barbarian onslaught. The Macrinii, their names suggest, may have been of Celtic origin, perhaps from Cologne, or even from Colchester in Britain.[38]

In spite of Lucius' reluctance – he had settled in for a season's hunting and banqueting, while he hoped to persuade Marcus to return to Rome – Marcus was adamant, and both emperors crossed the Alps to inspect the frontier provinces. It was – apparently – the first time in his life that Marcus had been outside Italy. Lucius, already familiar with many of the eastern provinces, may even have been to these northern ones as a boy thirty years before, when his father, L. Aelius Caesar, had governed both Pannonian provinces. Marcus and Lucius stayed at Carnuntum, the base of the legion XIV Gemina and headquarters of the governor of Upper Pannonia. Their presence is recorded by a dedication for their health at the shrine to Jupiter outside Carnuntum. Marcus maintained that it was essential to carry out the intended programme, for the retreat of the barbarian peoples appeared to him to be a deliberate manoeuvre to gain time. Realizing that the vast expeditionary force could overwhelm them they hoped to lull the Romans into a false sense of security. Marcus and Lucius 'dealt with everything relevant to the protection of Italy and Illyricum' (the old name for the Pannonian provinces). These measures included the setting up of a new command, the *praetentura Italiae et Alpium* – 'the Italian and Alpine front'. The man appointed to take command of this was an African senator, Quintus Antistius Adventus, who had served with distinction in the eastern wars. When they started, he had been in command of the Palestine legion VI Ferrata. He had been transferred to the Lower Pannonian legion II Adiutrix when it came to the east with Geminius Marcianus, and at the end of the war had governed Arabia in succession to Marcianus. Then he returned to become consul and curator of public works in Rome. Now he took charge of the two newly raised legions in the emergency zone.[39]

Servilius Fabianus Maximus, who had given faithful service in the north for seven years, governing Lower and Upper Moesia successively, was replaced in Upper Moesia by Claudius Fronto, and evidently came to Aquileia himself, presumably as *comes* of the emperors. He brought his personal doctor with him, which was a wise precaution; but the doctor himself died. Marcus had persuaded Galen to join the imperial staff at Aquileia, no doubt hoping that he could do something about the plague. Another expert present at imperial headquarters was an Egyptian priest, Harnouphis, presumably one of those whose aid had been invoked in the previous year, to combat the plague with religious rites. At Aquileia he dedicated an altar to Isis, and records his title, 'sacred scribe of Egypt'.[40]

Other measures were taken to reorganize the administration of northern Italy on a war footing. The experienced legal expert Arrius Antoninus, who had already had service in the north as one of the new *iuridici*, was made curator of Ariminum (Rimini). This normally straightforward post must have acquired enhanced importance now. The town was the roadhead of the *via Flaminia*, the main arterial route from Rome to the north-east. A procurator who had served as a regimental officer in the Parthian war, and in Britain with Calpurnius Agricola, among other appointments, Publius Helvius Pertinax, was given a procuratorship to deal with the *alimenta* along the *via Aemilia*, the main east-west route of northern Italy, an area he knew well, for his freedman father had settled in Liguria. Pertinax had two powerful patrons, Lollianus Avitus and Claudius Pompeianus. This minor post may have had an increased salary and additional duties on account of the war. Another procurator, Vehilius Gratus Julianus, was given a special task force.[41]

The emperors settled down to spend the winter of 168–9 at Aquileia, evidently planning to launch an offensive in the following spring. But the position was grim. The cold and the ever-present plague caused a large number of deaths, as Galen records. He recommended that the emperors should return to Rome. In midwinter they finally set off, at Lucius' insistence, having sent a letter to the senate announcing their intentions. After only two days' journey Lucius took a stroke in the carriage, near Altinum, where he died three days later. Marcus returned to Rome with the body.[42]

The biographer in the Augustan History has various sordid rumours to retail about the death of Lucius. It is said that Marcus had, in effect, murdered him, either by cutting a piece of pork with a knife smeared on one side with poison and handing the poisoned piece to Lucius, eating the other one himself; or by getting a doctor named Posidippus to perform a bloodletting at the wrong time. It was alleged, alternatively, that his mother-in-law Faustina had murdered him by sprinkling poison on some oysters, 'because he had betrayed to Lucilla the fact that they [Lucius and Faustina] had had sexual intimacy'. It was said, again, that Lucilla was responsible, because of her jealousy of the influence that Lucius' sister Ceionia Fabia had over him. Fabia had even begun a conspiracy with Lucius, it was said, which was revealed to Marcus by the freedman Agaclytus; and it was supposed to be then that Faustina did away with Lucius. Even Cassius Dio recorded the story that Lucius perished for plotting against Marcus.[43]

The story that Lucius was murdered is of the kind dear to the heart of the biographer and can hardly be credited, as the biographer himself admits. Marcus may, in the long run, have been relieved to be free of Lucius. In the short term it left him with a number of problems, and meant that his strategy had to be emended.

The character of Lucius as given in the Augustan History is clearly something of a travesty. His faults were emphasized, to highlight the good qualities of Marcus, possibly with some ulterior motive, such as an allusion to contemporary figures at the time of writing; but perhaps simply for literary effect. It was a stroke of luck for the biographer to have discovered the fascinating detail that Lucius' birthday was the same as that of Nero, and he made full play with this. If the account given by the biographer is ignored, a different picture emerges. The testimony of Marcus himself in the *Meditations* and of Fronto must be set aside too, perhaps, as biased in favour of Lucius. What is left – Dio, Aelius Aristides, Lucian, an anonymous panegyrist of Constantine, and the emperor Julian – gives little ground for the verdict that Lucius was a worthless libertine, or even a dull and indolent fellow. He quite clearly had faults, which Marcus may have attempted to cover up. But the atmosphere of the time would not have made it possible for him to be a second Nero.[44]

· 8 ·

THE NORTHERN WARS

THE FUNERAL CEREMONIES of Lucius had to be performed immediately Marcus returned to Rome. Marcus made generous provision for the support of Lucius' sisters, aunts, other relatives and freedmen. Lucius himself was deified under the name of Divus Verus. The worship of the new god in the Roman pantheon was conducted by the priesthood of Antoninus Pius, whose members (or some of them) now became *sodales Antoniniani Veriani*. This emphasized the unity of the family. It also saved trouble and expense. No separate temple is known to have been built for Divus Verus. The rites of commemoration in his honour were no doubt conducted in the temple of Antoninus and Faustina. Inscriptions record several men, who, already priests of Antoninus, became priests of Verus too. One was the friend of Marcus, Aufidius Victorinus. Another was M. Nonius Macrinus, who describes himself as 'chosen out of the closest friends'. He was from northern Italy, as were the Ceionii, Lucius' original family, and he had been consul in 154, the same year as the much younger Lucius. The following year, 170, Macrinus was to go to Asia as proconsul, but he was probably present at the deification ceremonies at Rome in early 169.[1]

Once the family business had been transacted, Marcus turned his attention to a financial crisis. A major cause of this was the plague, since it would have greatly diminished the governmental revenues from taxes and imperial estates. But the raising of new legions at the same time meant a vast increase in capital expenditure; and more troops still had to be raised, to plug the gaps revealed in the northern defences. The plague had also created vast gaps in the ranks of existing units. In the case of one legion, VII Claudia, stationed in Upper Moesia at Viminacium on the Danube, a record is preserved. At least twice the normal annual intake of recruits was necessary in 169. Only the number of those from this intake who survived the wars and the succeeding years, to be demobilized in 195, is known: but this is more than 240 men. Besides replenishing existing legions and recruiting new ones, fresh auxiliary units were enrolled. Slaves were accepted as volunteers for military service and received their freedom on enrolment. Gladiators were formed into special units. Bandits were conscripted as well, especially the wild hillmen of Dalmatia and Dardania – a country which has always bred ideal guerrilla fighters. Where possible, mercenaries were hired from Germanic peoples. The police forces maintained by the Greek cities of the east were brought under direct governmental orders.[2]

Not all these measures necessarily belong to the year 169. But the event of which they were the cause certainly took place in this year – the famous auction of imperial property in the Forum of Trajan. 'So that this [the recruitment] should not be a burden to the provinces he held an auction of palace property in the Forum of the Deified Trajan, as we have related, in which, apart from clothes and drinking cups and gold vases he also sold statues and paintings by great artists.' The biographer had already included a reference to this auction in a passage borrowed from another late writer, Eutropius, which gives more details and a less specific, but more acceptable cause. 'When he had drained the whole treasury for this war, and could not induce himself to impose any extraordinary taxes on the provincials, he held an auction in the Forum of the Deified Trajan of imperial furnishings, and sold gold, crystal and myrrhine drinking vessels, even royal vases, his wife's silk and gold-embroidered clothing, even certain jewels in fact, which he had discovered in some quantity in an inner sanctum of Hadrian's. Indeed, the sale went on for two months, and such a quantity of gold was acquired that after he had carried through the remainder of the Marcomannic war in accordance with his intentions, he gave permission to buyers to return their purchases and get their money back, if they wanted. He did not cause trouble to anyone, whether he returned what he had bought or not.'[3]

Marcus must have realized that new taxation would be extremely unpopular and not very productive. A gesture like the palace auction had more than a practical benefit – it demonstrated that the emperor was willing to make sacrifices. As a Stoic, Marcus cannot have found it any great hardship to get rid of some of the trappings of power. (Faustina may have resented losing some of her jewels and dresses.) This auction was not the only measure taken. C. Vettius Sabinianus, an experienced senator of modest origin (he had been promoted from the equestrian order), who had already commanded one of the two new legions, III Italica, was sent to Gaul 'to examine the accounts' in the three Gallic provinces under direct imperial rule. It sounds as if the council of the sixty Gallic states was in financial difficulties. To judge from events some eight or nine years later it did not prove possible to overcome them. Both the palace auction and the book-keeping exercise in Gaul had little more than symbolic significance. Another measure, however, had more serious and far-reaching effects: the imperial currency was debased. In other words, Marcus found it essential to strike more coinage without being able to increase the supply of bullion.[4]

Marcus was clearly determined to return to the front in 169. The precise chronology of events in this year, as in others in the war, is very obscure, but there seems little doubt that heavy fighting was going on, concentrated

1 Hadrian. Sestertius, 134–8 (HADRIANVS AVG COS III PP). *RIC* II Hadrian 845

2 Sabina. Sestertius, 128–36 (SABINA AVGVSTA HADRIANI AVG PP). *HCC* II Sabina 35

3–4 Aelius Caesar. Sestertius, 137: Obverse: L. AELIVS CAESAR, reverse: TR POT COS II – PANNONIA S C. The personification of Pannonia, turreted and draped, holding a *vexillum* (flag). *HCC* II Aelius Caesar 27

5 Antoninus Pius. Medallion, 145–61 (ANTONINVS AVG PIVS PP TR P; on the reverse, not illustrated, COS IIII). Gnecchi III Antoninus 136

6 Faustina I. Dupondius, 141 onwards (DIVA AVGVSTA FAVSTINA). *HCC* II Faustina I 78

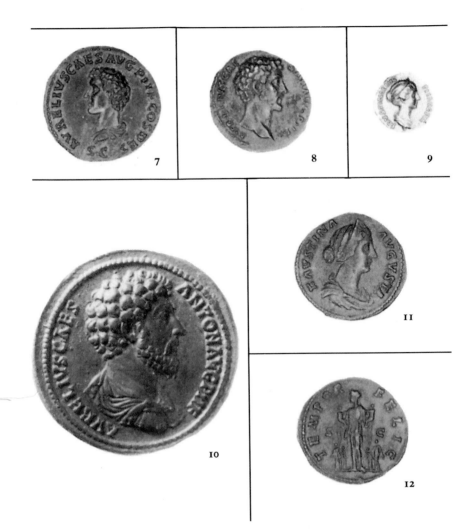

7 Marcus aged seventeen. Sestertius, 139 (AVRELIVS CAES AVG PII F COS DES S C). *HCC* II Marcus Caesar 13

8 Marcus aged twenty-six. Sestertius, 147 (AVRELIVS CAESAR AVG PII F; on the reverse, not illustrated, TR POT COS II). *HCC* II Marcus Caesar 48

9 Faustina II. Aureus, probably late 147 (FAVSTINAE AVG PII AVG FIL; the reverse, not illustrated here, has VENERI GENETRICI with an apple and child in swaddling clothes; the portrait of Faustina is Fittschen 34 ff., type 1) *HCC* Faustina II 6

10 Marcus aged thirty-seven. Medallion, 159 (AVRELIVS CAES ANTON AVG PII F; on the reverse, not illustrated, TR POT XIII COS II). Gnecchi II Marcus 44

11–12 Faustina after the birth of her second set of twins. Sestertius, 161–2: obverse: FAVSTINA AVGVSTA (Fittschen 34 ff., type 5), reverse: TEMPOR FELIC S C (Felicitas holds a twin in each arm; on each side two small girls). *HCC* II Faustina II 74

13, 14

16

17

18

15

13–14 Lucius Verus. Sestertius, 162: obverse: IMP CAES L AVREL VERVS AVG, reverse: CONCORD AVGVSTOR TR P II S C COS II. *HCC* II Lucius Verus 48

15 Lucilla. Medallion, perhaps c. 168 (LVCILLA AVGVSTA; the reverse, not illustrated here, shows Cybele riding on a lion). Gnecchi II Lucilla 9

16–17 Marcus aged forty-eight. Medallion, 170: obverse: M ANTONINVS AVG TR P XXIIII, reverse: PROFECTIO AVG COS III. Marcus is shown galloping, with another horseman on his left, preceded by a soldier with shield and *vexillum* (flag); another soldier with a standard follows behind. Gnecchi II Marcus 28

18 Marcus, aged fifty-six, Commodus aged sixteen. Medallion, 178 (M AVREL ANTONINVS AVG L AVREL COMMODVS AVG; the reverse, not illustrated, has PONT MAX TR POT XXXII COS III and shows Mars with spear and trophy). Similar to Gnecchi II Marcus & Commodus 5 – not illustrated by Gnecchi – except that he gives IMP after the first AVG on the obverse

19 Crispina, wife of Commodus.
Sestertius, probably c. 180–2 (CRISPINA
AVGVSTA; the reverse, not illustrated here,
has HILARITAS S C). *RIC* III Commodus
668

20 Commodus aged thirty. Medallion,
192 (L AELIVS AVRELIVS COMMODVS AVG
PIVS FELIX; the reverse, not illustrated
here, has HERCVLI ROMANO AVG P M TR P
XVIII COS VII PP). Gnecchi II Commodus 4

21 Pertinax. Sestertius, 193 (IMP CAES P
HELV PERTINAX AVG; the reverse, not
illustrated here, shows a distribution of
largesse with the legend TR P COS II S C
LIB AVG). *RIC* IV.1 Pertinax 19

22 Caracalla. Medallion, 213 (M AVREL
ANTONINVS PIVS AVG BRIT; the reverse, not
illustrated here, has the legend P M TR P
XVI IMP II COS III P P S C and shows the
Circus Maximus). Gnecchi III Caracalla 8

23 Bronze equestrian statue of Marcus Aurelius, Rome (see Appendix 5, p. 266).

24 Left-hand side of scene II of Aurelian column (see Appendix 5, p. 267). The personified river god, Danuvius, is shown extending his right arm, inviting the Roman army to cross into enemy territory. In the background, above the god's head, are buildings, probably at Carnuntum. The soldiers, at the rear of the column, are legionaries, wearing the *lorica segmentata* and plumed helmets, carrying lances and oval shields.

Petersen Tafel 9A (part); cf. Petersen 52 f.; Caprino 82 f.

25 The Lightning Miracle, scenes X–XI. A Roman fort in enemy territory is under siege; the barbarian siege tower is destroyed by a thunderbolt.
Petersen Tafel 17B; cf. Petersen 56 f.; Caprino 85 f.

26 The Rain Miracle, right-hand side of scene XVI. The mysterious Rain God, with water streaming from his arms and wings, smites Rome's enemies; barbarians and their horses lie dead, their weapons swept together in a heap by the deluge. On the left, Roman soldiers look on unharmed.

Petersen Tafel 23A; cf. Petersen 58 f.; Caprino 88 f.

27 Right-hand side of scene XXV. Barbarians, hands bound, are brought before
Marcus, cuirassed and carrying a lance; the figure behind him may be Pertinax. In the
background Roman soldiers accompany a mule-drawn wagon loaded with weapons
and barrels.
Petersen Tafel 33B; cf. Petersen 63; Caprino 92.

28 Scenes XXX–XXXI: a Roman camp. In the right foreground a sentry stands guard before a tent. Above him is Marcus making an agreement with a German chief; behind Marcus stand two of his advisers.
Petersen Tafel 39A (part);/Petersen 65; Caprino 94.

29 Scene XLIII: at the top a young German of high rank is about to be transfixed by a mounted Roman. This has been identified by Rossi as the killing of the chief of the Naristae, Valao, by Valerius Maximianus. In the foreground another high-ranking German vainly defends himself. At left a native house.
Petersen Tafel 50A (part); cf. Petersen 69; Caprino 97; L. Rossi, *Quad. tic.* 6 (1977) 223 ff.

30 Scene XLIX: a German chief begs for pardon, his cloak covering his outstretched arms, looking up at Marcus, who is accompanied by two men (that on the left could be Commodus, the other Pertinax); on the left are Roman guards and a German, who watch.

Petersen Tafel 56A (part); cf. Petersen 70; Caprino 98.

31 Scene LXVI. Marcus, on a cushioned seat, listens to a man standing at his side, perhaps a German chief. Two soldiers hold out severed heads, while a third drags a prisoner by his hair; other soldiers look on.
Petersen Tafel 75B; cf. Petersen 75; Caprino 103 f.

32 Scene LXXV. Marcus, wearing the general's cloak (*paludamentum*) and carrying a roll (*rotulus*) in his left hand, pours a libation on a flaming altar. His two companions could be Pompeianus (behind him) and Commodus (to his left). On the right, bareheaded guards look on, apparently speaking, to judge from their gestures and partly open mouths. At the back one soldier carries a flag (*vexillum*), decorated with ribbons for the ceremony, while others hold the horses.
Petersen Tafel 83B; cf. Petersen 77; Caprino 105 f.

33 Scene LXXVIII (right-hand side). The army crosses a pontoon bridge with Marcus at
its head; he is half turning as if to listen to the man behind him, perhaps Pompeianus.
The *vexilla* (flags) wave in the breeze; legionaries follow.
Petersen Tafel 88B; cf. Petersen 78; Caprino 106.

34 Scene LXXX. A sentry stands guard at the gate while Marcus and two men, perhaps Pertinax (left) and Pompeianus (right) confer.
Petersen Tafel 92A; cf. Petersen 80; Caprino 107.

35 Scene XCVIII. Marcus confers with two advisers, perhaps Pertinax (left) and Commodus (with lance). He holds a roll (*rotulus*) in his left hand and gestures with his right, as if to authorise the destruction of a native village by praetorian guardsmen wielding pickaxes.
Petersen Tafel 107A; cf. Petersen 86 f.; Caprino 112.

36 Scene CIV (right-hand side). Captured
barbarian women are led to a fort by
praetorian guardsmen; those at the top are
submissive, the two below are still distressed.
Petersen Tafel 113A; cf. Petersen 89; Caprino
113 f.

37 Scenes CX–CXI. Marcus and two
companions, perhaps Pertinax, left,
and Commodus, on the march with
legionaries and guardsmen.

38 The top of the Aurelian column, described from the bottom upwards: scenes XCVIII–XCIX: Marcus consults two of his staff; destruction of native village; and infantry attack.

CIV–CVI: barbarian women under escort; two high-ranking barbarians, fleeing on horseback, are caught by Roman infantry, two other barbarians lie dead; arrival of Marcus.

CXI: Marcus at the head of his troops, an adviser by his side; two ox-drawn wagons transport boats loaded with shields, helmets, cuirasses and lances – the wagons are moving over a bridge of some kind.

CXV: migration of barbarians escorted by Roman troops.

in the Hungarian plain, the re-entrant of barbarian territory crossed by the valley of the river Theiss, surrounded on the west by Lower Pannonia, on the south by Upper Moesia and on the east by Dacia. In the course of 169 – if not before – the governor of Dacia, Calpurnius Agricola, gave up his command hurriedly. Possibly he died in action, or from the plague. Claudius Fronto, governor of neighbouring Upper Moesia, was ordered to take over part of Agricola's province, namely Dacia Apulensis, the central sub-province. One of the other two Dacian sub-provinces, Malvensis, was now probably assigned to the command of its procurator, Macrinius Avitus, the man who had been decorated for his spectacular defeat of the Langobardi and Obii two years before, when he had been a cavalry commander. Another man evidently in Dacia as procurator at this time was the future emperor Pertinax, but his exact position is unknown. His conduct in Dacia won him unpopularity in some quarters, and his dismissal from office was brought about. Not long after this, although it is unknown whether it was in 169 or 170, Claudius Fronto took over the whole province of Dacia, the united 'Three Dacias'.[5]

There is thus every reason why Marcus should have been anxious to get back to the front. But he had first to consider the problem of what to do with his daughter Lucilla, the widow of Lucius. A young widow with the title Augusta (and with an infant daughter) was in need of protection. Not only that, however. She might be used by some unscrupulous and ambitious person for his own ends. Marcus solved the problem in a radical way. 'Although the period of mourning [for Lucius] had not expired, he gave his daughter in marriage to Claudius Pompeianus, the son of a Roman knight, of advanced age, a native of Antioch and of not sufficiently noble birth.' Faustina was opposed to the marriage – and so was Lucilla. The obligatory period of mourning of a Roman widow at this period is not certain. It is likely that it was twelve months, and this marriage took place by September or October at the latest, just before Marcus was setting out for the war. The biographer may exaggerate the age of Pompeianus somewhat (the word used is *grandaevo*), for he was still alive twenty-four years later. But he was a good deal older than Lucius, perhaps over fifty. To Lucilla, who was only nineteen, this may have seemed disagreeably elderly. What was worse was his origin. His father had not even been a senator, and he was a Syrian. In fact, the only other senator from Syria known at this period is the victorious general Avidius Cassius. But Cassius' father had been an intimate in court circles, and if not a senator, had been prefect of Egypt. Besides which, the family of Cassius was descended from kings of the east. There is no suggestion of anything romantic of this kind in the ancestry of Pompeianus. But Pompeianus had served in the north – he had been governor of Lower Pannonia in 167 – and Marcus had decided to make him his chief military adviser. His very origin was an advantage in the long view: it would not give him any dangerous ambitions, of the kind which men of nobler origin married to an Augusta might acquire. The marriage therefore took place.[6]

Immediately before his departure for the war, Marcus withdrew from the late summer heat of Rome to Praeneste (Palestrina). Here he suffered a family tragedy. His younger son, Annius Verus, had a tumour below the ear. He had an operation, but did not recover, and died, at the age of seven. Marcus' conduct showed that he was fully imbued with Stoic self-discipline. He mourned his son for five days only, during which time he gave some attention to public business. The games of Jupiter Best and Greatest were then in progress – which indicates a date in September. 'Because he did not want to have them interrupted by public mourning he merely ordered that statues of his son should be decreed, that a golden image of him should be carried in procession at the Circus games and that his name should be inserted in the hymn of the Salii.'[7] Now, it seems, only one son, Commodus, and four daughters were left. Another son had been born after Annius Verus, but his presumably brief existence is known only from two inscriptions, one at Ephesus, the other probably from Cyzicus, which give his name as Hadrianus. No fewer than four of Marcus' sons had been named after Antoninus Pius, and all had died young. Commodus and Annius Verus had survived longer. Faustina was to be pregnant again. Her last known child was born about the year 170. It was another daughter, who was given the names of Hadrian's empress, with the addition of Marcus' family name: Vibia Aurelia Sabina.[8] Perhaps the late appearance of the names of Hadrian and Sabina in the numerous progeny of Marcus and Faustina may indicate that Marcus' attitude to Hadrian's memory was becoming more favourable – yet it cannot be accident that he receives no mention in the first book of the *Meditations*.

After this private grief Marcus was perhaps grateful for the prospect of action. But it was almost autumn when he left Rome for the front, accompanied by a picked staff. The campaigning season was virtually over. Pompeianus certainly went with him, probably Lucilla too. Faustina was at the front with Marcus at a later stage, but it is probable that she remained in Rome now. Not only was she expecting a child. There may have been anxiety about the health of Commodus. Marcus had ordered Galen to accompany him, but, Galen recorded, 'I was able to persuade him, good-natured and charitable as he was, to leave me at Rome – for, indeed, he would soon return.' This optimistic forecast is surely useful confirmation that the major crisis of the war had not yet arrived – as it turned out, Marcus was to be away from Rome for over seven years. He instructed Commodus' *educator* or *tropheus*, Pitholaus, to send for Galen 'to attend his son, should he ever fall ill'.[9]

Other advisers as well as Pompeianus accompanied Marcus again, such as the veteran Pontius Laelianus and Dasumius Tullius Tuscus, both ex-governors of Upper Pannonia. The son of old Pompeius Falco, Q. Sosius

Priscus, apparently also came. Julius Verus may have been called on to give Marcus the benefit of his wide experience. He had not served on the Danube, but his family was from the Dalmatian hill-country and he must have had a good personal knowledge of the terrain and conditions in which the Roman armies would have to operate (during their deployment within the empire, that is, for an offensive campaign was planned, to carry Roman arms beyond the Danube).[10]

The location of Marcus' headquarters for the winter of 169–70 is unknown. A likely base would have been Sirmium on the river Save, a tributary of the Danube (modern Sremska Mitrovica in Yugoslavia), possibly even Singidunum (Belgrade), at the confluence of the Save and Danube. The main fighting was presumably in the area where Claudius Fronto was in command. Marcus' base a few years later, when there was further fighting in the same region, was Sirmium, so it is a strong possibility for the winter of 169–70.

The campaigning season of 170 was to open with a massive Roman offensive across the Danube. The creation of new legions had generally in the past been the prelude to conquest and annexation of new territory for the empire, and there seems little doubt that Marcus felt that the policy implied by the raising of two legions must be carried out. How he occupied himself in the winter of 169–70 is not recorded. Much of his time would be spent in the normal round of legal and administrative duties and decision-making, which would have followed him to the camp. In addition to this he would have had to supervise the maintenance of good health, discipline and training in the vast force under his personal command. It was his first full season in winter-quarters. It may well have been at this time that he began keeping the philosophical notebook which he left behind him at his death.

The events of 170 and the years of warfare that followed are nowhere fully recorded, and any account that can be pieced together must be in considerable part hypothetical.[11] Coins of the year 170 give some assistance. The *profectio* of Marcus from Rome, the official departure for the expedition in the previous autumn, is announced. Another issue depicts the emperor addressing troops and bears the legend *adlocutio*, the normal sign of the opening of a campaign. Other coins herald Roman victories, but must be regarded as aspirations of future success, at best as general statements of confidence arising out of some successes won by Claudius Fronto. It must be doubted whether the offensive directed by Marcus was successful. On the contrary, there is every suggestion that it met with disaster. The only clear statement of this is found in the satirist Lucian's attack on Alexander the false prophet of Abonutichus. This curious figure apparently provided the armies of Rome with an oracle, which forecast success if they began their offensive by casting two lions into the Danube. The advice was adopted. The beasts swam across to the enemy side and were dealt with by the barbarians without difficulty. They were taken for an unusual kind of dog or wolf and despatched with clubs. 'Immediately our side incurred its greatest blow, with the loss of almost 20,000 men. Then followed what happened with Aquileia, and the city's narrow escape from capture.' There is no need to believe Lucian's implication that the disastrous Roman defeat would not have occurred if it had not been for Alexander's oracle. But the conclusion that a Roman offensive met a disastrous setback, and was followed soon after by a barbarian invasion of Italy, is inescapable.[12]

The siege of Aquileia is also referred to by the late fourth-century historian Ammianus Marcellinus. Speaking of the Quadi in his own time, he goes on to recall their former strength, demonstrated by 'plundering raids once carried out with headlong speed, and Aquileia besieged by the same people, with the Marcomanni, and Opitergium wiped out, and many bloody deeds carried out in extremely swift military engagements, against which, when the Julian Alps had been breached, the earnest emperor Marcus could hardly make any resistance. . . .' The breaching of the Julian (i.e. Carnic) Alps by the invaders must therefore have occurred before Marcus could cut them off. The Marcomanni and Quadi with their allies, coming from Bohemia and Slovakia, had used the Amber Route. Antistius Adventus, if he was still in the Alpine zone as commander of the *praetentura*, failed to stem their advance. He may have moved elsewhere by now, and as Marcus had been attempting to launch an offensive into the barbarian lands across the Danube, northern Italy may no longer have been strongly garrisoned. The invaders had at any rate been able to slip through a gap, while the main Roman forces were facing in the opposite direction. Marcus must have made a desperate effort to get up the valley of the Save, but the invaders managed to enter Italy.[13]

The province of Upper Moesia was also in trouble at this time, for Claudius Fronto, governor of the Three Dacias, was obliged before the end of 170 to take Upper Moesia under his command again, combining the governorship of both provinces. This can only mean that the governor of Upper Moesia was put out of action suddenly, with no time to replace him in the normal way. Before the end of 170 Claudius Fronto himself was dead. His monument, which provides much of the information about the vicissitudes of the provinces under his command, recorded that 'after several successful battles against Germans and Jazyges, he fell, fighting for the republic to the last'. His successor in the Dacias was Sextus Cornelius Clemens. To Upper Moesia came the governor of neighbouring Thrace, Caerellius.[14]

Whether or not Italy was invaded in 170, it is clear that in this year barbarian forces burst into the Balkans, overrunning the frontier provinces, Thrace and Macedonia and even reaching Achaea, coming as far as Eleusis, where they destroyed the shrine of the Mysteries. Athens was lucky to escape. The tribe named as entering Macedonia and Achaea is the Costoboci, a people of uncertain origin who lived to the north or north-east of Dacia. Once the frontiers had been breached they met with virtually no opposition. The cities – which Aristides had depicted in such glowing terms – were unwalled and ungarrisoned. In one or two places vigorous resistance was hurriedly organized by local levies, but the general picture was one of pillage, burning and slaughter. Claudius Fronto had tried in vain to stem the onslaught which came on after the disastrous failure of Marcus' offensive. Marcus had been caught in the middle, somewhere on the middle Danube, while two tides of invasion flowed into the Empire.[15]

To meet the crisis Pompeianus was chosen to deal with the invasion of Italy and the Alpine region. He made Pertinax one of his principal assistants, thus vindicating his recently tarnished reputation. Another procurator, Vehilius Gratus Julianus, was sent with a task force to clear Macedonia and Achaea. Valerius Maximianus was given a task force composed of marines from various fleets, with strong cavalry support, to conduct supplies down the Danube to the Pannonian armies, cut off from their supplies to the south.[16]

The raid of the Costoboci was not so serious as the invasion of Italy. The invaders of Greece were too far from their homeland, in difficult country, and by the time they reached Attica much of their force must have been spent. The dislodgement of the Marcomanni and Quadi and their allies from northern Italy and the Alpine provinces was more difficult, however, and must have been a protracted task. Communications between Marcus' headquarters and Rome by the land route would have been extremely tenuous for some months, and it is therefore not surprising to find evidence that in 170 the port of Salona, chief city of the province of Dalmatia, was fortified by detachments of the new Second and Third legions. It was essential to maintain the alternative sea-link with Italy: the crossing from Split to Ancona is a short one.[17]

Many of the towns in the empire, uneasy after what had happened, must have begun to want walls for themselves. Many towns and forts had been destroyed. During this period Marcus found it necessary to lay down that towns which wanted walls should seek the emperor's permission. This would discourage panic measures in areas where they were unnecessary. But in the danger zone steps were taken, as at Philippopolis (Plovdiv) in Thrace.[18]

Marcus probably spent the winter of 170–1 moving from place to place. But in 171 he moved his headquarters to Carnuntum on the Danube. He had clearly realized that the Marcomanni and their allies were the chief enemy. In the course of 171 the invaders were trapped at the river crossing as they attempted to make their escape, laden with booty. Their force was destroyed, and the booty was returned to the provincials. Marcus was hailed by the troops as Imperator for the sixth time. This salutation is

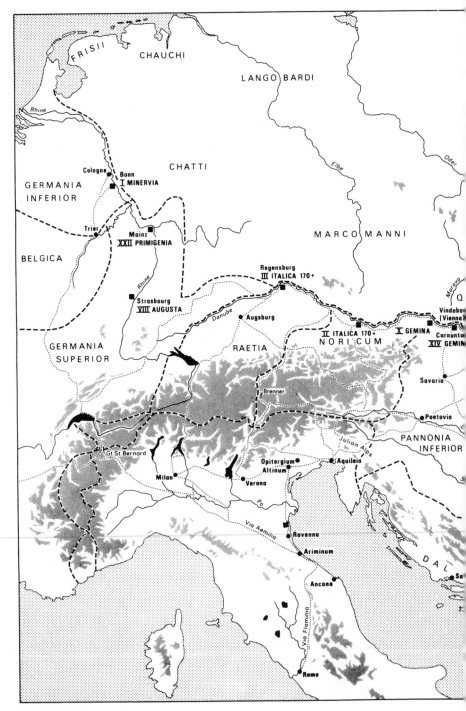

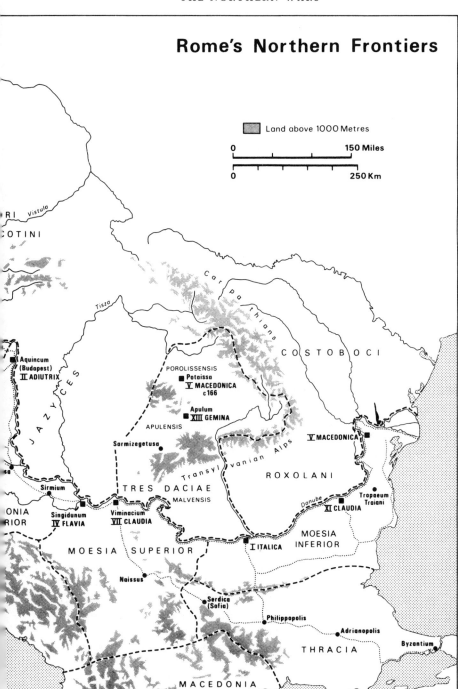

Rome's Northern Frontiers

Land above 1000 Metres

0   150 Miles

0   250 Km

Vistula

RI

COTINI

Carpathians

Tisza

COSTOBOCI

Aquincum
(Budapest)
II ADIUTRIX

J A Z Y C E S

POROLISSENSIS
Potaissa
V MACEDONICA
c 166

Apulum
XIII GEMINA

APULENSIS

Sarmizegetusa

V MACEDONICA

Transylvanian Alps

ROXOLANI

sa

Sirmium

TRES DACIAE

MALVENSIS

Danube

Tropaeum
Traiani

ONIA
RIOR

Singidunum
IV FLAVIA

Viminacium
VII CLAUDIA

XI CLAUDIA

MOESIA
INFERIOR

M O E S I A   S U P E R I O R

I ITALICA

Naissus

Serdica
(Sofia)

Philippopolis

Adrianopolis

Byzantium

T H R A C I A

M A C E D O N I A

167

recorded on the coinage in late 171, together with a 'German victory', i.e., over the Germans, but for most of the year the coinage bore no claims of Roman victory. On the contrary, appeals were made to the loyalty and unity of the armies, fighting under extremely difficult conditions. It is possible that the expulsion of the invaders from the Pannonian provinces occurred on 11 June. At any rate, on this day in the following year, both at Carnuntum and at Aquincum (Budapest), the principal cities of the Upper and Lower Pannonian provinces, dedications were made to Jupiter – and similar dedications continued to be made on 11 June at Carnuntum for over a century. A preferable interpretation might be that on 11 June 171, the barbarians were still in north-eastern Italy, cutting off Pannonia, and that the provincials made vows to Jupiter on that day, that they would make annual sacrifice to him if he saved them from this danger.[19]

This reconstruction of events is not the only possible one. The invasion of the Costoboci reaching far into Greece clearly occurred in 170, as did the death of Claudius Fronto. What is not certain is how long after the failure of Marcus' offensive the Marcomanni invaded Italy. It may not have been until early in 171. But the fact that Marcus did not record any victory on the coinage until late in 171 suggests that the operations of Pompeianus and Pertinax in clearing the invaded areas cannot have been completed until then.

Italy had not been invaded by a foreign enemy for hundreds of years. Nevertheless Marcus regarded it as essential to press on with his plans for an offensive, an offensive which was to be not merely a punitive campaign, but a campaign of conquest. Meanwhile, in 171 there was disquieting news from another part of the empire. The Iberian peninsula had been invaded by Moorish rebels who had crossed the Straits of Gibraltar. The area which met the full brunt of their assault was Baetica, one of the senatorial provinces, governed by a proconsul, and with no garrison to defend it. Marcus despatched his friend Aufidius Victorinus to Spain, to govern both Tarraconensis and Baetica simultaneously. This deprived the senate of a province, and to compensate it, Marcus assigned Sardinia to its sphere. A young man who had been going out to Baetica to serve as quaestor, after a term as quaestor in Rome went to Sardinia instead. The double service was another sign of the shortage of personnel. This was L. Septimius Severus, the future emperor. Aufidius Victorinus had only one legion, VII Gemina based at Legio (León) in the north of the peninsula. To strengthen his army, Marcus sent the procurator Gratus Julianus there from Greece. He must by now have completed his task of clearing out the remnants of the Costoboci, and his men would have become highly experienced in this kind of warfare.[20]

Fragments of Cassius Dio's account of the war have been preserved. One describes briefly the invasion of Italy, and its repulse by Pompeianus and Pertinax. It adds an interesting comment: 'Among the barbarian dead were found even the bodies of women wearing armour.' This indicates that the enemy peoples were on the move in a serious way. If they had their womenfolk with them, they wanted land. This detail, with its implications, is confirmed by the biographer of Marcus, who recorded that before Marcus and Lucius set off together (168) the Marcomanni and Victuali had been demanding to be allowed to enter the empire. In a later passage, describing the great invasion, the biographer says that 'all the peoples from the frontier of Illyricum right as far as Gaul had conspired together'. This common policy had indeed already been seen in 166 or 167 when ten tribes chose Ballomarius the king of the Marcomanni as their spokesman in negotiations with Iallius Bassus. Taken together, with the background of archaeological evidence to illuminate them further, these items of evidence help to explain why Marcus thought it necessary to depart in a radical way from the policy of his predecessors over the German question. He was faced with quite new problems.[21]

After the first victory he had won in person, although he accepted the salutation as Imperator, he refused the troops' request for a donative, 'saying that whatever they got from him over and above their regular pay would be wrung from the blood of their parents and families; as for the fate of the sovereignty, God alone could determine that. So temperately and firmly did he rule that even when engaged in so many and so great wars, he never did anything unworthy by way of flattery or as the result of fear.' The biographer gives a slightly less dramatic picture of Marcus as commander-in-chief: 'Always, before he did anything, in both military and civil affairs, he consulted with the foremost men. This was an especially frequent saying of his: "It is fairer that I should give way to the advice of so many friends – and such friends – than that so many of these friends should follow my advice, the advice of one man." Certainly, because he seemed hard, from his devotion to philosophy, both in his military discipline and in his whole way of life, he was bitterly criticized. But he answered all his critics in speeches or pamphlets.' The biographer adds, however, that because many noblemen had lost their lives in the war, Marcus' friends urged him to abandon it and return to Rome. But this advice he disregarded.[22]

In late 171 a period of intense diplomatic activity began. Marcus, probably at Carnuntum, met envoys from the barbarian peoples. He was aiming to detach some of the members of the barbarian 'conspiracy', so that the most dangerous members of it could be isolated. In this he was partly successful. Shortened extracts of some of Dio's account of the negotiations have survived. 'Marcus Antoninus remained in Pannonia to receive the barbarian embassies. For many of them came to him at that time, some of which, led by a twelve-year-old boy named Battarius, promised alliance. They were given money, and succeeded in restraining Tarbus, chieftain of a neighbouring people, who had entered Dacia, demanding money and threatening war if he was not given it. Others asked for peace, like the Quadi. It was granted them, first, in the hope that they could be detached from the Marcomanni, second, because they gave Marcus many horses and cattle, and promised to surrender all deserters and captives as well – 13,000 at first, the rest later. But they were not given the right to attend markets, because it was feared that the Jazyges and the Marcomanni, whom they had sworn not to receive and not to allow to pass through their country, would mingle with them, pretend to be Quadi themselves, spy out Roman positions and buy provisions. As well as those that came to Marcus, many others sent envoys, some by tribes and some by nations, offering to surrender. Some of them were sent on campaigns elsewhere, as also were the captives and deserters who were fit; others received land in Dacia, Pannonia, Moesia, Germany and Italy itself. Some of the ones settled at Ravenna revolted and even dared to try seizing the city. For this reason Marcus did not bring any barbarians into Italy again, but even banished those who had come there previously.'23

Some of the statements about land settlement in this passage are anticipatory, but it is probable that some barbarian settlers were accepted at this time. Marcus has been severely criticized for this step. It is regarded as the beginning of the barbarization of the empire. But if the statement of Orosius concerning the depopulation of the countryside can be accepted, there was some justification. It could even be argued that depopulation of the countryside, especially in Italy, had been beginning before the plague, to an alarming extent. Besides this, if the settlers were from peoples which Marcus intended to incorporate within the empire, the criticism has less point in any case. They were to be romanized sooner or later, by one means or another.

Diplomatic activity also went on in Dacia, conducted by Claudius Fronto's successor as governor, Cornelius Clemens. Another extract from Dio describes this. 'The Astingi, led by their chieftains Raüs and Raptus, entered Dacia with their entire households, in the hope of obtaining money and land in return for their alliance. They failed to obtain what they asked for, and left their wives and children under the protection of Clemens, while they went to take possession by force of the land of the Costoboci. But when they had defeated that people, they continued to inflict damage on Dacia. The Lacringes were afraid that Clemens, through fear of the Astingi, might bring them into the land which they inhabited. So they attacked them while they were off their guard and achieved a decisive victory. As a result, the Astingi undertook no further military action against the Romans, but in response to urgent appeals to Marcus obtained money and the promise of land in return for any damage they might inflict on his enemies.' The Astingi and Lacringes were both branches of the people whose name was later to become notorious – the Vandals. Their exact location at this time is unknown. The choice of the lands of the

Costoboci by the Astingi suggests that this attack came after that people had been weakened by their great raid of 170. The acquisition of these two tribes as allies was valuable to Rome, enabling Marcus to concentrate with more confidence on the subjugation of Bohemia.

'This tribe [the Astingi] did in fact fulfil some of its promises,' the extract from Dio continues, 'whereas the Cotini, although they made similar offers, on deceiving Tarrutenius Paternus, the secretary in charge of the emperor's Latin correspondence, with the pretence that they were willing to make a campaign with him against the Marcomanni, not only failed to do this, but handled Paternus very roughly, thereby bringing about their own destruction later.' The Cotini were neighbours of the Marcomanni and Quadi, a people with strong Celtic elements. Their adhesion to Rome would have provided a valuable base. Besides this, they controlled iron mines which may have been an important source of raw materials for weapon making among the barbarian peoples of the region. Taruttienus [as the name is more correctly rendered] Paternus was later to play an important military role as praetorian prefect at the end of the reign. He was also a jurist, who wrote on military law. The choice of a man of this type for the vital post of *ab epistulis Latinis* shows that Marcus still preferred to fill this post with military men rather than with the literary figures who had occupied it in the past. In spite of the failure with the Cotini, the neutralization of the Quadi meant that Rome had knocked out one of the three major enemies, and had driven a wedge between the other two.[24]

In 172 the offensive into enemy territory, which had been so many times postponed by the turn of events, at last took place. The coins of the year show another *adlocutio* scene, marking the opening of a new campaign; and a coin bearing the inscription *virtus Aug.* – 'the valour of the emperor' – depicts Roman troops crossing a bridge. This is the scene shown at the beginning of the column of Marcus Aurelius in the Piazza Colonna at Rome. The benign personified figure of Father Danube looks on while a Roman army marches across a bridge of boats. The fighting was not all in Rome's favour. It may have been in this campaign (unless it occurred in the fighting on Roman soil in the previous year) that 'the Marcomanni were successful in a certain battle and killed Marcus [Macrinius] Vindex the [praetorian] prefect.' Marcus found it difficult to replace Vindex. He would have liked to appoint Pertinax, but Pertinax had only recently been promoted to the senate for his outstanding achievements with Claudius Pompeianus, and was now commanding the legion I Adiutrix. The prefect of Egypt, Calvisius Statianus, who would have been a normal selection in other circumstances, was too far away and in any case had problems of his own to face. Marcus may have left the post vacant and have continued with one prefect only, the tough if somewhat illiterate Bassaeus Rufus.[25]

Two extraordinary episodes seem to belong to 172. Marcus is said to have 'summoned a thunderbolt from heaven by his prayers and destroyed an enemy military engine'. This episode is depicted in an early scene on the Column; and a remarkable series of coins of 172 shows Marcus, in full general's uniform, being crowned by the goddess Victory – and carrying, in addition to his lance, the thunderbolt of Jupiter, which seems a clear allusion to the occurrence. It is not hard to reconstruct what happened. Marcus may indeed have prayed during a thunderstorm, for lightning to strike the enemy.[26] The other story is even more remarkable and receives full attention from a variety of sources. A detailed account of a most unusual battle is given in an extract from Dio, which his epitomator, the Byzantine monk Xiphilinus, felt gave an inadequate record, and therefore supplemented with observations of his own. Various chroniclers also give a few details. This is the famous battle of the Rain Miracle. 'A great war against the people called Quadi also fell to his lot, and it was his good fortune to win an unexpected victory – or rather, victory was granted by God. For when the Romans were in danger in the course of the battle, the divine power saved them in a most unexpected way. The Quadi had surrounded them in a place favourable to themselves, and the Romans were fighting bravely with their shields fitted close together. The barbarians held back from fighting, expecting that they would easily overcome the Romans, who were worn out by the heat and by thirst. They hemmed them in on all sides, so that they could not obtain water from anywhere. For they themselves were far superior in numbers. Consequently the Romans were in a bad way, from their exhaustion, wounds, the sun and their thirst, and could neither fight nor retreat, but were standing in line and in their positions, scorched by the heat, when suddenly a great many clouds rolled up and a great downpour burst over them – not without the assistance of the gods. In fact, there is even a story to the effect that Arnouphis, an Egyptian magician, who was a companion of Marcus, had invoked by enchantments various deities, in particular Hermes Aërios [Mercury, the god of the air], and by these means brought on the rain. . . . When the rain poured down, at first all turned their faces upwards and let the rain fall into their mouths, then some held out their shields and helmets to catch it, and not only took great gulps of it themselves, but gave it to their horses to drink. When the barbarians charged them, they drank and fought at the same time. Some, already wounded, actually gulped down the blood that poured into their helmets, along with the water. In fact, most of them were so eager to drink that they would have suffered seriously from the enemy's onslaught, if a violent hailstorm and several thunderbolts had not fallen on the enemy. . . .' Dio continues with a purple passage describing the effect of this utter confusion in the barbarian ranks.

Xiphilinus, as mentioned, found Dio's account unsatisfactory. The reason for this was that within a very few years of the incident a firm tradition had been established that it had been the prayers of Christian soldiers of the Twelfth legion that had brought the rain, not the efforts of the Egyptian priest Harnouphis. Xiphilinus gives the Christian version. Unfortunately, one of the items of evidence which he cites is valueless. The Twelfth legion had the name 'Fulminata', 'bearer of thunder', probably because its emblem was the thunderbolts of Jupiter. The legion had been called this for well over a century, but Xiphilinus and other Christian writers allege that it was awarded the title 'Thundering' because of this battle. That is false. XII Fulminata was in fact a legion of Cappadocia, and it is not absolutely certain that it was fighting in the northern wars (although this is quite possible). Besides this, eastern legionaries were likelier than any others to have been Christian at this time. There may therefore have been some Christian soldiers involved in the battle.[27]

Unfortunately there is no reason to suppose that they were given any credit for the victory by Marcus, as is also alleged. On the contrary, coins of the year 173 portray the god Hermes, and it seems likely that Marcus built a temple to this god in gratitude. A medallion shows Jupiter in a four-horse chariot destroying barbarians with his thunderbolts. On the Aurelian column the event is depicted in graphic detail. The weary Romans are exhibited in marching order. A legionary points at the sky and immediately to the right rain is seen falling. One man waters his horse, another drinks, some hold up their shields to collect the water. The downpour is personified as a frightening and semi-human figure, with gloomy face and long beard, whose hair melts into descending streams of water. The rain-spirit rushes forward over men and animals, while beneath him appears a prospect of dead barbarians and stricken horses. If the personification had a name, it can only have been the name of one of the gods whose aid was acknowledged on the coinage – presumably Hermes Aërios, although the grim and frightening figure is very unlike the normal youthful winged-footed Hermes or Mercury. The god described by Dio as 'Hermes Aërios' is apparently a native Egyptian deity, Thoth-Shou, whose aid was invoked by the exotic Egyptian priest Harnouphis. There was, indeed, a rival non-Christian claimant for the credit of obtaining divine assistance, the 'Chaldaean' Julianus. In any case, Marcus recognized the assistance of pagan gods only.[28]

Neither the column nor the account of Dio-Xiphilinus indicate that Marcus himself was present at the Rain Miracle. In fact, if the remark of the fifth-century Christian historian Orosius, that there was only a small force involved on the Roman side, could be accepted, it may have been a minor action not involving the main army. The *Chronicle* of Eusebius asserts that the Roman commander was Pertinax, which it is tempting to believe – it is difficult to see how such a detail could have been invented. Further, the forged Christian letter (included in the manuscript of Justin's *Apology*) in which Marcus is supposed to have attributed the Miracle, in a letter to Senate and People, to the prayers of Christian soldiers, locates the event 'in Cotinum', in other words, among the Cotini. This detail, likewise, suggests access to an authentic account. The Cotini, after their treatment of the *ab epistulis* Paternus, would have been due for punitive action. However, the mention of the Quadi in Dio-Xiphilinus cannot be dismissed as a mistake. The conclusion must be that, after the defeat of the Marcomanni, Marcus turned at once against the Quadi – who, as another passage in Dio records, 'had received in their own land any Marcomannian fugitives who were hard pressed while that tribe was still at war with Rome'.[29]

By the end of the campaigning season of 172, the victory over the Marcomanni led to Marcus being given the title 'Germanicus', 'conqueror of the Germans', presumably at the request of the senate. Commodus too received the title, and the biography of him in the Augustan History supplies the date, 15 October. The coins of 172 did not carry the title, although they continued to record the sixth imperatorial salutation and now began to proclaim not merely 'German victory' but 'subjugation of Germany', *Germania subacta*. They also advertised the clemency of the emperor in his treatment of the enemy: a female figure, carrying a hexagonal shield, the personification of Germania, is portrayed kneeling before Marcus. A treaty was granted to the Marcomanni, imposing severe restrictions on them.[30]

The award of the title Germanicus to Commodus had always suggested that he was by this time with Marcus, and the dedication from the precinct of Jupiter outside Carnuntum made on 11 June 172 confirms that he and Marcus were both residing there on that day. An undated dedication at Lilybaeum in Sicily is a prayer for the safety and return of Marcus 'and of his children'. Marcus is not given the title Germanicus, which makes it probable that the dedication was made no later than 172. The children mentioned may have been just Commodus and Lucilla, but it is possible that the other married daughter, Annia Faustina, was also there.[31]

The year 172 saw problems in the east. In Egypt there was rebellion, recorded in an extract from Cassius Dio. 'The so-called Bucoli [i.e., 'herdsmen', the population of a district of the Delta of the Nile], under the leadership of a certain priest, Isidorus, began a disturbance in Egypt, and caused the rest of the Egyptians to revolt. First, dressed in women's clothes, they had deceived the Roman centurion into believing that they were going to give him gold as ransom for their husbands, and then struck him down when he came near. They sacrificed his companion too, and after swearing an oath over his intestines, ate them. Isidorus surpassed all his followers in bravery. Then, having defeated the Romans in a pitched battle, they nearly captured Alexandria – and would have succeeded if Cassius had not been sent against them from Syria. His strategy was to destroy their mutual harmony and to split them up, for because of their desperation as well as their numbers he had not dared to attack them while they were united. Thus, when they began quarrelling, he defeated them.' Cassius' entry into Egypt required special authority, for as a senator he was automatically excluded from Egypt by a regulation of Augustus. He received special powers over all the eastern provinces, placing him on a footing similar to that which Lucius had held during the Parthian war.[32]

There was also trouble in Armenia. Sohaemus, the pro-Roman king installed by Lucius in 164, was expelled by elements favourable to Parthia. He was restored by P. Martius Verus, governor of Cappadocia. The man responsible for the trouble may have been a certain Tiridates who, according to Dio, 'stirred up trouble in Armenia and killed the king of the Heniochi, and then thrust his sword in Verus' [i.e. Martius Verus'] face, when he rebuked him for it'. Tiridates' punishment was not severe: 'Marcus did not put him to death, but only sent him to Britain' – which makes it sound as if Britain was then the Roman equivalent of Siberia. However, it was chosen merely as a conveniently distant place from Armenia. Dio took the opportunity, when recording the restoration of Sohaemus, to give a character sketch of Martius Verus: 'Martius not only had the ability to overcome his opponents by force of arms, to be a move ahead of them by his speed or to outwit them by surprise action, which is the true strength of a general, he could also persuade them by plausible promises, conciliate them by magnificent gifts and tempt them by bright hopes. There was a grace about all his actions and words, a charm that soothed the annoyance and anger of everyone, while raising their hopes even more. He knew the proper time for flattery and presents and for entertaining people with his hospitality. Since in addition to these talents he showed perseverance in his undertakings and energy coupled with speed in his dealings with the enemy, he made it clear to the barbarians that it was worth more to aim for his friendship than his enmity.' When he arrived in Armenia, Martius Verus found that the garrison of Roman soldiers left in the New City (the new capital which replaced Artaxata) were in a mutinous state, and he took steps to remedy the situation. If some of the eastern legions, or detachments drawn from them, were now serving in the Danubian war – perhaps including men from XII Fulminata – it can easily be understood that the Parthians and those in Armenia who favoured her may have hoped to undermine the settlement of 166.[33]

Marcus may well have hoped to return to Rome in 173, having defeated the Marcomanni. In fact, his return is even announced on a medallion struck in that year. His sons-in-law, Claudius Severus and Claudius Pompeianus, were the consuls for the year, both for the second time, and he may have hoped to be present in Rome to lend his prestige to their tenure of the *fasces*. But as it turned out, even Pompeianus is unlikely to have been able to return. The war with the Quadi proved to be difficult, and other tribes were involved. Rome won striking success against the Naristae, a smaller neighbour and ally of the Quadi, when the Pannonian cavalry commander Valerius Maximianus slew with his own hands their chieftain Valao. The lengthy inscription set up in honour of Maximianus ten years later, by the councillors of Diana Veteranorum in Numidia, supplies the information. Maximianus was 'publicly praised by the emperor Antoninus Augustus and presented with a horse, *phalerae*, and arms'. This native of Poetovio (modern Ptuj in Yugloslavia) in the province of Upper Pannonia had already given, and was to give more, vital service in this war against an enemy that directly threatened his own homeland. In addition to this decoration, he was promoted to command the crack double strength cavalry regiment (*ala milliaria* – a unit of which there were at most twelve in the entire army, less than half as many as there were legions), the *ala I Ulpia contariorum* stationed at Arrabona (modern Györ in Hungary). It had done good service in the war from the very start, when under Macrinius Avitus is repulsed the invasion of the Langobardi and Obii in 166 or 167.[34]

The war that Marcus and the Roman armies were fighting was a desultory affair, as the visual record of it on the Aurelian column illustrates. Apart from the Rain Miracle episode, there were scarcely any pitched battles, but a succession of minor engagements against an enemy that had to be fought section by section. As a result, new methods of deploying the troops had to be worked out. Instead of fighting as a legion, the legionary troops were split up into special detachments (*vexillationes*). The chance record of inscriptions has preserved details of some of the special commands necessary in the war and of careers of outstanding generals. Vettius Sabinianus was now legate of XIV Gemina, but his real task was to be acting governor of Upper Pannonia while the governor was fighting beyond the frontiers with Marcus. A young senator named Julius Pompilius Piso was given a task force composed of the First Italica and Fourth Flavia, legions of Lower and Upper Moesia respectively, with their auxiliary units. He was given the powers of a governor. This may have been to administer newly conquered territory. But it is not possible to date this most unusual command very precisely.[35]

The year 173 was the third year in succession that Marcus had spent at Carnuntum. The second book of his *Meditations* is headed 'at Carnuntum'. The third is headed 'On the Granua'. The Granua, the modern Hrón or Gran, is one of the northern tributaries of the Danube, and flows through Slovakia, the confluence being a little to the west of the great southward bend of the Danube, just within the confines of Upper Pannonia. If Marcus came near the source of the Hrón, he would have been close to the headwaters of the northward-flowing River Vistula – which he might even have seen, for the Vistula rises in the lands of the Cotini. The River Hrón flows near the boundaries of the Quadi and the Sarmatian Jazyges, the fierce horsemen of the Hungarian Plain. These were to be Marcus' next antagonists.

The Quadi had had the same terms imposed upon them as the Marcomanni (full details are not recorded). In the course of 174 they broke their word again, by giving assistance to the Jazyges. In addition to this, they were not returning all the captives and deserters as promised – 'only a few,' according to Dio – those that they could neither sell nor usefully employ for any work. Or, if they ever did hand over any of those who were in good physical condition, they kept back relatives of these men, 'so that the men handed over would desert again in order to rejoin them'. This situation in itself argues a severe lowering of morale on the Roman side, and the mention of deserters goes a long way to explain why coins were issued in 171 appealing to the loyalty and harmony of the armies. It had always been a principle of Roman law that a captive regained his legal status as a Roman citizen when he returned from captivity. But this meant that there was no obligation on him to repay the ransom money. It seems to have been the case that, as a result of the enormous numbers who fell into enemy hands by one means or another at the beginning of the 170s, Marcus enacted that ransomed captives did not regain their rights until they had repaid their ransom money. This somewhat inhumane enactment was probably designed to encourage private individuals to undertake the ransoming of captives as a business proposition, as the only means of getting substantial numbers back.

Another development caused further anxiety. The Quadi expelled their pro-Roman ruler Furtius and the hostile Ariogaesus took power. Marcus refused to recognize Ariogaesus – in fact set a price on his head, alive or dead – and rejected the conciliatory offer of the surrender of 50,000 captives in return for renewal of the peace treaty. (All Roman treaties were made with individuals, and the Quadic treaty would require renewal on the change of ruler.) However, when Ariogaesus was captured, Marcus treated him mildly. His punishment was exile in Alexandria. On the same principle that had been followed when Britain was made the place of exile of an Armenian dissident, somewhere as far away as possible was selected. Ariogaesus' subsequent fate is not recorded.[36]

For his campaign against the Jazyges Marcus selected Sirmium on the River Save as his base. Virtually nothing is recorded of this second, 'Sarmatian' phase of the war. Cassius Dio does report a winter battle on the frozen Danube, which he regarded as something of a military curiosity. The Jazyges had obviously attempted a surprise attack. The Romans reacted vigorously and pursued them back over the ice. The enemy expected that the Romans could easily be outmanoeuvred in a battle under such conditions, as their own horses had been trained to go well even on ice. 'The Romans on observing this were not worried, but formed together in a compact body, facing the enemy all at once. Most of them laid down their shields and supported one foot on them, so that they would not slip.' With their superior discipline they were able to get the better of the Jazyges. This battle belongs to the winter of 173–4 or 174–5.[37]

At some stage in the fighting of 174 the Jazyges sued for peace, but it was refused them. After his experience with the Quadi, Marcus was unwilling to take chances. It would seem, in fact, that the Jazygian envoys had represented only part of their people, the supporters of one of their kings, Banadaspus, who was imprisoned by his own people for making overtures to Marcus. It may have been in 174 that the Marcomanni appealed for a relaxation of the terms imposed on them. 'In view of the fact that they had fulfilled all the conditions that had been imposed on them, even if grudgingly and unwillingly, Marcus restored to them half of the neutral zone along their borders, allowing them to settle up to five miles from the Danube; and he fixed places and days for mutual trade (which had not been settled before), and exchanged hostages with them.'[38]

During 174 Marcus accepted a seventh imperatorial acclamation, evidently for the submission of the Quadi, and at the same time Faustina was given the title 'Mother of the Camp', *mater castrorum*, which incidentally indicates that she had by this time joined Marcus in the north. Dio records two incidents from the war – he himself was doubtful about their historical importance, but they do convey something of the atmosphere. 'A boy who had been taken prisoner was questioned by Marcus. "I cannot give you a reply," he said, "because of the cold. So if you want to gain any information give orders for a coat to be given me, if you have one." A soldier who was on watch one night on the Danube heard a shout from his fellow soldiers who were prisoners on the other side. He at once swam across just as he was, set them free, and came back.'[39]

The column of Marcus provides the best commentary on the wars. It may never be possible to use it as a guide to the exact chronology of events, but it portrays the actuality of the fighting in a far more vivid way than any written description ever could. There is a change of atmosphere from the aggressive martial confidence of the column of Trajan, which extolled the disciplined achievement of the armies of Rome. There is a note of pathos that is only too clear, when the burning and destruction of enemy villages, the execution of rebels and the remorseless onset of battle are displayed, carved on the winding panels. The only unity that it possesses is the ever present figure of Marcus, generally accompanied by a faithful counsellor who is surely Claudius Pompeianus. The war was a grim and sordid necessity. Marcus knew it, and the artists of the column clearly felt it.[40]

Marcus carried on his judicial business as uninterruptedly as possible during the war. 'Whenever he had spare time from the war he held court.' Dio states, 'he used to order that an abundant supply of water should be measured out for the speakers on the water-clocks used in court, and he went into the preliminary inquiries and examinations at great length, so as to administer strict justice from every point of view. As a result, he often spent as many as eleven or twelve days trying the same case, in spite of holding sessions at night sometimes. For he was hard-working and applied himself with detailed care to all the responsibilities of his office. He never said, wrote or did anything as if it were an unimportant matter, but would sometimes spend whole days over some tiny point of detail, thinking that it was right that an emperor should never do anything hurriedly. For he believed that, if he should overlook even the smallest detail, it would result in criticism of all his other actions. Yet he was so weak physically that at first he could not endure the cold and, even after the soldiers had assembled at his command, would withdraw without addressing a word to them. He ate very little food, and that always at night. He could not take anything in the daytime, except some of the medicine called *theriac*. This he took not so much because he was afraid of anything, but because he was suffering from a chest and stomach condition. It is said that the practice of taking this drug enabled him to endure both this and other illnesses.' The point of Dio's remark about *theriac* is that the word means literally 'antidote', and emperors and other rulers in antiquity not infrequently took some form of antidote to give them immunity from poison. The medicine which Marcus took was prescribed for him by Galen. It contained opium. Galen records that Marcus stopped taking because it made him drowsy, but then found he could not sleep, and had to take a regular dose again. This *may* indicate that he had become an opium addict. But Marcus did not become a helpless addict like Thomas de Quincey, and the attempt to discover traces of the opium eater's confused and distorted imagination in the *Meditations* has not been very convincing. It is reasonable to suppose that he took the opium as a pain-killer and as a sleeping-draught. The illness he suffered from sounds like some form of ulcer.[41]

Since Dio introduces Marcus' close attention to his legal business at this stage of his narrative, this is an appropriate point to mention one or two cases which required his attention at this time. But first a statement of administrative interest from the biographer may be mentioned. 'Marcus enrolled many of his friends in the senate, with the rank of aedile or praetor. He bestowed the rank of aedile or praetor on many senators who were poor but undeserving of blame – and he did not appoint anyone as a senator whom he did not know personally.' His law-tutor Maecianus had of course been enrolled in the senate at an early stage in the reign. But it was during the heavy fighting which led to severe loss of life in all ranks that he was obliged to make men like Pertinax and Macrinius Avitus senators and give them immediate positions of high military responsibility. There was indeed a severe shortage of suitably qualified men for high command. In the reign of Pius men like Statius Priscus who had been promoted to the senate had to serve a long apprenticeship in junior posts before attaining to the responsibilities which their talents deserved. The crisis of the Marcommanic or northern wars made such a procedure inadvisable. Marcus was no respecter of persons – as his choice of Claudius Pompeianus as son-in-law indicates. He judged strictly on merit.[42]

An interesting case came up during this period involving the family life of a senator. 'A certain Brasidas, a Spartan senator of praetorian rank, had emancipated his sons from his control when a legacy had been left to them by his divorced wife' (which they could receive only on condition that they were *sui iuris* by their father's death). 'Therefore', Scaevola recalls, 'the deified Marcus decreed that the legacy must be handed over to them, having understood the wishes of their mother, who had put off their receiving the legacy until their father's death because she did not believe that their father would emancipate them. But she would have done so if she had hoped that he would emancipate them. Scaevola heard Marcus adjudicating on such a case in his audience hall (*auditorium*).' One may wonder whether Brasidas had made some arrangement with his sons, to share some of their mother's inheritance with them, on condition that he emancipated them from his authority so that they could obtain it in the first place. But Marcus evidently felt that the action was reasonable.[43]

Scaevola, one of Marcus' main advisers on legal questions, does not reveal where the hearing was held. It may have taken place at Marcus' headquarters, at Carnuntum or at Sirmium, as did another celebrated case involving a Greek senator, which although of insufficient legal interest to have been recorded by the lawyers, is reported in some detail by Philostratus in his *Lives of the Sophists*. The senator was Marcus' former tutor Herodes Atticus. The exact background to the case is somewhat obscure, in spite of the details given by Philostratus in his biography of Herodes. It had its origin, apparently, in the hostility shown to Herodes by the Quintilii brothers, who had been acting as special commissioners in the province of Achaea. The family of the Quintilii was from Alexandria Troas, a Roman colony in the province of Asia near the site of Troy – and therefore Latin in origin. They had risen to some prominence by the reign of Pius, and the brothers Maximus and Condianus achieved the exceptional honour of being consuls together for the year 151. Their sons were also in high favour. Maximus, the son of Condianus, was consul in 172, and his cousin the younger Condianus was also obviously having a successful career. Herodes disliked the two brothers and indulged in the luxury of calling them 'Trojans', which for a Greek may have been a pleasant private joke. But the Quintilii encouraged Herodes' enemies, and hostility to him at Athens grew. Herodes brought a charge of 'conspiracy to set the people against him' before the proconsul. But his adversaries, Demostratus, Praxagoras and Mamertinus, appealed to Marcus. They hoped to find him favourable to their side, Philostratus says, because Marcus suspected Herodes of having intrigued treasonably with Lucius against him. This assertion may be somewhat exaggerated. 'Now the emperor was based among the peoples of Pannonia, with his headquarters at Sirmium, and Demostratus and his friends lodged near the imperial residence. Marcus provided them with supplies and often asked them if they needed anything. He was in any case disposed to treat them favourably, and his wife and his little daughter, who still could not speak properly, urged him to do so. His little daughter especially used to fall at her father's knees and implore him with many blandishments to save the Athenians for her.' This must be Vibia Aurelia Sabina, Marcus' and Faustina's youngest child, as is apparent from a later reference to the daughter being three years old.

Herodes had brought with him to Sirmium two twin girls whom he had brought up from childhood (they were the daughters of his freedman Alcimedon) and had made his cupbearers and cooks. Shortly before the tribunal met, they were killed by lightning while they were asleep in the tower where Herodes and his party were lodging in the suburbs of the town. The emotional Herodes was driven frantic with grief, and when he appeared before the emperor all his usual eloquence deserted him. Instead he attacked Marcus violently. 'This is all I get in return for my hospitality to Lucius – though it was you who sent him to me! These are the reasons on the basis of which you judge me – and you are sacrificing me to the whim of a woman and a three-year-old child!' The praetorian prefect Bassaeus Rufus felt that only one conclusion was possible: Herodes obviously wanted to die. 'Herodes replied: "My good fellow, an old man fears little"', and swept out of the court before his allotted time was up. Marcus 'did not frown or change his expression', but told the other side to make their defence, '"even though Herodes does not give you leave"'. Marcus listened for some time without showing his feelings, but eventually the whole attack on Herodes moved him to open tears. However, the attack was not only on Herodes personally, but also on his freedmen. These Marcus punished, although mildly, and Alcimedon was pardoned, on the grounds that the loss of his daughters had already caused him sufficient suffering. Philostratus could not be absolutely certain what happened to Herodes, but concludes that a suggestion that he was exiled was unfounded. He did in fact live for a while after the trial at Oricum in Epirus, a city that had benefited from his generosity, but this was not exile, says Philostratus. It is probable that Marcus advised Herodes to live away from Athens for a time.[44]

The biographer records a number of administrative measures which Marcus took in his absence from Rome. 'He left forceful instructions while absent that the entertainment of the Roman people should be provided by the richest givers of public spectacles. For there had been popular rumours that he intended to deprive them of their entertainments after he had taken the gladiators away to the war – and to drive them to take up philosophy. He had in fact ordered that the ballet-dancers (*pantomimi*) should start their performances nine days later than usual, so that business should not be disrupted. There was talk, as we mentioned earlier, about his wife's love-affairs with ballet-dancers, but he cleared her of these charges in his letters.' The effect of the calling-up of the gladiators for military service was in fact, it appears, to bring an enormous increase in the prices demanded by the *lanistae*, the trainers and promoters. This price-increase was intensely unpopular. It perhaps had tragic effects – as a by-product – a few years later. Faustina's alleged dalliance with undesirable lovers was the subject of a good deal of malicious gossip. She was also rumoured to have a fancy for gladiators. Her only opportunity for indulging such fancies must have been at the beginning of the 170s, and it may have been partly to put a stop to the gossip, however much truth or otherwise there was in it, that Marcus summoned her to the front with their youngest child.[45]

Commodus was by now back at Rome, continuing his education under the supervision of Pitholaus, and there were a number of relatives at hand as well, not least his older sisters and their husbands – for Fadilla and Cornificia were probably by now married as well as Annia Faustina. Fadilla's husband was Plautius Quintillus, a nephew of Lucius, and Cornificia married Petronius Sura Mamertinus, grandson of Pius' guard prefect and kinsman of Fronto.[46] There was an occasion during this period for Galen to display his medical skills in attending the heir apparent.

Galen's treatment of Commodus was regarded as 'highly remarkable', Galen records, but 'in fact it is far from it', he modestly adds. After leaving the *palaestra* (wrestling-school) 'he was seized with quite a hot fever'. Galen took his pulse and diagnosed inflammation. 'Pitholaus expressed surprise that inflammation of the tonsils could alter the boy's pulse.' But so it proved. Galen established that the gargle prescribed had been too strong and ordered a change 'to a solution of honey and rosewater'. On the morning of the third day the boy's fever had almost passed. Marcus' cousin, Annia Fundania Faustina, called to see Commodus, and was enormously impressed by Galen's success. She took the opportunity of praising him to one of his rivals, from the so-called 'Methodist' school of medicine. In the same work, *On Prognosis*, Galen tells the story of his cure of Sextus Quintilius Condianus the younger. This is a further reminder, incidentally, by mention of the close interest in Sextus' health taken by Pitholaus and by Marcus' son-in-law Claudius Severus, that the Quintilii family enjoyed great favour at court. Clearly the odds had been against Herodes in the trial at Sirmium.[47]

The biographer adds a few further glimpses of Marcus's pronouncements on public matters. 'He prohibited riding and driving within the city boundaries; abolished mixed bathing; reformed the morals of married women and young nobles, which were growing lax, and separated the sacred rites of Serapis from the miscellaneous ceremonies of the Pelusia. There was a rumour, as a matter of fact, that certain persons masquerading as philosophers had been making trouble both for the state and for private citizens, but Marcus refuted this charge. It was his custom to give lighter sentences for all offences than those usually inflicted by the laws, although on occasion he showed himself implacable towards those who were clearly guilty of serious crimes. He himself conducted trials of distinguished men for capital offences, and with complete fairness. Once he rebuked a praetor who had heard the pleas of the defendants in a hurry, and ordered him to hold a retrial, saying that it was a matter of honour for the accused that they should be tried by a judge who judged on behalf of the people. Marcus always acted with equity, even in his dealings with enemy prisoners of war. He settled an immense number of foreigners on Roman soil.' With the brief mention of the two miracles that follows, this miscellaneous summary by the biographer of his activity in the years 169–75 is almost concluded.[48]

The campaigning season of 175 brought a renewed assault on the Sarmatians. Marcus was now determined to make their territory and that of the Marcomanni and Quadi into a province. He is in fact credited with the wish to exterminate the Sarmatians utterly. It is not quite clear how literally this statement (in Cassius Dio) should be taken. But the territory of the Marcomanni was already partially occupied, by a detachment of troops from the African legion III Augusta, and it may well be that Julius Pompilius Piso with his special force and special powers was occupying part of the Sarmatian lands. But the campaign can barely have been under way for a few weeks, in early spring, when news was brought to Marcus that Avidius Cassius, the governor of Syria and by Marcus' order virtual ruler of the whole east, had raised the standard of rebellion, and had been recognized as emperor in most of the eastern provinces, including Egypt.[49]

· 9 ·

THE LAST YEARS

THE NEWS OF Cassius' rebellion reached Marcus like a bolt from the blue. He ought to have had some warning of it, for example through the head of the Greek Secretariat, the *ab epistulis Graecis*. For a time during the wars this post was held by an expert on Plato named Alexander, from whom, Marcus records in the *Meditations*, he learned 'not often and only from necessity to say to anyone and to write in a letter that "I am too busy", and not to get out of the duties involved in our relationship with those who live with us by some expression like that, with the excuse of "pressure of business"'. Alexander is said to have died at his post. Criticism of him would be unfair. It may seem a little suprising that such a man was chosen by Marcus, considering his choice for the Joint Secretariat or the Latin Secretariat of tough men with a military background such as Varius Clemens and Taruttienus Paternus. But the functions of the head of the Greek Secretariat at the time of the northern wars had no doubt been expected to be, more or less, concerned with peaceful matters. In any case, other holders of the post are known from this period. One of them, Ti. Claudius Vibianus Tertullus, was in office at some time in the period 172–5. He received promotion, as well, so fault was not found with him. Another, T. Aius Sanctus, was later made Commodus' tutor in oratory.[1]

Whatever the cause, Marcus was totally unprepared, and extremely disturbed by the news, which reached him in the form of a despatch from Martius Verus, governor of Cappadocia, who had remained loyal. The rebellion is a highly puzzling episode. Both Dio and the biographer assert that Cassius proclaimed himself emperor at the wish of Faustina. With more convincing detail it is explained that she had expected Marcus to die – 'she was in despair over her husband's health' – or that 'seeing that her husband had fallen ill and expecting that he would die at any moment, she was afraid that the empire would fall to someone else as Commodus was young and rather naïve – and that should would be reduced to a private station. Therefore she secretly persuaded Cassius to make his preparations so that, if anything should happen to Antoninus, he might take over both her and the empire. So, while he was considering this, a message came that Marcus was dead (in such circumstances rumours always make things out to be worse than they actually are). At once, without waiting for confirmation, he laid claim to the empire, on the grounds that he had been elected by the soldiers then in Pannonia. In spite of the fact that he not long after learned the truth, nevertheless, having once made a beginning, he did not change course, but within a short time took control of all the region south of the Taurus, and began preparations to seize the throne by war.' The biographer springs into the breach to defend Faustina's reputation in his largely fictitious biography of Cassius, but his advocacy is tarnished by the bogus letters which he produces to support his case. Cassius Dio and the biographer's source for the anti-Faustina version which he records, Marius Maximus, were both young men at the time of the event they described, and must be given some credence, even if, it must be admitted, very few persons can have had the opportunity of learning the truth.[2]

Marcus had certainly been unwell, as Dio himself records. Some at least of his *Meditations* had been composed already. That work is full of references to the nearness of death. Marcus clearly did not expect to live long. Avidius Cassius can hardly have been able to know that a short while before his emperor had written of himself in his private notebook as 'one already on the threshold of death', had thought of suicide, and had then calmly resolved to 'wait for death with a good grace'. But Marcus' ill-health and weakness must have been common knowledge. Faustina was with Marcus. Commodus was in Rome. If Marcus had in fact died when he was thought to have, with Commodus a boy of thirteen who had not yet assumed the toga of manhood, it is clear that some other person would have needed to take on the role of his protector. Even Nero had been older (nearly seventeen) at the death of Claudius – not that he was a likely choice as a precedent. The days of child-emperors were yet to come. If Marcus died in 175, one man was in a stronger position than any, his son-in-law Tiberius Claudius Pompeianus, twice consul, husband of the junior Augusta, popular with the senate, and, having been with Marcus and the armies throughout the four previous campaigning seasons, well known, at the least, to the most powerful armies in the empire. But Faustina – and Lucilla – felt an antipathy to Pompeianus. Avidius Cassius was the only available counterweight to him. There is no need to suppose any personal relationship between the empress and the rebellious general. But Cassius was probably the same age as Faustina, who could well have met him when they were both young. Cassius, as the son of a Greek intellectual who had achieved high rank in the imperial service, had doubtless been in favour in court circles in the 150s. And Faustina surely met him again at the end of the Parthian war, when his fame was at its height, and she was in the east.[3]

Cassius was declared a public enemy by the senate as soon as the news reached it, and it ordered his property to be confiscated. His position was not strong, but neither was it hopeless. He had a strong personal following in his native Syria and in much of the east, due partly to his royal origin, partly to his successes in the Parthian wars and in suppressing the revolt of the Bucoli. He had powerful marriage connections with an extremely rich and extensive family group of Lycian notables through his son-in-law, Claudius Dryantianus. In terms of actual power he could count on, at most, seven legions, his own three in Syria, two in Palestine, one in Arabia, and one in Egypt – for Calvisius Statianus, the friend of Fronto (who could not 'find sufficient praise for him'), had acceded to him. Statianus may, of course, have had little choice. It must be remembered however that Cassius had been in Egypt in 172, and the two men may have had the opportunity of speculating together about possible future action. Statianus had been *ab epistulis Latinis* during the early years of the reign, and therefore may have had a great deal of highly valuable intimate knowledge about the previous behaviour of men whose support might be sought. Statianus' freedom of action must have been increased by the fact that his family was, probably, with him. At any rate his son Faustinianus, the same for whom Fronto, who 'loved him like a son', had obtained a military commission in Lower Germany some fifteen years before, now held an important post in the Egyptian administration, as *idiologus* at Alexandria.[4]

Cassius was certainly accepted as emperor in Egypt by 3 May, when a document is dated by the 'first year' of his reign. But a papyrus from Oxyrhyncus makes it probable that he was confident of Egyptian support as early as April or even March, and indeed may even have been there in person. It is part of a letter written in the month of Pharmouthi (which ended on 23 April) 'in the first year'. The writer – convincingly identified as Cassius – commends the good will shown towards him and announces his arrival, 'having been elected emperor by the most noble soldiers'. Then, he goes on, 'being about to come into the sovereignty among you', he looks forwards to commencing his beneficence by favour to 'my paternal city' – or, indeed, 'fatherland'. The city is Alexandria – for 'the Alexandrians' are mentioned at the beginning of the papyrus, and Cassius may indeed have been born there, when his father Heliodorus had accompanied Hadrian in the year 130, as the emperor's *ab epistulis*. Further, he probably spent several years in Egypt when his father was prefect. Cassius may not yet have entered Egypt, but it was undoubtedly a logical step that he should make it his base.[5]

With Egypt in his power Cassius controlled the main granary of Rome, and the opportunity to exert economic blackmail existed. But he had failed to win over Martius Verus, his former associate in the Parthian War and governor of Cappadocia, to his cause. Verus should have had two legions under his command, although both of these were probably depleted by the demands of the Danubian front. Cassius may at first have hoped for some support from the Danube armies, especially if some of the eastern legionaries were there, and some of the men in northern legions must have served under him against the Parthians. But his strict discipline may not have endeared him to them. At any rate, no support for him seems to have been forthcoming from any of the European provinces. Herodes Atticus is reported to have sent him a letter celebrated for its brevity. It contained one Greek word: *emanēs* ('you are mad').[6]

At Rome there was panic. It was thought that Cassius would arrive during Marcus' absence and that he would ravage the city 'like a tyrant' in revenge for his having been declared a public enemy. Marcus took immediate steps. Vettius Sabinianus, at the time serving as governor of Lower Pannonia, was sent with a special force 'to protect the city' (*ad tutelam urbis*). Marcus also summoned Commodus to his side.[7] Commodus had taken a step towards entering public life a few months earlier. On 20 January 175, he had been admitted to the colleges of priests. Before his departure for Pannonia, still wearing the *toga praetexta* of boyhood, he distributed bounty to the people in the Basilica of Trajan. The event was commemorated on coins, which symbolically depict the event: the seated Commodus holds out his right hand; the personified figure of Liberalitas stands before him holding an *abacus* and *cornucopiae*, while a citizen holds up a fold of his toga to catch the falling coins; behind Commodus stands a figure who may be the prefect of the city (probably T. Vitrasius Pollio at this time, husband of the emperor's cousin). This giving of bounty was probably not so much to commemorate the entry into the priesthood of the young prince, as to celebrate in advance his assumption of the *toga virilis*. Marcus had decided that this should take place at once, at the front, instead of waiting for the traditional date, the Liberalia of 17 March. Thus the giving of largesse to the people probably came immediately after the summons from Marcus and before Commodus' departure. The benefaction was in any case a useful insurance of public support among the volatile urban populace. At the same time, the coins somewhat anxiously proclaimed the loyalty and unity of the armies.[8]

At first Marcus tried to keep the news of the uprising secret, but when he could conceal it from the army no longer – 'the troops were strongly disturbed by the rumour and were talking a lot' – he addressed a speech to them, Dio records. As Dio had the opportunity of knowing something of the events of 175 from personal experience and from eye-witness accounts, there may be some echoes in his version of an actual speech of the emperor.

'It is not to express anger, fellow soldiers, but to lament my fate, that I have come before you. For why become angry at the deity, to whom all power belongs?' He lamented the horrors of war, and the greatest horrors of civil war, and the discovery of disloyalty 'by a dearest friend'. This last expression may be technically accurate. Cassius may well have been one of those co-opted into the priesthood of the *sodales Veriani, ex amicissimis*. Marcus said, Dio continues, that if the danger had been his personal danger alone, he would have been willing to set before the army or the senate the issue between himself and Cassius, and would gladly have yielded the empire to him without fighting, 'if this had seemed to be for the common good. For it is for the common good that I continue to labour and undergo danger, and have spent so much time here outside Italy, although I am already old and weak, and unable to take food without pain or sleep undisturbed.'⁹ This has the ring of truth. One may wonder, however, what issue there was between Marcus and Cassius which either might have considered susceptible to public debate. It can only have been the question of peace or war. There was, as the biographer records, a peace party among the emperor's advisers which was reluctant to continue the war. In the eastern provinces, there must by now have been considerable opposition to its continuance. Cassius might well have won support on a promise to end for good a war against northern barbarians to whom the eastern empire was indifferent, a war which can only have seemed unproductive and was an actual drain on their resources. Marcus was still bent on expanding the empire in the north.

Marcus' speech went on, according to Dio, with an appeal to the loyalty and fighting spirit of the Danubian armies. Cassius' armies of the east were fewer in number than their own forces, he said, but even had they been greater by thousands, they never had and never would prove superior. He reminded them that the loyal Martius Verus had been as successful as Cassius against the Parthians, if not more so. Cassius was likely to change his mind when he heard that he (Marcus) was in fact alive. However that might be, he hoped that Cassius would not kill himself or be killed on learning that he was coming against him, for that would deprive him (Marcus) of the opportunity of giving an example of mercifulness 'for surely goodness has not completely perished among men, but a fragment of the ancient virtue remains'. Marcus wrote to the senate in similar terms, 'never abusing Cassius in any way, except that he constantly referred to him as ungrateful. Nor did Cassius say or write anything insulting to Marcus.'¹⁰

The biographer of Cassius includes in his unconvincing farrago the statement that Cassius proclaimed at the outset, when he still believed, or wanted it to be believed, that the emperor was dead, the deification of Marcus. But the temptation to the biographer to insert 'documentary evidence' at other points, to pad out his scanty information, was too great, and 'letters of Cassius' are produced, which include derisive comment about Marcus. These are quite worthless. Marcus was clearly in a much stronger position than Cassius. The armies of the Rhine and Danube now possessed a combined strength of sixteen legions, and with Britain, Spain and Numidia, Marcus had another five on which he could count, not to mention the élite corps of the praetorian guard. On the other hand his troops were perhaps battle-weary, and he could only take a proportion of them with him.¹¹

Commodus left Rome on 19 May. It cannot have taken him much more than two or three weeks at the most to reach his father at Sirmium. The ceremony of the *tirocinium fori* obviously did not take place at once. A suitable day had to be chosen. July 7 was selected – 'the Nones of July, the day that Romulus disappeared from the earth'. Thus Commodus entered the ranks of the *cives Romani* under the protection of Rome's founder. Marcus commended his son to the army. At the same time he became *princeps iuventutis*, leader of the knights – and, by the same token, his position of heir-apparent was publicly proclaimed. The ceremony was a demonstration to Cassius and to Rome that Commodus was, after all, ready to take the purple if Marcus should die.[12]

The news that Marcus was facing civil war in the east inspired various barbarian tribes to offer assistance. This Marcus declined, declaring that 'the barbarians ought not to know of any trouble arising between the Romans'. During his preparations for departure, news was brought him that Cassius was dead, slain by a centurion named Antonius, after 'a dream of empire lasting three months and six days'. His head was sent to Marcus who refused to see it and had it buried. Martius Verus had taken control of Syria. One of his first acts was to burn the correspondence of Cassius, containing, no doubt, material which could incriminate many in high position (not least, perhaps, Faustina).[13]

In spite of the abrupt downfall of his adversary, Marcus still felt that it was necessary to go to the east in person, to inspect the eastern provinces and to try to restore their loyalty to the dynasty. It was therefore necessary to conclude peace with the Jazyges. As it is recorded that news of Cassius' death came to Marcus 'at the same time as news of many victories over different barbarians', it would seem that peace was made after Cassius' death. Marcus was recognized once more as emperor in Egypt by 28 July. It was probably in July or August that he received the title Sarmaticus, 'conqueror of the Sarmatians', and the eighth salutation as Imperator. Curiously, however, it is reported that because of his alarm he made peace with the enemy, most exceptionally for him, without consulting the senate over the terms.[14]

'The Jazyges were defeated and came to terms,' wrote Cassius Dio. 'Zanticus himself came as a suppliant. Previously they had imprisoned Banadaspus, their second king, for making overtures to Marcus, but now all their leading men came with Zanticus and accepted the same terms as the Quadi and Marcomanni had been given, except that they were required to live twice as far away from the Danube. The emperor, in fact, had wanted to exterminate them utterly. It was obvious that they were still strong at this time and that they had caused the Romans great damage, from the fact that they surrendered 100,000 captives that were still in their hands, even after the many who had been sold, had died or had escaped; also from the fact that they at once provided as their contribution to the alliance 8,000 cavalry, 5,500 of which Marcus sent to Britain.'[15]

Although it is obvious that sending the Sarmatians to Britain was a convenient means of placing them far from home where they would not be dangerous, at the same time, the mere fact that the already enormous garrison of that province was reinforced with soldiers (probably mainly cavalry) equal in numbers to a legion or to eleven normal sized auxiliary cohorts or *alae*, must indicate that the trouble in Britain which began in 162 was not yet over. The governor at this time was probably Q. Antistius Adventus, soon to be succeeded by Caerellius, both veterans of the Danubian wars. Other parts of the empire were also in a disturbed state. Aufidius Victorinus and Vehilius Gratus Julianus had evidently dealt with the Moorish invasion of Baetica – Julianus had been back from Spain in two other posts before peace was concluded on the Danube in 175. But there was more trouble to come in Spain.[16]

There had been danger in northern Gaul also: disturbances of an unknown nature among the Sequani in the Jura, and an invasion of Belgica presumably near the coast, by the North Sea German tribe of the Chauci. They were repulsed by the governor of Belgica, Didius Julianus, with hastily raised local levies. Didius became consul in 175 at the age of forty-two, by no means early for one who had been brought up for a time by the emperor's mother Domitia Lucilla. He went on to be governor of Dalmatia, not a province of the first importance by now; but he had some fighting to do in the suppression of brigandage in the wild hinterland. Julianus' colleague as consul was Helvius Pertinax, now aged forty-nine and at the height of his powers. Marcus had become extraordinarily impressed with this freedman's son from Liguria, who had once tried to make a career as a centurion. After his worth had become apparent when Pompeianus had rescued him from disgrace, he went from strength to strength. According to his biographer, Marius Maximus preserved a eulogy of him by Marcus on the occasion of his appointment as consul. The speech related 'all that he had done and had suffered'. Some however expressed their distaste that a man of such origin should hold the *fasces* (not that he in fact went to Rome to perform the duties of his office – he did not enter the senate-house until some ten years after becoming a senator). The line of Euripides was quoted: 'Such things are forced on us by wretched war.' However, Marcus chose him as his *comes* to accompany him to the east.[17]

Another officer chosen to accompany Marcus was M. Valerius Maximianus, who, with the rank of procurator, was put in charge of a special force of Marcomanni, Quadi and Naristae – the latter being the people whose chief he had killed in battle not long before – 'to punish the Oriental rising'. This description of Cassius' revolt, revealed by the inscription in honour of Maximianus at Diana Veteranorum, appears to indicate that it really was a widespread rebellion. The information that Marcomannic and other barbarian troops were taken to the east at first sight contradicts Dio's statement that Marcus refused barbarian offers of assistance. But the Marcomanni and their neighbours probably did not offer this assistance.

Tribes allied to Rome by choice, such as the Astingi and Lacringes, might have done so. The Marcomanni and the others named here were, like the Sarmatae, providing men under the terms of an agreement dictated by Rome, as much by way of hostages as anything else.[18]

Marcus probably set out for the eastern provinces no later than the end of July 175, accompanied by Faustina and Commodus and other members of the family. In addition to Pertinax and Valerius Maximianus, other officers in the party included the Quintilii brothers. Their home was in the Troad and they will thus have been familiar with Asia Minor. In the meantime their sons were evidently left on the Danube holding the key positions as governor in the two Pannonian provinces. Arrius Antoninus, Fronto's friend and fellow-Cirtensian, was to take over Cappadocia from Martius Verus, and may have travelled on ahead. The prefect of the guard, Bassaeus Rufus, with a strong force of guardsmen, will also have been in attendance. It is probable that the first part of the journey was by boat, down the Save to Singidunum, then down the Danube, perhaps as far as Novae, before taking the road south across the Balkans into Thrace and on to Byzantium. Claudius Pompeianus may have remained in the Lower Danube area for some time.[19]

After crossing into Bithynia, Marcus' route seems to have been across central Anatolia, eastwards first, perhaps to Ancyra, and then south-east towards the Taurus mountains. A little way beyond Tyana in Cappadocia, at a village called Halala, Faustina died. Cassius Dio takes the opportunity of making various insinuations about the cause of her death. Suicide is suggested, the motive being to avoid the penalty for having made an 'agreement' with Cassius. The story is unverifiable, but, given the character of Marcus, and his attitude to Faustina, it seems unlikely. The expectation of life for a woman in antiquity, even one of exalted rank, was low. Faustina had borne at least fourteen children, and was forty-five years old. Dio does at least give an alternative explanation – gout. It is even possible that she was pregnant yet again and this time succumbed. In a passage in Book 9 of his *Meditations*, which seems to carry allusions to Cassius' revolt, Marcus, as so often preparing himself for death, writes: 'Just as now you wait for the moment when the child emerges from your wife's womb, likewise stand by for when your soul will escape from its shell.' Whatever the cause, the long journey cannot have done her health much good – it was by now presumably mid-winter – and in any case she had been with the armies at least since the previous summer. She was deified by the senate, and Marcus renamed Halala, where she died, after her, 'Faustinopolis'. A large number of coins were issued in her memory and various other commemorative measures taken. Marcus was doubtless aware of some at least of the stories about his wife, and it seems that he deliberately took steps to vindicate her reputation. He was certainly very distressed by her death, as Dio himself records.[20]

Shortly after this bereavement he had occasion to write to the senate on the question of the treatment of Cassius' supporters. One of Cassius' sons, Maecianus, had been killed soon after the rising had ended. The other, Heliodorus, was banished. His daughter Alexandria and son-in-law Dryantianus were given freedom of movement, and 'entrusted to the protection of their uncle by marriage', presumably the wealthy Lycian senator Claudius Titianus. Marcus emphasized with great vigour in his despatch to the senate that he wanted to keep his reign 'unstained by the blood of any senator'. Dio places this request immediately after the death of Faustina, and adds, somewhat enigmatically, 'as if from this alone he might be able to gain some consolation for losing her'. In fact, this principle was established over a century before, probably through the efforts of the Stoic senators Helvidius Priscus and Junius Mauricus; and Nerva and his successors, if not the Flavians as well, swore an oath that they would not put any senator to death, on their accession. Marcus must have become anxious that this principle might now be in jeopardy. A practical step was now taken in the form of a decree forbidding a man to govern the province of his origin. This had had a dangerous effect on Cassius.[21]

It was presumably at about this time that Marcus received a letter from Herodes Atticus, asking 'why the emperor no longer wrote to him, although in the past he had written so often that on one occasion three letter-carriers had arrived at his house in one day'. Marcus now wrote back, Philostratus records, 'at length and on several subjects, infusing what he wrote with a marvellous urbanity'. Philostratus then quotes part of the letter: It began, 'Greetings, dear Herodes'. Then, after discussing the military winterquarters where he then was, and lamenting his wife whom he had just lost by her death, and some comments on his own bad health, he continued as follows: 'As for you, I wish you good health, and that you should regard me as well-disposed towards you. And you should not regard yourself as unjustly treated if – after I detected their crimes – I punished some members of your household, as lightly as possible. So don't feel resentment against me for this. But if I have hurt you in any way or am doing so still, demand recompense from me in the temple of Athena in your city at the time of the Mysteries. For I made a vow, when the war was blazing particularly fiercely, that I too would be initiated, and I would like you to initiate me.'[22]

After Halala Marcus must have gone south through the Cilician Gates and on to Tarsus. Here he stopped to hear the boy prodigy Hermogenes, the fifteen-year-old sophist, who delighted Marcus with his formal speech and astonished him by his extempore declamation. He rewarded him with splendid presents. Now Marcus was close to Syria, the seat of the uprising against him. He apparently avoided Antioch, the chief city of the province, where Cassius had lived as governor for nine years. Nor did he wish to see Cyrrhus, Cassius' home town. In that case it is possible that he sailed across from Cilicia to a port further south. In any case, he was aiming for Egypt. On his journey through Palestine he commented unfavourably on its people. On more than one occasion he apparently found their riotous behaviour and lack of concern with hygiene something of a trial, Ammianus records, adding that Marcus 'exclaimed with a groan: 'O Marcomanni, Quadi and Sarmatae, at last I have found people more excitable than you!'' '[23]

A very different tradition of Marcus' contact with the Jews is preserved in the Talmud. A Roman emperor named as 'Antoninus son of Asverus' is said to have been on terms of intimacy with the celebrated Rabbi Juda I. The legendary Jewish teacher began his office as patriarch in the year 175, and is likely to have sought and received an audience with the emperor when he travelled south through Palestine early in 176. In the Talmud the emperor and the patriarch are represented as lifelong friends who had known each other since infancy and had carried on a lengthy correspondence, discussing such matters as the nature of the soul. It would accord well with the character of Marcus and with the report of his visit to the eastern provinces – where 'he left many traces of his philosophy behind him' – to engage in philosophical discussion with the most learned man in Palestine. Hence, even if much of the detail in the Talmud is fiction, a kernel of truth may lie behind it.[24]

The date of Marcus' entry into Egypt is not recorded. No doubt an advance force of loyal troops had gone in well before his own arrival. The prefect Calvisius Statianus received very light punishment – only banishment to an island, and the records of the case were burned. His associates were released from custody. In spite of the city of Alexandria's fervent adherence to Cassius' cause, Marcus treated it with moderation. 'While in Egypt he conducted himself like a private citizen and a philosopher at all the schools and temples, in fact everywhere.' It seems that it was while he was at Alexandria that 'he conducted much negotiation and ratified peace with all the kings and ambassadors of the Persians (i.e. Parthians), when they came to meet him'.[25]

In the spring he left Egypt to tour the Asian provinces. He left one of his daughters at Alexandria, which may have been a token of his forgiveness. It is not known whether he went to Syria by land, going through Palestine again. He might have gone by sea from Alexandria to the mouth of the Orontes. It seems clear, however, that he did go to Syria again, for the biographer notes that he did after all visit Antioch in spite of his earlier avoidance of the city. The return journey was by a different route, naturally, for he was now making for Rome. His last stop in Asia seems to have been at Smyrna, where he stayed for some time. Philostratus records the story of his meeting there with Aelius Aristides, who, Marcus was surprised to find, allowed three days to pass without calling. The Quintilii brothers arranged for him to come the next day, when he explained that he had been engaged in such deep meditation that he had been unable to allow himself any interruption. Marcus liked this answer, and he asked when he could hear the great orator declaim. 'Give me my subject today, and hear me speak tomorrow', was the reply. Aristides explained that he was not one of those extempore orators who 'vomit up their speeches'. He asked Marcus to allow his pupils to be present in the audience as well, a request which Marcus granted – 'for that is democratic'. Aristides then asked that the pupils should be permitted to shout and applaud as loud as they could. 'The emperor smiled, and replied: "That depends on you".'[26]

From Smyrna Marcus and Commodus and their party crossed to Athens on their way back to Rome. Marcus must have had many motives for wanting to visit the intellectual capital of the empire, the home of philosophy, including his own Stoicism, and of all the liberal arts; and of course he wished to be initiated. The mysteries of Demeter and Persephone took place at Eleusis every September. Marcus and Commodus were both duly initiated. There is no record of Herodes having taken a part in the ceremony, although he was probably present. The initiator of Marcus and Commodus was a certain Julius, and the priest was the same L. Memmius who had initiated Lucius fourteen years previously. The biographer mentions Marcus' initiation and states that he had himself initiated 'to demonstrate his innocence of wrong-doing' – an essential prerequisite for admission – 'and he entered the sanctuary unattended'.[27]

At the very time of Marcus' induction into this ancient cult, he may have been invited to consider the merits of a newer religion. A Christian named Athenagoras, described as being 'of Athens, a Christian philosopher', composed a defence of the faith which he addressed to 'the Emperors Marcus Aurelius Antoninus and Lucius Aurelius Commodus, conquerors of Armenia, [Media, Parthia, Germany,] Sarmatia, but, greatest of all, philosophers'. The last phrase recalls the *Apology* of Justin, and the imperial titles clearly belong after the summer of 175. Further, since he refers to the whole world enjoying profound peace, he could hardly have written later than mid-178. He certainly appears to have hoped for a personal hearing – for he directly addresses Marcus and Commodus. Since he had proved that the accusations of atheism, cannibalism and incest were quite false, but that the Christians were on the contrary god-fearing, reasonable and well-behaved, 'you who are in every way, by nature and by upbringing, good, moderate, beneficent and deserving of kingship, show your assent by a royal nod of the head'. But he may not have gained admittance.[28]

Marcus no doubt had a great many who sought an audience with him at Athens. The biography of Herodes by Philostratus is evidence enough that Marcus had already been obliged to concern himself with Athenian affairs. This is supplemented by a massive marble plaque on which is inscribed the text of an edict issued after the hearing at Sirmium, in which he gave rulings on a whole series of matters (including those involving Herodes).

'What great enthusiasm I have for the glory of Athens, that she may continue in possession of her ancient majesty, has, I think, been sufficiently made plain,' he writes at one point. He added, close to the end of the edict, his personal hope that 'Herodes, with his famous enthusiasm for education, should in future, together with the Athenians, share the enjoyment of their festivals, both religious and secular'. Since the causes of conflict were removed, 'would it not be possible for them to love my Herodes, who is also their Herodes?' He added the explanation that this last comment was a postscript: 'In fact, this occurred to me after all these orders had been set out together in the Greek language. . . . I added it because it was omitted from my formal statement; though it could be inferred from my verdict . . . it needed some further clarification.'[29]

Cassius Dio records an important action of Marcus at Athens. 'He bestowed honours on the Athenians, and he established teachers at Athens in every academic discipline, for the benefit of mankind, and he granted them an annual salary.' Philostratus relates that Marcus asked the advice of Herodes for several of the appointments, namely the four chairs of philosophy for a Platonist, an Aristotelian, a Stoic and an Epicurean. But he appointed one, Theodotus, to a chair of rhetoric on his own initiative. This man had been involved in the 'conspiracy' against Herodes, so advice from that quarter would have been heavily biased. Philostratus elsewhere mentions another professor of rhetoric at Athens at the time, Adrianus of Tyre, a pupil of Herodes. Adrianus had been appointed to his chair by Marcus before his arrival in Athens, on the strength of his reputation alone. 'The consular Severus' (who must be Marcus' son-in-law Cn. Claudius Severus) had made some severe criticism of Adrianus' style, so Marcus went to hear for himself; Adrianus was to speak on a theme which the emperor had set for him. Marcus was impressed, and the sophist received a number of gifts and privileges. The criticism of Claudius Severus had probably been made in a friendly spirit, as he was the patron of Adrianus, and together they had attended Galen's anatomical demonstrations in Rome some twelve or more years before, along with Vettulenus Civica Barbarus and other distinguished personages of intellectual inclinations.[30]

Back in Rome, in the late autumn, Marcus addressed the people. He referred to his many years of absence, and some of his audience called out 'eight' (that is, 169–76 inclusive), and held up all four fingers of both hands – to indicate that they should be given eight gold pieces. Marcus smiled and said 'eight'; and they did later receive this sum. Preparations were made for the triumph. Marcus was determined that Commodus should participate in it with him, so on 27 November the young prince, who had as yet no other official position, was granted *imperium*, which gave him the necessary status. At the same time Marcus requested that he should be excused from the provisions of the *lex annalis*, which governed the minimum age at which magistracies might be held. Obviously it had been intended for

some months that Commodus should take office as consul in January 177 –
probably since the previous spring. In January Commodus was fifteen,
younger even than Nero had been when consul for the first time in AD 55,
and was, in fact, the youngest consul of the Romans hitherto. His colleague
was to be his brother-in-law, Fadilla's husband, the nephew of Lucius, M.
Peducaeus Plautius Quintillus.[32]

The mother of Quintillus, Ceionia Fabia, apparently tried at this time to
interest Marcus in a second marriage, to herself. But Marcus rejected the
overtures of his former fiancée. He was unwilling to marry again and 'give
so many children a stepmother', the biographer records. But he took a
mistress instead, the daughter of one of Faustina's procurators. Her name is
unknown. Pius had done likewise after his wife had died. In fact, the excuse
was not very plausible if it was made. Only two of the surviving six
children now remained unmarried, Commodus and Vibia Aurelia Sabina,
the two youngest. Meanwhile Lucilla had borne, or was soon to bear, a son
from her marriage to Pompeianus. He survived, and was to be consul in the
year 209, when he is recorded with the names Aurelius Commodus
Pompeianus. Lucilla had had three children from her marriage to Lucius,
but two, a boy and a girl, died in infancy. The third, a daughter, whose
names are not known, was later betrothed to her stepbrother, a son of
Pompeianus by a previous marriage.[33]

It was probably not long after the return to Rome that Marcus fell ill and
was treated by Galen, a cure which the great doctor describes in his *On
Prognosis* as 'genuinely remarkable'. Marcus himself and the doctors who
had been with him on campaign believed that it was a violent attack of
fever, but they were to be proved wrong. 'He had taken a dose of bitter
aloes the day before at the first hour, and then *theriac*, as was his practice
every day, at about the sixth hour. Then he had a bath at sunset and a little
food, and there ensued colic pains and diarrhoea, which made him
feverish.' His doctors saw him at dawn, and advised rest, then gave him
some thick gruel or porridge at the ninth hour. 'Although I was called in
after this, to sleep at the palace myself, when the lamps had just been lit,
someone came to summon me, who had been sent by the emperor.' Three
other doctors had already examined the emperor at dawn and at the eighth
hour and agreed that the symptoms indicated the onset of an illness. Galen
remained silent, to the emperor's surprise, and was asked why he had not
taken his pulse as well. Galen explained that the other doctors, having been
with him on campaign, were better placed to diagnose him. Nonetheless,
when asked to do so, Galen took Marcus' pulse, and pronounced that there
was no fever, merely a stomach upset. Marcus was pleased by the diagnosis
and praised it three times in these words: 'That's it! It's exactly what you've
said it is! I feel as if I'm weighed down by some rather cold food.' The
prescription would normally have been peppered wine, Galen said, but 'for
you kings, when doctors are are accustomed to use the safest remedies, it is

sufficient to apply a pad of scarlet wool, smeared with warmed ointment of nard, to the rectum'. Marcus replied that this was his own usual remedy, and asked Pitholaus to apply it. Then he had his feet rubbed by masseurs, 'ordered Sabine wine, sprinkled pepper in it and drank it, after which he said to Pitholaus: "We have one doctor, and he is a free man"'. Thereafter Marcus regularly referred to Galen as 'first among physicians and unique among philosophers'.[34]

The triumph was celebrated on 23 December. Only one detail is recorded. Marcus ran beside the triumphal chariot in which his son sat, in the Circus Flaminius. This was to do honour to the spectators, and Commodus presumably had to stay in the chariot to control the horses. Still, some clearly found the scene rather striking. Marcus had been voted a triumphal arch by the senate the previous month, in honour of his victories: 'because, surpassing all the glories of all the greatest *imperatores* before him, having wiped out or subjugated the most warlike peoples' – and here the record breaks off. The arch itself has not survived, although some of the reliefs which adorned it seem to have. (It may have been at this time also that the senate voted for the erection of the column to commemorate his achievements.) Coins were issued in honour of the triumph – 'De Germanis, De Sarmatis'. Members of Marcus' staff received decorations for the part that they had played. Such are recorded for Bassaeus Rufus and Pontius Laelianus, for example, both of whom were near the end of their service, and Julius Verus and Sosius Priscus were probably honoured as well. Pertinax was back on active service and could not attend, but he, Maximianus and others also received their marks of honour.[35]

After the triumph Marcus went to Lavinium to rest. However he was back in Rome for Commodus' entry into his consulship on New Year's Day. On the same day, evidently, Commodus was granted the tribunician power, and later in the year, the name Augustus and all the other titles, honours and powers of an emperor (except the office of *pontifex maximus*). He was now joint ruler, in the same position that Lucius had been from 161 to 169. If Marcus died, Commodus would need no further powers. His succession was now completely assured – he would merely continue to rule. Largesse – the 'eight gold pieces' – and 'wonderful spectacles' were provided in honour of the occasion.[36]

Commodus was still receiving education. Only three of his teachers are named in the biography, the Greek and Latin elementary teachers Onesicrates and Antistius Capella, otherwise unknown, and T. Aius Sanctus the orator (whose name is given incorrectly as 'Ateius' Sanctus). The name of his *educator* or *tropheus*, Pitholaus, is recorded by Galen. But he must have finished with the attentions of Onesicrates, Capella and Pitholaus long since, and have begun oratory with Sanctus by 176. It is not known what *grammatici* instructed him in the interim. Marcus himself had given Commodus some lessons, in the best old tradition, and had procured for him the best available teachers. In fact in the *Meditations* Marcus records his gratitude that he had been able to find such good teachers for his children. Aius Sanctus was probably from Campania, and hence could have been an Italian of Greek origin and culture, a possibility to which some support is given by his having held the post of *ab epistulis Graecis*. It may well be that he held this post during the tour of the east when the head of the Greek Secretariat would need to be with Marcus, and his tuition of Commodus thus could have begun very soon after Commodus assumed the *toga virilis*. Back in Rome Sanctus served successively as the head of two of the financial departments, as procurator of the *ratio privata* and as *a rationibus*. It may reasonably be supposed that he was able to continue his instruction of the prince at the same time.[37]

Various unfavourable criticisms of Commodus' character as a boy are retailed in the Augustan History. The faults criticized are described mostly in a general way, and the specific habits listed are not particularly discreditable – an interest in pottery-making, dancing, singing and whistling might in certain circumstances be regarded as positively commendable. An early fondness for vulgar jokes and for performing as a gladiator may have been unfortunate tastes, but not necessarily disastrous. One detailed story is given, of a piece of boyish fury at the age of eleven: he ordered a bathkeeper, who had let the bath at Centumcellae go lukewarm, to be thrown into the furnace. The slave to whom the order was given burned a sheepskin instead. This might be true: Marcus would then be away, for it belonged to the period August 172–August 173, when Commodus might well have got out of hand. But it is the type of story that the biographer and some of his sources were particularly fond of inventing. If it were true, it would not be revealing of a sensationally evil and odious character, merely of impetuous bad temper. After all, the order was not carried out, and was probably only shouted out in a tantrum. Dio's statement should be preferred, that Commodus was not naturally wicked. Still, the contrast with the grave eleven-year-old Marcus, who tried to live the philosopher's life, is very striking.[38]

Fighting was evidently still going on in the north in 177, or at any rate broke out again in that year. There was a Roman victory, presumably gained by the Quintilii cousins. Marcus was saluted as Imperator for the ninth time and Commodus for the second time. What was equally serious was the amount of brigandage that was going on still. Before Marcus' return to Rome he had despatched Valerius Maximianus on a new special mission. His salary was increased, and he was given the post of procurator of Lower Moesia, and the task of 'capturing a band of Brisean bandits on the borders of Macedonia and Thrace' – that area where the boundaries of Bulgaria, Greece and Yugoslavia now meet, through which the rivers Axios or Vardar and Strymon flow, on the western fringes of the Balkan mountains. Meanwhile Didius Julianus, as governor of Dalmatia, was facing similar problems. The bandits he was fighting were probably based in Albania or Montenegro. However, by 177 he had been promoted to Lower Germany, and was succeeded by Vettius Sabinianus, who had at long last been made consul.[39]

In Rome Marcus now turned his attention to the civilian administration; and a considerable number of his legal decisions from the period of his joint rule with Commodus (177–80) have been preserved. Interesting cases of murder came up. In a reply to Scapula Tertullus, Marcus and Commodus wrote: 'If you have ascertained that Aelius Priscus is so insane that he is permanently mad and thus that he was incapable of reasoning when he killed his mother, and did not kill her with the pretence of being mad, you need not concern yourself with the question how he should be punished, as insanity itself is punishment enough. At the same time he should be kept in close custody, and, if you think it advisable, even kept in chains. This need not be done by way of punishment so much as for his own and his neighbours' security. If however, as often happens, he has intervals of sanity, you must investigate whether he committed his crime on one of these occasions and thus has no claim to mercy on the grounds of mental infirmity. If this is so, refer the case to us, so that we may consider whether he should be punished in accordance with the enormity of the crime – if he did in fact commit it in a rational interval. But since we learn by letter from you that his position in respect of place and treatment is such that he is in the hands of friends, even, in fact, confined to his own house, your proper course is to summon those in charge of him at the time and to enquire how they were so remiss, and then to pronounce on each case separately, according as to whether there is any excuse or aggravation for their negligence. The object of keepers for the insane is not merely to stop them from harming themselves, but from destroying others, and if this happens, there is some justification for casting the blame for it on those who were somewhat negligent in their duties.'[40]

Two decisions concern *crimes passionels*. A father had killed the lover of his married daughter, but the daughter herself had survived his attack. The *lex Cornelia* laid down that homicide in such a situation was justifiable only if both members of the adulterous couple were killed. But, as the woman was seriously injured, the emperors granted the father a pardon, as he had clearly acted under provocation, and had not spared his daughter deliberately. In another case a husband who was found to have killed his wife when he caught her in the act of adultery was adjudged not guilty of capital murder.[41]

A rescript of general application issued at this time is very significant of the prevailing social conditions. It was expressly laid down that 'governors and magistrates and police are bound to assist slaveowners in searching for their runaway slaves and that they are bound to give them up if they find them. Also that persons on whose land slaves are in hiding are to be punished if any unlawful behaviour can be brought home to them. Anyone whatever who apprehends a runaway slave must bring him forward publicly. Magistrates are enjoined to keep any such slaves carefully in custody so as to prevent their escape.' This illustrates the growing seriousness of a problem which developed into full-scale war within a few years, and was to continue almost indefinitely until the fall of the western empire. Another rescript of Marcus and Commodus, to Piso, mentioning a particular case, again illustrates the atmosphere of the times. 'Since it is established by you, dearest Piso, that Julius Donatus, after being terrified by the arrival of brigands, had fled to his villa, and was wounded, and then, soon afterwards, making his will, repaid the services of his slaves, neither the family loyalty of his wife's grandmother nor the anxiety of the heir ought to have the effect of summoning to punishment those whom their master himself absolved.' The details of the case are slightly obscure (the text needs emendation and it is not clear quite what happened after Donatus' death), but the picture of the country landowner fleeing in panic to his villa, and his slaves rushing to tend his wounds, is vividly present.[42]

An important decision was made at this time affecting the position of slaves. In reply to an official query put to him by his old friend Aufidius Victorinus, Marcus, with Commodus, gave a ruling concerning the manumission of slaves, which is cited nearly twenty times in the legal collections (mostly naming Marcus only and not Commodus, and only naming Aufidius Victorinus on a few occasions). The most frequent citation includes the words: 'He attains his liberty in accordance with the ruling of the Deified Marcus' (*ex constitutione divi Marci venit ad libertatem*). This *constitutio*, also referred to as 'the so-called law of liberty', is nowhere quoted in full, but from the cases where it is cited as the basis of a judgment, it seems that it was designed to make sure that slaves did obtain their freedom if their masters had intended that they should have it, whatever legal obstacles might be put in their way by third parties. This had particular application to the case of slaves sold on the understanding that they would be set free after a stated period. This provision was, quite obviously, often evaded by buyers of slaves. Although the general rescript concerning runaway slaves quoted earlier reveals the harsh realities of the situation in which an economy based on slave-labour was liable to find itself, it is fair to say that Marcus' attitude, as revealed not only by the much-quoted reply to Victorinus, but by other decisions made earlier in his reign, was one of deep compassion for the position of individual slaves, and that he did take some steps to improve their position.[43]

Some time after his return, Marcus initiated a piece of legislation in the senate involving a matter for which he had always felt some distaste, namely gladiatorial spectacles. Probably largely as a result of his own action in conscripting gladiators into the armed forces some years previously, the costs of putting on public performances had soared enormously. The shortage of trained gladiators meant that the professional promoters (*lanistae*) had raised their prices to a prohibitive level. This development affected the pockets of the upper classes throughout the empire, for on them fell the duty of providing entertainment for the masses. As a result, evidently, an appeal went to Marcus from the council of the Three Gauls. Here it was the duty of one of the council, chosen in annual rotation, as High Priest of the three Gallic provinces, to provide public entertainment at the annual festival at Lugdunum (Lyons) beginning on 1 August, in honour of Rome and Augustus.

The priest appointed for the following year had already resigned himself to squandering his entire fortune, when news of the proposed legislation arrived. Marcus had decided to allow his procurator in the Gallic provinces to supply criminals condemned to death, at a cheap price, for use as gladiators. This special concession was made, it seems, not only because of the economic crisis in the world of mass entertainment, but because some archaic religious ritual in the Gallic provinces had involved the use of human sacrificial victims, known as *trinqui*. The state was now in effect to supply *trinqui* at six gold pieces a head.

The Gallic priest was overjoyed that his financial burden was to be lightened, and declared that he now positively welcomed the duty of putting on a spectacle, which he had previously repudiated. In the course of that year Marcus and Commodus brought in a decree in the senate to fix prices for gladiators throughout the empire, and the special provision for the Gallic provinces was embodied in it. The provisions of the senatorial decree which was passed are known from two inscriptions, at Sardis in Asia Minor and at Italica in the Spanish province of Baetica. That at Sardis, inscribed on marble, is only preserved in part, but it can be supplemented by the bronze tablet from Italica containing much of a speech by an unknown senator. This senator not only quotes extensively from the imperial proposals, but describes the grateful reception which they had received in the Gallic provinces. It is of course very rare to have a verbatim record of a speech by a senator. In particular, although the speech does not represent anything approaching modern concepts of free debate, it nevertheless demonstrates considerable latitude in the amount of expression of opinion allowed. The senator himself presumably had some connection with Gaul. The fact that the minutes of this senatorial business were set on record in two places at opposite ends of the empire, neither of them in Gaul, where there was particular interest in the proposals, indicates that this was done on governmental instructions. Marcus must have decided that it would be valuable to make widely known the fact that he had taken steps to lighten the burdens of the wealthy classes, whose support, at a time when the empire was in difficulties, was more than ever essential.[44]

Lugdunum, whence the initiative for the senate's decree evidently originated, was not long afterwards the scene of a sickening spectacle. Eusebius, the historian of the church, quotes at length at the beginning of his fifth book from a letter sent by 'the servants of Christ dwelling at Vienne and Lyon in Gaul to those in Asia and Phrygia'. It describes a violent outbreak of persecution, resulting in a number of brutal martyrdoms. Eusebius appears to assign the event to the year 177 – 'the seventeenth year of the emperor Antoninus Verus'.[45] But it may be simply that he knew it took place after Eleutherus became bishop of Rome in that year, and before the death of Marcus. The reasons behind the outbreak are not clear, but it is not surprising that anti-Christian feeling was running high in this period. War and plague had been taking a heavy toll, economic difficulties followed, and scapegoats were wanted: the pagans believed that the gods were angry. The names of the martyrs of Lyon include several that are Greek and two are specifically described as immigrants, Attalus from Pergamum and Alexander the doctor from Phrygia. Thus xenophobia, often a potent ingredient in such outbreaks, probably played a part here too. It could even be that the decree on gladiators was cynically exploited. If criminals condemned to death could be used in place of normal gladiators, officials of the Gallic council might have been tempted to add to the supply by accusing Christians.[46] Public confession of the faith and refusal to recant was still a capital offence.

At any rate, whatever the spark which ignited the 'rage of the heathen against the saints', the Christians were hounded by the mob and dragged into the town forum by the tribune commanding the cohort of police and by the civic authorities. They were then accused, and, on confession, were placed in custody until the governor of Lugdunensis arrived. A Christian named Vettius Epagathus, 'a man of position', tried to intervene on behalf of the accused when the governor arrived, but was howled down by the mob. The governor ignored his appeal and asked him if he were a Christian. When Epagathus confessed 'in a clear voice', he was placed under arrest himself. The governor then ordered all the Christians to be prosecuted, and the testimony of pagan slaves belonging to some of them was accepted, accusing them of cannibalism and incest. This increased public frenzy against them. They were subjected to torture of the most brutal kind. Some died before the spectacle was put on, including Pothinus the bishop, a man of over ninety, who died in prison from the effects of the beating he had received from the crowd after his interrogation.

Finally the executions by ordeal in the arena began. 'Maturus and Sanctus and Blandina and Attalus were led out to the wild beasts as a spectacle of inhumanity for the public and for the council of the provinces [*koinon tōn ethnōn*, i.e. the *concilium Galliarum*], the day of fighting against wild beasts having been specially appointed for our people.' Maturus and Sanctus met their deaths heroically: after a day of 'being made a spectacle to the world as a substitute for all the variations of gladiatorial combats', they were at last 'sacrificed' – precisely as the *trinqui* were in the barbarous Gallic ritual. Blandina had been hung on a stake for the beasts to attack, but none would touch her, and she was finally taken down for use on a later occasion. Attalus was then brought into the amphitheatre and was led round with a placard bearing, in Latin, the words, 'This is Attalus, the Christian'. But the governor was informed that he was a Roman citizen, and ordered him to be sent back to jail. He was awaiting instructions from the emperor as to how Roman citizens should be treated.

In the meantime the resolution of the surviving Christians had been strengthened, and some of those who had at first denied the faith were spurred on to confess themselves Christians. They were led out for interrogation by the governor, 'at the beginning of the festival there, at which there is a heavy attendance as all the [Gallic] provinces gather together for it'. The emperor had apparently written back to the governor with the instructions that any Roman citizens who recanted should be released, but that the rest should be beheaded. A few recanted, but most stayed firm, and the governor had the sentence carried out. Beheading was the death that Paul had suffered under Nero, for it was a Roman citizen's privilege to die in this way. The non-citizens were sent to the wild beasts. In order to please the mob the governor included Attalus in their numbers, which was a definite breach of the law. The people wanted to watch him being tormented in the amphitheatre, which duly happened. He was finally burnt to death. Then Blandina and a boy of about fifteen named Ponticus, both of whom had been led in every day to watch the others being tortured, were sacrificed.

No burial was permitted for the mangled corpses. The authorities must have known that Christians attached great importance to burial, and attempts made by surviving Christians were thwarted. After six days the remains were burned and the ashes thrown into the Rhône.[47]

Marcus' personal attitude to the fate of the Christians must remain largely undiscoverable: the *Meditations* provide limited and uncertain guidance. But as a Stoic, who by his training and by the necessity of his position believed profoundly in the duty of the individual towards the state, he cannot have viewed kindly the activities of people who professed complete lack of concern with worldly life. Also, hostility to Christianity was growing. It is no coincidence that the first written attack on the faith of which much is preserved, that of Celsus, dates from just this moment. There is no need to suppose that Marcus actively approved of persecution any more than had Trajan, for example. But the precedent had already been established, that to be a Christian was in itself a capital crime. Marcus clearly did not initiate the persecutions personally. But equally he would have seen no reason to obstruct the course of law. What remains an enigma is that, in spite of the existence of this fixed legal attitude, Christianity still survived and flourished. There was never any legal obstacle to persecution, yet it was only when times were hard, and scapegoats were wanted, that it broke out.[48]

Marcus had many other preoccupations at this time. The Moors, for example, were still giving active trouble. Only a few years after Marcus' friend Aufidius Victorinus had been despatched to Spain with a special command to combat a Moorish invasion, a similar incursion took place. This time it was judged sufficient that the procurator of Mauretania Tingitana, Vallius Maximianus, should pursue them across the Straits. He was able to wipe out the invaders, but they had penetrated far inland, up the R. Baetis to Italica, and as far as Singilia Barba, which they had subjected to a 'long siege', as an inscription at the town reveals.[49] The longstanding problem of the unpacified Moors no doubt made Marcus the more willing to conciliate pro-Roman elements in Tingitana. In the 160s he and Lucius had granted citizenship to Julianus, chieftain of the Zegrenses, his wife Ziddina, and their four sons, 'even though Roman citizenship is generally not given to those tribesmen except for very great services, by imperial favour', as their letter to the procurator of that time put it. In 177 Vallius Maximianus forwarded another request, from the younger Julianus, supported by testimony on his behalf from a previous procurator. Maximianus was asked to supply details for the imperial records. Then an imperial letter was duly drawn up, granting citizenship to the younger Julianus' wife Faggura and their two sons and two daughters. What gives this episode particular interest and importance is that the whole dossier was engraved on a large bronze tablet and set up in the town of Banasa. The grant was made on 6 July 177. An imperial freedman, Asclepiodotus, checked the entry in 'the register of Roman citizens' who had received their grant from previous rulers. The list starts with Augustus and names all his successors, except for Otho and Vitellius, down to Marcus and Commodus. This impressively prefaced extract from the register was added to the text of the two letters to procurators of Tingitana, and the whole document was them witnessed by twelve members of the imperial *consilium*, or advisory council. First named is M. Gavius Squilla Gallicanus, who had been consul in 150, then M'. Acilius Glabrio, consul of 152, T. Sextius Lateranus, consul of 154, C. Septimius Severus, consul in 160 (and a kinsman of the future emperor Severus). The next two are also probably ex-consuls, P. Julius Scapula Tertullus and T. Varius Clemens – the latter presumably the former *ab epistulis*, now a senator. Then come Bassaeus Rufus, still in office as prefect of the guard, it can be assumed, and P. Taruttienus Paternus, the former *ab epistulis*, who will be the colleague of Rufus as second prefect. The remaining four consellors may all be identified as high-ranking equestrians: Sex. Tigidius Perennis, later to be guard prefect himself, Q. Cervidius Scaevola, the eminent jurist, at this time prefect of the *vigiles*, Q. Larcius Eurupianus and T. Flavius Piso.[50]

An important legal measure was taken in the following year, the *Senatusconsultum Orfitianum*, named after one of the consuls of 178, which gave preference to a woman's children as to her inheritance, over her brothers, sisters and other relatives of her own family (*agnati*). This may seem of relatively minor significance, but it was in fact a great step forward in the recognition of a woman's individual existence apart from her family.

It may also have been at this time that Marcus made a decision arising out of Cassius' rebellion and its aftermath. The property of a certain 'Depitianus, a senator, who had participated in the Cassian frenzy' was ordered to be seized by the *fiscus* after his death, according to the Severan jurist, Paulus. 'Depitianus' is generally identified with Cassius' son-in-law Dryantianus, who had been liberally treated at first. The reasons behind this decision are not stated, and no hint is given as to the cause or manner of his death – which might have been from natural causes.[51]

Whatever the motives for this treatment of a pardoned traitor's estate, they cannot have been fiscal, for the economy had now been placed on a securer basis. In this year Marcus cancelled all debts incurred to the treasury and *fiscus* over the past forty-six years reckoned inclusively, that is from the year 133. Hadrian had likewise cancelled debts in 118, but it is not known why the interim period was not included. Perhaps the years 118–33 had already been dealt with. Documents concerning the years 133–78 were publicly burnt in the Forum.[52]

In this year there was a disastrous earthquake at Smyrna. An appeal went from the ruined city to ask for assistance from the emperor. The eloquent Aelius Aristides composed their plea, and he bewailed Smyrna's fate so movingly that Marcus 'groaned on many occasions at passages in his "lament", but when he came to the words: "She is a desert and the west winds blow through her," he shed tears over the letter.' Inspired by Aristides he consented to rebuild Smyrna. Cassius Dio, more prosaic than Philostratus, does not mention Aristides, but includes the detail that a senator of praetorian rank was appointed to supervise the work. This generosity towards Smyrna, Dio states, was only one example of 'the gifts of money that he made to various cities. . . . Therefore I am surprised that even now [i.e. the 220s] people criticize him on the grounds that he was not open-handed. For although, in general, he was very economical, yet he never avoided a single necessary expenditure – in spite of the fact that he did not burden anyone by financial levies and that he had of necessity to pay out very large sums beyond the normal regular expenses.' In fact the *congiaria* in Marcus' reign were very liberal.[53]

Unfortunately, at the same time as the economic position was showing signs of recovery, the situation on the Danube was deteriorating. It is noticeable that the titles of victory *Germanicus* and *Sarmaticus* disappear from the coinage of this year. Dio records that 'the Quintilii had been unable to bring the war to an end, although the two of them possessed much shrewdness, courage and experience'. By the middle of the year Marcus must have realized that his own presence was required once again, to give a new impetus.[54]

Commodus was to go north with Marcus, and for this reason it was decided to bring forward the date of his marriage. The chosen bride was Bruttia Crispina, granddaughter of the friend of Hadrian and Pius. Her father Bruttius Praesens had been consul in 153, and hence was probably a year or two older than Marcus. It was too late in the year for Praesens to be selected as the colleague for his son-in-law in the consulship in 179. That honour had already been bestowed on Martius Verus, still, no doubt, in Syria at the time. However, Praesens was to be consul for the second time in 180, instead, with Julius Verus as his colleague. The wedding was a modest occasion. 'The marriage was celebrated in the manner of private citizens.' But largesse was given to the people and the event was commemorated on the coinage. An *epithalamium*, or wedding hymn, for Commodus was written by the sophist Julius Pollux, who had shortly before this dedicated a Lexicon to the young prince. However poor his style, he had a winning voice and Commodus later made him professor of rhetoric at Athens.[55]

The biographer records that before Marcus set off he swore a solemn oath on the Capitol that he had not knowingly been responsible for the death of any senator, and that he would even have preserved the rebels if he had known in time. Aurelius Victor describes another remarkable scene. Marcus was 'so outstanding for his wisdom, lenience, innocence of character and literary attainments that when he was about to set off against the Marcomanni with his son Commodus, whom he had made Caesar, he was surrounded by a crowd of philosophers, who were protesting that he should not commit himself to the expedition and to battle, before he had expounded the difficulties and obscurities of the philosophical schools. Thus it was feared, from zeal for philosophy, that the uncertainties of war would affect his safety. And so greatly did the liberal arts flourish in his reign that I would think it the glory of the times.'[56]

A third event immediately preceding the departure is noted by Cassius Dio. Marcus had asked the senate for funds from the treasury, as a mark of formal deference, because these funds were always at his disposal in any case. '"As for us," he said, speaking to the senate, "we are so far from having any possessions of our own that even the house we live in is yours." After this speech, he threw the bloody spear kept in the Temple of Bellona into ground symbolically regarded as enemy territory (as I have heard from people who were there), and set off.' This latter action would have been taken by Marcus in his capacity as one of the *fetiales*. These priests had had the regular duty of declaring war from the earliest days of Rome's existence. Marcus had probably only continued, rather than revived, a traditional practice. If the statement about his 'possessions' is genuine,

Marcus was exaggerating, in view of his considerable inherited wealth. But it probably represents fairly his attitude to the imperial property.[57]

Marcus and Commodus finally left Rome on 3 August 178, on the *expeditio Germanica secunda*, as it was officially named. Among those who accompanied them were Claudius Pompeianus, Vitrasius Pollio and Bruttius Praesens from those related by marriage to the Antonine house. Taruttienus Paternus was by now probably senior prefect of the guard, following the retirement of Bassaeus Rufus, with Tigidius Perennis as his colleague. Paternus is recorded as actively involved in the war before long. Some of the best generals were certainly in the north already, for example Helvius Pertinax, who was on the Danube, and probably moved in this year to take over the key province of the Three Dacias. Meanwhile, Syria seems to have been entrusted to Marcus' close friend Aufidius Victorinus, to ensure that the east remained calm.[58]

The imperial headquarters for the winter of 178–9 is not known (there can have been little time left for campaigning when Marcus reached the front). One significant decision was probably made soon after Marcus arrived. The redoubtable M. Valerius Maximianus was 'chosen by the Most Sacred Emperors to be a member of the Most Honourable Order [*a sacratissimis imperatoribus in amplissimum ordinem allectus*] and straightway appointed legate of the legion First Adiutrix'. Maximianus had held three procuratorships since participating in the expedition to the east. Now he finally entered the senate. This man's career is in many ways even more striking than that of Pertinax. It illustrates once again Marcus' ability and willingness to recognize worth. 'It is impossible to make men exactly as one wishes them to be,' he said once, 'but it is our duty to use them, such as they are, for any service in which they may be useful to the state.'[59]

The promotion of Maximianus will have been only one among hundreds of appointments that required Marcus' attention, wherever he was. Each would require a formal letter, *codicilli*. The only specimen of the text of such an imperial 'codicil' that happens to be preserved is one that Marcus issued at this time to a certain Q. Domitius Marsianus on his appointment as procurator of crown property in Narbonensis. It was inscribed on the base of a statue set up in Marsianus' honour at his home town of Bulla Regia in Africa: 'Caesar Antoninus Aug(ustus) to his own Domitius Marsianus greeting. Having long been eager to promote you to the splendour of a ducenary procuratorship [i.e. one at a salary of 200,000 sesterces a year], I seize the opportunity which now offers. Succeed therefore to Marius Pudens with every hope of my continued favour, as long as you know yourself to retain your integrity, diligence and experience. Farewell, my Marsianus, very dear to me.'[60]

In the campaigning season of 179 supreme command in the field was assigned to Taruttienus Paternus. He engaged the enemy in a battle that lasted for a whole day. Marcus was acclaimed Imperator for the tenth time (and Commodus for the third time). No further details are recorded, but the enemy was probably the Quadi.[61]

Marcus' activity during the second expedition seems to be described in various extracts of Cassius Dio which have survived. 'The Jazyges sent envoys and asked to be released from some of the terms that they had agreed to. Some concessions were granted to them so that they should not become completely disaffected. However, neither they nor the Buri were willing to ally themselves to the Romans until they had been given assurances by Marcus that he would definitely carry the war through to its conclusion, for they were afraid that he might make a treaty with the Quadi as he had done before – and thus leave them with enemies on their borders.' The conditions granted to the Jazyges are detailed in another passage. Most of the restrictions imposed in the treaty of 175 were lifted, except for those concerning their public assemblies and markets, and, in particular, the ban on the use of boats of their own, as well as a total prohibition against landing on the islands in the Danube. He made them one important concession. They were to be allowed, subject to the approval of the governor of Dacia on the particular occasions, to pass through Roman territory to the lands of their Sarmatian cousins the Roxolani, on the Black Sea.[62]

Meanwhile powerful pressure was being exerted on the two most powerful German tribes, the Quadi and Marcomanni. Twenty thousand men were stationed in forts in the territories of each of these tribes. That is the equivalent of more than six legions, but a large proportion of the troops were undoubtedly auxiliaries and the legions were in any case operating in detachments (*vexillationes*) at this time. Whatever the composition of the force it is certain that a large number of semi-permanent forts were constructed, and eventually remains of some of them may be recovered in Bohemia and Slovakia. Dio even records that the soldiers stationed in the embryo province of Marcomannia had 'baths and all the necessities of life in abundance'. The Romans were in fact now firmly on top. It was they who were now receiving deserters from the Germans, in contrast to ten years or so previously, and they were able to recover many of their own men who had been taken prisoner. The Germans were kept constantly harassed, unable to pasture their flocks or cultivate the land. Finally the Quadi attempted to emigrate en masse to the north, hoping to find a home among the Semnones, another Suebic people. 'But Antoninus learned of their intention in advance and prevented them by blocking the roads. Thus he showed that he wanted not to acquire their land but to punish the people.' This judgment by Dio is faulty. To Marcus land without inhabitants would be useless. The empire itself was no longer in need of fresh areas to settle – rather the reverse, as the settlements of barbarians in Italy itself and the provinces demonstrate. Indeed, an instance arose at this very time. The Naristae, the smaller neighbours of the Marcomanni and Quadi, came over in large numbers (three thousand, according to Dio) and were given land within the empire. Marcus wanted to romanize the Marcomanni, Quadi and Jazyges, not merely to acquire their land.[63]

The occupation of enemy territory went on throughout the winter of 179–80, as is proved by an inscription carved high on a crag above the River Váh (Waag) at Trenčin in Slovakia, eighty miles north of the Danube frontier, which records the presence there of Valerius Maximianus, now with the Second Adiutrix; and that is confirmed by Maximianus' own inscription from North Africa, describing him as 'commander of the *vexillationes* wintering at Leugaricio' (the Roman version of the native name for Trenčin). During the winter, before the New Year of 180, Cn. Julius Verus died. His place as consul with Bruttius Praesens was taken by young Quintilius Condianus.[64]

The fulfilment of Marcus' intention to create two new provinces was now in sight, but early in March of 180, when the campaigning season was about to begin, he fell seriously ill. When Marcus realized that his condition was serious he sent for Commodus, according to the biographer. He asked him not to regard the completion of the war as a task beneath his dignity. If he did this, it would seem like a betrayal of the interests of the state. Commodus replied that his own health was his first consideration. Marcus consented but asked that he should 'wait for a few days and not set off at once'. This can only mean that Commodus had some justification in thinking that his health was in danger. These had been the sentiments of Lucius at Aquileia, when plague was rife in the army. A slightly different version of the conversation is given by another fourth-century writer according to whom Commodus replied that 'tasks can be completed by a man in good health, even if only gradually. A dead man can complete nothing.'

Marcus 'then began to abstain from eating and drinking in his desire for death, which made his condition worse. On the sixth day he called his friends, and, smiling at the concerns of men and despising death, said to them: "Why do you weep for me instead of thinking rather of the plague and death in general?" And when they wanted to withdraw, he groaned, and said: "If you give me leave to go now, I say farewell to you, as I go on ahead." And when he was asked to whom he commended his son, he replied: "To you, if he prove worthy, and to the immortal gods."' In another passage, drawn from a different source, the biographer relates that Marcus on this occasion expressed the same sentiments about Commodus that Philip had about Alexander, and that he regretted that he was leaving such a son behind him. But this story is suspect.

When the army learnt of their emperor's serious condition, the men were deeply moved with grief, 'for they loved him as none other'. 'On the seventh day his condition worsened and he allowed only his son to see him. But he sent him away at once, in case the disease should be passed on to him.

Having sent his son away, he covered his head, as if he wanted to sleep, but during the night he breathed his last.' Dio gives a different, and briefer, version. At the point of death he is said to have commended Commodus to the protection of the soldiers. 'To the tribune who asked him for the watchword he said: "Go to the rising sun. For I am already setting."'

The exact cause of his death is not known. From his own reported mention of the plague, from his sending Commodus away from his sickbed to avoid the risk of infection, and even from Commodus' preoccupation with his own health, it sounds as if Marcus had caught the plague. However, Dio states that his death was deliberately brought about by his doctors – 'as I have been plainly told' – to gain favour with Commodus, and implies that Marcus knew his son to be in some way responsible. But Dio also says, when stating his own view of the cause of death, that it was not 'as a result of the disease from which he was still suffering'. This refers to the stomach and chest condition which he had described earlier. It might have been cancer. But speculation is unprofitable. Marcus died on 17 March 180, two days before the traditional date for the opening of the campaigning season, and just over a month before his fifty-ninth birthday. Aurelius Victor, writing in the year 360, and his so-called epitomator over thirty years later, say that he died at Vindobona (Vienna). But Tertullian, in his *Apologeticum* composed less than twenty years after the event (probably in 197), says that 'Marcus Aurelius was taken from the republic at Sirmium'; and he has the correct date. The answer may be that Marcus died at Bononia on the Danube, less than twenty miles north of Sirmium. In that case, one may suppose that the campaign planned for 180 was to have been against the Sarmatians of the Hungarian plain.[65]

· 10 ·

MARCUS TO HIMSELF

DURING MARCUS' LAST STAY at Rome, reports the biographer, 'the saying of Plato was always on his lips, that states flourish if philosophers rule or if rulers are philosophers.' The story may be apocryphal, but if true would be ammunition for those who view the *Meditations* as the musings of a self-conscious prig. Self-conscious Marcus certainly always was, and sometimes he recognized that he was in danger of being priggish. If he was really quoting Plato frequently at that time, it may have been to justify to sceptics and critics his continued public preoccupation with philosophy, of which the culmination was the extraordinary scene on the eve of his departure in August 178. He knew he had critics. 'Penetrate inside their guiding reason,' he writes, 'and you will see what critics you fear – and what sort of critics they are of themselves.' Again, a little later, 'Whenever someone else blames or hates you . . ., approach their souls, penetrate inside and see what sort of people they are. You will see that you shouldn't torment yourself so that they should think in a certain way about you.' But, he adds, 'you must, however, think kindly of them, for by nature they are friends.' This kind of reflection crops up in the later books. In one, more elaborate, passage in Book 10 he allows himself some gentle satire. 'No one is lucky enough not to have some people standing by his death-bed welcoming the evil that is happening to him. Say he was virtuous and wise, won't there be someone at the last to say of him: "we shall breathe more freely now this schoolmaster has gone. Even if he wasn't hard on any of us, still I felt that he was silently condemning us." So much for the virtuous man – but as for us, how many other reasons are there for many to want to be rid of us! Think of this then when you're dying and you will depart the easier if you consider: "I am leaving a world in which even my companions, for whom I struggled, prayed and worried so much, wish me gone, hoping for some relief thereby." Why then should anyone cling on to a longer stay? Still, don't leave them in a less friendly spirit for this reason: be consistent to your own character, loving, good-natured, gracious. And don't leave as if being wrenched away, rather your departure from them should be like that gentle slipping away of soul from body of one who dies well. It was nature that bound you and united you to them and now she releases you. I am released as from my own kinsfolk, not dragged away and not compelled. For this too is a part of nature.'[1]

No one knows who preserved Marcus' manuscript after his death or how and when it first found a wider readership. Two of his oldest friends, Aufidius Victorinus and Seius Fuscianus, who survived him for some years, could have played a part. Or one might think of his daughters and sons-in-law. The last words of one daughter, Cornificia, before her death on the orders of Caracalla in 213, seem to show that she subscribed to Marcus' beliefs. But this does not prove that she had been responsible for circulating his writings, or even that she had read them. One of his freedmen, Chryseros, who wrote a chronicle from the foundation of Rome to the death of Marcus, has been suggested. But this too is pure speculation. Nor can it be detected how soon copies of the manuscript became more widely available. The Christian writer Clement of Alexandria and the historian Cassius Dio, both writing in the early third century, appear to be familiar with Marcus' thought. But they could have come across passages in his speeches or letters that echo what he wrote 'to himself' in the private notebooks we call the *Meditations*.[2] Herodian, writing in the 250s, says of Marcus that 'he was a lover of old-fashioned language . . . as is witnessed by what has come down to us of his sayings and writings'. This may include the *Meditations*. At any rate, by the fourth century the work was undoubtedly well known. The orator Themistius, friend of Marcus' great admirer and imitator Julian, addressing the emperor Valens, told him (flatteringly): 'You have no need of the *Precepts* of Marcus, or of any excellent sayings of any particular emperor.' This was in the year 364. Over thirty years later, the author of the Augustan History, in the life of Avidius Cassius, with his embroidered version of the scene from August 178, shows his familiarity with Marcus' *Meditations*, which he calls *paraeneseos*; and he alleges that Marcus spent three days giving public lectures to interpret them. This is one of the Augustan History's pleasanter inventions. The subsequent history of the *Meditations* is not relevant here. But the letter of Arethas, deacon of Patras (later Archbishop of Caesarea), to Demetrius, Archbishop of Heracleia, written in the late ninth or early tenth century, deserves partial quotation: 'Marcus the Emperor's most profitable book I have had for some time, an old copy though, not to say completely tattered, which spoils its usefulness to those who want to use it. However, I have been able to have a new copy made and can send it on to posterity in a new dress.' The deacon charitably passed on his old copy to the Archbishop.[3]

The *Meditations* are divided into twelve 'books', of which the first, in which Marcus summarises the benefits he has received from his family, friends and teachers, was probably written separately, when he was near to death. It provides a clue to what Marcus was trying to do in the other eleven: to remind himself, while far from home, in difficult and often exhausting circumstances, of the lessons he had learned in happier times. Rusticus, Apollonius, Sextus, Claudius Severus and Claudius Maximus receive long tributes, but far and away the fullest is that given to his adoptive father Antoninus Pius. It looks as if it is a development of a briefer reminicence of Pius in the sixth book, beginning with the words 'In all things Antoninus' disciple'. This particular reflection may have led him to set down, in summary fashion, but more systematically, all his debts to his mentors, in a separate notebook.[4]

There can be no doubt that Marcus wrote for himself alone, in his tent 'among the Quadi' as in Book 2, or 'at Carnuntum', as Book 3 is headed, in the camp of the legion XIV Gemina, and wherever else he found himself in the years from 172–180. Some passages are indeed like short formal essays. Others are collections of aphoristic quotations or near-quotations. That what he wrote has in places a decidedly literary cast is hardly surprising, considering his long and elaborate education. Nor is it surprising that some of what he wrote could have been spoken as philosophical 'precepts' to others. This may be because it represents his distilled recollections of the teaching of Apollonius or Rusticus or his other tutors. In any case, as he reveals, he tried to train himself to think thoughts that he would never be ashamed to express to anyone who suddenly asked him: 'What are you thinking now?' In the form in which it is transmitted the work is inevitably scrappy, repetitive, often concise to the point of obscurity, with frequent changes of subject. Sometimes, no doubt, he had time for only a few sentences, and may have resumed writing after a gap of some days or weeks. There are few personal allusions, other than in the first book.[5]

It is ironic that Marcus, whose name is most familiar to posterity through the medium of the *Meditations*, dwells frequently in them on the uncertainty of posthumous fame. 'Little then is each man's life and little the corner of the earth he lives in, and little even the longest survival of his fame with posterity, and that too passed on through a succession of poor mortals, each one of them soon to die, with no knowledge of themselves even, let alone of a man who has died long ago.' 'Shall mere fame distract you? Look at the speed of total oblivion of all and the void of endless time on either side of us and the hollowness of applause. . . . For the whole earth is but a point, and of this what a tiny corner is our dwelling-place, and how few and how paltry are those who will praise you.' 'The man whose heart flutters for fame after death does not picture to himself that every one of those that remember him will also very soon die. Then again their successors, until finally the entire remembrance of the man is extinguished. . . . But even supposing that those who are to remember never die and their remembering is thus immortal – what is that to you? To the dead praise means nothing, I need not say – and what is it to the living, except for some practical purpose?' 'In a short space of time will come for you obliviousness of everything – and everything will be oblivious of you.' Further similar passages could be quoted.

In several other passages he reflects on the transience of human history:

'Consider for example the times of Vespasian, and you will see all these things: people marrying, rearing children, falling ill, dying, making war, holding festivals, trading, farming, flattering, asserting themselves, suspecting, plotting, praying for other people's death, muttering about present conditions, making love, hoarding money, wanting the consulship, wanting the throne. Now that life of theirs exists no more anywhere. Pass on, again, to the times of Trajan. Again, all the same. That life is dead too.' 'Words familiar once are now obsolete. So too are the names of those once renowned in song, now obsolete in a sense, Camillus, Caeso, Volesus, Dentatus, and a little later Scipio and Cato, then Augustus too, then Hadrian and Antoninus. For everything fades away and quickly becomes a myth; and soon complete oblivion covers them over. And this I say of those who shone in some remarkable way. For the rest, as soon as the breath left their bodies, they were "unnoticed and unwept".' 'How many a Chrysippus, how many a Socrates, how many an Epictetus has eternity already devoured.' 'Watch the stars in their courses as if you were running about with them and think constantly of the changes of the elements into one another. Mental images of these things wash away the filth of life on the ground. And, indeed, when writing about mankind look on earthly things as if from some place on high – assemblies, armies, farms, marriages, divorces, the din of law-courts, deserts, varied barbarian peoples, festivals, mournings, market-places, a mixture of everything and an order made up of opposites. Look back at the past, how many changes of dynasties. And you can foresee what is to come, for it will be of totally similar pattern and it is impossible for it to escape the rhythm of the present. So to study human life over forty years is the same as studying it over ten thousand.'[6]

Although Marcus was writing in the middle of a terrible war, with other external preoccupations such as the plague and the revolt of Cassius, it has struck many how little obvious reference there is to external events. 'Yet here we find no echo of these great struggles. There is only one reference to the Sarmatian War' is the understandable complaint of a modern scholar who has wrestled with the scanty evidence for the history of the northern campaigns. If the literary-minded emperor had had tastes like Julius Caesar, then *Commentaries* on the Marcomannic and Sarmatian Wars might have appeared. It is better not to regret that it happened otherwise. In any case the view that there is 'no echo' of the wars is mistaken. To the reader with some imagination many pages of the *Meditations* can be seen to have an intensity and a special choice of imagery for which the wars were responsible. The wars in fact were the reason for their being written. They are full of thoughts of death. A tranquil Marcus Aurelius, happy in Rome or in the country with his family and his books, living like Pius to a ripe old age, would probably never have put pen to paper, or would have contented himself with completing his *Deeds of the Ancient Greeks and Romans*.[7]

The second Book of the *Meditations* is headed 'Written among the Quadi on the Granua' and the third 'Written at Carnuntum'. In Book 10 comes the famous sole explicit reference to his wars. 'A spider is proud when it catches a fly, a man when he snares a hare, another when he nets a fish, another wild boars, another bears, another Sarmatians. If you test their principles, aren't they all brigands?' Marcus did not exult in his victories. But some of his men must have taken pride in their personal prowess against the enemy. The artists of the Aurelian column in Rome have authentically recaptured the resignation and sympathy which motivated Marcus, in their portrayal of the northern wars.[8]

Apart from specific mention of names, there are many places where the influence of personal contact with the grim realities of war is apparent. The sentiments expressed in 'Despise the flesh, gore, and bones and a network, a wickerwork of nerves, veins, arteries', from the beginning of the book written on campaign in enemy territory, may have been polished by attendance at Galen's dissections. But it must have been consciousness of the body heightened by witnessing death and wounding that made him use the word 'gore' (luthros). Experience of battle inspires other passages. 'When a man's understanding has been chastened and purified, you will find no trace of a festering wound, gangrene, abscess, beneath the skin.' 'Just as surgeons always keep their instruments and lancets ready to hand for emergency operations, so you too should keep your beliefs ready, for the diagnosis of things divine and human.' 'Even what is closest [to the reason], the body, is cut, cauterised, suppurates, becomes gangrenous – yet let the part which makes judgments about these things be silent: that is, let it judge nothing to be good or bad which can happen equally to a good man or to a bad man.' This is faithfulness to Epictetus' teaching. The vivid language surely reflects personal experience, as another passage certainly does: 'if you've ever seen a dismembered hand or foot or a head cut off, lying apart somewhere from the rest of the body. . . .' The reliefs on the columns of Trajan and of Marcus spring to mind, depicting soldiers holding up the heads of their decapitated foes; and, likewise (on the column of Trajan), army surgeons attending to wounded Romans on the battlefield.[9]

In a section reflecting on the common lot of all men, death, he recalls Alexander the Great, Pompey and Caesar, who 'utterly destroyed whole cities so many times, and on the field of battle cut to pieces many tens of thousands of cavalry and infantry – and they themselves one day left the field of life'. The word 'gore' recurs shortly afterwards. Pursuing a philosophical conceit for a while he wonders 'how the earth can contain the bodies of those who have been buried in it, through countless ages'. The thought was one in which a man who had seen many of his friends and officers die, and, if Lucian can be believed, 20,000 men from his army fall in one battle, may be excused for indulging.[10]

The sources do not speak of Marcus being wounded personally. It is unlikely that he was. But Dio speaks of his weakness and of the pain in his chest. It is probably this which was at the back of the jotted comments on pain which occur here and there. 'In the case of every pain, be ready with the thought that it is not dishonourable and doesn't harm the mind that holds the helm. . . . This saying of Epicurus should help you – pain is neither unbearable nor unending, so long as you remember its limitations and don't add to it with your imagination.' 'On pain: what we cannot bear takes us away [from life]; what lasts can be borne.' 'Pain in the hand or foot is not against nature, provided that the foot and hand are fulfilling their own tasks. Hence not even for a man as man is pain contrary to nature. If it's not contrary to nature, it's not evil for him.' Thus he tried to apply the Stoic criteria to his own position.[11]

Sleep was a problem for him, as Dio and Galen record. He found it difficult to pull himself out of bed at dawn, after a disturbed night perhaps, when he had finally used Galen's *theriac* to help him get to sleep. 'At daybreak, when you are getting up with reluctance, let this be before your mind: "I am getting up to man's work".' 'When you are stirred from your sleep with difficulty, recall to mind the thought that acts in the service of the community are part of your constitution, but sleeping is what you have in common with dumb animals.' 'Let it make no difference to you whether you are shivering or warm, so long as you are doing your duty, whether you are drowsy or have had sufficient sleep, whether you are hearing ill or good spoken of yourself, whether you are dying or doing something else – for dying too is one of the actions of life. So in this too it is enough to "make the best use of the present".' His sleep was not always tranquil: 'be sober again and recall yourself, shake off sleep again – and realize that it was dreams that disturbed you, and now that you are fully awake again, look at these things as you looked at those'.[12]

His consciousness of his duties as emperor and commander-in-chief are never far from his mind. 'Each hour decide firmly, like a Roman and a man, to do what is to hand.' 'And let the divinity within you be the master of a being that is manly, and mature in years, a statesman and a Roman and a ruler – who has taken up his post, as would one who is waiting for the retreat to be sounded, from life.' 'Don't be ashamed to be helped. The task in front of you is to carry out your allotted duty, like a soldier in a storming-party. Suppose that you're lame and can't scale the wall by yourself. Yet it is possible with another's help.' He quoted Plato's *Apology* to strengthen his determination. 'Wherever a man takes up his post, either because he thinks it is the best place or because his officer has placed him there, there, I think, he should stay, and face the danger, taking nothing else into account, neither death nor anything else, in comparison with dishonour.'[13]

The military metaphors seem to recur in a passage from the book written 'Among the Quadi'. 'Do things breaking in on you from outside distract you? Well, give yourself some free time to learn some new good thing, and stop leaving your post. But now you must guard against another sort of wandering off course also: those who are weary of life and have no target at which to aim every impulse, or, in general, every mental impression (*phantasia*), are triflers, in their actions as well [as their words].' 'Just as those opposed to you in your progress in agreement with right principle will not be able to divert you from right conduct, so you must not let them divert you from good will towards them. Be equally on your guard in both respects, both in steady judgment and behaviour and in gentleness to those who try to hinder you or are difficult in other ways. For to be hard on them is a weakness, just as much as to abandon your course and surrender from fear – for the man who panics and the man who is alienated from his natural kinsman and friend are both deserters from their post.' 'Always run the short way', he says near the end of the fourth Book, 'and nature's way is short. So do and say everything in the most healthy way, for a determination like this is a release from troubles and warfare and every care and affectation.' His detached attitude in the middle of the fighting, and his reliance on his Stoic creed are powerfully summed up in Book 2. 'Of human life, time is a point, existence is a moving stream, sensation is dim, the whole fabric of the body susceptible to decay, fame uncertain – briefly, all the things of the body are as a river, all the things of the spirit a dream and a tomb, life is like war and a sojourn in a foreign land. What then can escort man? One thing and one alone, philosophy.' Some of these ideas derive ultimately, perhaps, from Heraclitus. They would be impressive in any context. But the fact that they were written during war, during 'a sojourn in a foreign land', adds considerably to their effect on the reader.[14]

The image of the river, first used by Heraclitus, recurs several other times. 'Time is like a river composed of all things that happen, a rushing torrent.' 'In such a fog and filth, in so great a flowing past of being and of time, of movement and of things moved, what can be respected or be pursued with enthusiasm I do not know.' 'All being is like a river in ceaseless flow, its activities in continual change, its causes constantly varying, scarcely anything stable.' 'The world-cause is like a river in flood. It carries all before it.' Marcus had seen rivers before he went to Pannonia – and the Tiber in destructive flood. But he had never seen a great river like the Danube, and this must have had its effect on him. The eerie flat landscape of Burgenland, around the Neusiedlersee, in particular, which has had a perceptible effect on great creative artists (Haydn and Liszt), can hardly have failed to impress him, likewise the flat lands of the Marchfeld and the Hungarian plain.[15]

References to other external events occur also, detached as always, but vivid. He talks of 'fleeing from the plague', but applies it to the corruption of the mind, 'far more corrupting' than the plague itself. He has a passing reference to 'treaties and armistices in war', and a little further on reflects on treachery. 'Turn inwards to your own self whenever you blame a traitor or an ungrateful person, for it is clearly your own fault, if you trusted such a man to keep loyal.' A little earlier there is an enigmatic passage: 'If he did wrong, the evil is on that side; but perhaps he did no wrong.' These passages may reflect the events of 175, when Marcus made peace with the Sarmatians because of the rebellion of Cassius. Dio records that Marcus never publicly abused Cassius, but constantly referred to him as 'ungrateful'. 'If *he* did wrong' might equally be translated 'if *she* did wrong', and could allude to Faustina's supposed implication. One may also note the reference to 'loss' in an adjacent passage: 'Loss (*apobole*) is nothing else but change (*metabole*).' This might perhaps have reflected the death of Faustina. In a few places one might detect references to Commodus, for example, 'If you can, convert him by teaching; if not, remember that kindliness was given to you for this very thing;' 'if he makes a mistake, teach him with kindliness and point out what is being overlooked; if you fail, blame yourself, or not even yourself;' 'kindness is invincible . . . what can the most insolent do if you continue to be gentle with him and quietly show him a better way at the very moment when he tries to do you harm – "No, child, we were born for other things, I shall not be harmed, you are harming yourself, child".'[16]

Two further possible echoes of contemporary preoccupations may be mentioned here. 'He who runs away from his master is a runaway slave. But law is a master and the lawbreaker is a runaway slave too.' This recalls the increasing prevalence of slaves running away, and the 'general rescript' concerned with this some time in the years 177–80. 'Visualize to yourself every man who gives way to pain or discontent at anything at all is like the pig being sacrificed, kicking and squealing.' Marcus had to perform the military sacrifice of the *suovetaurilia* on several occasions during the wars. (It marked the official opening and closing of a campaign.) Marcus is shown performing such a sacrifice on one of the reliefs which were on his triumphal arch.[17]

Marcus is much preoccupied with death in the *Meditations*. The subject recurs again and again, especially in the last few books. Metaphor after metaphor, simile after simile, are brought in as the emperor struggles to reconcile himself with the prospect that his life was nearing its end. 'The governor of the universe' has 'set a time-limit' on you, he tells himself. 'Do each act as if it were your last.' The concept of his life nearing its close is one that recurs again and again. The 'winding of the threads ordained by providence' or by Clotho, one of the three Goddesses of Fate, was nearing its conclusion.[18]

Sometimes he says, briefly, 'life is short'. On one occasion he puts it to himself that one of the gods might tell him: 'tomorrow you will be dead'. Later he goes beyond this and tells himself to think of himself as already dead, and to regard what remains as a bonus – to be lived 'in accordance with nature'. A man's death is not the same as an actor having to break off in mid-performance. Death must not come as a surprise. It must not be despised either: 'smile at its coming'.[19]

Above all he reminds himself again and again that death is natural. 'Death is like birth, a mystery of nature.' He thinks of the great men of the past who are dead, of men who clung greedily to life, of cities like Pompeii that are, in a sense, now dead. 'Alexander the Great and his stable-boy both met their death in the end.' 'Soon enough you will vanish into nothing, like Hadrian and Augustus.' He quotes Euripides and Plato on death. 'The court of Augustus, his wife, his daughter, his grandsons, stepsons, sister, Agrippa, his kinsmen, his friends, Areius, Maecenas, his doctors and sacrificial attendants – the whole court is dead. Then pass on to other courts – and the death not of a single man but of a whole family, like that of Pompey. And that epitaph: "The Last of his Line".' He thinks of mourners, such as Lucilla his mother mourning his father Verus, and of Panthea mourning her lover Lucius. 'And if they were still sitting by the tomb, would the dead notice? And if they did notice, would it please them?'[20]

The simile of the retreat from the battlefield of life, and the idea of the river of time, have already been mentioned; and also his views on posthumous fame. His ideas on life after death were not fixed. He reviews the possibilities as dispassionately as he can. Sometimes he thinks of death in the orthodox Stoic way, as a dissolution of the body's material into the whole from which it came. He tells himself not to speculate. 'Either there is a random interlocking of atoms, and a scattering again, or there is unity, order, providence. If the first, why do I even desire to wear myself out in a world formed by chance, and in such a confusion . . .? And why am I disturbed? The scattering of the atoms will come upon me whatever I do. But if the alternative be true, I worship and I am calm, I take courage in the governor of all.' 'On death: either dispersal, if we are merely atoms; or if we are a true unity, either extinction or a change of dwelling-place.' In the last book he turns to the question more than once. How can the gods have allowed this, the gods who ordained everything, with love for mankind; that truly good men should be utterly extinguished? But, he tells himself, if it ought to have been ordered differently, 'the gods would have made it so; for if it were just, it would be possible also, and if it were in accordance with nature, nature would have brought it about'. He argues with himself whether there is an inexorable destiny, whose decrees cannot be transgressed, or a divine providence that listens to human prayer, or simply an ungoverned chaos. If it is inexorable destiny, why resist? If a divine providence, he should make himself worthy of assistance. If nothing but random chaos, then he should be glad that amid the flood of waves, he has a mind that can direct. In the last words of the *Meditations* he masters his fears. 'Man, you have been a citizen in this great city. What does it matter to you whether it is for five years or for fifty? For what is in accordance with the laws is equal for every man. Why then is it terrible, if it is not a tyrant nor an unjust judge, but nature herself who brought you in, that sends you away from the city – as if the praetor who engaged an actor were to dismiss him from the stage? "But I have not spoken my five acts yet, only three." "Quite true – but in life three acts are the whole play." For he defines the perfect whole, the cause yesterday of your composition, today of your dissolution; you are the cause of neither. Go away then, gently. For he who releases you, releases you gently.'[21]

Death was for Marcus a release, a 'lying down to rest'. 'Remember that the story of your life is finished and your service is completed.' The theme of service to others was always present. He had no illusions about those around him: 'At dawn say to yourself first: "I shall meet the interfering, ungrateful, insolent, treacherous, envious, uncharitable".' This passage, from the opening of Book 2, was perhaps the first he wrote – but he adds that 'all these qualities come from their ignorance of good and evil'. The thought recurs in a later passage: 'next pass on to the characters of those living around you, even the best of whom it is hard to put up with'. But again he qualifies this: 'not to say that it is hard for a man to put up with himself', and elsewhere he tells himself to 'think of the good qualities of those around you, when you want to cheer yourself up: the energy of one, the modesty of another, the generosity of another, and so on. For there is nothing so cheering as the images of the virtues shining out in the character of one's contemporaries, and meeting as far as possible in a group. So you should keep them ready.' The biographer in the Augustan History stresses that 'he always conferred with the leading men not only on matters of war but on civilian affairs as well, before he did anything. Indeed, this was always his particular saying "It is fairer that I should follow the advice of so many and such good friends, than that they should follow the wishes of a single man, myself".' This is borne out by several passages in Marcus' own *Meditations*. 'If anyone can prove and bring home to me that an idea or an action of mine is wrong, I will amend it gladly. I seek the truth, which never harmed anyone.' 'What need for surmise when you can see what should be done and if you can see your course to take it gladly and not turn aside – but if you cannot, suspend judgment and use the best men to advise you.'[22]

Sometimes he yearned for the chance to withdraw from it all. 'Men search out retreats for themselves, in the country, by the sea, in the mountains – you yourself, more than most, are in the habit of longing for such things. But all this is most unlike a philosopher – you can retreat inside yourself any hour you like.' His thoughts must have returned wistfully to the quiet days of his youth spent at Lanuvium or Baiae. It may even be that when he told himself never to let anyone 'hear you finding fault with court life again, not even yourself', there was a conscious or unconscious realization that his life in the palace had been, if nothing else, preferable to life in army headquarters. On occasion he told himself that his 'station in life' made his profession of philosophy difficult. But later he says that 'no other calling in life is so fitted for philosophy as this in which you now find yourself.' 'If you had a stepmother as well as a mother,' he writes at one point, you would do your duty to your stepmother but would constantly return to your mother. So for you with the court and philosophy – return frequently to philosophy and be refreshed, and this way court life will seem more bearable to you, and you to it.'[23]

A frequent image that Marcus uses is that of the city of the world, the universal city of which all men are citizens, 'the most venerable of all cities and constituted societies', obedience to whose laws is the 'aim of all rational beings'. 'Test everything one meets in life,' he says, 'in accordance with its "value in reference to the whole, and to man, who is a citizen of the highest city, of which all other cities are like individual houses". A man who "cuts off his own soul from the soul of reasonable creatures" is a fragment cut off from the city, which is a unity.' 'What does not harm the city does not harm the citizens either.' 'What does not benefit the hive does not benefit the bee.' 'The poet sings: "Dear City of Cecrops" – and you will not say "Dear City of God"?'[24]

Marcus had no illusions about himself. 'This too can make you despise vain glory, the fact that you can no longer achieve the aim of having lived your whole life, or at least, your life from manhood, as a philosopher. To many other people as well as to yourself you have plainly fallen far short of philosophy. So you are tainted and it is no longer easy for you to gain the reputation of a philosopher.' 'Will you, my soul, one day be good, simple, single, naked, plainer to see than your surrounding flesh?' At one point he tells himself, with a kind of impatience, 'Don't go on discussing what a good man should be, just be one'.[25]

The philosophy of life expressed in the *Meditations* is not orthodox Stoicism. It is the individual attitude to life of a man who has studied and thought for a long time about the problems of conduct and the different teachings of the philosophical schools, and has made his own selection, strongly influenced by his own experiences. Stoic doctrines predominate, as is not unexpected in the case of one so closely associated with Stoics like Junius Rusticus and Claudius Maximus, not to mention his philosophy tutor Apollonius. The idea of the 'city of God' and the constant effort to 'live in accordance with nature' express the essence of Stoic doctrines. 'Be free,' he tells himself, as Epictetus had taught. 'It is what is hidden within you that controls the strings.' 'Keep yourself every hour for freedom, contentedly, simply and reverently.' 'The understanding that is free from passions is a citadel.' 'Bear and forbear,' he says, as Epictetus did. Again and again he sets out reasons for following this precept, and avoiding anger. He is also much concerned with 'truth', not merely in the philosophical sense, of the reality of things, but in its simple meaning, telling the truth. This was a quality which Fronto had stressed, and it was no doubt one which Marcus had striven for from early boyhood, conscious of his name 'Verus' and its meaning – hence, no doubt, Hadrian's nickname for him 'Verissimus'.[26]

The deepest impression left on Marcus by the teaching of any single Stoic predecessor was that made by Posidonius' concept of the world as a unified organism, in which the inner tension in everything preserves it as a composite whole. 'Meditate often on the bond between all things in the universe, and their mutual relationship to one another. For all things are in a way woven together and all are because of this dear to one another. For one thing follows on another in order because of the stress movement and common spirit and the unity of all being.' This concept was closely related to that of the world-city, which Posidonius, living in the first century BC when Rome's predominance had at last begun to unify the Mediterranean world, had eloquently expressed. It is difficult to define Marcus' religious position. To some he appears deeply imbued with traditional piety. But at times in his writings he seems more like an agnostic, although believing that it was right to carry out formal acts of religious cult. He quotes an old Athenian prayer for rain, and comments: 'Either don't pray at all, or like this, simply and frankly'. But later, in a passage questioning whether the gods have any power, he writes: 'If they have no power, why pray to them? But if they do have power, why not rather pray that they should give freedom from fear for these things or lust for these things or grief at these things, rather than they they should grant or not grant the thing itself?'[27]

It is difficult to select any one passage which summarizes Marcus' philosophy. But in one written at Carnuntum, in Book 3, the essence of his attitude to life comes out clearly. 'If you do the work on hand following the rule of right with enthusiasm, manfully and with kindheartedness, and allow no side issues to interrupt, but preserve the divinity within you pure and upright, as if you might even now have to return it to its Giver – if you make this firm, expecting nothing and avoiding nothing, but are content with your present activity in accordance with nature and with old-fashioned truthfulness in what you say and speak – you will live a happy life, and there is no one who can prevent this.'[3] Reading the *Meditations* for long periods can be conducive of melancholy. The atmosphere is certainly strongly tinged with darkness, although in many places it is lightened by vivid imagery – figs and olives, the drooping heads of ripe corn, rosebuds and saplings, vines bearing another summer's grapes, scuffling puppies or quarrelsome children. But he was not trying to achieve 'fine writing'. 'Forget your thirst for books, or you will die muttering.'[28]

The *Meditations* are the self-expression of a ruler of a great empire who could see further than his empire. 'Asia and Europe are corners in the Universe. Every sea is a drop in the Universe – Mount Athos is a clod of earth in the Universe. Every instant of time is a mere point in eternity.' 'I have a city and a fatherland. As Antoninus, I am a Roman, as a man, I am a citizen of the Universe.' He wanted his Rome to be as near to his ideal city as he could. He knew it was difficult – 'don't hope for Plato's Utopia, but be content to make a very small step forward and reflect that the result of even this is no trivial success'. But the man whose friends had made him familiar with the lives of Thrasea and Cato, and able to 'conceive the idea of a state based on equity and freedom of speech, and of a monarchy which cherishes above all the liberty of the subject', had aspirations that were capable of realization. His hope was not fulfilled. But the verdict on his reign of Ammianus Marcellinus, admirer in his turn of Marcus' admirer Julian, is one that Marcus deserved: 'after calamitous losses things were restored anew, because the temperance of old had not yet been infected with the irresolution of negligence and laxity . . . with unanimous ardour highest and lowest hastened, as if to a calm and peaceful haven, to an honourable death in the service of the republic'. Cassius Dio, who experienced for himself the reign of Marcus and of his successors, gives explicit credit to the emperor himself. 'He did not have the good fortune that he deserved, for he was not physically strong, and for almost his whole reign was involved in a series of troubles. But I for my part admired him all the more for this very reason, that amid unusual and extraordinary difficulties he both survived himself and preserved the empire.'[29]

· II ·
EPILOGUE

IN THE JUDGMENT of his contemporaries, Marcus Aurelius had been the perfect emperor. Posterity confirmed the verdict. There was one qualification: his choice of successor. Commodus, the first emperor born in the purple, became 'a greater curse to the Romans than any pestilence or any crime', in the words of Dio. He was hated by his own class, and was continually plotted against. Only interested in his pleasures, he let his favourites rule, first the chamberlain Saoterus, then Tigidius Perennis, as praetorian prefect a coldly efficient Grand Vizier, then another freedman chamberlain, Cleander. When these three were gone, Commodus began to break loose (in 190) and to indulge his fantasies to the full. A new plot was formed and on New Year's Eve 192 he was strangled in his bath. The 'royalest of all emperors' was replaced by Helvius Pertinax, the freedman's son and former schoolmaster, who proclaimed a return to the policies of Marcus. Less than three months later he too was dead from assassination, succeeded, after the notorious auction of the empire at the praetorian camp, by Didius Julianus, the one-time protégé of Domitia Lucilla. Didius began under a cloud and never had a chance. The men who had backed Pertinax acted, and their nominee, Septimius Severus, marched on Rome from Pannonia. It took four years, from 193–197, for Severus to secure the throne, in two more civil wars.[1]

Severus, for political reasons, proclaimed himself 'son of the deified Marcus' and renamed his elder son 'Marcus Aurelius Antoninus'; then even deified Commodus (whose memory had been condemned) and added 'brother of the deified Commodus' to his titles. This demonstrates the dilemma of Marcus. The notion of hereditary succession was deeply imbedded. Only the adoption of Trajan by Nerva had broken the pattern. Thereafter kinship counted a great deal. Hadrian had been Trajan's closest male relative, and had also married his grand-niece. To be sure, Hadrian himself had then rejected his own grand-nephew in favour of a remoter connection, the young Marcus and his family group. But the cementing of a dynastic system had been made manifest under Antoninus Pius, with the marriage of Marcus and his cousin Faustina. Marcus is even said to have regarded his wife as the source of his claim. When advised to divorce her for infidelity, it is alleged in the Augustan History, he replied that in that case 'he would have to return the dowry as well' – the empire.[2]

Marcus' toleration of Faustina's affairs has certainly been held against him. Most of the stories about her must probably be discounted. It was the subsequent behaviour of their son which led someone to suggest that she had had a liaison with a gladiator. It was the only way that they could explain the discrepancy in character between Marcus and Commodus. Perhaps Faustina strayed later. But in 160, when she was only thirty, the mother of four young children (the two youngest born in 159 and 160), who had lost several others in infancy, it is hard to believe that she was unfaithful. When Marcus was away from her for three years or more (autumn 169–autumn 172, perhaps up to 173), until she joined him at the front, things may have been different. There were stories about affairs with ballet-dancers (*pantomimi*) then. She might have met temptation in the east in 165–6. Lovers of rank are named also, one of whom paid her court when Marcus was at home, it was said. Finally, there was the story of the messages to Cassius – passion combined with treason. This last is probably untrue. But it may be that at some time she had let it be known that if Marcus died before Commodus reached his majority, she would prefer Cassius as her own and Commodus' protector, rather than her uncongenial son-in-law Pompeianus. Although the Stoic emperor could view the act of physical love as merely 'friction of innards and convulsive ejaculation of mucus', he thanked the gods that his wife was 'so docile, so affectionate, so unaffected'. A few escapades would not have been enough to destroy the memory of thirty years of marriage.[3]

Septimius Severus faced a similar problem with his own succession. His son 'Antoninus' – better known as Caracalla – was marked out as heir at a much younger age than even Commodus had been: he was only nine years old when he was made Augustus. He was a little older in 211 (twenty-one), when Severus died, than Commodus had been in 180. But Severus knew his faults only too well. Dio reports that 'he allowed his love for his offspring to outweigh his love for his country' – even though 'he had often blamed Marcus for not putting Commodus quietly out of the way.'

The rising of Cassius must have made Marcus aware of the problem. If he himself died with a youthful and untried heir, there would be civil war. He must have hoped that by giving Commodus the powers of co-emperor, making him known to the armies and surrounding him with tried and trusted advisers, he could avert another armed rebellion at his death. As it turned out, Commodus' reign and the civil wars that followed it cut a swathe through the ranks of the old élite. It had already been weakened in Marcus' own time through plague and external warfare, but Marcus had been able to recruit new men like Pertinax and Valerius Maximianus. His own careful respect for the prerogatives of the senatorial order ensured that there was a broad consensus within the ruling élite. By the end of the second century this consensus had collapsed. The attempt of Septimius Severus to weld his own family on to the Antonine dynasty could not repair the damage.[4]

APPENDIX I

Sources

A. ANCIENT EVIDENCE

Marcus Aurelius presents a unique opportunity to an ancient historian.

1. His correspondence with his tutor Fronto gives insight into his life from his late teens until his mid-forties, c. 138–66; and his *Meditations* offer us his private thoughts during the last years, c. 172–180. The Codex containing Fronto's correspondence was rediscovered by Angelo Mai in 1815, and further portions of it a few years later. Mai's original publication of the damaged and fragmentary MS was improved on several times in the nineteenth century, the best edition being that of S.A. Naber in 1867. In 1919–20 C.R. Haines produced the Loeb edition, with English translation, in which he rearranged the correspondence in chronological order (naturally, this was to a considerable extent conjectural), and took account of improved readings, notably by E. Hauler. The most recent edition is that by M.P.J. van den Hout (1954), who gives the text in the original order of the Codex, with readings in many cases superior to those of Haines. A promised second volume, with commentary, ancient *testimonia*, and full *index verborum* (p. lxxx) has not materialised. In 1974, E. Champlin tackled the chronology of the letters in a fundamental new study in *JRS*, and followed this up with his monograph, *Fronto and Antonine Rome* (1980). These two investigations are now indispensable guides to any study of Fronto and of Marcus. Naturally, there are some interpretations which have been corrected by subsequent discoveries. In two particular cases, I have been unconvinced by Champlin's arguments. First, on the trial in which Fronto and Herodes appeared on opposite sides, I have been swayed by W. Ameling, *Herodes Atticus* (1983) to retain the earlier date. Second, there is the very important question of Marcus' 'conversion' to philosophy. I am totally persuaded by Champlin's case, *JRS* 64 (1974) 144, that the letter written by Marcus when he was twenty-five, *Ad MC* 4.13, refers to (Titius) Aristo, the jurisconsult and friend of Pliny, rather than to the third century BC Stoic philosopher Aristo of Chios. But the conclusion that he draws seems to me slightly excessive. I accept that there was 'no sudden conversion to philosophy' and that 'there was no abandonment of literature and eloquence' (*Fronto and Antonine Rome* 121; cf. 77). On the other hand, the letter does indicate very plainly that Marcus had been undergoing some inner 'crisis', was dissatisfied with himself and how he was spending his time, and felt the need for higher things. On the date of Fronto's death I am totally in agreement with Champlin's conclusion that 'there can be little hope that the unhappy orator survived the year 167' (*Fronto and Antonine Rome* 142). Finally, it may be noted that in van den Hout's edition, the five books of correspondence with Marcus as Caesar occupy pp. 1–87; then come 4 books to him as emperor (88–110); 2 books to Lucius Verus as emperor (111–30); miscellaneous

pieces addressed to Marcus as emperor (*De eloquentia*, 131–48; *De orationibus*, 149–55); letters to Antoninus Pius (156–162); 2 books of letters to friends (163–90); the *Principia Historiae* (191–200); *Laudes fumi* etc. (201–5); *De bello Parthico* (206–11); *De feriis Alsiensibus* (212–19); *De nepote amisso* (220–4); *Arion* (225–6); and the *Additamentum* (mainly letters in Greek, 227–39), followed by fragments (240–4).

2. The so called *Meditations* of Marcus have been edited and translated many times, and only a brief selection can be noted here. C.R. Haines published a Loeb text and translation (1924), which I have found helpful, but the most important contribution is that of A.S.L. Farquharson, in two volumes: I, introduction, text and translation, and English commentary; II, commentary on the Greek text (1944). Unlike Farquharson, I am persuaded by H. Schenkl, *WS* 34 (1912) 82 ff. that Book 1 was the latest to be written. At any rate, there are strong grounds for thinking that it was not written first. Haines attempted, in *Journal of Philology* 33 (1914) 278 ff., to date the different parts of the *Meditations*, almost an impossible task, although some passages do offer strong hints of allusions to particular events, e.g. to the revolt of Cassius; and Books 2 and 3, headed 'among the Quadi' and 'at Carnuntum', may legitimately be assigned for that reason to the period c. 171–4. P.A. Brunt, *JRS* 64 (1974) 18 f., tackled the question again without being able to offer much that was new. (Oddly, on p. 19 he attributed to Haines an attempt to connect *Med.* 5.7 with the Rain Miracle, an idea which Haines, *JPhil.* 33 (1914) 283 called 'purely fanciful', and to myself the idea that 4.28 referred to Cassius – no reference is given, and I cannot find such an attribution in anything that I – or for that matter anyone else – wrote). Brunt's article, *JRS* 64 (1974) 1–20, is a most valuable contribution to the interpretation of Marcus' thought, with particular stress on his Roman qualities, and the importance of Antoninus Pius in his development. J.M. Rist (1982) re-examines the extent of Marcus' commitment to Stoicism.

3. The legal compilations (*Digest*, *Code* of Justinian, etc.) preserve a great many of Marcus' pronouncements from his reign, examined at length by P. Noyen (in Flemish in 1954 and in English in 1955). G.R. Stanton, *Hist.* 18 (1969) 570 ff., questioned Noyen's claim that Marcus' Stoicism was a dominant influence in this sphere. There have been a number of other contributions to the debate, but I find most instructive the article by W. Williams, *JRS* 66 (1976) 67 ff., in which he analyses the differences between Hadrian, Antoninus, and Marcus revealed by the legal sources.

4. The orator Aelius Aristides is an important source for the age of the Antonines, the *Roman Oration* being the principal basis for the favourable verdict of posterity on the era. Considerable advances have been made in the dating and interpretation of Aristides' life and writings. G.W. Bowersock, *Greek Sophists in the Roman Empire* (1969), supplies a sensitive and illuminating examination of Aristides' world – as well as of Herodes, Galen, Philostratus and others. A particularly valuable step was taken when C.P. Jones demonstrated, in *JRS* 62 (1972) 134 ff., that *Or.* 35 K was indeed by Aristides, and that it offers fascinating evidence for the early years of Pius. (Note also his reply to criticism, in *CQ* 31 (1981) 224 f.) Meanwhile, the edition of *Or.* 26 K, the *Roman Oration*, by J.H. Oliver (1953) remains immensely valuable.

5. The writings of the great doctor Galen contain a great deal of information on the elite of the Antonine era. The edition, translation and commentary produced by V. Nutton, of Galen, *On Prognosis* (1979), marks a great advance. There has been no comparable work on other writers who were Marcus' contemporaries (Aulus Gellius – but cf. Champlin's *Fronto*; Apuleius; Lucian). But the two volume study of *Herodes Atticus* (1983) by W. Ameling is of great value. This depends not only on the mass of contemporary epigraphic evidence but on Philostratus' *Vitae sophistarum*, which Bowersock's *Greek Sophists* had already made so much better appreciated and understood.

6. Coins, inscriptions and papyri supply vital primary evidence. For the former, H. Mattingly's *Coins of the Roman Empire in the British Museum*, vol. IV (1940) remains the most up to date comprehensive collection; and for the medallions, there is nothing more recent than F. Gnecchi (1912). Naturally, later studies, particularly of chronological questions, have modified some interpretations. For another aspect of numismatics, the analysis of the Roman silver coinage by D.R. Walker has disclosed a period of debasement 161–66, followed by improvement 166–70, then further debasement 170–80; also, it is something of a surprise, debasement under Pius, in 148 (*BAR Supp. ser.* 40, 1978, 124 ff.). In the field of epigraphy one may single out the full publication of the *Fasti Ostienses* (*Inscr. It.* XIII.1, 1947; L. Vidman, *Fasti Ostienses*[2], 1982); the improved text of the *SC de sumptibus gladiatoriis minuendis* in the edition of J.H. Oliver and R.E.A. Palmer (1955); the *cursus* inscriptions of M. Valerius Maximianus (*AE* 1956. 124) and Pertinax (*AE* 1963. 52); the letter to Q. Domitius Marsianus (*AE* 1962. 183); Marcus' letter to the Athenians (*Hesperia*, Supp. 13, 1970); the *tabula Banasitana* (*AE* 1971. 534); the dedications for Marcus and Lucius and for Marcus and Commodus at Carnuntum (*AE* 1982. 777–8). But it is above all the combining together of a mass of material, as by H.G. Pflaum in his *CP* (and the *Supp.*), by R. Syme in a series of major articles (cf. App. 2), and by G. Alföldy, especially in his *Konsulat und Senatorenstand* (1977), that makes progress possible. Of papyri, one may note in particular A.K. Bowman's identification, in *JRS* 60 (1970) 20 ff., of a letter from Avidius Cassius as emperor, to the Alexandrians, and the publication by J.D. Thomas (1972) of a letter of Pius which lists both Marcus and Lucius among his *consilium*. (On the evidence of archaeology, particularly the historical reliefs, cf. App. 3.)

7. The major narrative historian of the period was Cassius Dio, a senator from Nicaea in Bithynia, who wrote a history of Rome from earliest times to his own day, the 220s (he was *cos. II ord.* in 229, one of the latest events mentioned). Unfortunately, his treatment of Hadrian and of Marcus is preserved only in abbreviated epitome and in excerpts, and of Pius is virtually completely missing. Dio, whose father was also a senator, was born in the 160s and greatly admired Marcus, whose death, in his view marked the end of an age of gold and the onset of an age of rusty iron. The standard edition is that by U.P. Boissevain (5 vols., 1895–1931; repr. 1955), while the Loeb edition with English translation is also convenient – but adopts a different numbering of the later books (in particular, book 71 of Dio is numbered 72 in Loeb vol. 9, from 71.3.1). Boissevain's numbering is followed here. F. Millar's study of Dio (1964) is the essential introduction to the man and his work (but takes an eccentric position regarding the time of composition, criticised by most reviewers; for a new view, cf. now T.D. Barnes, *Phoenix* 38 (1984) 240 ff., whose case for a later date, in the 220s, looks promising). Dio's evidence is vital, but allowance has to be made for his prejudices (not least concerning questions of expanding the empire, cf. App. 3). Further, the way in which his excerptors and epitomators, principally the eleventh-century Byzantine monk John Xiphilinus of Trapezus, treated his work, is open to varying interpretation (in particular over the Rain Miracle, cf. App. 3).

8. The other third-century historian of any substance, Herodian, is certainly inferior to Dio; and in any case refers to the period of Marcus only by way of flashbacks. Although he has been defended, e.g. by his Loeb editor C.R. Whittaker (1969) – and has on occasion been vindicated, e.g. over Lucilla's standing as Marcus' eldest daughter (App. 2) – his value is rather small for the present work, particularly as he takes the death of Marcus as his starting-point. On that subject he has nothing useful to contribute, cf. G. Alföldy, *Latomus* 32 (1973) 345 ff.; and for the identity, status and date of Herodian, cf. id., *Ancient Society* 2 (1971) 204 ff.

9. The *Historia Augusta* (Teubner ed. by E. Hohl, 1927, repr. with *corrigenda* 1955; Loeb ed. and trans. by D. Magie, 1921–32) is a source of a very different kind, a set of biographies of emperors, Caesars, and usurpers, from Hadrian to the sons of Carus. It was ostensibly the work of six biographers, of whom 'Aelius Spartianus' wrote lives of Hadrian, Aelius, Didius Julianus, Severus, Caracalla, Pescennius Niger and Geta; 'Julius Capitolinus' those of Pius, Marcus, Lucius Verus, Pertinax, Clodius Albinus, Macrinus and some other third century emperors; 'Vulcacius Gallicanus V.C.' produced only the life of Avidius Cassius; and 'Aelius Lampridius' the lives of Commodus, Diadumenianus, Elagabalus and Severus Alexander. (The later third-century lives were supposedly the work of 'Trebellius Pollio' and 'Flavius Vopiscus of Syracuse'.) H. Dessau, in an epoch-making article, 'Über Zeit und Persönlichkeit der *Scriptores Historiae Augustae*', *Hermes* 24 (1889) 337 ff., argued that the *HA* was the work, not of six authors, from the age of Diocletian and Constantine (as numerous – although mutually inconsistent – references in the work assert), but of one man writing c. 395. Dessau further led the way in demonstrating that much of the 'information' it contained was fiction, above all in the third century lives, but also in the 'minor lives' of figures such as Aelius Caesar, Avidius Cassius, and later usurpers. There is still some disagreement about the details of Dessau's thesis, but it now appears to be generally accepted. This is due not least to the series of *Colloquia* begun in 1963 and still in progress; and to the writings of R. Syme (*Ammianus and the HA*, 1968; *Emperors and Biography*, 1971; *Historia Augusta Papers*, 1983). I give a more detailed account of the problem in the introduction to my Penguin Classics translation of the lives from Hadrian to Elagabalus (*Lives of the Later Caesars*, 1976).

One as yet unresolved – and perhaps insoluble – question is that of the sources of the *HA*, tackled in a monograph by T.D. Barnes (*Collection Latomus* 155, 1978). Barnes there maintains the view which he first expressed in *JRS* 57 (1967) 65 ff., that the principal source of the factual information in the second century lives was an unknown good biographer, labelled *Ignotus*, a view also argued forcibly by R. Syme (especially in *Emperors and Biography*, 30 ff.). I have elsewhere stated my preference for the view that Marius Maximus, cited fairly frequently in the *HA* and clearly the author of a continuation of Suetonius, was the main source: cf. my *Septimius Severus* (1971) 308 ff. It must be conceded that the *Verus* is wrongly labelled a 'minor life', as it is clearly not full of fiction, like the *Aelius* and *Avidius Cassius*. However, it does not follow that the author of the *HA* used a source that provided a separate life of Verus. It is easy to see how the material in the *Verus* could have been excerpted from a life of Marcus by Marius Maximus, and then reworked; this would also help to account for the confusion in the *Marcus* from the end of section 14. I. Marriott's computer study tends to confirm this view: 'with the exception of the *Verus*, the "primary" lives group together . . . [Verus] may not have received separate treatment in the common source' (*JRS* 69 (1979) 69 f.). The *HA* is therefore something of a minefield, or as Mommsen put it, 'not just a contaminated source: a sewer'. But it has to be used, and fortunately there are now helpful guides, even if the hoped for commentary, to which the *Colloquia* are aiming, has not yet materialised. On the *Marcus*, the monograph by Schwendemann remains vital, even though it was composed in 1913–14 and not published until after the author's death, in 1923; and it labours under the preconceptions of its time, somewhat arbitrarily dividing up the *vita* into three parts: 'biographical', 'annalistic' and 'compiler's' own contribution (with the section lifted from Eutropius). The lack of index makes consultation difficult, and some passages receive no commentary at all. H.W. Benario published *A Commentary on the Vita Hadriani* in 1980, which has some uses but is unreliable in detail (cf. *JRS* 73, 1983, 242 f.). For the *Verus*, there is T.D. Barnes' study in *JRS* 57 (1967) 65 ff. Avidius Cassius has received full treatment in the biography by M.L. Astarita (1983); but it must be noted that she is tempted in places to accept bogus data in the *HA vita*. Attention must be drawn here to four articles by H.G. Pflaum, analysing the persons mentioned in the lives from Hadrian to Avidius Cassius: *HAC* 1964/65 (1966) 143 ff.; 1968/69 (1970) 173 ff.; 1972/74 (1976) 173 ff.; 189 ff. Note also G. Kerler, *Die Aussenpolitik in der Historia Augusta* (1970).

For ancient Christian evidence, cf. App. 4.

B. MODERN WORK

G.R. Stanton, 'Marcus Aurelius, Lucius Verus, and Commodus: 1962–1972', in *ANRW* 2.2 (1975) 478–549 has a full bibliographical survey of fairly recent work. R. Klein, ed., *Marc Aurel* (1979) contains twenty chapters on different aspects of the subject, all but two reprinted versions, but in some cases with addenda; and a lengthy bibliography (pp. 503–529). From the point of view of the present work one must underline the importance of *PIR²* (now covering the letters A–M); of R. Syme's *Tacitus* (1958) and *Roman Papers* I–II (1979); III (1984); IV (forthcoming); and his studies of the *HA* mentioned above; H.G. Pflaum's *CP* (with the *Supp.*); G. Alföldy's *Konsulat und Senatorenstand* (1977); and the work of Ameling, Astarita, Barnes, Bowersock, Brunt, Champlin, C.P. Jones, Oliver and Williams mentioned above. (Note also, in App. 2, the work of R. Bol and K. Fittschen; and in App. 3 of J. Guey and W. Zwikker). Finally, F. Millar, *The Emperor in the Roman World (31 BC–AD 337)* (1977), is a truly monumental examination of what emperors did. Its relevance to the study of a particular man who was emperor hardly needs stating. Marcus, indeed, features frequently in its pages – and the opening chapter, by way of prologue, is entitled 'Marcus Aurelius at Sirmium'. However, Millar's concept of the emperor's role differs somewhat from my own; and one key aspect of it found no place (another volume would have been required) in his pages: the emperor at war. Little though he can have liked it, Marcus spent his entire reign dealing with military matters, and much of it actually in the field.

APPENDIX 2
The Antonine Dynasty

The dynasty labelled 'Antonine' runs from Nerva to Commodus. Only Marcus was succeeded by his own real son; he himself and his three predecessors had been adopted. Yet, while Nerva's choice of Trajan as heir was not influenced by any tie of kinship whatever, it was otherwise with Hadrian's succession to Trajan, and with that of Marcus to Pius. Hadrian was Trajan's nearest male relative – son of a first cousin – and the link had been reinforced early on when Hadrian married Sabina, Trajan's grand-niece, granddaughter of Hadrian's father's cousin. Marcus was the nephew of Pius' wife and married Pius' much loved daughter. Hereditary considerations thus played a clear role; and Marcus, by making sure his son Commodus succeeded him, followed precedent. It is true that on his accession in 161 he made his adoptive brother Lucius co-emperor, giving the empire joint rulers for the first time (although the difference from the situation of Tiberius at the end of Augustus' reign, or of Titus under Vespasian, was in reality slight: Tiberius and Titus had lacked only the name *Augustus*). In 166 Marcus made his sons, Commodus and Annius Verus, Caesars. What was envisaged, should Marcus – at least nine years older – have died before Lucius, cannot be known – by 166 Lucius had children of his own, his wife, Marcus' daughter, was Augusta.

However that may be, the real residual puzzle, and debate, regarding the Antonine dynasty, continue to revolve around Hadrian's arrangements for a successor. Hadrian had no children. But his sister had a daughter, Julia Paulina (A). Julia's husband Pedanius Fuscus – from a distinguished family, also deriving from Spain, albeit from a different part to Hadrian's – was brought into instant prominence after Hadrian's accession. He held the consulship with Hadrian as his colleague in Hadrian's first full year, 118. Hadrian himself held the *fasces* only one more time, the next year. His colleague in 119 was another man related to him, although more distantly, P. Dasumius Rusticus (D). Neither Pedanius and Julia, nor Dasumius, are mentioned in the surviving ancient sources for Hadrian's reign. They may not have survived long. But Julia had a son; and her father Servianus lived on. It may be imagined that the emperor's grand-nephew was regarded as a likely heir.

In the meantime, however, others received favour, most notably M. Annius Verus, another Roman of Spanish colonial extraction. His second consulship in 121 presumably went with his prefecture of the city (an important role, especially as Hadrian was so much abroad). A second consulship was a considerable honour; but another man, L. Catilius Severus (D), had enjoyed it a year earlier, even though his first consulship had been in 110, thirteen years later than Verus' first. Then in 126 Verus held office again, thus equalling Hadrian's own total, and the first *privatus* to have a third consulship since Licinius Sura in 107. Catilius and Annius

Verus both had links with the Dasumii, Hadrian's kinsmen (D); and Verus may even – it is doubtful – have married a half-sister of Hadrian's wife (C). Servianus seems to have conceded primacy to Verus in the 'glass-ball game' of politics, if E. Champlin's ingenious interpretation of a poem is correct (*ZPE* 60 (1985) 159 ff.). Eight years on, in 134, Servianus, by then in his late eighties, at last received equivalent recognition from his brother-in-law. Yet in 136 he and his grandson Pedanius Fuscus, the obvious heir (cf. E. Champlin, *ZPE* 21 (1976) 78 ff.) were forced to suicide. 'All, in the end, whom he had considered for the imperial position, he detested as though they were emperors-to-be', says the biographer (*HA Had.* 23.6). (Another victim may have been Servianus' original colleague as consul in 134, cf. A. Degrassi, *I Fasti consolari* (1952) 38 f.).

Late in 136 (cf. *PIR²* C 605 for the timing) Hadrian announced his heir: L. Ceionius Commodus, one of that year's consuls. This is the order of events given by the biographer (*HA Had.* 23.8–11). Cassius Dio puts the adoption first, and makes it cause Servianus' death, and his grandson's, 'on the grounds that they were displeased at it' (69.17.1). One might reconcile the two versions by supposing that Hadrian's intention was known within a small circle – which included Servianus – before it was announced and implemented; that Servianus expressed his resentment, and that his death was imposed, before the public act. (T.D. Barnes, *The Sources of the HA* (1978) 45, accepting the evidence of a horoscope supposedly that of young Fuscus, assigns his death and that of Servianus to a moment after Antoninus' adoption in 138 – but the horoscope only puts Fuscus' death between 6 April 137 and 5 April 138; and its validity is doubtful). Commodus, aged about 36 at most, perhaps as young as 33, was the son and grandson of *consules ordinarii*; and his mother Plautia (E) was from a distinguished family, the Plautii of Trebula Suffenas, near Tibur (L.R. Taylor, *MAAR* 24 (1956) 9 ff.; A.R. Birley, *The Fasti of Roman Britain* (1981) 37 ff.). Why this man? Remorse for the execution of Avidius Nigrinus, Commodus' stepfather and father-in-law has been suggested (by R. Syme, *Tacitus* (1958) 601). The *HA Had.* 23.10 suggested it was his personal beauty. A modern scholar proposed something more startling, that Commodus was Hadrian's bastard son (J. Carcopino, *REA* 51 (1949) 262 ff.); but the 'evidence' adduced is invalid (R. Syme, *HSCP* 83 (1979) 301 = *RP* 1170 f.). Commodus, who became L. Aelius Caesar, had a son, aged at most seven, perhaps only four (E), and two daughters. One of them, Ceionia Fabia, had been betrothed, in 135 or early in 136, 'at Hadrian's wish' to the grandson of old Annius Verus – Marcus (*HA Marc.* 4.5); and soon after Marcus held the office of prefect during the *feriae Latinae*, appointed, it may be inferred, by the consul Ceionius Commodus (4.6). Marcus had been greatly favoured by Hadrian (*HA Marc.* 4.1–2 – at latest from the age of five or six). Given the high favour shown to old Verus, Marcus' grandfather – and Marcus' uncle Libo (C) was consul in 128 – this is not surprising. Further, Aelius Caesar was the cousin of Libo's wife Fundania; and Fundania's brother had married Marcus' cousin Aurelia Fadilla (B, E). The fourth-century chronicler Eutropius actually asserts that Hadrian wanted to make Marcus his successor; but that he was not old enough (8.11) – this statement reappears in the *HA Marc.* 16.6, but has no independent value: *HA* 16.3–17.7 is a passage repeated from Eutropius, with some slight variations in wording. Eutropius cannot be relied upon, as he can be seen to be making an inference from what happened later (as pointed out by T.D. Barnes, *JRS* 57 (1967) 78). Aelius Caesar was known to be consumptive, as Dio reports

A: TRAJAN AND HADRIAN

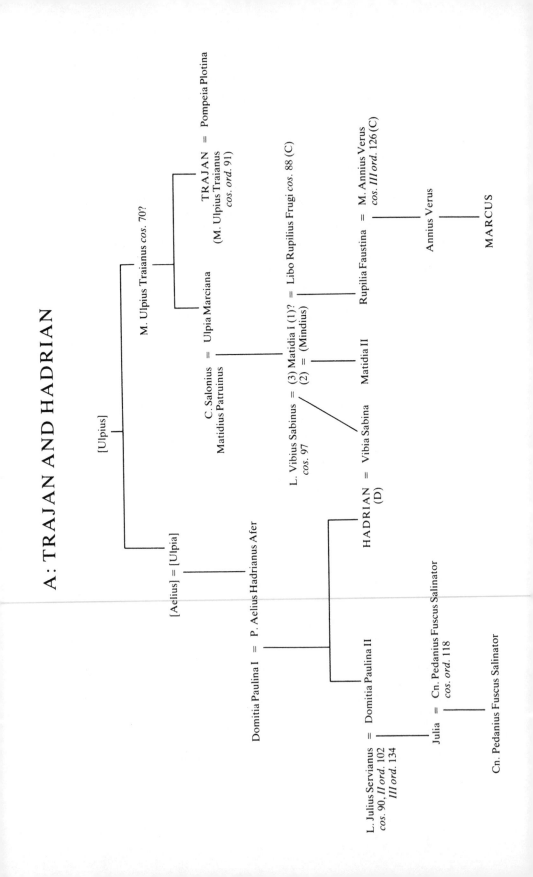

B: ANTONINUS PIUS

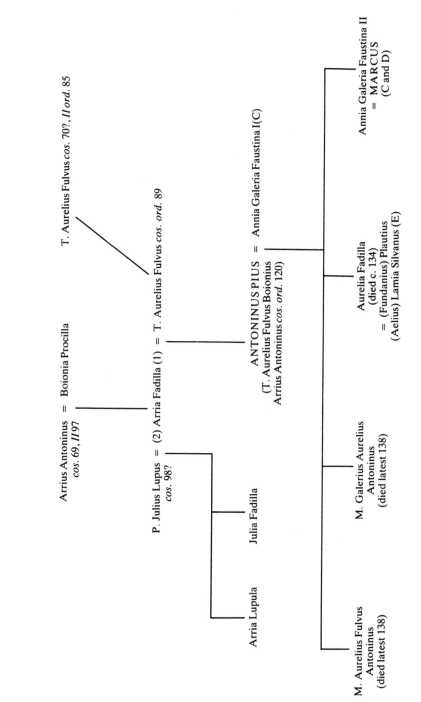

T. Aurelius Fulvus *cos. 70?, II ord.* 85

Arrius Antoninus = Boionia Procilla
cos. 69, *II* 97

P. Julius Lupus = (2) Arria Fadilla (1) = T. Aurelius Fulvus *cos. ord.* 89
cos. 98?

ANTONINUS PIUS = Annia Galeria Faustina I(C)
(T. Aurelius Fulvus Boionius
Arrius Antoninus *cos. ord.* 120)

Arria Lupula

Julia Fadilla

M. Aurelius Fulvus
Antoninus
(died latest 138)

M. Galerius Aurelius
Antoninus
(died latest 138)

Aurelia Fadilla
(died c. 134)
= (Fundanius) Plautius
(Aelius) Lamia Silvanus (E)

Annia Galeria Faustina II
= MARCUS
(C and D)

C: ANNII VERI

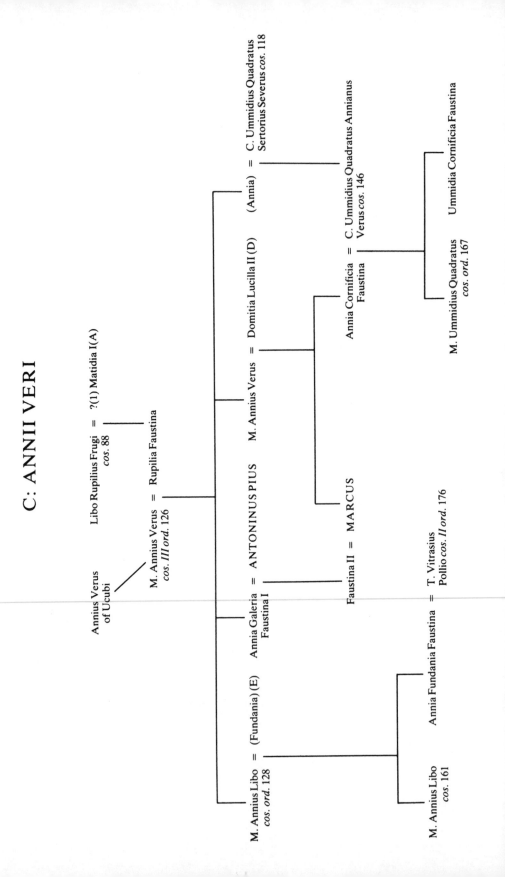

D: DOMITIA LUCILLA

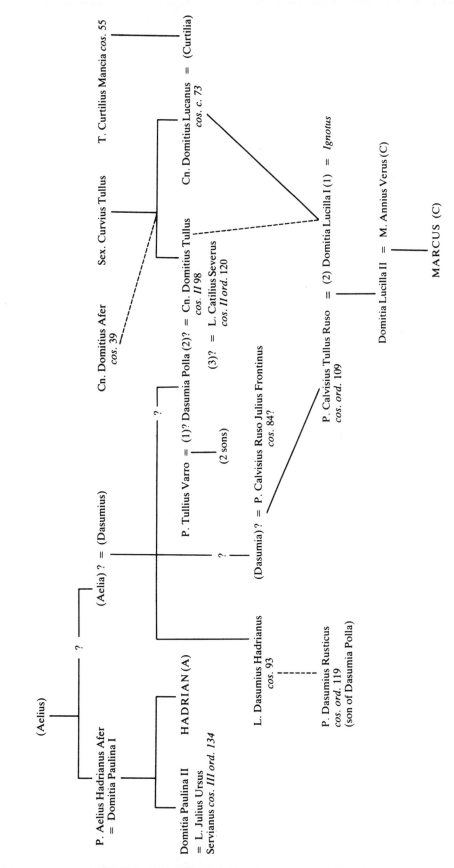

E: LUCIUS

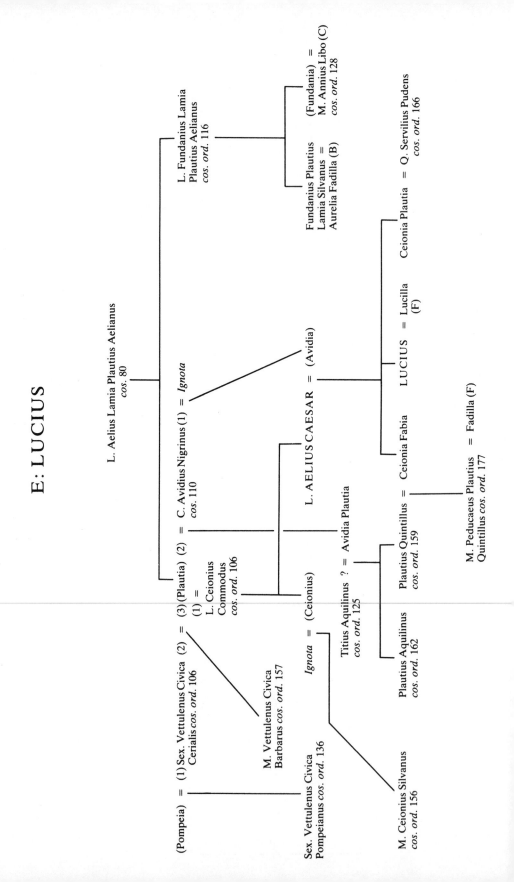

F: THE CHILDREN OF FAUSTINA II

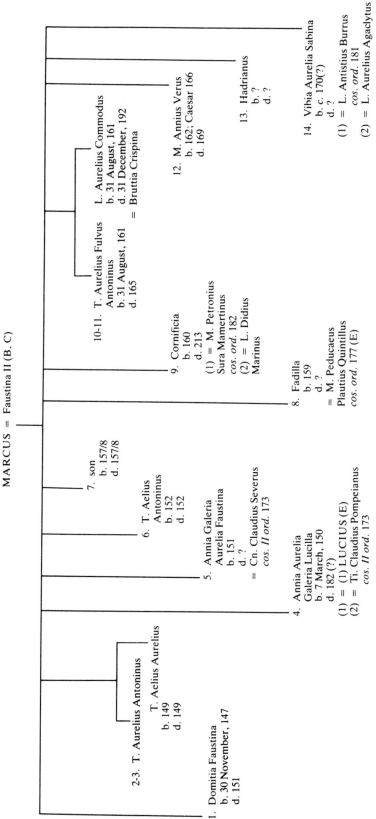

MARCUS = Faustina II (B. C)

1. Domitia Faustina
   b. 30 November, 147
   d. 151

2-3. T. Aurelius Antoninus
      b. 149
      d. 149
      T. Aelius Aurelius
      b. 149
      d. 149

4. Annia Aurelia
   Galeria Lucilla
   b. 7 March, 150
   d. 182 (?)

   (1) = (1) LUCIUS (E)
   (2) = Ti. Claudius Pompeianus
         cos. II ord. 173

5. Annia Galeria
   Aurelia Faustina
   b. 151
   d. ?
   = Cn. Claudius Severus
     cos. II ord. 173

6. T. Aelius
   Antoninus
   b. 152
   d. 152

7. son
   b. 157/8
   d. 157/8

8. Fadilla
   b. 159
   d. ?
   = M. Peducaeus
     Plautius Quintillus
     cos. ord. 177 (E)

9. Cornificia
   b. 160
   d. 213

   (1) = M. Petronius
         Sura Mamertinus
         cos. ord. 182
   (2) = L. Didius
         Marinus

10-11. T. Aurelius Fulvus
       Antoninus
       b. 31 August, 161
       d. 165

L. Aurelius Commodus
b. 31 August, 161
d. 31 December, 192
= Bruttia Crispina

12. M. Annius Verus
    b. 162; Caesar 166
    d. 169

13. Hadrianus
    b. ?
    d. ?

14. Vibia Aurelia Sabina
    b. c. 170(?)
    d. ?

    (1) = L. Antistius Burrus
          cos. ord. 181
    (2) = L. Aurelius Agaclytus

(69.17.1), a fact elaborated by the author of the *HA* in his largely fictional life of Aelius – leading H.G. Pflaum to conclude that Hadrian deliberately selected as immediate heir a man who would not live long, so that Marcus would then succeed (*HAC 1963* (1964) 103 ff.). This might be so – although *HA Ael.* should not be invoked to support the thesis. At any rate, it would be over a decade after the adoption that Aelius' own son – Lucius – could conceivably succeed. Marcus, on the other hand, the destined son-in-law, was already in his sixteenth year.

After Aelius' death on New Year's Day 138, Hadrian waited for eight weeks before announcing his replacement: Aurelius Antoninus, Marcus' uncle, who was instructed to adopt young Lucius, now seven (or perhaps only four, cf. E), and also Marcus. But, Dio says, Hadrian favoured Marcus 'because of his kin [or: kinship] and his age and because he was already giving indication of having an exceptionally strong character; whence he used to call him "Verissimus"' (69.21.2). T.D. Barnes claims that Dio originally said that it was Antoninus, not Hadrian, who 'favoured Marcus'; yet this conflicts with the second half of the sentence, about *Verissimus*, which Xiphilinus should not have misunderstood (*JRS* 57 (1967) 78). The *HA* may indeed name Lucius first in its version (*Had.* 24.1), although giving him the wrong names. But this hardly supports Barnes' assertion (op. cit. 77 ff.) that Lucius, and not Marcus, was intended by Hadrian as the eventual heir. No more do his other arguments. First, that Lucius 'had the better of the proposed dynastic matches', since he was betrothed to Antoninus' daughter Faustina. But Ceionia Fabia and Faustina were both the daughter of a Caesar, and Fabia of the first one chosen. Even less relevant to this case is the stone relief from Ephesus, depicting Lucius between Antoninus and Hadrian, with Marcus to one side. As Barnes concedes (78 n. 84), with one exception the art historians date the making of the relief to the 160s, when Lucius was at Ephesus. If a local artist at that time chose to magnify Lucius' role in a series of reliefs portraying his life, the fact has no value in determining Hadrian's intentions in 138. Thus, although, certainly, it cannot be proved exactly what Hadrian had in mind for Marcus – or for the much younger Lucius – between the adoption of Lucius' father late in 136 and the adoption of Antoninus on 25 February 138, there is no doubt that *both* were then adopted by Hadrian's new heir. And Dio says – or Xiphilinus' epitome of Dio – that Hadrian favoured Marcus. (It is odd that Barnes attaches weight to Lucius' selection as Antoninus' son-in-law, op. cit. 77 and *corrigendum*, 79, since he earlier denies significance to Marcus' status as son-in-law of Ceionius Commodus, 74 f.; 77). It is thus not surprising that most scholars before Barnes (cf. his list, op. cit. 75 n. 41) interpret Hadrian's intentions in the period 136–138 as having been, all along, to ensure the ultimate succession of Marcus (one of the two exceptions, B.W. Henderson, *The Life and Principate of the Emperor Hadrian* (1923) 261 is a weak support indeed: he swallows the fiction and mistakes of the *HA* whole; and makes Lucius eleven years old). One must now add the more detailed reconstruction of Marcus' 'kinship', stressed by Dio (69.21.2; 71.35.2). The fact that two of the men who incurred Hadrian's disfavour in his last years, C. Ummidius Quadratus (C) and L. Catilius Severus (E), were also Marcus' kinsmen, should not be overlooked. It surely suggests the possibility of competition for the role of placeholder for Marcus: Ceionius was his father-in-law to be (and linked by other ties to the Annii); Antoninus was his uncle by marriage – so too was Ummidius, it now seems; and Catilius was his great-grandfather. The above remarks depend heavily on the writings of R. Syme, above all in his *Tacitus* (1958) 600 ff.; 791 ff.; and his several remarkable articles, quoted below in the annotation of the stemmata. It must be recorded that the interpretation here offered does not quite match Syme's own. In conclusion, it must be admitted that Hadrian's intentions remain obscure, except that in late February 138 he imposed on Antoninus joint heirs, Marcus and Lucius, or, some might prefer, Lucius and Marcus. It can then be added that, while Antoninus later scarcely acknowledged Lucius' equal status, this was at once repaired by Marcus when Antoninus was dead.

Special comment is required on stemma F, the children of Faustina II. By great good fortune two scholars were independently able to demonstrate, by different routes, that the order of birth of these children had been mistakenly set out by modern historians: K. Fittschen, *Die Bildnistypen der Faustina minor und die Fecunditas Augustae* (1982), from study of the coinage; R. Bol, *Das Statuenprogramm des Herodes-Atticus-Nymphäums* (1984), from examination of the copious epigraphic record at Olympia. They concerted their efforts, and the results are followed here; with minor divergence, notably that made possible by G. Petzl's redating, in *Chiron* 13 (1983) 33 ff., of a letter from Marcus, recording the birth and death of an unnamed son (no. 7). It hardly needs to be added that much uncertainty remains.

Note: 'A 185', 'J 569', etc. refer to *PIR²*

A: TRAJAN AND HADRIAN

P. Aelius Hadrianus Afer. A 185. From Italica, descendant of a senator called Marullinus; first cousin of Trajan; died in 85–6 aged 39, of praetorian rank.

Domitia Paulina I. D 185. From Gades.

Domitia Paulina II. D 186.

Julia Paulina. Not in *PIR²*. Her full name revealed in the 'Testamentum'; cf. R. Syme, *Chiron* 15 (1985) 49; and *RP, passim*; married in 106 (Pliny, *Epp.* 6.26).

L. Julius Ursus Servianus. J 569, 631. Originally Ser. Julius Servianus, adopted by L. Julius Ursus (J 630). Probably from Narbonensis.

Matidia I. M 367. Also recorded as Salonia Matidia. Augusta from 112. Niece of Trajan, mother-in-law of Hadrian. Died in 119 and deified. Her marriages are a problem. Her first seems to have been to a man called Mindius, father of Matidia II; she was also married to L. Vibius Sabinus, it seems, father of Hadrian's wife Vibia Sabina. In his funeral speech for Matidia, Hadrian referred to her long widowhood (*CIL* XIV 3579), which suggests that Sabinus died soon after 97, when he was consul. This leaves the problem of a possible marriage, to Rupilius Frugi, *q.v.*

Matidia II. M. 368. Apparently a Mindia, from the names of *liberti*. Not known to have married. Still alive in 161, as Marcus' daughters stayed with her after he was emperor. Her death gave rise to a complex legal wrangle, alluded to by Fronto. Called *matertera*, 'aunt' of Pius on inscriptions, either because her sister was wife of Pius' adoptive father Hadrian; or, just possibly, as half-sister of Rupilia Faustina, *q.v.* (C), and 'aunt-in-law' of Pius.

Matidius Patruinus, C. Salonius. M 365. From Vicetia. Died in 78.

Cn. Pedanius Fuscus Salinator cos. ord. 118. From Barcino. Linked by Pliny (*Epp.* 6.11) with C. Ummidius Quadratus (*cos.* 118): an '*egregium par*'. Not mentioned in ancient sources for Hadrian's reign, but as husband of the emperor's niece, and *cos. ord.* 118, clearly a key figure early in the reign. Perhaps adopted by the

polyonymous senator whose names included 'Velleius Blaesus', cf. E. Champlin, *ZPE* 21 (1976) 84 ff. Discussed in several places by Syme, cf. *RP passim*, esp. 1158 ff.
Cn. Pedanius Fuscus Salinator. Cf. under his father. Forced to suicide with his grandfather Servianus in 136.
Pompeia Plotina. Evidently from Nemausus. Her family was perhaps already related to that of Trajan, cf. an 'Ulpia Plotina' (AD 70: *AE* 1955. 198). Cf. esp. Syme, *Tacitus* 604; 794.
Rupilia Faustina, Libo Rupilius Frugi: cf. under C, below.
Ulpia Marciana. *RE* Supp. 15 (1978) 932 f. Her *cognomen* permits the inference that Trajan's mother was a Marcia; on her family (perhaps that of Titus' wife Marcia Furnilla, cf. E. Champlin, *Athenaeum* 61, 1983, 257 ff.). Augusta from early in Trajan's reign; died in 112 and was deified.
M. Ulpius Traianus cos. 70. *RE* Supp. 10 (1965) 1032 ff. (unsatisfactory). Cf. Syme, *Tacitus* 30 f.; *RP*, *passim*. Vidman 74 assigns his consulship to 72.
Vibia Sabina. *RE* Supp. 15 (1978) 909 ff. Born at latest c. 85, since she was married to Hadrian before 101. Augusta under Hadrian, exact date uncertain. Died in 135 or 136, although regarded as alive in *AE* 1951. 43–4 of December 137. Deified.
L. Vibius Sabinus cos. 97 (?) Syme, *Tacitus* 795; Schumacher, *Priesterkollegien* 111 f. (Cf. under *Matidia I*, above).

B: ANTONINUS PIUS

Annia Galeria Faustina: see under C.
Arria Fadilla. A 1119. The *cognomen* was given to a daughter, granddaughter and great-granddaughter. It was very rare, presumably derived from the even rarer Fadus, cf. Kajanto 168; 178. She seems to have had two daughters by her second marriage.
Arria Lupula. Recorded only as owner of a brickworks in 139, but presumably another half-sister of Pius rather than Julia Fadilla under another name, cf. J 667. She might, however, be a daughter of Julia Fadilla.
Arrius Antoninus cos. 69, II 97. A 1086. Generally reckoned to derive from Nemausus, like his son-in-law, cf. Syme, *Tacitus* 605; 792, Cn. Arrius Augur (*cos. ord. 121*, as colleague of M. Annius Verus *cos. II*) may be a kinsman, R. Syme, *Hist.* 17 (1968) 86 = *RP* 673.
Aurelia Fadilla. A 1653. Died before Pius was proconsul of Asia (c. 134).
M. Aurelius Fulvus Antoninus. A 1511. Assumed to have died before Pius became emperor.
T. Aurelius Fulvus cos. 70 (?), II ord. 85. A 1510. From Nemausus. His wife's name is unknown. Cf. Syme, *Tacitus* 605; 793.
(T.) Aurelius Fulvus cos. ord. 89. A 1509. Syme, *Tacitus* 793.
T. Aurelius Fulvus Boionius Arrius Antoninus (Pius). A 1513.
Boionia Procilla. B 142. Her *gentilicium* is 'patently Celtic in origin' (Syme, *Tacitus* 792).
M. Galerius Aurelius Antoninus. G 26. Presumed to have died before his father became emperor (but G.R. Stanton, *Hist.* 18 (1969) 583 f. argues that he was still alive in 141. He supposes that Dio 69.21.1, stating that Pius had no male child living at the time of his adoption, need not exclude the birth of a son after it; and that the single Greek coin naming him along with his mother after her death shows him

still alive then. It seems very implausible). On the name 'Galerius', cf. under
Faustina I (C).

Julia Fadilla. J 667. No husband known, but she may be mother of Julia Lupula (J
676 and perhaps of Arria Lupula, cf. above).

P. Julius Lupus cos. 98 (?). J. 389. Perhaps from Nemausus.

C: ANNII VERI

(Annia). Postulated by Syme, *Hist.* 17 (1968) 98 = *RP* 686; *HSCP* 83 (1979)
308 = *RP* 1177, from the nomenclature of the consul of 146 (below).

Annia Cornificia Faustina. A 708. Younger than Marcus, i.e. born no earlier than
122; married soon after his betrothal, i.e. c. 136. Died in 152. Her husband is
identified by Syme, op. cit., with the *cos.* 146. Her name 'Cornificia' may suggest
descent from the republican senatorial family, from Lanuvium (e.g. the *cos.* 33
B.C., C 1503; but no descendants are otherwise known); or as Syme suggests,
Ancient Society 13/14 (1982–3) 260 f. (= *RP* IV, forthcoming) it may indicate a
claim, genuine or otherwise, by the Annii Veri of Ucubi, to Lanuvium as their
ultima origo.

Annia Fundania Faustina. A 713. Mentioned by Galen. She had two children, T.
Fundanius Vitrasius Pollio and Vitrasia Faustina. Probably the cousin of his father
whom Commodus *complexibus suis iniunxerat* (*HA Comm.* 5.8) and later killed
(ibid. 7.7).

Annia Galeria Faustina I. A 715. The date of her marriage to Pius is unknown, but as
she had a daughter who herself married before 134 it must have been well before
120. She died in October or November 140 (Vidman 49 f.; 121 f.) and was deified.
The name 'Galeria' which one of her sons, her daughter and two of her
granddaughters bore may derive from Galeria Fundana, wife of Vitellius (G 33)
through the daughter whom Vespasian 'spendidissime maritavit' (Suet., *D. Vesp.*
14). But if so, Fundana could only be the wife of Libo Rupilius Frugi, *q.v.*

Annia Galeria Faustina II. A 716. The date of her receipt of the title Augusta is now
known to be 147, not 146 (cf. under F).

M. Annius Libo cos. ord. 128. A 667. He takes his *cognomen* from his grandfather
Rupilius, *q.v.* It is uncertain whether he or Marcus' father Verus was the elder son.
His wife is assumed to be a Fundania from the name of his daughter.

M. Annius Libo cos. 161. A 668. The date of his consulship is given by *AE* 1972. 657,
permitting the inference that he was born no earlier than c. 128. His widow, whose
name is unknown, was given in marriage by Lucius – against the wishes of Marcus
– to Lucius' freedman Agaclytus. A son of this marriage became the second
husband of Marcus' youngest daughter Vibia Aurelia Sabina. The senator M.
Annius Sabinus Libo (A 688) and the *cos. ord.* 204 M. Annius Flavius Libo (A 648)
may be Libo's son and grandson. The names 'Flavius' and 'Sabinus' suggest descent
from the imperial Flavian family, perhaps through one of the seven children of T.
Flavius Clemens *cos. ord.* 95 (F 240).

Annius Verus. A 694. His wife is unknown.

M. Annius Verus cos. III ord. 126. A 695. Syme, *Tacitus* 791 f. His apparently
effortless rise remains not fully explained. The theory that his wife was a half-sister
of Hadrian's wife can be invoked (cf. below on Rupilius). So what? Hadrian
'detested his wife' (R. Syme, *JRS* 43 (1953) 155 f. = *RP* 244 f.). Still, he was

devoted to her mother. The Annii of Ucubi may have had their own links with the Aelii Hadriani of Italica (apart from those shown in stemmata A and D). Syme, *Tacitus* 792 notes the *cos.* c. 67, M. Annius Afrinus (A 630); his unique *cognomen* (Kajanto 205) recalls that of Hadrian's father, Afer.

(M.) Annius Verus. A 696. Died when praetor, and thought to have been still alive in 128 or 129 when Marcus became a *salius*, since *salii* were supposed to have both parents living. But the fact that Marcus' enrolment is stated to have been by Hadrian (*HA Marc.* 4.2) may suggest that the rule was waived. If Verus were older than Libo, *cos.* 128, he should have been eligible to be consul himself in 126 or 127; and as he died when praetor can hardly have lived later than 124 or 125.

(Fundania). Assumed to be the wife of the *cos.* 128 from the name of his daughter: Syme, *HSCP* 83 (1979) 307 = *RP* 1175, who further presumes her a daughter of the *cos. ord.* 116 (E).

Rupilia Faustina. 'Avia paterna' of Marcus (*HA Marc.* 1.4).

Libo Rupilius Frugi. His name to be restored, 'Rupili [Li]boni[s] consularis filia' in *HA Marc.* 1.4, cf. A.R. Birley, *Hist.* 15 (1966) 249 f., citing *AE* 1940. 39 and Pliny, *Epp.* 3.9.33, reporting him speaking aggressively in the senate in 101. Cf. *PIR²* L 166, where he is assumed to have been (L. Scribonius) Libo etc. At all events, his first and third names advertise descent from Scribonia and M. Crassus Frugi (*cos. ord.* 27), the former a descendant of Pompeius Magnus. Perhaps his daughter's *cognomen* suggests that there was a connection also with Sulla's family, through his twins Faustus and Fausta. Of course, the name 'Faustus' is also found with an Annius (a disreputable knight under Nero, A 645); and note the *cos. suff.* of 121, M. [A]nnius Faustus (Syme, *Tacitus* 792; *RP* 673 n. 6). Further, one should note the Libo *cos. suff.* in 118 (*CIL* VI 207; perhaps a son of Libo Frugi. For the latter's own consulship, cf. Vidman 81). Libo Frugi's wife is unknown, but J. Carcopino, *REA* 51 (1949) 262 ff. argued that she was Matidia I (cf. under A). This was supported by H.G. Pflaum, *HAC* 1963 (1964) 106 f. However, Schumacher, *Priesterkollegien* 195 points out that Libo Frugi's daughter Rupilia Faustina can hardly have been old enough, in that case, to be the mother of Marcus' father. The only way out would be to suppose that Matidia married Libo before her other two husbands; and was divorced from him (as he was still alive in 101). The theory becomes increasingly implausible. A preferable putative wife for Libo might be Vitellius' daughter, cf. above on Annia Galeria Faustina I.

Ummidia Cornificia Faustina. Cf. A 709, her daughter Annia Faustina, recorded with her on their estates in Anatolia. No other evidence, and no husband attested. E. Champlin, *AJP* 100 (1979) 295 suggests M'. Acilius Glabrio *cos. ord.* 152, to account for the appearance of the name 'Faustinus' in the next generation of Acilii. However, cf. Syme, *Chiron* 10 (1980) 445 = *RP* 1333 (and in any case the Acilii could perhaps claim descent from Fausta, Sulla's daughter, cf. A 75).

M. Ummidius Quadratus Annianus cos. ord. 167. Syme, *Hist.* 17 (1968) 100 = *RP* 687 f. He adopted a son of Cn. Claudius Severus (F); cf. Syme, op. cit. 102 f. = 689 f.; H.G. Pflaum, *JS* 1962, 33 f.

C. Ummidius Quadratus Annianus Verus cos. 146. Syme, op. cit. 98 ff. = *RP* 685 ff. convincingly identifies the *cos.* 146, C. Annianus Verus, with Cornificia's husband Ummidius Quadratus.

C. Ummidius Quadratus Sertorius Severus cos. 118. His full name and governorship of Moesia Inferior c. 120, as revealed by an inscription at Tomis, are discussed by

Syme, *HSCP* 83 (1979) 287 ff. = *RP* 1158 ff. Syme points out that his father was probably a Sertorius. His family may have been linked by marriage with the Pedanii (A).

T. Pomponius Proculus Vitrasius Pollio cos. II ord. 176. G. Alföldy, *Fasti Hispanienses* (1969) 33 ff. has a full discussion of his family and career.

D: DOMITIA LUCILLA

P. Calvisius Ruso Julius Frontinus. C 350. Syme, *ZPE* 56 (1984) 173 ff. = *RP* IV re-examines the evidence and argues convincingly that this man was consul c. 84, and should be distinguished from the P. Calvisius Ruso consul in 79. His last two names suggest his mother was a sister of Sex. Julius Frontinus (J 322). That his wife was a Dasumia seems the only way of explaining *HA Marc.* 1.6, the legendary descent from 'Malemnio, Dasummi filio, qui Lopias condidit'. Cf. further, Syme, *Chiron* 15 (1985) 41 ff., esp. 46 ff.; 50; 55. He was later, apparently, married to Eggia Ambibula (*AE* 1914. 247), perhaps sister of the *cos. ord.* 126 (E 5–6), colleague in that office of M. Annius Verus. The Calvisii may derive from Narbonensis, cf. Syme, loc. cit.

P. Calvisius Tullus Ruso cos. ord. 109. C 357. Syme, *Chiron* 15 (1985) 41 ff., esp. 55 ff. As son-in-law and heir of Domitius Tullus (identified as the testator formerly thought to be a Dasumius) he took the name 'Tullus' in accordance with the terms of the will.

L. Catilius Severus Julianus Claudius Reginus cos. II ord. 120. C 558. As suggested by Syme, *Hist.* 17 (1968) 95 f. = *RP* 683; *Chiron* 15 (1985) 54 f., he may be presumed to have married the widow of Domitius Tullus, thereby becoming stepfather of Domitia Lucilla I – and in due course 'great-grandfather' of Marcus. The widow in question is now identified as Dasumia Polla, *q.v.* For Catilius' origin (perhaps Apamea in Bithynia) and career cf. H. Halfmann, *Die Senatoren aus dem östlichen Teil des Imp. Rom.* (1979) 133 ff.

T. Curtilius Mancia cos. 55. C 1605; cf. Syme, *Chiron* 15 (1985) 52.

Sex. Curvius Tullus. C 1623.

(Dasumia). Postulated by Syme, *Chiron* 15 (1985) 41 ff., esp. 55; cf. 43 and his stemma (p. 62) – which does not, however, suggest what degree of relationship there might be between this person's assumed mother (Aelia) and Hadrian himself.

Dasumia Polla. Syme, *Chiron* 15 (1985) 41 ff., esp. 48 ff.; 53 ff.; 62 (stemma), identifies her as the widow of Tullus, previously married and with children; and suggests that she married again, to Catilius Severus.

L. Dasumius Hadrianus cos. 93(?). Cf. D 14; Syme, *Chiron* 15 (1985) 41 ff.; 47 ff.; 62 (stemma). He argues that Dasumius adopted one of the two sons of his sister Polla and P. Tullius Varro.

P. Dasumius Rusticus cos. ord. 119. D 15; Syme, *Chiron* 15 (1985) 41 ff.

Domitia Lucilla I. D 182; Syme, *Chiron* 15 (1985) esp. 52 ff. Previously married before she became the wife of Calvisius Tullus Ruso, with sons and a granddaughter (unknown), and probably several years older than Tullus Ruso. The principal beneficiary of the testament of Domitius Tullus. Cf. also Syme, *JRS* 43 (1953) 156 = *RP* 246 for the emendation of *HA Marc.* 1.3.

Domitia Lucilla II. D 183.

Cn. Domitius Afer cos. 39. D 126. From Nemausus. Died in 59.

Cn. Domitius Lucanus cos. c. 77. D 152. Died c. 93.

Cn. Domitius Tullus cos. ca. 77, II 98. D 167; Syme, *Chiron* 15 (1985) 51 ff.

P. Tullius Varro. Syme, *Chiron* 15 (1985) 41 ff.; 54. One son was P. Dasumius Rusticus *cos. ord.* 119; the other, his homonym, was *cos.* 127. The family was from Tarquinii.

E: LUCIUS

L. Aelius Caesar, cf. below under L. Ceionius Commodus *cos. ord.* 136.

L. Aelius Lamia Plautius Aelianus cos. 80. A 205. Descendant of the Plautii Silvani and Aelii Lamiae prominent under the Julio-Claudians. Obliged to surrender his wife to Domitian.

(Avidia). Inferred from her father being father-in-law of Aelius Caesar.

Avidia Plautia. A 1412; Syme, *Athenaeum* 35 (1957) 311 = *RP* 328 f., conjectures that she was the wife of Titius Aquilinus *cos. ord.* 125 and mother of the Plautii consuls in 159 and 162.

C. Avidius Nigrinus cos. 110. A 1408; Syme, *Ath.* 35 (1957) 310 = *RP* 327 f. Put to death for alleged conspiracy in 118, said to have been Hadrian's intended heir. From Faventia.

Ceionia Fabia. C 612. Syme, *Ath.* 35 (1957) 312 = *RP* 329, suggests that 'Fabia', and 'Barbarus' in the name of M. Vettulenus, derive from Q. Fabius Barbarus *cos. c.* 64 (*RE* Supp. 14 (1974) 117). If so, perhaps another wife of the *cos.* 80 was a Fabia Barbara. Ceionia Fabia was originally betrothed to Marcus. Her son married a daughter of Marcus, presumed to be Fadilla (F).

Ceionia Plautia. C 614.

L. Ceionius Commodus cos. ord. 106. C 604; Syme, *Ath.* 35 (1957) 306 ff. = *RP* 325 ff. His father, the homonymous *cos. ord.* 78 (C 603), was governor of Syria under Titus. His mother, Appia Severa (A 955), probably came from Narbonensis (Syme, op. cit. 306 n. 2 = 325 n. 2: tribe Voltinia, *ILS* 1003 f.). The Ceionii were Etruscan.

L. Ceionius Commodus cos. ord. 136 (L. Aelius Caesar). C 605. Date of birth unknown but as son and grandson of *cos. ord.* he should have been consul at 32, i.e. born c. 103. However, he was supposedly praetor in 130 (*HA Verus* 1.8, 2.10), for Lucius, born in his father's praetorship, was adopted by Pius 'post septimum annum', in February 138, his seventh birthday then being 15 December 137. A more plausible year for Aelius Caesar's praetorship would be 133 or 134, and it is possible that *HA Verus* 2.10 originally read 'post IIII annum', corrupted to 'post VII annum'; and that Lucius was born in 133. Otherwise, unusually for a patrician, the future Aelius Caesar might have commanded a legion or even governed a province after his praetorship.

M. Ceionius Silvanus cos. ord. 156. C 610; Syme, *Ath.* 35 (1957) 310 = *RP* 328.

L. Fundanius Lamia (Plautius) Aelianus cos. ord. 116. A 204; 'Fundanius' is known from *AE* 1947. 4. It may derive from his mother, unknown (but Syme suggests she was a Fabia Barbara, cf. above under *Ceionia Fabia*). Or perhaps the consul of 80 had a daughter, married to a Fundanius, who were parents of the *cos.* 116. Cf. Syme, *Ath.* 35 (1957) 310 = *RP* 327; *HSCP* 83 (1979) 306 = *RP* 1175 on his sister, daughter and son.

Fundanius Plautius Lamia Silvanus. A 206; cf. Syme, op. cit. on his father.

Plautius Aquilinus cos. ord. 162. Syme, *Ath.* 35 (1957) 312 = *RP* 329. His parentage is made more probable by the fact that he was also called L. Titius (*AE* 1948. 115).

Plautius Quintillus cos. ord. 159. Syme, op. cit. For his son, cf. F.

Q. Servilius Pudens cos. ord. 166. ILS 330; cf. G. Alföldy, *Konsulat und Senatorenstand* (1977) 264 n. 314.

L. Epidius Titius Aquilinus cos. ord. 125. A mysterious figure, whose conjectured marriage is the only explanation for his being honoured with the ordinary consulate.

Sex. Vettulenus Civica Cerialis cos. ord. 106. Syme, *Ath.* 35 (1957) 306 ff. = *RP* 325 ff. Son and nephew of two prominent supporters of Vespasian, who were probably his fellow-townsmen. Cf. *RE* 14 (1974) 845 ff.

M. Vettulenus Civica Barbarus cos. ord. 157. Cf. C 602 (wrongly assuming him to be a Ceionius); Syme, op. cit.; *RE* 14 (1974) 845.

Sex. Vettulenus Civica Pompeianus cos. ord. 136. Syme, op. cit.; *RE* Supp. 14 (1974) 847.

F: THE CHILDREN OF FAUSTINA II

1. *Domitia Faustina.* Born 30 November 147: *Inscr. It.* XIII.1 207. Previously thought to have been no. 5; but cf. Bol 31 f.; Fittschen 23 n. 8; 26 f. Her birth brought Faustina the title Augusta, Marcus the tribunician power, on 1 December 147. She died in 151.

2., 3. The twins, *T. Antoninus* and *T. Aelius Aurelius.* Bol 32 f.; Fittschen 23 ff.

4. *Annia Aurelia Galeria Lucilla.* A 707; Bol 33 f.; Fittschen 26. Bol and Fittschen demonstrate *inter al.* that Herodian 1.8.3 is correct in describing Lucilla as Marcus' eldest daughter (excluding the short-lived Domitia Faustina). This also explains why she, not no. 5, was chosen as bride for Lucius. Her date of birth was 7 March (*IGR* I 1509), and the year must be 150. Fitschen 32; 72 ff. argues that she had three children by her marriage to Lucius: two daughters, the first of whom died young, while the second was involved in a plot against Commodus in 182 (Dio 72.4.4); and a son, also presumed short lived. From her marriage to Ti. Claudius Pompeianus she had further children, including a son called Aurelius Commodus Pompeianus, *cos. ord.* 209, probably born c. 176, cf. H.G. Pflaum *JS* 1962, 33 f., who also deals with later descendants. The full name of the *cos.* 209 is supplied by J.F. Oates, *Phoenix* 30 (1976) 282 ff. Lucilla was exiled in 182, then killed.

5. *Annia Galeria Aurelia Faustina.* A 714; Pflaum, *JS* 1962, 29 ff. – still regarding her as the first born; cf. now Bol 34; Fittschen 27. Her husband Cn. Claudius Severus, fully discussed by Pflaum, op. cit., had been married previously; a son by this earlier marriage was adopted by M. Ummidius Quadratus *cos. ord.* 167 (C). Her descendants are recorded well into the third century.

6. *T. Aelius Antoninus.* The birth of a son in this year (152) is registered by the *Fasti Ostienses: Inscr. It.* XIII.1 207; identified by Bol 34 f. and Fittschen 27 f. with T. Aelius Antoninus.

7. *IGR* IV 1399, redated by G. Petzl, *Chiron* 13 (1983) 33 ff. Bol 35 and Fittschen 27 n. 34 mistakenly assign to no. 6 this document, Marcus' reply to good wishes for the birth of a son, from Smyrna, indicating that the child was already dead. This birth and early death must belong to late 157 or early 158; and the name of the child is unknown.

8. *Fadilla.* F 96; Pflaum, *JS* 1962, 34 ff. (on her husband, perhaps adopted by the *cos. ord.* 141, M. Peducaeus Stloga Priscinus); Bol 35; Fittschen 29.

9. *Cornificia.* C 1505; Pflaum, *JS* 1962, 36f. on her marriages. Her first husband was

murdered by Commodus in 190 or 191; she supposedly had an affair with Pertinax; was remarried under Severus to an equestrian procurator; and herself forced to die by Caracalla in 213.

10.–11. *T. Aurelius Fulvus Antoninus.* A 1512.

L. Aurelius Commodus. A 1482; and cf. F. Grosso, *La lotta politica al tempo di Commodo* (1964). On his wife Bruttia Crispina: B 170; Fittschen 82 ff.

12. *M. Annius Verus.* A 698. Fittschen 31.

13. *Hadrianus.* Known only from two inscriptions, one at Ephesus, *CIG* 2968, the other from the Propontis, ibid. 3709, calling him son of Marcus as emperor. Hence he was alive in the period 161–180. Bol 35 n. 145 and Fittschen 31, cf. 42 f., agree that he cannot have been born before 161.

14. *Vibia Aurelia Sabina.* Pflaum, *JS* 1962, 37 ff. discusses her marriages. Philostratus, *VS* 2.1.11 refers to a three year old daughter of Marcus being at Sirmium when Herodes was there. If this was Sabina, she must have been born c. 170 (Pflaum overlooks the information on age). Fittschen 31 f. puts her birth in 166, but his arguments seem rather insecure, since he is unaware e.g. of J.H. Oliver, *Hesp.* Supp. 13 (1970) 83, dating the stay of Herodes to 174. The daughter that Fittschen postulates, from the coinage, c. 166, may be yet another child, otherwise unknown.

APPENDIX 3
The Marcomannic Wars

The 'German or Marcomannic war – or rather, war of many nations' (*HA Marc.* 22.7) is generally regarded as marking a major turning-point for the empire, as the harbinger of what finally took place in the fifth century. From the accession of Trajan until the 160s the Germans seem to have been quiescent. Trajan's great new Dacian bastion neutralised a large area north of the lower Danube; and, while Hadrian abandoned transdanubian territory attached to Moesia Inferior, he was able to reduce the legionary establishment in Dacia itself to a single unit, XIII Gemina. Likewise, the Sarmatians, the Jazyges of the Hungarian plain and the Roxolani between Dacia and the Black Sea, caused little trouble under Trajan, Hadrian and Pius. Under Marcus the whole northern frontier seemed to explode: 'all the peoples from the limit of Illyricum as far as Gaul had conspired together', says the biographer (*HA Marc.* 22.1). Trouble began with Marcus' accession – at the western end (*HA Marc.* 8.9: the Chatti) – but was to centre on the upper and middle reaches of the Danube, whence Italy itself was most vulnerable. The Parthian war diverted three of the northern frontier's thirteen legions to the east for four years (162–6) and the peoples beyond the Danube showed clear signs of disturbance: the governors were instructed to hold them off (*HA Marc.* 12.13: *Dum Parthicum bellum geritur, natum est Marcomannicum, quod diu eorum, qui aderant, arte suspensum est, ut finito iam orientali bello Marcomannicum agi posset.*). Two new legions were raised in 165–6 (II and III Italicae) as part of the preparations for a Roman campaign of major proportions. But a group of tribes from northern Germany (Dio 71.3.1a says six thousand Langobardi – Lombards – and Obii) invaded Pannonia. Marcus and Lucius were to lead the Roman offensive in 167, the year after the triumph for the eastern war was celebrated; but the plague which came back to Rome with the returning troops made them postpone their departure until 168. In that year the emperors went north and crossed the Alps; they stayed at Carnuntum (*AE* 1982. 777) 'and settled everything concerned with the protection of Italy and Illyricum' (*HA Marc.* 14.6) before going to winter at Aquileia (*HA Verus* 9.10, claiming pressure from Lucius – *urgente Lucio* – for this move: this suggests that Marcus had wished to remain on the Danube). The plague was rampant there: it may have claimed many victims already, for, the biographer asserts, Lucius had wished to return to Rome without even making the northward crossing of the Alps, 'because the prefect of the guard Furius Victorinus had been lost and part of the army had perished' (*HA Marc.* 14.5). No cause of death is given, but plague is more likely than enemy action (as Zwikker 66 showed): the biographer speaks of tribes causing trouble ('cuncta turbantibus'), or threatening war if they were not taken into the empire, being pressed by 'remoter barbarians'; but the initial arrival of Marcus and Lucius at Aquileia ended all this; hence Lucius thought the task finished; and to remain further undesirable in view of the prefect's death. Marcus insisted on crossing the Alps (*HA Marc.* 14.1–5). The return to Aquileia was clearly intended as a return to winter-quarters, with a further mission planned for 169. But the plague made them decide to depart (Galen 19.17 f.) and Lucius died on the journey south, at Altinum (*HA Verus* 9.11; *Marc.* 14.8). Marcus returned to Rome for the funeral and consecration, and did not resume campaigning until Lucilla had been found a new husband, Ti. Claudius Pompeianus (*HA Marc.* 20.6). Just before Marcus set off again for the north, his younger son Annius Verus died; it was during the games of Jupiter Optimus Maximus, hence in mid-September (*HA Marc.* 21.3–5, cf. *Inscr. It.* XIII.1 506 ff.).

In spite of the detail supplied by the *HA* – albeit in somewhat incoherent fashion, and split between the lives of Marcus and Lucius – its author nowhere directly mentions, either in the sections already quoted, covering the period from the end of the Parthian war until the autumn following Lucius' death, or in the rest of the life of Marcus, the most alarming episode in the reign: the invasion of Italy. Instead, there is merely an oblique reference to the fact that Marcus trapped the Marcomanni 'at the very crossing of the Danube and restored the booty to the provincials' (*HA Marc.* 21.10). Reference to booty must indicate that the invaders were being driven out, a process already mentioned in an earlier passage borrowed, with modifications, from Eutropius 8.13 (*HA Marc.* 17.3). It may be that the author of the *HA*, having dissected the material in his source, a biography of Marcus, so as to produce separate lives of Marcus and of Lucius, became confused or negligent over the presentation of events after 169 (cf. App. 1), and inadvertently omitted a proper account of what transpired in 170–1. After Lucius' death and consecration he leaps on, to Cassius' rebellion and then to Commodus' share in the triumph of 176 (14.8–16.2); there is suddenly recourse to a chunk of Eutropius (8.11 ff., slightly reworded, as 16.3–17.7) and then a piece of vapid and inaccurate reflection, topped up by scandal about Faustina (18.1–19.2). At last, from the beginning of 20, the author tries again. It is as if he had lost his notes or mislaid the factual source which he had been plagiarising, had resorted first to memory, then to the inferior Eutropius, finally to empty verbiage, before at last feeling obliged to take his task more seriously for a time. One may even wonder if the invasion of Italy was deliberately omitted: it would have shed, perhaps, an unfavourable light on the emperor he had introduced as a saint (*HA Marc.* 1.1).

However this may be, it is at least clear from the three sources that do record the invasion, Lucian, Cassius Dio and Ammianus, that when it happened Marcus alone was emperor. The point was made by Zwikker, *passim*, and clearly reiterated by J. Fitz, *Historia* 15 (1966) 336 ff. Zwikker favoured 171, or perhaps 170, for the invasion, while Fitz prefers 169. In *Festschift R. Laur-Belart* (1968) 214 ff. I pressed the case for 170. One part of that argument (op. cit. 221 f.) was that in *HA Pert.* 2.4 Pompeianus is labelled *generum Marci*, son-in-law of Marcus, in the reference to his role in expelling the invaders (not there spelt out, but inferred from Dio's account, 71.3.2 ff.). Fitz reasonably objects, *Alba Regia* 19 (1981) 289, that the phrase is used only to identify Pompianus, as elsewhere in the *HA*, and cannot be used as a dating indicator. But that is not the only argument against dating the invasion to 169. More fundamental is the behaviour of Marcus. Lucian shows (*Alex.* 48) that the invasion followed the disastrous failure of a Roman offensive across the Danube, led by Marcus. Ammianus (29.6.1) speaks of the Quadi and Marcomanni 'breaking through the Julian Alps' on their way to besiege Aquileia and sack Opitergium, with 'Marcus scarcely able to check them'. Yet there is no sign in the *HA* of Marcus doing anything military in 169 until his departure back to the front at earliest in September, let alone trying to launch an expedition over the Danube. And if Pompeianus, with Pertinax, were involved in the repulse of the invaders in 169 (Dio 71.3.2), it is difficult to see how he could be at Rome in late summer, marrying Lucilla. Hence it seems logical to place Marcus' failed offensive, and the invasion of Italy by Quadi and Marcomanni, in 170, the year when the Costoboci certainly invaded Greece and sacked the sanctuary at Eleusis, the year also when M. Claudius Fronto, legate of both Moesia Superior and the reunited Three Dacias simultaneously, died 'fighting to the last for the republic' (*ILS* 1098; cf. Zwikker 165 ff.). His death surely occurred during the debacle described by Lucian.

Much weight has been placed by all students of these wars on the role of Q. Antistius Adventus, *legatus Augusti* at *praetenturam Italiae et Alpium expeditione Germanica* (*ILS* 8977). The title of his special command reflects the phrase in the *HA*, that Marcus and Lucius (in 168) took measures pertaining to the defence of Italy and Illyricum (*Marc.* 14.6). Further, the natural approximate date for Adventus assuming this command is c. 168. He was consul after receiving decorations in autumn 166, then curator of public works at Rome before going north. Yet most scholars have felt constrained to assume that the *praetentura* was only established after the invasion, assuming that if it had existed before, the Marcomanni could not have reached Aquileia. Zwikker (162 f.) therefore tried to date Adventus' command to 171 or even 172. J. Šašel, on the other hand, *MH* 31 (1974) 225 ff., an article which gives by far the best analysis of the topographical extent of the *praetentura*, accepting the natural dating to 168 of Adventus' arrival, felt obliged to date the invasion to 167 or 168 – ignoring the silence of the sources over Lucius. A possible solution, put forward in *Festschr. Laur* 219 f., is that Adventus was indeed there from 168, that he resisted the invaders as best he could, but failed to keep them out: 'the Julian Alps were broken through' (Amm. 29.6.1). The newly raised legions II and III and some auxiliary regiments would not have been sufficient to block their passage.

There is further controversy over the next few years, centred on the date of the Rain and Lightning Miracles. On the whole, the careful and thorough examination by J. Guey, *MEFR* 60 (1948) 105 ff.; 61 (1949) 93 ff., remains the most convincing. He dates both to 172, following and supporting with new arguments the case established by Zwikker, esp. 206 ff. It is necessary to add, however, that the account in chapter 8 differs from Zwikker and Guey in some respects: in particular, there seems no good reason to accept that the Quadi were attacked first, then the Marcomanni. The latter – who had killed the guard prefect Macrinius Vindex (Dio 71.3.5) – and were caught with their booty at the Danube (*HA Marc.* 21.10) surely incurred the initial onslaught. As for the Quadi, it was because they had 'received Marcomannian fugitives . . . while that tribe was still at war with the Romans' (Dio 71.13.2) that Marcus attacked them. Earlier (Dio 71.11.2), they had been granted peace (presumably in 171, when Marcus received embassies in Pannonia) 'in the hope that they might be detached from the Marcomanni'. The Marcomanni killed the prefect of the guard Macrinius Vindex, another excerpt from Dio records; then Marcus overcame them and received the title Germanicus (71.3.5), clearly in 172 (*HA Comm.* 11.14). Scrappy and confused though the evidence is, it seems possible to reconstruct the opening years of the war as follows:

167 Langobardi and Obii invade Pannonia; gold-mines in Dacia attacked; expedition of Marcus and Lucius deferred on account of plague.

168 Marcus and Lucius proceed to Aquileia; the tribes treat for peace, but Marcus insists on proceeding north; the emperors stay at Carnuntum; then return to winter at Aquileia, until forced to leave by the plague.

169 Lucius dies *en route*; Marcus returns alone, conducts funeral and deification and takes emergency measures; in the autumn he returns to the north.

170 A Roman spring offensive across the Danube is defeated; the Quadi and Marcomanni penetrate Italy and the Costoboci reach Eleusis; Pompeianus, Pertinax and others begin repulse of invaders.

171 The last invaders are expelled from the empire; Marcus, based at Carnuntum, receives barbarian envoys and makes peace with some tribes, including Quadi.

172 The Roman offensive begins, with invasion of Marcomannian territory; Roman victory gives Marcus the title Germanicus; the Quadi, after breaking agreement by harbouring fleeing Marcomanni, are in turn attacked; in the course of this campaign – in the second half of the season – the Rain and Lightning miracles take place.

Much new light has been shed on the details by new evidence on the careers of those involved, elucidated notably by H.G. Pflaum in his *CP* and by G. Alföldy in his *Konsulat und Senatorenstand*. Two inscriptions recording the presence of Marcus at Carnuntum, in 168, with Lucius, and in 172, with Commodus (*AE* 1982. 777–8), offer some welcome precision. But the attempt by W. Jobst, *Sb. Wien* 335 (1978), to use the second of these to date the Rain Miracle precisely to 11 June 172 is unconvincing. Certainly, 11 June must have marked an important occasion for Pannonia, where the day was commemorated in other years as late as the end of the third century. Yet it is illogical to suppose that those who dedicated for Marcus' and Commodus' welfare at Carnuntum on that date in 172 could have known of a Miracle taking place in the lands of the Quadi (or Cotini). A preferable explanation might be that they were commemorating the expulsion of the Marcomanni in the previous year, perhaps on 11 June.

The two miracles are represented prominently on the column of Marcus, in scenes 11 (Lightning) and 16 (Rain). It could be argued that they are depicted out of chronological order so that they might be visible from ground level. But the column remains difficult to interpret in any case. It is clear that it begins with the offensive of 172, but still uncertain whether it covers only the period 172–5, or whether the final stage of the wars, 178–80, is also portrayed. Some small progress is offered by L. Rossi, *Quaderni ticinesi* 6 (1977) 223 ff., who plausibly suggests that scene 43 shows the feat of arms by M. Valerius Maximianus – who 'killed Valao leader of the Naristae with his own hand' and was decorated in the field and publicly praised by Marcus (*AE* 1956. 124). The most thorough examination of Maximianus' career, by G. Alföldy, *Situla* 14/15 (1974) 199 ff. (not cited by Rossi) assigns the action to 173. If this date is correct, Rossi's suggestion would lend support to the view (challenged by J. Morris, *JWI* 15 (1952) 32 ff.) that the victory scene (55) represents the end of the war with the Quadi; and that the remainder principally covers the fighting in 174–5. At all events, the column does confirm the evidence of epigraphy, that the northern wars were fought largely by *ad hoc* army corps, composed of vexillations (cf. P. Romanelli, in C. Caprino et al., *La Colonna di Marco Aurelio* (1955) 61 ff.).

It is hard to be sure about the causes of the great upheaval. Movement by the Goths, commencing their long migration from Baltic to Black Sea, has been invoked: the *HA* speaks of 'tribes which had fled before the pressure of remoter barbarians, threatening war unless they were taken into the empire' (*Marc.* 14.1). Appian, a contemporary, writing his *Roman History* c. 160, had seen ambassadors from 'poor and unprofitable barbarian peoples at Rome, offering themselves as subjects – but the emperor [presumably Pius] would not accept men who would be no use to him' (*praef.* 7). Marcus was to settle vast numbers on Roman soil (*HA Marc.* 24.3), specified in a fragment of Dio: Dacia, Pannonia, Moesia, Germany and Italy itself – but some given land at Ravenna seized the town, hence no more barbarians were let in to Italy and those already installed were expelled (Dio 71.11.4–5).

Did Marcus have an alternative strategy to solve this problem? The author of the *HA* attributes to him the intention of annexing the lands of the Marcomanni and Jazyges, as the provinces of 'Marcomannia' and 'Sarmatia'. This is stated explicitly in *Marc.* 24.5 as an intention thwarted by the rising of Cassius in 175, and again, as a plan within one year of its fulfilment when he died (27.10). Cassius Dio appears to corroborate the latter statement: 'and if he had lived longer, he would have subdued all that region' (71.33.4[2]). In reference to the last year of the war Dio also records the presence of 20,000 troops in forts among each of two peoples [Quadi and Marcomanni? The mention of these tribes may be an addition by the excerptor, according to Boissevain, ad loc., vol. III 274]; the men had bath-houses, suggesting that occupation was intended to be permanent. When the Quadi tried to migrate northwards to escape this military presence, Marcus, forewarned by intelligence reports, barred the passes. Dio adds his own comment: 'Thus he was eager, not to take possession of the land, but to punish the people' (Dio 71.20.1–2). The comment cannot be taken as decisive. Dio was hostile to further expansion of the empire (cf. esp. his critical verdict on Severus' new province of Mesopotamia, 74.3.2–3), but admired Marcus fervently. It may have suited him to claim that a policy of which he himself disapproved, and which had not been carried to fulfilment, had in fact never existed. Dio's views have swayed some modern scholars, also influenced – it is understandable – by the questionable status of the *HA* as a source (especially for unfulfilled plans). Herodian, who attributes to the young Commodus the aspiration, in a speech to the troops in March 180, of 'advancing Roman rule as far as the ocean' [sc. the Baltic] (1.5.6), has no independent value. Some other considerations may be put forward. A medallion found in Cyprus, published by D.H. Cox, *Coins from the Excavations at Curium 1932–1953* (Numismatic Notes and Monographs of the American Numismatic Society, 1959) 114, no. 230 and plate VIII, deserves attention:

'*Obv.* No inscription. Busts of Marcus r. and Commodus l., laur., confronted.
    Rev. PROPAGA/TORIBUS/IMPERII in wreath.'

Cox regards it as being 'perhaps a little earlier' than two examples in Gnecchi, II.1 44, nos. 5–6, the first dated to 178. She herself offers two interpretations of *propagator*, either 'one who continues the empire' (in a dynastic sense), comparing PROPAGO IMPERI on coins of Caracalla and Plautilla, or 'somewhat less convincingly, because without numismatic parallel, but more in keeping with the other medallions with two busts . . . as "one who enlarges the boundaries of empire"'. The latter is greatly to be preferred. As Dr J.P.C. Kent kindly informs me (by letter): 'Plautilla is not a true analogy; I would suggest that PROPAGO IMPERI is "poetic" for FECVNDITAS AVG or the like, using a straight gardening metaphor. PROPAGATOR is properly an epithet of Jupiter, and its adoption by a second century emperor would be quite in line with the regular use of OPTIMVS MAXIMVS, etc., at that period.' The term PROPAGATOR IMPERII as an imperial epithet is attested only once before this, applied to Lucius is an inscription of 166 (*CIL* XIV 106, Ostia). It is extensively used by Severus and Caracalla, mainly in African inscriptions. The policy of Severus, indeed, may shed some light on that of Marcus, for the African emperor attached great weight to the connection, styling himself 'divi Marci filius' and giving his wife Julia the title 'mater castrorum' which Faustina had been awarded in 174.

The aim of annexing Bohemia and Moravia was not new. Tiberius Caesar had launched an invasion with this aim in AD 6, only to be turned back by the Pannonian revolt (Velleius 2.110). At that time the Jazyges did not occupy the Hungarian Plain and Dacia was still free. By the time of Marcus conditions were in some respects more favourable. The provinces along Rhine and Danube were prosperous and flourishing; the Dacian bastion provided security on the east. Marcus raised new legions in 165, which could be taken as a sign that he planned expansion then (thus e.g. J.C. Mann, *Hermes* 91 (1963) 483 ff.). Hence some have accepted that there may have been an annexation policy in the mid-160s, later abandoned in the face of plague and heavy losses. I prefer to believe that Marcus clung on to the notion that to revive, in some form, the Tiberian (or late Augustan) initiative could neutralise the northern threat, not least because the mountain frontier thereby attained would be superior to the river line. Why deny the natural inference from Dio's description of the occupation army of 179–180? It is usefully exemplified by the inscription of Valerius Maximianus, *AE* 1956. 123, showing him commanding vexillations wintering at Leugaricio-Trenčín – where 855 or a few more soldiers of II Adiutrix under his command celebrated the imperial Victory on the cliff, *CIL* III 13439, suitably restored in the light of the new evidence: *CP* no. 181 *bis*.

It remains to catalogue summarily contributions to the study of the wars and of Marcus' war aims. The monograph by W. Zwikker, intended to prepare the ground for his detailed investigation of the Column, remains fundamental, even though the full work was never completed. H.W. Böhme, *JRGZ Mainz* 22 (1975) 153 ff., offers the fullest examination of the archaeological evidence for the entire northern frontier at this period. G. Alföldy, *Noricum* (1974), 143 ff., and A. Mócsy, *Pannonia and Upper Moesia* (1974) 183 ff., supply ample treatment of these provinces during the wars. A general survey is provided in the slim volume by G. Langmann, *Die Markomannenkriege 166/167 bis 180* (1981). Criticism of the view that Marcus intended to annexe new provinces was launched by F. Hampl, *Festschr. Heuberger* (1960), 33 ff., who was supported by E. Swoboda, *Carnuntum* (4th ed., 1964) 55 f.; 250 f. J. Dobiáš, in *Corolla Swoboda* (1966) 115 ff., defended the traditional interpretation; likewise A.R. Birley, in *Proceedings of the Seventh*

International Congress of Roman Frontier Studies 1967 (1971) 7 ff.; and id., *Trans. Durham & Northumberland* 3 (1974) 13 ff.; but G. Kerler, *Die Aussenpolitik in der Historia Augusta* (1970) 74 ff., regards the story of the plan for new provinces as the invention of Marius Maximus. G. Alföldy, *Historia* 20 (1971) 84 ff., lent his support to Hampl and Swoboda; his paper is reprinted in R. Klein, ed., *Marc Aurel* (1979) 389 ff., with *addenda*, 425 ff., in which *inter al.* he disputes the interpretation of the medallion with PROPAGATORES IMPERII, cited by Birley in *Trans. Durham*, loc. cit. Meanwhile A. Mócsy, *ACD* 7 (1971) 63 ff., argued that there was a plan to annexe new provinces c. 164–5, but that this was subsequently given up. The case is repeated in *Pannonia and U. Moesia*, 183 ff., but seems unsupported by the evidence (cf. Alföldy, op. cit. 427 f.). The case defended in this book is set out more fully in R. Klein, ed., *Marc Aurel* (1979) 473 ff. Among other discussions one may also note A. Chastagnol, *Ktéma* 7 (1982) 151 ff., who regards the statement in *HA Marc.* 24.5 as hardly believable and that in 27.10 as a repetition. But the case is not argued, and the evidence of Dio insufficiently considered. J. Fitz, in *Festschr. Vetters* (1985) 123 ff., attributes an important role in the planning of a province of 'Sarmatia' to Ti. Claudius Pompeianus, governor of Pannonia Inferior, as consular, in 167, but argues that the plan was aborted by the Marcomannic invasion and not taken up again. Once again, this not only sets aside the *HA*'s evidence but ignores that of Dio on 179–80.

APPENDIX 4
Christianity

1. It is unnecessary to stress the immense importance of developments in Christianity during the lifetime of Marcus. Justice cannot be done to such a subject here. All that is intended is a summary – difficult though even that is – of the main features, in particular of chronological problems. The status of Christians was definitively established (whatever had been the case earlier) by Trajan's rescript to Pliny nine or ten years before Marcus' birth. During the remainder of the second century Christian literature proliferated, and a good deal of it has survived. The first Apologists belong to the 120s or 130s. Major heretics – Marcion, Valentinus, Basilides, Montanus – were at work, provoking vigorous reaction and response. The earliest authentic accounts of 'trials' (the word may perhaps be misleading) and martyrdoms belong to the 150s; others, among the most important in the history of the early churches, survive from the 160s and 170s. Pliny's letter is the earliest surviving 'pagan' record. The account of the Rome Christians' savage execution by Nero was written by Pliny's friend Tacitus a few years later (*Ann.* 15.44; perhaps c. 118); likewise, early in Hadrian's reign, Pliny's former protégé Suetonius briefly alluded to their execution (*Nero* 16.2). All three regarded Christians as pernicious and deserving death. There is a variety of comment in the later literature of the second century: a faint (and disputed) reference in Arrian's *Discourses of Epictetus*; possible allusions in Apuleius; a fragment from a speech of Fronto, retailing the standard charges of cannibalism and incest; an amusing vignette by Lucian of a bogus Christian, Peregrinus (and a useful indication of hostility towards Christians by Alexander the false prophet of Abonutichus) (*Pereg.* 11–14; *Alex.* 25; 38); four comments by Galen (R. Walzer, *Galen on Jews and Christians* (1949) 14 f.); the full-scale attack by a man called Celsus; and a brief comment by Marcus himself in his *Meditations* (cf. below).

2. Our knowledge of the pre-Constantinian church depends to an extraordinary degree on the writings of Eusebius of Caesarea, especially his *Historia Ecclesiastica*. Understanding of Eusebius has been greatly enhanced by the work of T.D. Barnes, culminating in his *Constantine and Eusebius* (1981): cf. esp. ch. 7, 'Biblical Scholarship and the Chronicle' (106–25) and ch. 8, 'The History of the Church' (126–47). Fundamental is Barnes' analysis (esp. 131 ff.) of Eusebius' 'general interpretation' – regrettably echoed to a greater or lesser extent by some modern writers. The first Roman persecution had been launched by Nero, followed by another wicked emperor, Domitian; but even a good emperor, Trajan, permitted persecution. 'From Trajan onwards, Eusebius attempts to trace each emperor's attitude towards Christianity' (Barnes 137); and where he found evidence of martyrdoms and persecutions he assigned them to a particular persecuting emperor – 'unaware of this basic fact about the persecution' (Barnes 143) that the attitude of provincial governors (or, at Rome, the city prefect) was of far greater importance. Eusebius' great value lies in his ample quotation of earlier documents, above all, for present purposes, in Book Five, the letter of the Gallic churches about the Lyon martyrs, and the material on Montanism. 'A danger exists, however, that the evident care and honesty of his scholarship may be assumed to guarantee the accuracy of his results' (Barnes 141). For the Antonine period he had a particular problem in distinguishing between emperors called 'Antoninus' – not merely Pius and Marcus; Caracalla and Elagabalus were also called 'Marcus Aurelius Antoninus'. He was particularly at sea with Marcus, who he believed – because Tertullian and Apollinarius vouched for it – had publicly acknowledged the merits of Christian soldiers in the 'Thundering Legion' (App. 3). Hence he distinguishes between 'Marcus Aurelius Caesar' who gave Christians the credit for the Rain Miracle (*HE* 5.5.1–6) and his brother, 'Antoninus Verus', to whose seventeenth year he dates the Lyon martyrdom (5.*pr*.1; cf. 5.2.1; 5.4.3). Earlier, he had quoted a bogus decree supposedly issued by Pius, but bearing the name of 'Marcus Aurelius Antoninus Augustus Armeni(ac)us' and a date equivalent to 161 (4.12.1–13.1 – naturally, it has been possible to explain this particular confusion rationally). He takes Melito's *Apology* to have been addressed to 'the emperor Verus' (4.13.8; when it is quoted, in 4.26, the emperor is not named, but Hadrian is called his grandfather and allusion is made to his joint administration with his father, unnamed, but clearly Pius). In 4.14.10 he records the death of Pius and the succession of 'Marcus Aurelius Verus, also called Antoninus, his son, together with his brother Lucius'. He at once gives a full account (4.15), closely matching the extant *Martyrium*, of the trial and death of Polycarp – but lacking the date given in *Mart. Pol.* 21 (cf. below), which dates it to the reign of Pius. Then comes (4.16 ff.) the martyrdom of Justin, already cited earlier (4.8), Eusebius does not quote from the *Acts of Justin and his Companions* (cf. below) which, however, show – because of the prefect Rusticus – that he has placed Justin's death correctly under Marcus. However, he quotes extensively from Justin's *Apology* which he was misled – perhaps by Melito – into treating as two separate *Apologies* (cf. below). Other problems deriving from Eusebius are referred to below.

3. Quite what the legal status of 'Christian' had been during the first three decades of the religion's existence remains unclear. In 64 'a huge multitude' was executed at Rome (Tacitus, *Ann.* 15.44) and Christians subsequently regarded this as the start of the persecutions. Thereafter, it seems, being a Christian was a capital offence. But it was only when Pliny, as governor of Pontus-Bithynia in the second year in his province (which he probably entered in September 110: W. Eck, *Chiron* 12 (1982) 349 n. 275) obtained an answer from Trajan, that this became unambiguous (*Epp.* 10.96–7). It was not relevant to guilt or innocence whether Christians committed 'abominable acts', *flagitia* – Pliny found none had (*Epp.* 10.96.8: torture of two female slaves revealed nothing but *superstitionem pravam, immodicam*). The name alone, *nomen ipsum* (10.96.2), was sufficient to incur death; yet full pardon was granted to Christians who apostatised by sacrifice 'to our gods'; no search was to be made; and action should only follow open, not anonymous, denunciation (10.97). No subsequent modifications were made to this position. It clearly still applied at the end of the century, when Tertullian attacked and ridiculed it as unjust and inconsistent (*Apol.* 2.6–20). Nor were there any centrally directed persecutions until the mid-third century. This case was carefully and convincingly put by G.E.M. de Ste Croix, *Past & Present* 26 (1963) 6 ff. (reprinted in M.I. Finley, ed., *Studies in Ancient Society* (1974) 210 ff.). Post-Trajanic rescripts dealing with Christians are found only in Christian sources. They must all be rejected as forgeries – some very plausible in their details. Thus Hadrian's rescript to Minicius Fundanus, proconsul of Asia (datable, if he actually was proconsul, to 122–3: W. Eck, *Chiron* 13 (1983) 156 n. 362), often mistakenly said to follow the Trajanic line, was, on the contrary, intended to show that Hadrian had lifted the punishment from the 'name', and was designed to scare off accusations by its threats of penalties for false charges (Eusebius, *HE* 4.9): cf. the demonstration by H. Nesselhauf, *Hermes* 104 (1976) 348 ff. The very fact that Apologists are found at this time attempting to have the status of criminality lifted is demonstration that Hadrian did not make any change – and has misled modern scholars into claiming that the letter to Fundanus merely reaffirmed Trajan's position. As Nesselhauf pointed out, Trajan effectively placed the fate of Christians in the hands of the society in which they lived, of their neighbours. Since they refused to honour pagan gods, they were likely to be blamed for unexplained calamities (cf. Tertullian's famous statement, *Apol.* 40.2); and in times of difficulty Christians who were immigrants – as at Lyon – were victims of xenophobia. When trouble broke out, governors had to intervene: the governor's job was to keep his province *pacata atque quieta* (*Digest* 1.18.13). Occasionally, Trajan's instruction that Christians were not to be hunted out (*conquirendi non sunt*: 10.97.1) was infringed, as with Polycarp; and the Lyon governor went beyond the normal bounds. Further, the behaviour of Christians changed, and their numbers increased. The tendency to seek martyrdom actively was no doubt not a new phenomenon. But the 'Phyrgian heresy' of Montanus and his followers made voluntary martyrdom much commoner. It is all the more regrettable that the date when Montanus began to prophesy remains uncertain (cf. below).

4. Many of the major Apologists for Christianity were at work in the lifetime of Marcus. Quadratus and Aristides are assigned to Hadrian's reign by Eusebius who states they addressed that emperor (*HE* 4.3.3); but he may have confused Hadrian with Pius (who included Hadrian's names in his full style). A Syriac version of Aristides' work, and part of an Armenian one, are extant (*ODCC*[2] 84). Eusebius quotes a few words from Quadratus – whose *Apologia* was 'composed because some wicked men were trying to trouble the Christians' (*HE* 4.3.1–2) – but nothing else of his survives, unless, as has been suggested, he is the author of the anonymous *Epistle to Diognetus* (*ODCC*[2] 1149). Justin, as already mentioned, is also drawn on by Eusebius. His *Dialogue with Trypho* and *Apology*, both written in the 150s, are of major importance (*ODCC*[2] 770). The *Apology*, which incorporated (originally in Latin) the letter of Hadrian to Fundanus, was before long revised and further 'documents' added, including the bogus letter of Marcus on the Rain Miracle. In the process the *Apology* was divided into two parts and Eusebius, followed by a majority of writers ever since, refers to a *First* and *Second Apology*. In fact there was only one, written under Pius, when Lollius Urbicus as prefect had recently sentenced two Christians to death and not long after the Egyptian prefecture of Munatius Felix. For the problem, cf. W. Schmid, 'Die Textüberlieferung der Apologie des Justin', *ZNT* 40 (1941) 87 ff. and id., 'Ein Inversionsphänomen und seine Bedeutung im Text der Apologie des Justin', in *Forma Futuri. Studi in onore del Card. M. Pellegrino* (Turin 1975) 253 ff. Cf. for further bibliography *ODCC*[2] 770. The other Apologists of the period include Hegesippus, Tatian, Theophilus, Melito, Apollinarius and Athenagoras. For the three first named, not directly relevant to the present subject, cf. *ODCC*[2] 628; 1341; 1364. Melito of Sardis and Athenagoras of Athens both addressed *Apologies* to Marcus, which may be assigned to his stay in the east, probably in 176. For Melito, cf. M. Sordi, *StudRom* 9 (1961) 368ff., who argues that the quotation from the work in Eusebius, *HE* 4.26, esp. the reference to the emperor's son in section 7, best fits this moment. The same may well apply to Apollinarius of Hierapolis, treated as a contemporary of Melito by Eus., 4.26.1. Athenagoras of Athens is not mentioned by Eusebius, but his *Legatio*, 'embassy' addresses Marcus and Commodus in terms which would fit in well with their visit to Athens in 176, cf. T.D. Barnes, *JTS* 26 (1975) 111 ff. It remains doubtful whether Athenagoras or the other two actually had an audience, let alone the chance to read out an *Apology* – *Ath.*, *Leg.* 37.1 may imply this, but cf. Barnes 111 and n. 6. Such touches may well have been added to give the impression that the author had been in the imperial presence. Cf. also M.L. Astarita, *Avidio Cassio* (1983) 123 ff., who quite properly suggests that the revolt of Cassius in 175 may have made conditions more difficult for Christians in the aftermath (cf. further below).

5. Heresy – a peculiarly Christian concept – flourished greatly in this period. The Roman authorities may well have failed to appreciate differences between different types of 'Christian'. However, attitudes to authority and to persecution varied between a readiness to compromise with and to evade persecution – as with some 'Gnostics' (a rather wide term which included many groups) – and active eagerness for martyrdom, as with Montanists. The orthodox view was certainly as much against this (cf. *Mart. Pol.* 4: 'we do not commend those who give themselves up, brethren, since the Gospel does not give this teaching') as it was, of course, insistent on endurance and refusal to sacrifice when the test did arise. Gnosticism is not of direct relevance in the present context: cf. *ODCC*[2] 573 f. But the importance of Irenaeus, a disciple of Polycarp and bishop of Lyon after the martyrdoms (which occurred in his absence), deserves stressing, as 'the first great Catholic theologian' and as an important link between east and west; his best known work is the *Adversus omnes haereses*, preserved in a Latin version, with parts of the original Greek, and of Syriac and Armenian translations, also surviving (*ODCC*[2] 713 f.). As well as attacking Gnostics, Irenaeus tackled the 'millenaristic' tendencies, of which Montanists were prominent exponents. Montanus, said to be a recent convert, indeed a former priest of Apollo, from a small village in western Phrygia (probably from the region north-west of Apamea), proclaimed his 'new prophecy' some time in the second century. With two women, Priscilla and Maximilla, he won a fervent following which spread rapidly in Asia Minor, and beyond (Tertullian of Carthage became a Montanist in the first decade of the third century). The sect was not stamped out by Christian emperors until the ninth century. There is a problem over the date at which it began. In his *Chronicle*, Eusebius set its appearance under Marcus, in his eleventh year (Armenian version) or twelfth (Jerome's Latin version), i.e. 171 or 172. In the *HE*, he devotes considerable space (5.14–19) to Montanism, quoting at length from writers of the second or early third century, one of whom, unnamed but addressing his work to Avircius Marcellus of Hieropolis, assigns Montanus' 'ecstasy' to the time 'when Gratus was proconsul of Asia' (5.16.7). As it happens, no senator of this name is known from the Antonine period. However, a later fourth century writer, Epiphanius of Salamis, who also has considerable knowledge of Montanism, dates its inception to the 'nineteenth year of Antoninus Pius' (*Panarion* 48.1), i.e. the year 156 or 157. The date given by Epiphanius has been favoured by most scholars: e.g. *RE* 16.1 (1933) 206; *PIR²* G 224; G. Alföldy, *Konsulat und Senatorenstand* (1977) 143 f. But T.D. Barnes, *JTS* 21 (1970) 403 ff., argued that Epiphanius' other dates for the second century are so mistaken (e.g. for Justin) that Eusebius must be preferred; further that his date is indirectly confirmed by evidence about Tertullian. After becoming a Montanist Tertullian wrote a defence of the movement, *De Ecstasi*, in six books; then added a seventh, in refutation of Apollonius' attack on Montanism. This is cited by Eusebius in the *HE*, and Apollonius there states that he was writing forty years after Montanus began to prophesy (5.18.12). As Tertullian's Montanism seems to begin c. 207/8, Barnes, assuming that he got to know Apollonius' work soon after it was published, dates Montanus' first prophesying c. 170, Apollonius' attack c. 210 and Tertullian's reply soon after. Unfortunately, this is not decisive: Apollonius' attack could easily have been written c. 196, but only brought to Tertullian's notice ten years or more later, e.g. by a Catholic opponent wishing to demolish the *De Ecstasi*. Besides this, since so many of Eusebius' dates for the Antonine period are questionable (cf. above; and note also that in *HE* 5.15.47 he puts Pionius' martyrdom under Marcus – instead of under Decius), it seems rash to accept him for Montanus. In certain respects an earlier date than 171/2 makes better sense of the data (even if the Montanism of the Phrygian Quintus in *Mart. Pol.* 4 is ruled out, Montanist tendencies among the Lyon Christians cannot be so easily denied; further, Bishop Soter of Rome, who died only two or three years after 172, is supposed to have written against the Montanists: Praedestinatus, *Haer.* 26). It is tempting, although A. Stein (*PIR²* G 224) warned against it, to ask whether the proconsul 'Gratus' might not indeed be the same L. Statius Quadratus under whom Polycarp was martyred c. 156 (cf. below): *kata Kodraton* corruptly transcribed as *kata Graton*. For a recent study of the local origins of Montanism, cf. A. Strobel, *Das heilige Land der Montanisten* (1980).

6. The martyrdoms of the period are important and instructive. H. Musurillo, *The Acts of the Christian Martyrs* (1972) supplies Greek text and translation of five supposedly from the reigns of Pius and Marcus; and cf. the discussion of their authenticity and date by T.D. Barnes, *JTS* 19 (1968) 509 ff. Those of Carpus, Papylas and Agathonice, are assigned to the 160s by Eusebius, *HE* 4.15.48; but a third century date seems more likely, cf. Barnes, op. cit. 514 f. (and this is certain for Pionius, Barnes 529 ff. Eusebius also places the martyrdom of Sagaris, Bishop of Laodicea, under the proconsul 'Servillius Paulus', in the 160s. No such senator is on record; the name might be amended, but the date must remain doubtful). Two cases are quite clear. Justin reports that of Ptolemaeus and Lucius in his *Apology* (2.2; also in Eusebius, *HE* 4.17; Musurillo 38 ff.), and it must fall in the 150s, at Rome. Justin himself and his companions were also martyred at Rome, under the prefect Q. Junius Rusticus, thus in the 160s (Musurillo 42 ff.; cf. Barnes, op. cit. 515

ff.). The case of Polycarp remains controversial. In the *Martyrium Polycarpi* 21 a date is given which may be either February 22 or 23 – 22, if a leap-year, otherwise 23; at the eighth hour; 'on a great Sabbath'; when Philippus of Tralles was high priest and Statius Quadratus was proconsul. Statius Quadratus was consul in 142, and can hardly have been proconsul earlier than 154 or 155 – or later than c. 159. The information about the high priest does not fit – the man is on record in the office no later than 149–50; but as Barnes, op. cit. 512 suggests, this may be a mistaken inference from *Mart Pol.* 12, where he is referred to as 'Asiarch' (i.e. 'ex-high priest'). Attention has been focused on the 'great Sabbath', and attempts made to explain it in terms of a Jewish festival: thus A. Strobel, *Ursprung und Geschichte des frühcristlichen Osterkalenders* (1977) 245 ff., who assigns the martyrdom on these grounds to 167, about the date indicated by Eusebius, *HE* 4.15. But cf. W. Rordorf, in *Pietas. Festschr. B. Kötting* (1980) 245 ff., who points out the circularity of Strobel's argument, and himself suggests an interesting alternative: that the 'great Sabbath' was a Roman festival, the *Terminalia*. At all events, the case for c. 155–7, when the proconsul Quadratus must have held office, seems strongest (157–8 is now ruled out by another proconsul; R. Syme, *ZPE* 51 (1983) 276; 280). Finally, there are the martyrs of Lyon, whose remarkable conduct is recorded in the anonymous letter from the churches at Lyon and Vienne to their brethren in Asia and Phrygia, reproduced by Eusebius, *HE* 5.1. Eusebius, *HE* 5.pr.1 clearly dates the event to 177; but this is doubted by T.D. Barnes, *JRS* 19 (1968) 518 f.; and in the proceedings of the conference *Les martyrs de Lyon* (1978) 137 ff., he notes that in the *Chronicle* the event is put under Marcus and Lucius (i.e. 161–9), and argues that in the *HE* Eusebius merely inferred a date from the fact that the martyrs commended Irenaeus to Eleutherus (5.4.1–2), bishop of Rome from c. 175 (Jerome, *Chron.* 207b), and that (as he thought) persecution ceased for a time with the death of Marcus (*HE* 5.21.1). Proof is certainly lacking, and as Barnes concludes (*Les martyrs* 141): 'we should, therefore, leave open the possibility that the correct date might be several years later than 177.' Apart from the date, there are other controversial questions. The attempt by J. Colin, *L'empire des Antonins et les martyrs gaulois de 177* (1964), to demonstrate that the whole affair took place in Asia Minor and not in Gaul at all, must be rejected as misplaced ingenuity. It is less easy to dismiss the thesis of J.H. Oliver and R.E.A. Palmer, *Hesperia* 24 (1955) 320 ff., that the passing of the decree of the senate on reducing the prices of gladiators – which should belong to 177 or 178 – indirectly sparked off the persecution at Lyon. The decree particularly affected Gaul; and although T.D. Barnes, *JTS* 19 (1968) 519 curtly claims that the letter of the Gallic churches 'does not so much as mention the priests of the imperial cult', there are in fact phrases in it which evoke the *Concilium Galliarum* and its games. Cf. Eus., *HE* 5.1.37 (*eis koinon tōn ethnōn theama*: did the text originally refer to '*the koinon* of the tribes'?); 1.40; 1.47. The argument is that the decree permitted those who were obliged to put on gladiatorial games in Gaul to purchase condemned criminals for the purpose – and that they began accusing Christians to boost the supply. This must remain uncertain. At all events, causes for pagan hatred of Christians are not in fact hard to seek at a time of crisis such as this. Finally, one may note, in addition to the papers printed in *Les martyrs de Lyon*, the valuable study by H. Kraft, 'Die Lyoner Märtyrer und der Montanismus', in *Festschr. Kötting* (1980) 250 ff.

7. In the fragment of his *Apology* quoted by Eusebius, Melito of Sardis complains of 'new decrees' which resulted in Christians being harassed throughout Asia (*HE* 4.26.5–6). Various explanations have been put forward. M. Sordi, *StudRom* 9 (1961) 365 ff. suggested that measures intended to combat other problems (brigandage, etc.), attested in *Digest* 1.18.13 and 48.13.4.2, were being applied to the Christians. P. Keresztes, *HTR* 61 (1968) 321 ff. suggested that the decree on gladiators was being applied in Asia as well, with Christians as the easy target to supply cheap condemned men; it is indeed the case that one copy of the *SC* comes from Sardis itself (the other derives from Italica in Spain). Proof is lacking; but Keresztes' article does not inspire confidence (he ignores much modern work). More plausible is the suggestion of T.D. Barnes, *JRS* 58 (1968) 39, that a proconsul of Asia, in his edict on entering the province, had 'for the first time explicitly included Christianity among the offences of which he proposed to take cognisance'. This would also explain, as he points out, why Melito was uncertain whether the 'decrees' were from the emperor or not. Finally, one must note the pertinent comments of M.L. Astarita, *Avidio Cassio* (1983) 123 ff., who quite reasonably sees the rising of Cassius, and the resultant upheaval in the east, as a likely source of difficulties for groups such as Christians. (Not all her speculation may be justified.)

8. A variety of other Christian material requires brief mention. Much is made by some modern scholars of a series of imperial letters, from Hadrian, Pius and Marcus, referring to Christians. The majority receives summary discussion by T.D. Barnes, *JRS* 58 (1968) 37 ff. While generally sceptical, Barnes does accept Hadrian's letter to Fundanus as genuine; but cf. H. Nesselhauf, *Hermes* 104 (1976) 348 ff., who shows good reason to doubt this as well as all those recorded only in Christian sources. It is, nonetheless, quite possible that factual information is preserved, e.g. that Minicius Fundanus was proconsul of Asia; or – in the letter about the 'Thundering Legion' – that the 'Rain Miracle' took place in the territory of the Cotini; and that Vitrasius Pollio was prefect [*sc.* of the city] at the time. Some genuine material is also incorporated in the *Vita Abercii*: *Acta Sanctorum: Octobris, Die Vigesima Secunda* (Brussels, 1858) 485 ff.; ed. T. Nissen (Leipzig, 1910). This was demonstrated when W.M. Ramsay discovered the original epitaph, composed for himself by Abercius and quoted in the *Vita*. The Greek text is given, with discussion, in the *Reallexikon für Antike und Christentum* I (1950) 11 ff.; English translation, with bibliography, in J. Quasten, *Patrology* I (1950) 171 ff.; cf. also *ODCC*² 4 f. Barnes, op. cit. 39, notes that the *Vita* itself cannot be earlier than 361 from its mention of the emperor Julian; but that the author 'had some reliable information at his disposal.' He seems to have used it for a characteristically edifying, rather than historical, purpose. The inscription, on the other hand, sheds valuable light on the nature of Christianity, in Phrygian Hieropolis in particular, and in the empire generally, in the later second century. It seems reasonable to identify Abercius with the addressee of Eusebius' source, Avircius Marcellus (cf. above). But it seems unwise to use the *Vita* as an independent means of dating events such as the marriage of Lucius and Lucilla, or the invasion of Italy.

9. Comments on Christians by 'pagan' writers require some separate discussion. S. Benko, *Pagan Rome and the Early Christians* (1985), together with his article,

ANRW 2.23.2 (1980) 1055–1118, provides a convenient conspectus, although there are some gaps in his coverage of modern scholarship. Epictetus, *Disc.* 4.7.6 is generally thought to refer to Christians when he speaks of 'Galilaeans' being intent on death and totally fearless, 'from habit. (*ethos*). However, S. Applebaum, *JRS* 61 (1971) 164 argues that he referred to the Zealots, members of the Jewish resistance movement founded by Judah of Galilee. This view (not known to Benko) is also taken by P.A. Brunt (cf. below). Fronto's attack on Christians for cannibalism and incest, quoted by Minucius Felix, *Octavius* 9.6, is most plausibly explained by E. Champlin, *Fronto and Antonine Rome* (1980) 64 ff. (not known to Benko): it would have been part of a speech attacking a certain Pelops, against whom charges of 'Thyestean banquets', etc., would be ideal for the Roman forensic orator. Hence it would be mistaken to claim that Fronto devoted a special speech to attacking Christians: he merely tried to slur a defendant whom he was prosecuting by associating him with anti-Christian propaganda that may have been already commonplace (cf. Benko 54 ff.). Fronto's contemporary and fellow-African, Apuleius of Madauros, is thought to allude to Christians in a similarly hostile way in his novel, *Met.* 9.14; and in his *Apologia*, delivered before Marcus' friend Claudius Maximus, then proconsul of Africa (probably autumn 158), at Sabratha, he describes his opponent Sicinius Aemilianus in terms which might have been intended to make him seem a Christian (cf. A.R. Birley, *Septimius Severus* (1971) 46 ff., esp. 58). On Apuleius and Christianity cf. further M. Simon, in *Mélanges H.C. Puech* (1974) 299 ff. Lucian wrote a sustained attack on a famous figure of the Antonine age who was for a time a Christian, but turned into a notorious Cynic 'philosopher', and committed a spectacular suicide at the Olympic games of 165, Peregrinus Proteus. Lucian's *De morte Peregrini* (esp. 11–14) above all guarantees the fact that Christians were commonplace in the east at least; likewise the passing references in *Alexander* 25 and 38. Cf. Benko 30 ff. for a spirited account of Peregrinus. Galen mentions Christians four times (R. Walzer, *Galen on Jews and Christians* (1949) 14 f.; Benko 142), in three cases lumping them together with Jews – 'followers of Moses and of Christ' – as people who use faith rather than reason; in the fourth passage the stress is on Christians 'drawing their faith from parables and miracles, and yet some acting in the same way as philosophers. For their contempt for death and of its sequel is obvious every day; and likewise their restraint in sexual intercourse. . . .' In comparison with the preceding, the sustained onslaught by Celsus is in a quite different category. His *True Discourse*, evidently composed c. 178, has to be reconstructed from the reply of Origen, *Contra Celsum*, written c. 248, on the eve of the Decian persecution; but some ninety per cent of Celsus' work is reckoned to be thus preserved. The text of Celsus is edited by R. Bader (1940; and in the *Kleine Texte* series, no. 151 by O. Glöckner, 1924). Origen's work, including the quotations from Celsus, is edited with French translation in the *Sources chrétiennes* series, vols. 132, 136, 147, 150, 227 (1967–76), by M. Borret. An English translation, with introduction, by H. Chadwick, *Origen: Contra Celsum* (1953), distinguishes typographically between Celsus and Origen. Although praising some aspects of Christian thought and morality, Celsus criticised and ridiculed the miracles and the central teaching of the incarnation, objected to Christian intolerance and appealed to Christians to support the empire, not to undermine it. Last of all, there is Marcus' own reference to the Christians, in his *Meditations* 11.3. He is writing about readiness for death (indeed about suicide):

'What a soul is that [or: how admirable is the soul] which is ready to be released from the body at any requisite moment, either to be extinguished or to be scattered or to persist! But this readiness must come from a specific decision, not in accordance with a simple lining up, like the Christians, but after reflection and with dignity, and so as to convince others, without stage-heroics.' This brief comment, presumably written not long before Marcus' death (from its position in the second last book of the *Med.*, cf. p. 218, above), opens up fascinating perspectives, which cannot be explored in detail here. However, P.A. Brunt, in C. Deroux (ed.), *Studies in Latin Literature and Roman History* I (1979) 483 ff. has discussed the passage at length and concludes that the words 'like the Christians' are a later addition; and that Marcus was not referring to them at all. I am totally unconvinced by his arguments. Here only one or two comments are possible. His criticism centres on the phrase translated above 'in accordance with a simple lining up', *kata psilēn parataxin*. This has usually been rendered 'out of sheer (or: mere) opposition', which, it may be agreed, is unsatisfactory (influenced by Pliny's 'pervicaciam certe et inflexibilem obstinationem' (*Epp.* 10.96.3). But Brunt also objects (488) to giving *parataxis* 'its normal meaning . . . "battle-array"'. He finds this 'absurdly inappropriate'. Yet references to Christians e.g. in Galen rather support it; and cf. Tertullian, *De spect.* 1, 'Sunt qui existimant Christianos, expeditum morti genus, ad hanc obstinationem abdicatione voluptatium erudiri' (the use of 'obstinatio' here should not mislead: the important words are 'expeditum' and 'erudiri': Christians ready for death after training). He does discuss (493) passages cited by Farquharson in which *antiparatattesthai* and *antiparataxis* are used, but finds them inconclusive. However, he has missed a better one. In the beginning of the letter of the Gallic churches, the author states that, while the 'adversary' had attacked the faithful, 'practising his own adherents and training them against the servants of God', yet 'against them the grace of God was our general, and rescued the weak, while it marshalled against them (*sc.* the devil's adherents) steadfast pillars able by patience to draw themselves the entire onslaught of the evil one' (Eusebius, *HE* 5.1.5–6). The military metaphors could not be clearer; 'marshalled against' translates *antiparetasse*. Of course, the conception of Christians as the *milites Christi* is too well known to need further exemplification. It may be added that *psilos* has a military connotation, meaning 'unarmed' or 'light-armed'. Thus Marcus thinks of Christians as 'lined up unarmed' for death, as soldiers in battle array: but not as persons who had really made an individual reasoned choice – they were drilled, trained to die (cf. Tertullian's 'erudiri'; better, from the letter of the Gallic churches, again, cf. on Attalus, who 'went in a ready combatant', *hetoimos eisēlthen agonistēs*, 'since he was nobly trained in the Christian order (*sc.* of battle)', *epeidē gnēsiōs en tēi Christianēi suntaxei gegumnasmenos*. Brunt (487 n. 11) cannot understand Marcus' *atragōidōs*, 'without histrionic display', as referring to Christians either. The *Acta Martyrum* provide instructive evidence which might explain this perfectly. Even the defiant dialogue between Polycarp and the governor (*Mart. Pol.* 9 ff.) might seem like histrionics; cf. also *Acts of Justin* 6: the martyrs went to their death 'glorifying God' (i.e. singing?); Eusebius, *HE* 5.1.35, the confessors going to their death at Lyon wearing their chains like jewellery, with gladness – may this not have seemed like actors in a tragedy? Students of the period – it might appear – have veered between two extremes: some (e.g. C.R. Haines, and many of the translators of the *Meditations*) tend to assume that Christianity preoccupied Marcus a great deal; others are reluctant to believe that he noticed it at all. It is difficult to imagine that the city prefects Urbicus and Rusticus failed to discuss the cases of the Christians that they sent to their death; and surely the case of Polycarp was sufficiently striking for the cultivated Statius Quadratus (an Athenian, and a friend of Aelius Aristides, thus likely to have moved in court circles) to have said something about it after his return from Asia. On the other hand, the appalling Lyon martyrdoms – even if, as still seems most probable, they took place in or soon after 177 – may not have been reported on in person by the (unnamed and unknown) legate of Gallia Lugdunensis: Marcus had probably left for the Danube before the governor's tour of duty ended. There remain some other passages – 1.6; 3.16; 7.68; 8.48; 8.51 – which C.R. Haines (Loeb ed. 318 ff.) thought to allude to Christians. Farquharson (440; 587; 779) was unconvinced; as is Brunt, op. cit. Perhaps rightly; but J.M. Rist, in B.F. Meyer and E.P. Sanders, edd., *Self-Definition in the Greco-Roman World* (1983) 190 n. 15 is 'still inclined to think [Marcus] refers to [Christians] among others at 3.16.'

APPENDIX 5
The Illustrations

The face of Marcus Aurelius is unusually well recorded on the imperial coinage, from his first appearance as 'Aurelius Caesar, son of Pius Augustus, consul designate' in 139, to his last in the year of his death forty-one years later. There were in his lifetime and subsequently very numerous portraits in other materials too, as we would know even without the much-quoted passage in Fronto's letter to him (*Ad MC* 4.12.6 = H.i 207 = vdH 67) about the cheap painted busts in clay or wood that he came across everywhere in the shops and markets of Rome. Cf. M. Wegner, *Die Herrscherbildnisse in antoninischer Zeit* (Berlin 1939); M. Barg-mann, *Marc Aurel* (Frankfurt 1978). I have preferred to select coins rather than sculpted portraits, both of Marcus and of other members of the imperial family, since they can be more precisely dated – giving in the case of Marcus himself, a series showing him at the ages of seventeen, twenty-six, thirty-seven, forty-eight and fifty-six. The other coins are intended to illustrate the principal figures in the dynasty: Hadrian and his empress, Aelius Caesar, Antoninus and Faustina I, Faustina II, Lucius and Lucilla, Commodus and Crispina. I have added portraits of Pertinax, who played a not insignificant role in Marcus' wars and of Caracalla, whose name was changed to that of Marcus. I have also included the equestrian statue of Marcus now in the Piazza del Campidoglio, one of the most celebrated imperial images of all time, and as copious a selection as was possible of scenes from the Aurelian Column, focusing mainly on those in which Marcus himself appears Brief comment on these may be helpful.

The original location of the bronze equestrian statue was perhaps next to the barracks of the imperial horse guards (*equites singulares Augusti*), e.g. on their parade ground in the *campus Caelimontanus*. It could have been placed on top of a triumphal arch to commemorate the victory over Parthia, for the portrait fits a date c. 166. From the 10th century onwards it is recorded as located this area north of St John Lateran; by then it was mistakenly identified as representing Constantine the Great. It was moved to its present position on the Campidoglio by Pope Paul III in 1538.

Marcus is leaning slightly forward but completely relaxed. His extended left hand originally held reins with the little finger and ring finger, while the other fingers and thumb would have carried a globe surmounted by a statuette of Victory. He is wearing a short-sleeved tunic and short leather boots and sits on an elaborate horse-cloth (but, apparently, no saddle). The scale of the rider is rather exaggerated compared with his spirited mount, perhaps to compensate for the fact that the statue (which was originally gilded) would be seen from below.

A comprehensive discussion of the statue and its vicissitudes may be found in E.R. Knauer, 'Das Reiterstandbild des Kaisers Marc Aurel', *Werkmonographien zur bildenden Kunst*, ed. M. Wundram, no. 128 (Stuttgart 1968) 3–32, repr. in R. Klein, ed., Marc Aurel (1979) 304–346.

The Aurelian column in the Piazza Colonna at Rome was officially known as the 'columna centenaria divorum Marci et Faustinae', as it is called on an inscription of the year 193, recording the authorisation to the imperial freedman Adrastus, custodian of the Column, to build himself a hut (*CIL* VI 1585 = *ILS* 5920). This suggests that the work had only recently been completed, indeed may still have been in progress, thirteen years after Marcus' death. The interpretation of what it depicts is still uncertain in some respects: the Victory between scenes L V and L VI obviously marks the end of one campaign – but is this a subdivision of the war of 169–175 (as most have believed), or does it mark the armistice of 175, with the top part of the Column recording the second war, which terminated only with Marcus' death in 180? Petersen, Domaszewski, Caprino and others believed that Commodus was not portrayed anywhere. But this is questionable – for one thing, it is probable that he would appear looking as he was at the time the Column was being made. Hence, in the captions to the selection of scenes here shown, Commodus is tentatively recognised among his father's high-ranking companions, as well as Pertinax and Pompeianus. John Morris, *JWI* 15 (1952) 33 ff. argued this case long ago. I believe that the new evidence (*AE* 1982. 777), conclusively demonstrating that Commodus was at the front in 172, should encourage further study of the Column.

For abbreviations used in the captions to coin illustrations, see p. 290f.

Finally, thanks are due to the following for permission to reproduce the illustrations appearing in this book:

The Hunterian Museum Glasgow for figs 2–4, 6–9 and 11–14

Prof. G.D.B. Jones for fig 38

University of Manchester (photos Keith Maude) for figs 1, 5, 10 and 15–22

Mansell Collection for fig 23

Figs 24–37 are taken from Petersen's edition of the Aurelian column (1896).

References and Notes

For abbreviaton used in the Notes see page 290

1 The Age of the Antonines *(pages 11–27)*

1 E. Gibbon, *The History of the Decline and Fall of the Roman Empire* (1776), ch. 3; Dio 71.36.4.

2 Tacitus, *Agr.* 3.1; Pliny, *Pan.* 2.3; 3.4; Tacitus, *Hist.* 4.74.2 (Cerialis); *HA Sev. Alex.* 65.5 (Trajan); 'one of us': Pliny, *Pan.* 2.4; cf. the classic paper by J. Béranger, *REL* 17 (1939) 171 ff.

3 Dio's Book 53 is the fullest account of the establishment of the new order; Velleius 2.89.3; cf. above all R. Syme, *The Roman Revolution* (1939); on his names, id., *Hist.* 7 (1958) 172 ff. = *RP* 361 ff.

4 On senatorial careers, E. Birley, *PBA* 39 (1953) 197 ff.; A.R. Birley, *The* Fasti *of Roman Britain* (1981) 5 ff.; equestrians: H.-G. Pflaum, *Les procurateurs équestres* (1950), with his *CP*; P.A. Brunt, *JRS* 73 (1983) 42 ff. Cf. also F. Millar, *The Emperor in the Roman World* (1977) 275 ff.

5 R. Syme, *Roman Revolution* viii.

6 Ruler-cult: D. Fishwick, *ANRW* 2.16.2 (1978) 1201 ff.; S.R.F. Price, *Rituals and Power. The Roman imperial cult in Asia Minor* (1984).

7 'Chameleon': Julian, *Caes.* 309 A. On the downfall of the Julio-Claudians, cf. esp. M. Griffin, *Nero. The End of a Dynasty* (1984).

8 Tacitus, *Hist.* 1.4.2; 2.7.1.; Suetonius, *D. Vesp.* 25; Dio 65.12.1; Suetonius, *Dom.* 8.1–2; 1.3.2; Tacitus, *Agr.* 45.

9 R. Syme, *Tacitus* (1958), esp. ix–xii, 1–58, 627–33 (Nerva and Trajan); 236–52; 481–91 (Hadrian).

10 E. Birley, in E. Swoboda (ed.), *Carnuntina* (1956) 26 ff.

11 H.-G. Pflaum, *Les procurateurs équestres* (1950) and his *CP*.

12 A.R. Birley, *The* Fasti *of Roman Britain* (1981) 17 ff.; 28 ff.

13 J.A. Crook, *Consilium Principis* (1955); R.J.A. Talbert, *The Senate of Imperial Rome* (1984); secrecy: Dio 53.19.1–6.

14 G.R. Watson, *The Roman Soldier* (1969); H.-G. Pflaum, *Les procurateurs équestres* (1950).

15 F. Millar *et al.*, *The Roman Empire and its Neighbours*² (1981) offers a useful survey.

16 *Correspondance de Napoléon Ier*, vol. 30 (1870) 10.

17 E. Kornemann, 'Die unsichtbare Grenzen des römischen Kaiserreiches', in *Gestalten und Reiche* (1943), 323 ff.; D. Braund, *Rome and the Friendly King: the character of client kingship* (1984).

18 Aelius Aristides, *Or.* 30 K (ed. and trans. J.H. Oliver, *Trans. Amer. Philos. Ass.* 43 (1953) 971 ff.), sections 97, 99, 100, 82, 70, 10 ff., 58, 28 ff. Cf. further p. 86 ff., below.

19 Christianity: App. 4. Religion generally: cf. J. Beaujeu, *La religion romaine à l'apogée de l'empire* I (1955).

20 C. Wirszubski, *Libertas as a Political Idea at Rome* (1950); R. Syme, *Tacitus* (1958) 4; 59 ff.; 585 ff.

21 R. Syme, *Proc. Massachusetts Hist. Soc.* 62 (1957–60) 3 ff. = *RP* 566 ff.

22 Cf. A. Wallace-Hadrill, *Suetonius. The Scholar and his Caesars* (1983), esp. 198 ff. and E. Champlin, *Fronto and Antonine Rome* (1980), esp. 29 ff.

23 For detailed discussion of the main sources, App. 1 below.

2 Family and Early Years *(pages 28–32)*

1 Milo: *RE* 1 (1894) 2271 ff. – he had no known link with the consuls of 153 and 128 BC. Nor are the Annii Veri related to consular Annii of the first century AD, so far as is known (*PIR²* A 630, 637, 677, 701. But cf. App. 2 on A 630). Scapula: [Caesar], *B. Alex.* 55.2. Ucubi and first two Annii Veri: *HA Marc.* 1.2, 4. Rise of provincials: cf. esp. R. Syme, *Tacitus* (1958) 585 ff. See further App. 2.

2 Birth: *HA Marc.* 1.5. Family and ancestry: cf. App. 2. 'funerary address': *CIL* XIV 3579; cf. *HA Had.* 9.9.

3 On the year 97, R. Syme, *Tacitus* (1958) 1–18; 640 ff. Antoninus and Nerva: *Epit. de Caes.* 12.3.

4 On the family, App. 2. Pliny, *Epp.* 8.18.

5 On the *testamentum* see now esp. R. Syme, *Chiron* 15 (1985) 41 ff. = *RP* IV (forthcoming), discussing *CIL* VI 10229 with *AE* 1976. 77; and App. 2.

6 Brickworks: T. Frank, *ESAR* V (1940), esp. 207 ff.; H. Bloch, *I Bolli laterizi* (1947), esp. 204 ff.; 320 ff. Cf. also M. Steinby, *Epigrafia e ordine senatorio* I (1982) 227 ff. on ownership of brickworks.

7 Marcus on his real father: *Med.* 1.2; cf. *HA Marc.* 6.7–8; 12.7; 17.2.

8 Consulships under Hadrian: *HA Had.* 8.4 is mistaken. The 'glass-ball game': E. Champlin, *ZPE* 60 (1985) 159 ff. has produced the remarkable explanation of *ILS* 5173 summarised here.

9 Dio 69.21.2; 71.35.2–3; cf. App. 2.

10 *HA Marc.* 1.5–7; Fronto, *Ad MC* 2.8.2 (vdH 30) = Haines I 142.

11 J. Marquardt, *Das Privatleben der Römer²* (1886, repr. 1964) 10; 80 ff.

12 Tacitus, *Dial.* 28–9.

13 *HA Marc.* 2.1; *Med.* 5.4; Quintilian, *Inst.* 1.1. 12 ff.

14 A. Gellius, *NA* 12.1. Favorinus: *PIR²* F 123; G. W. Bowersock, *Greek Sophists in the Roman Empire* (1969) 35 f.; 41 f.; 51 f.

15 *HA Marc.* 1.7, 9; 10; cf. 1.4; *Med.* 1.17.2; 1.4. On Catilius' presumed marriage to widow of Tullus, App. 2. Origin and career: H. Halfmann, *Die Senatoren aus dem östlichen Teil des Imp. Romanum* (1979) 133 ff.

16 Cf. esp. R. Syme, *HSCP* 83 (1979) 287 ff.; 307 = *RP* 1158 ff.; 1175; Pliny, *Epp.* 7.24. Cf. App. 2.

17 Plautia: Syme, *Ath.* 35 (1957) 306 ff. = *RP* 324 ff. Aurelii Fulvi: *PIR²* A 1509; 1510; 1513. Arrii: ibid. 509; 1086. Lupus: J. 389. Cf. App. 2.

18 *Med.* 1.1; 1.17.2; *HA Marc.* 2.1. His mother: *Med.* 1.17.7; other references in *PIR²* D 183.

19 Quintilian, *Inst.* 1.1.16; Plutarch, *Cato Maior* 20. 2 ff.; Pliny, *Epp.* 3.3.3.

20 *Med.* 1.4. *HA Marc.* 2.2 (the mention of Andro here is misplaced, cf. Schwendemann 7); *Med.* 1.5; cf. *HA Pius* 10.5.

21 *HA Marc.* 4.1; cf. A. Stein, *Der römische Ritterstand* (1927) 31 ff.; 47 ff.; 159 f. Salii: *RE* 1 A (1920) 1874 ff.; R. Bloch, *The Origins of Rome* (Eng. tr. 1960) 134 ff. Marcus' enrolment: *HA Marc.* 4.2–4; cf. R. Dailly and H. van Effenterre, *REA* 56 (1964) 357 ff.

22 Andro: *HA Marc.* 2.2. Diognetus: ibid. 4.9; *Med.* 1.6; cf. Schwendemann 7; 20. 'austere way of life': *HA Marc.* 2.6.

23 S. Dill, *Roman Society from Nero to Marcus Aurelius* (1904, repr. 1956) 354 ff.; 443 ff.; D.R. Dudley, *A History of Cynicism* (1937) esp. 143 ff.

24 'Verissimus': *HA Marc.* 1.10; 2.1; *PIR²* A 697 (p. 120: coins); *AE* 1940. 62. Hadrian's travels: *HA Had.* 10.1–14.7 provides most detail; cf. H. Halfmann, *Itinera principum. Geschichte und Typologie der Kaiserreisen im Römischen Reich* (forthcoming). Antinous: *PIR²* A 737. *HA Had.* 23.1 places the onset of illness shortly after his return and before the death of Servianus, i.e. between 134 and 136; for his age, *HA Had.* 1.3; cf. *PIR²* A 184. The grand-nephew: cf. esp. E. Champlin, *ZPE* 21 (1976) 79 ff.; and App. 2. Servianus: *HA Had.* 15.8; 23.2–3, 8; 25.9; 8.11; Dio 69.17.1; cf. R. Syme, *Tacitus* (1958) 636; further references in App. 2.

25 S. Aurigemma, *Villa Adriana* (1961); G. Lugli, *Roma. I Monumenti Antichi* III (1938) 693 ff. Commodus: *PIR²* C 605. Nigrinus: *PIR²* A 1408; cf. App. 2.

26 App. 2.

27 *HA Marc.* 2.3, with the emendation by A.R. Birley, *HAC* 1966/67 (1968) 39 ff.

28 Ael. Aristides, *Or.* 32 K; *Med.* 1.10; cf. Farquharson II 453; *PIR²* A 502.

29 *HA Marc.* 4.5; cf. *RE* 6 A (1937) 1450 ff. on the *toga virilis*.

30 *HA Marc.* 4.6.

31 *HA Marc.* 2.7, reading *Commodi magistro* and deleting *usus est et* before *Apollonio*, following Obrecht's conjecture adopted in the Loeb ed. Schwendemann 12 regards it as misplaced, but 'adfinitas destinata' fits the period 136–7. On Apollonius, cf. *Med.* 1.8; 1.17.5; *PIR²* A 929 and p. 62, below.

32 *HA Marc.* 4.7; cf. App. 2.

33 *HA Had.* 23.1–3, 7–9; also 15.8; 25.8; Dio 69.17.1–3. cf. App. 2.

34 *HA Had.* 23. 10 ff.; Dio 69.17.1.

35 *HA Had.* 7.1–2; 23.10; Dio 69.2.5; *HA Had.* 23.11; Ael. 3.8–9 (cf. App. 1).

36 On the family nexus, App. 2. 'horoscope . . short-lived': *HA Ael.* 3.8; favoured by H.-G. Pflaum, *HAC 1963* (1964) 95 ff. 'illegitimate': the theory of J. Carcopino, *REA* 51 (1949) 262 ff.; disposed of by R. Syme, *HSCP* 83 (1979) 300 ff. = *RP* 1170 f.

37 Pliny, *Epp.* 6.26 (cf. also 3.17 and mentions in 7.6.8; 8.23.5; 10.2.1).

38 *PIR²* C 605. 'summi fastigii . .': Tacitus, *Ann.* 3.56.

39 E. Swoboda; *Carnuntum⁴* (1964); J. Klose, *Roms Klientel-Randstaaten* (1934).

40 *HA Had.* 23.15–16; Dio 69.20.1 (cf. 69.17.1).

41 Dio 69.20.1; *HA Had.* 24.1; 26.8–10; 26.6; Dio 69.20.1–4.

42 'Pius': *HA Pius* 4.1–2; Victor, *De Caes.* 14.11; cf. *HA Had.* 24.3; *Pius* 2.3 and p. 55 below. Omens: *HA Had.* 26.6–7, cf. B. Mouchová, *HAC 1968/9* (1970) 112 ff.

43 *HA Pius* 1.9–2.2; 2.9–11; 3.6–8; 2.11; *Had.* 22.13; cf. W. Eck, *Die . . Organisation Italiens* (1979) 247 ff. Omens: *HA Pius* 3.1–5.

44 Dio 69.21.1–2; *HA Had.* 24.1; *Pius* 4.5; *Marc.* 5.1; *Verus* 2.1–2; *Had.* 24.6–7. Scipio: *PIR²* C 1446.

45 Cf. H. Halfmann, *Die Senatoren aus dem östlichen Teil des Imp. Rom.* (1979) 133 ff.

46 *HA Had.* 15.7, cf. App. 2. Turbo: R. Syme, *JRS* 52 (1962) 95 ff. = *RP* 541 ff.

47 *HA Pius* 4.4; Dio 69.20.5; *Epit. de Caes.* 12.3; *HA Pius* 1.4.

48 *HA Pius* 4.6; *Verus* 2.3; *Ael.* 6.9; *Marc.* 5.6, 6.2. If *Marc.* 5.6 may be pressed, Marcus was not adopted before his seventeenth birthday (April 26, 138). Pius' titulature and powers: Hüttl I 45, 50 ff.

49 *HA Marc.* 5.2–4; Dio 71.36.1; *HA Marc.* 4.8–10; 7.1.

50 *HA Marc.* 5.6–8. On the various types of career, E. Birley, *PBA* 39 (1953) 197 ff. 'Faustina': *HA Pius* 4.8.

51 *HA Had.* 24.8–10; Dio 69.22.1–3; *HA Had.* 29.11–13; 25.1–4.

52 *HA Had.* 25.5–6, 9.

53 *HA Had.* 25.6; Dio 69.22.3–4.

54 Dio 69.2.5; 69.1; 69.9.4–6; 69.5.1–2; *HA Had.* 1.5. On Hadrian cf. above all R. Syme, *Tacitus* (1958), esp. 236 ff.; 481 ff.; id., in *Les Empereurs romains d'Espagne* (1965) 243 ff.; id. *JRS* 54 (1964) 142 ff. = *RP* 617 ff.; id., *JRS* 70 (1980) 64 ff. = *RP* 1276 ff.; id., *Ath.* 59 (1981) 273 ff. = *RP* 1436 ff.; id., *Ath.* 62 (1984) 31 ff. = *RP* iv (forthcoming). It should be observed that Hadrian receives no mention in Book 1 of the *Med.*, which suggests that Marcus' view of him was cool; cf. Fronto, *Ad MC* 2.1 (vdH 24 f.) = Haines I 108 ff.

3 Aurelius Caesar *(pages 53–68)*

1 *HA Had.* 25.7; *HA Marc.* 6.1.

2 *HA Marc.* 6.2, cf. *Verus* 2.4; *Ael.* 6.9; *Med.* 1.17.2; 1.17.7 (in spite of which R. Dailly and H. van Effenterre, *REA* 56 (1954) 53 f. believe that Benedicta and Theodotus were Marcus' first sexual partners). Marriage: cf. generally P.E. Corbett, *The Roman Law of Marriage* (1930) 1–23.

3 *ILS* 7190; cf. H.-G. Pflaum, *HAC* 1963 (1964) 110 ff.

4 *HA Pius* 5.1, 6.4–4; *Had.* 27.1–2; cf. *BMC* IV, pp. xl f., xlviii ff.

5 *HA Pius* 5.1–2; *Had.* 27.3; *ILS* 350–2; *HA Had.* 25.8; *Pius* 6.3.

6 Tacitus, *Ann.* 1.75; Pausanias 8.43.5; cf. *ILS* 341; Dio 70.2.1; *HA Had.* 24.3–5; 27.2–4; *Ael.* 7.9–10; *Pius* 2.3–7; *Av. Cass.* 11.6; Eutrop. 8.8.3. Medallions; Gnecchi IV 90; 158. Coins: *BMC* IV *AP* nos. 237, 1264, etc.

7 Praesens: see esp. R. Syme, *Hist.* 9 (1960) 374 ff. = *RP* 489 ff.; id., *Festschrift Kajanto* (1985) 274 ff. = *RP* iv (forthcoming). Son, and Crispina: *PIR²* B 165; 170. Vidman 123 conjectures that Praesens died in 140.

8 *HA Pius* 5.3 is mistaken; cf. A.R. Birley, *Corolla Swoboda* (1966) 43 ff. Orfitus: *HA Pius* 8.6; cf. R. Syme, *Hist.* 9 (1960) 375 ff. = *RP* 491. Nepos, Severus, Urbicus: A.R. Birley, *The Fasti of Roman Britain* (1981) 100 ff.; 106 ff.; 112 ff. Four consulars: W. Eck, *Die staatliche Organisation Italiens* (1979) 249.

9 *Med.* 6.30. P. Maas, *JRS* 35 (1945) 145, reviewing Farquharson, prefers the alternative reading *apokaisarianōtheis*, which he takes to mean 'do not become one of the *Caesariani*', which he renders 'courtiers'. But *Caesarianus* and its Greek equivalent both normally meant 'Caesarian', i.e. supporter of Caesar in the Civil War, as opposed to *Pompeianus*, cf. Appian, *BC* 3.91 for its use in this sense by a contemporary of Marcus. The normal word for members of the imperial household is *kaisareios*; cf. Dio 78.18. Both readings give otherwise unattested words. The one translated here gives the better sense. Dio 71.35.5.

10 *HA Marc.* 6.3; *CIL* VI 32; 379, cf. *ILS* 360.

11 *HA Pius* 6.6; cf. Hüttl I 63 ff.

12 *HA Marc.* 6.3; *Med.* 5.16; cf. 8.9; Lucan 8.493; *Med.* 1.17.3. 'duties': cf. M. Hammond, *The Antonine Monarchy* (1959) 288 ff. *HA Marc.* 6.5.

13 J. Crook, *Consilium Principis* (1955).

14 *HA Marc.* 7.1; 22.6; cf. *Med.* 5.3.

15 *PIR²* C 933–4; cf. *Med.* 1.15. The tribute to Pius forms *Med.* 1.16.

16 *HA Pius* 8.7. Maximus: *CP* no. 105 *bis* + Supp. pp. 32 f. Mamertinus: E. Champlin, *Fronto and Antonine Rome* (1980) 10.

17 Sisennae, Laelianus, Falco: A.R. Birley, *The* Fasti *of Roman Britain* (1981) 109 f.; 248 ff.; 273 f.; 95 ff. 'Three years ago': Fronto, *Ad MC* 2.6 (vdH 29) = Haines I 140. For other former senior officers who had served in Britain, available at this time for advice, cf. Fasti 239 ff.; 271 ff.; 292 ff.; 306 ff.

18 Cf. now esp. W.S. Hanson and G.S. Maxwell, *Rome's North-West Frontier: the Antonine Wall* (1983). *ILS* 340; *BMC* IV AP nos 1640 ff.; *Pan. Lat.* 8 (5). 14.2, quoted in Haines II 250.

19 *HA Pius* 5.4; cf. R. Syme, *JRS* 52 (1962) 87 ff. = *RP* 541 ff.; *BMC* IV *AP* no. 1274, cf. *ILS* 1058.

20 *BMC* IV *AP* no. 1272, etc. Hiberi: *HA Pius* 9.6; cf. *Had.* 13.9; Dio 69.15.3 = 70.2.1. Vidman 124 f. 'Firm action': *ILS* 1076; cf. K.F. Stroheker, *HAC* 1964/65 (1966) 241 ff.; R. Syme, *Ath.* 69 (1981) 278 = *RP* 1441.

21 *HA Marc.* 6.5; Quintilian, *Inst.* 12.1.1 (cf. 1.*pr*.4). Cf. H.I. Marrou, *A History of Education in Antiquity* (Eng. tr. 1956) 284 ff. Tutors: *HA Marc.* 2.4–5; 3.6 (cf. *CP* no. 141).

22 Quintilian 1.*pr*.13, cf. H.I. Marrou, op. cit. 210 ff.; 285; Tacitus, *Agr.* 4.4; *HA Pius* 10.4; cf. *Marc.* 3.1; *Med.* 1.8; 1.17.5.

23 Philostratus, *VS* 1.22.3; Aristides, *Or.* 50 K; *Med.* 8.25; cf. *PIR²* C 368 (Celer).

24 Philost., *VS* 2.1.1; 2.1.8; 1.25.3; 2.1.4–5; 2.1.8 ff.; 2.1. 14. W. Ameling, *Herodes Atticus* (1983) supersedes earlier treatments in many respects. But G.W. Bowersock, *Greek Sophists in the Roman Empire* (1969) is the essential introduction to Philostratus and the sophists.

25 A. Gellius, *NA* 1.2 (he also stayed at Cephisia when recuperating from dysentery, ibid. 18.10).

26 *NA* 9.2; 19.12.

27 *HA Pius* 10.5 (an *educator*, perhaps the unnamed one in *Med.* 1.5).

28 See esp. E. Champlin, *Fronto and Antonine Rome* (1980). *Pan. Lat.* 8 (5).14.2 and further ancient verdicts in Haines I ix f.; Dio 69.18.3.

29 *NA* 19.8; 2.26; 13.28; 19.10; 19.13; cf. *HA Pert.* 1.3; *NA* 1.21.L; 6.2.L; 7.3.L; 8.3.L; 15.10.L.

30 Cf. E. Champlin, *Fronto and Antonine Rome* (1980), esp. chs. 3 and 4. Tacitus, *Dial.* 38.2; 41.5; Juvenal 10. 147–67.

31 *PIR²* F 59 (Quintilian); 257; 397 (his pupils).

4 The Education of an Heir Apparent *(pages 69–88)*

1 Fronto, *Ad Ant. Imp.* 1.2.5 (vdH 90) = Haines II 38.

2 *Ad MC* 4.3 (vdH 56 ff.) = Haines I 2 ff.

3 *Ad MC* 3.12 (vdH 44) = Haines I 12 ff.

4 *Ad MC* 3.13 (vdH 44 f.) = Haines I 14 ff.

5 *Ad MC* 3.9 (vdH 42) = Haines I 18 f.

6 *Addit.* 8; 7.3 (vdH 234 ff.) = Haines I 20 ff.; 32.

7 *Ad MC* 3.7, 3.8.1 (vdH 40 f.) = Haines I 32 ff.

8 *Ad MC* 3.10–11 (vdH 43 f.) = Haines I 50 ff.

9 *Ad MC* 5.74 (vdH 86 f.) = Haines II 52 ff. Cf. Pliny, *Epp.* 6.31.15–17 on Centumcellae forty years earlier.

10 *Ad MC* 2.13 (vdH 33 f.) = Haines I 150 ff.

11 *Ad MC* 4.4 (vdH 60 f.) = Haines I 174 ff. Anagnia is SE of Rome, E of Lanuvium.

12 *Ad MC* 4.5 (vdH 61 ff.) = Haines I 178 ff.

13 *Ad MC* 4.6 (vdH 62 ff.) = Haines I 180 ff.

14 *HA Pius* 11.2, 5; *Med.* 1.5.

15 E. Champlin, *Fronto and Antonine Rome* (1980) 26 f. argues for the correctness of 'Cratia', citing *AE* 1945. 38 (the daughter); *AE* 1966. 44 for the Ephesian lady. Fronto's children: *De nepote amisso* 2.1 (vdH 220) = Haines II 222. Victorinus' marriage: Champlin, op. cit. 27 f. His career: G. Alföldy, *Fasti Hispanienses* (1969) 38 ff.; W. Eck, *Die Statthalter der germ. Provinzen* (1985) 67 ff. Marcus' friends: *HA Marc.* 3.8.

16 Vidman 49 f.; 121 f.; *HA Pius* 3.7; 6.7–8; 8.9; cf. *ILS* 1839; Julian, *Caes.* 312 A.

17 G.W. Bowersock, *Greek Sophists in the Roman Empire* (1969) 93 ff., followed by E. Champlin, *JRS* 64 (1974) 142 and *Fronto* (1980) 63 f., regards this dating of the case as unsatisfactory and argues for a period later in Pius' reign. But cf. now W. Ameling, *Herodes Atticus* (1983), who follows the traditional, earlier date in I 61 ff. and defends it in II 30 ff. See further App. 1. I accept Bowersock's argument that the case was a trial of Demostratus, not of Herodes, despite the doubts of Ameling, II 35.

18 Fronto, *Ad MC* 3.2 (vdH 36 f.) = Haines I 58 ff.

19 *Ad MC* 3.3 (vdH 33 f.) = Haines I 62 ff. I owe to E. Champlin, *Fronto* 105 the comment on the significance of Marcus having dictated the letter.

20 *Ad MC* 3.4 (vdH 38 f.) = Haines I 66. E. Champlin, *JRS* 64 (1974) 142 takes the reference to *Marcianus noster* as evidence that the date must be later than the early 140s, by identifying the man with Geminius Marcianus, consul c. 167 (*PIR²* J 340; G. Alföldy, *Konsulat und Senatorenstand* (1977) 182), hence assumed to have been too young to have been involved in a trial in the early 140s. But cf. Pliny, *Epp.* 5.8.8: Marcianus could have been a junior counsel aged eighteen c. 142, and legionary legate c. 160 aged thirty-six. However, a homonymous father may easily be postulated.

21 *Ad MC* 3.5–6 (vdH 39) = Haines I 66 ff.

22 Publication: Fronto, *Ad Ant. Imp.* 3.4 (vdH 106) = Haines II 220; *Ad Verum Imp.* 2.9 (vdH 130) = Haines II 234. E. Champlin, *Fronto* 64 assumes the success from publication, but cf. W. Ameling, *Herodes Atticus* II 35 n. 27. Mamertinus: Fronto, *Ad Am.* 1.10 (vdH 170) = Haines II 242, the significance of which was spotted by Champlin 10. His hypothesis, 80 f., that Fronto was in fact prefect of both treasuries in succession before being consul has no evidence to support it.

23 Fronto, *Ad MC* 1.3.2 (vdH 2 f.) = Haines I 84 ff. Ausonius, *Grat. act.* 7.32–3. On the *consules ordinarii*: G. Alföldy, *Konsulat und Senatorenstand* (1977) esp. 88 ff.; 100 ff.

24 *Ad MC* 1.4 (vdH 6 ff.) = Haines I 90 ff.

25 *Ad MC* 2.1 (vdH 24 f.) = Haines I 108 ff.

26 *Ad MC* 2.2 (vdH 25 f.) = Haines I 112 ff.

27 *Ad MC* 1.9 (vdH 17 f.) = Haines I 118 ff.

28 *Ad Ant. Pium* 2 (vdH 156 f.) = Haines I 126 ff.

29 *Ad MC* 2.3.3 (vdH 27) = Haines I 130; *Ad MC* 1.10 (vdH 20 ff.) = Haines I 130 ff.

30 *Ad MC* 2.5.2 ff. (vdH 28 f.) = Haines I 138 ff.

31 *Ad MC* 2.8 (vdH 30 f.) = Haines I 140 ff.

32 *Ad MC* 2.9 (vdH 31) = Haines I 144.

33 Quadratus: E. Champlin, *Fronto and Antonine Rome* (1980) 9 accepts E. Birley's suggestion, *JRS* 52 (1962) 225 that he was legate of Numidia; it is doubted by G. Alföldy, *Konsulat und Senatorenstand* (1977) 249 f. Lucilla's birthday: *Ad MC* 2.10–12; 14–15 (vdH 31 ff., 34 f.) = Haines I 144 ff.; 152 ff.

34 *Ad MC* 1.6–8 (vdH 10 ff.) = Haines I 154 ff.; 4.1 (vdH 53 f.) = Haines I 70 ff.

35 *Ad MC* 4.2 (vdH 54 ff.) = Haines I 74 ff. Champlin, *JRS* 64 (1974) 143 and *Fronto* (1980) 103 f., dates this letter later in Pius' reign, as with his chronology of the Herodes lawsuit, cf. nn. 17, 20 above.

36 Maecianus: *CP* no. 142. For his origin, cf. R. Syme, *ZSS* 97 (1980) 83 = *RP* 1397. Julianus: G. Alföldy, *Konsulat* (1977) 313.

37 Aristides, *Or.* 26 K. Cf. esp. the edition with introduction, commentary and translation by J.H. Oliver, *Trans. Amer. Philosoph. Ass.* N.S. 43 (1953) 869 ff. I prefer the traditional date, 144, rather than 143, which Oliver favours: cf. C.P. Jones, *JRS* 62 (1972) 150 n. 159. The passages summarised here and in some cases quoted are from sections 5 ff., 28 f., 34, etc. (size of city and empire); 15 ff. (Persia), 24 ff. (Macedon); 29 f. (perfection); 31 ('great governor'); 36 (free men); 38 f. (protects weak); 60 f. (one city-state); 72a/71b ff. (army); 70 ('war thing of past'); 80 ff. (frontiers); 106 ff. ('Golden Race'). Urbicus, Charax: A.R. Birley, *The Fasti of Roman Britain* (1981) 114, 251.

38 Aristides, *Or.* 35 K, discussed and interpreted by C.P. Jones, *JRS* 62 (1972) 134 ff., to whom I am indebted. The passages here quoted or summarised are: 5–10, 13–27, 30, 32–6, 38–9.

5 The Stoic Prince *(pages 89–115)*

1 Consulship: cf. esp. G. Alföldy, *Konsulat und Senatorenstand* (1977) 21; 88 ff.; 100 ff.; 149. Fronto, *Ad MC* 5.1 (vdh 71) = Haines I 188; 4.8 (vdH 64) = Haines I 184 ff.

2 Dio 71.36.3; 71.1.2; 71.6.3–4; 71.24.4; *Med.* 1.8; cf. 1.17.20. R. Dailly and H. van Effenterre, *REA* 56 (1954) 352 ff. offer a diagnosis. Cf. Galen 14 K 3 ff.; 201 ff.

3 G. Alföldy, *Chiron* 15 (1985) 91 ff. offers full bibliography, esp. 100 f. (add *AE* 1968. 28 for Quietus).

4 *Ad MC* 4.7 (vdH 64) = Haines I 184.

5 *HA Marc.* 4.5; *Verus* 3.1; cf. *BMC* IV pp. lxiv ff.; lxix; *HA Verus* 2.5–7, 9. Nicomedes: *CP* no. 163 (on *ILS* 1740).

6 *HA Marc.* 6.6; *Pius* 10.2, dated by *Inscr. It.* XIII.i 205. Coins: *BMC* IV pp. lxv, lxxxvii; *AP* nos. 611 f., 1236 ff., 1801. On the ceremonies, P.E. Corbett, *The Roman Law of Marriage* (1930).

7 *Ad MC* 5.20 (vdH 73 f.) = Haines I 192; *Ad Ant. Pium* 2 (vdH 157) = Haines I
  128; *Ad MC* 5.25 (vdH 75) = Haines I 144; *Ad MC* 5.26 (vdH 75) = Haines I
  194; 5.23 (vdH 74 f.) = Haines I 196, cf. 5.27–32 (vdH 75 f.) = Haines I 198 ff.
  This is not, however, evidence of hypochondria (prevalent among others in
  that age). See the comments of E. Champlin, *Fronto and Antonine Rome* (1980)
  141.

8 *HA Pius* 7.3–4; *Inscr. It.* XIII.i 205, cf. 235. Cf. also A.R. Birley, *The* Fasti *of*
  Roman Britain (1981) 115 f., suggesting that Priscianus might have governed
  Britain shortly before his 'hostile action' in Spain.

9 Clarus: *Inscr. It.* XIII.i 204 f.; cf. R. Syme, *Hist.* 9 (1960) 373 ff. = *RP* 488 ff.
  Praesens: ibid. 375 = *RP* 491. Urbicus: A.R. Birley, *The* Fasti *of Roman Britain*
  (1981) 112 ff. It is puzzling that Urbicus is not known to have held a second
  consulship, especially as he seems to have held the city prefecture for a fairly
  long period. Is it conceivable that he was *cos. suff. II* in 145 – even though no *cos.*
  suff. II is recorded after Trajan – in recompense for his British victory? The
  ordinarii were Pius (*cos. IV*) and Marcus (*cos. II*) – hence to be suffect consul to
  replace either would be almost as prestigious as being *ordinarius*. There is a gap
  in the *Fasti* at this point: G. Alföldy, *Konsulat und Senatorenstand* (1977) 149; and
  cf. his discussion of iterated consulships, 107 ff.

10 *Ad MC* 5.43 (vdH 79) = Haines I 208; 5.37–8 (vdH 77) = Haines I 210.

11 *Ad MC* 5.42 (vdH 78) = Haines I 214.

12 *Ad MC* 4.13 (vdH 68 f.) = Haines I 214 ff.

13 E. Champlin, *JRS* 64 (1974) 144 convincingly identifies this Aristo mentioned
   by Marcus with Pliny's friend the philosophical jurist, portrayed in *Epp.*
   1.22.1–7, rather than with the Stoic philosopher of that name as had been
   assumed by most students, including myself. However, in spite of Champlin's
   warning, I still believe that *Ad MC* 4.13 shows Marcus to be disillusioned with
   both rhetoric and law and yearning for higher things.

14 *Ad MC* 4.3.1 (vdH 56) = Haines I 2 ff.; 3.16 (vdH 47 f.) = Haines I 100 f.

15 *HA Marc.* 3.5–8.

16 *Med.* 1.17.5; 1.7; cf. *PIR²* J 814.

17 *Ad Ant. Imp.* 1.2.2 (vdH 90) = Haines II 36.

18 *De eloq.* 4.5; 5.4 (vdH 144, 147) = Haines II 74, 82.

19 *Med.* 1.14 (τοῦἀδελφοῦ is perhaps a gloss, though it could mean *consocer*)

20 *Med.* 1.15; Apuleius, *Apol.* 19 ff.; cf. *PIR²* C 933–4; G. Alföldy, *Konsulat und*
   Senatorenstand (1977) 143; 208; 236 – accepting the identification with the
   Maximus of *ILS* 1062, who had been *iuridicus* of both Pannonias when L.
   Aelius Caesar had charge there, then governor of Lower Pannonia, consul,
   curator aedium sacrarum. Since he had been decorated for service in the Parthian
   War of Trajan (as *tribunus laticlavius*) he can hardly have been born later than c.
   99. He may well have been of eastern origin.

21 *Med.* 1.9; cf. Dio 71.1.2; Philost., *VS* 2.1.9; Fronto, *Ad am.* 1.3.3 (vdH
   166) = Haines I 280; *Ad Verum Imp.* 2.7.7 (vdH 128) = Haines II 154; cf. *Med.*
   1.11; Fronto, *De fer. Als.* 4.2 (vdH 219) = Haines II 18.

22 Cinna Catulus: *Med.* 1.13; otherwise mentioned only in *HA Marc.* 3.2. These
   two names suggest, but do not prove, a claim to descent from great families
   assumed extinct, patrician Cornelii, and Lutatii. Cf. H.G. Pflaum, *HAC 1968–69*

(1970) 210 f. Athenodotus: *PIR²* A 1291, a Stoic, pupil of Musonius, teacher of Fronto.

23 Cf. for fuller and more expert discussion J.M. Rist, *Stoic Philosophy* (1969) and, on Marcus himself, Rist's contribution to B.F. Meyer and E.P. Sanders, edd., *Jewish and Christian Self-Definition* III (1982) 23 ff. Note also the valuable remarks of P.A. Brunt, *PBSR* 43 (1975) 7 ff., on Stoicism and the principate.

24 Fronto, *De fer. Als.* 3.6 (vdH 215) = Haines II 10; *De eloq.* 2. 17 f. (vdH 140) = Haines II 66; *Med.* 7.19; 6.42. Zeno is mentioned by Fronto, *De eloq.* 1.3; 2.14 (vdH 132, 138) = Haines II 48 ff.; 62 (in the latter place he also names Cleanthes).

25 Seneca: cf. esp. M.T. Griffin, *Seneca, A Philosopher in Politics* (1976). Lucan, *Pharsalia* 1. 128. Helvidii: *PIR²* H 69–70. Rusticus: *PIR²* J 730. Cf. generally R. MacMullen, *Enemies of the Roman Order* (1966), chs. 1 and 2.

26 Musonius: *RE* 16.1 (1933) 893 ff.; C.E. Lutz, *YCS* 10 (1947) 3 ff.

27 *PIR²* E 74; C.G. Starr, *CPh* 44 (1949) 20 ff.; F. Millar, *JRS* 55 (1965) 141 ff.

28 *Discourses* 1.13; *Ench.* 1.1–2; 8; 14.2; 21; 47; 53.4 (Plato, *Apol.* 30 C–D); *Discourses* 1.1.26 f.

29 Date of birth: *Inscr. It.* XIII.1 207 (previously put in 146). For the name of the daughter and other details of Faustina's children, cf. App. 2. *Med.* 1.17.8, cf. p. 225, below.

30 *HA Marc.* 6.6; *Inscr. It.* XIII.1 207.

31 *HA Pius* 7.11; *Marc.* 7.2.

32 *HA Marc.* 6.9; *Pius* 11.8; *Marc.* 6.7–8.

33 *Inscr. It.* XIII.1 207 shows no record of celebration in 147. Games: *HA Pius* 10.8–9. Coins: *BMC* IV *AP* nos. 1838 ff.; cf. pp. lv; lxvi. Numa: *HA Pius* 2.2; 13.4; *Epit. de Caes.* 15.3. D.R. Walker, *The Metrology of the Roman Silver Coinage* III (1978) 124 f. notes that there was a 5% debasement of the silver coinage in 148, which he explains by the high expenditure on celebrations.

34 Mauretania: see now G. Alföldy, *Chiron* 15 (1985) 100 f. Parthian king (Vologases III): N.C. Debevoise, *A Political History of Parthia* (1938) 244; cf. *HA Pius* 9.6; *Marc.* 8.6 and p. 61 above. 'several letters': *Ad MC* 3.14.5 (vdH 47) = Haines I 222. Note 3.14.1 (vdH 46) = Haines I 220: *tot negotiis, tot officiis, tot rescribendis per provincias litteris.*

35 *Ad MC* 4.11–12 (vdH 65 f.) = Haines I 202 ff.; cf. *HA Marc.* 18.5.

36 Details in App. 2; *Med.* 1.8; 8.49; 9.40; 10.34; 11.34.

37 Details in App. 2. *Ad MC* 5.34.2 (vdH 77) = Haines I 224; 5.57.2 (vdH 83) = Haines I 244; 5.60 (vdH 84) = Haines I 246. *CIL* XV 1090 indicates that his mother was still living in 155; cf. *Med.* 1.17.7. 'delight': *Ad MC* 5.67 (vdH 85) = Haines I 250.

38 App. 2.

39 Cornificia's death is registered by *Inscr. It.* XIII.1 207; cf. App. 2.

40 *HA Verus* 3.4–7; 2.9–11. Note *BMC* IV *AP* no. 239 depicting Marcus and Lucius in a *quadriga* with Pius. *Poxy* 3361 shows them both participating as members of Pius' *consilium*, cf. discussion by J.D. Thomas, *BICS* 19 (1972) 103 ff.

41 *HA Verus* 2.8; Fronto, *Ad MC* 5.53–4 (vdH 82) = Haines I 240; cf. *HA Pius* 11.3.

42 Victorinus consul: G. Alföldy, *Konsulat und Senatorenstand* (1977) 167. Fronto's preparations: *Ad MC* 5.51 (vdH 81) = Haines I 234. On the proconsuls of Asia

under Pius, R. Syme, *ZPE* 51 (1983) 271 ff. = *RP* IV (forthcoming).

43 *Ad Ant. Pium* 8 (vdH 161) = Haines I 236. Cf. *Digest* 4.4.2 on children and the *cursus honorum*.

44 *Ad MC* 5.55 (vdH 82) = Haines I 240 ff. 'Cholera' may be dysentery.

45 Cf. App. 2.

46 The *Apology* is not much later than 154, from the allusion (1.29.2) to the prefect of Egypt L. Munatius Felix, replaced in that year (*PIR²* M 723). Quadratus, Aristides, Justin: cf. App. 4, where it is pointed out that Justin wrote only one *Apology*, later mistakenly split into two. The text of the trial before Urbicus is printed, with translation, by H.I. Musurillo, *The Acts of the Christian Martyrs* (1972) 38 ff.

47 Fronto's accusations are quoted by Minucius Felix, *Octavius* 9.8 (also reproduced by Haines II 282 ff.). Cf. E. Champlin, *Fronto and Antonine Rome* (1980) 64 ff., who observes that they probably derived, not from a speech entirely devoted to Christianity, but from one attacking a defendant in a trial, whose conduct it suited Fronto to compare with that attributed to Christians – perhaps his speech *In Pelopem*.

48 Polycarp: dated by T.D. Barnes, *JTS* 18 (1967) 433 ff. and 19 (1968) 510 ff.; cf. on Quadratus R. Syme, *ZPE* 51 (1983) 280 ff. = *RP* IV (forthcoming). See further pp. 152 ff.; 202 ff., below; and App. 4.

49 Pius' health: *HA Pius* 13.1–2. Gavius and successors: ibid. 8.7–9. On Gavius: *CP* no. 105 + *Supp.* pp. 32 f. Tattius: *CP* no. 138. Victorinus: *CP* no. 139. Repentinus: his career emerges from *AE* 1980. 235 (Puteoli); cf. the comments of E. Birley, *HAC* 1982–3 (1985) 69 ff.; cf. *CIL* VIII 14628 + p. 2538 (Simitthu, for his origin), and Fronto, *Ad am.* 2.4 (vdH 180 f.) = Haines I 282 (Fronto calls him *frater Contucci*, presumably a *signum*).

50 *Ad Ant. Pium* 3; 7; 4 (vdH 157 ff.) = Haines I 254 ff.; 258 ff.; cf. E. Champlin, *Fronto and Antonine Rome* (1980) 100 f. Niger had been a friend of Marcius Turbo and Erucius Clarus: *Ad Ant. Pium* 3.3; cf. *PIR²* C 658; *CP* no. 97 *bis*.

51 Philost., *VS* 2.1.8–9; cf. W. Ameling, *Herodes Atticus* (1983) I 100 ff., II 7 ff.

52 Verus: A.R. Birley, *The Fasti of Roman Britain* (1981) 118 ff. Coins: *BMC* IV *AP* nos. 1971 ff., 1993 ff. Cf. W.S. Hanson and G. Maxwell, *Rome's North-West Frontier. The Antonine Wall* (1983), esp. 139 ff. However, the history of the Antonine Wall is so dependent on the uncertain evidence of pottery that it may require revision. The current view may be registered, that shortly after the withdrawal the Forth-Clyde frontier was briefly reoccupied, only to be abandoned again (for good), at latest by the governorship of Calpurnius Agricola (p. 123 below). Agricola, it is now known, had been governor of Upper Germany in 158, probably remaining there until his transfer to Britain: W. Eck, *Die Statthalter der germ. Provinzen* (1985) 65 ff.

53 G. Alföldy, *Fundber. aus Baden-Württemberg* 8 (1983) 55 ff.; W. Eck, op. cit. 60 ff.

54 Priscus: A.R. Birley, *The Fasti of Roman Britain* (1981) 123 ff. Prefects: *Inscr. It.* XIII.1 571 f.; cf. G. Alföldy, *Konsulat und Senatorenstand* (1977) 287.

55 *IGR* IV 1399, redated by G. Petzl, *Chiron* 13 (1983) 33 ff. Cf. App. 2.

56 App. 2.

57 Dio 71.33.4–5 gives the date; 70.3.3; *HA Pius* 12.4–8; *Marc.* 7.3.

58 *Med.* 6.30.

59 On Dio of Prusa cf. esp. C.P. Jones, *The Roman World of Dio Chrysostom* (1978).

6 The First Years as Emperor *(pages 116–139)*

1 *HA Marc.* 7.5; *Verus* 3.8. Tiberius: Tacitus, *Ann.* 1. 11 ff. Galba: id., *Hist.* 1.16. *horror imperii: HA Pert.* 13.1; 15.8. Lucius under Pius: *HA Verus* 2.11.

2 *HA Marc.* 7.6–7; *Verus* 4.1; cf. *Ael. passim*, and App. 1.

3 Cf. E. Kornemann, *Doppelprinzipat und Reichsteilung im Imp. Romanum* (1930).

4 *HA Verus* 4.2; *BMC* IV *MA & LV*, nos. 1 ff., 25 ff., etc.

5 *HA Marc.* 7.9; *Verus* 4.3. *ILS* 190 supplies the text of an oath of allegiance (to Caligula).

6 *HA Marc.* 7.10–11.

7 *HA Marc.* 7.11; *Pius* 13.3–4; cf. Dio 74.4–5 (deification of Pertinax); Herodian 4.1–2 (of Severus). Games: *HA Marc.* 8.2 (misplaced). Cf. on the college of priests H.-G. Pflaum, *Les sodales Antoniniani de l'époque de Marc-Aurèle* (1966).

8 *HA Marc.* 7.7. It might be, of course, that Lucius had already been married, and widowed; if so, no hint in the sources. 'poor children': cf. W. Eck, *Die Organisation Italiens* (1979) 146 ff., esp. 151 f.

9 *HA Pius* 12.8; *Marc.* 7.4; *Comm.* 1.1–4; 10.2 (cf. Suetonius, *Calig.* 8.1). The story in *HA Marc.* 19 is surely fiction. Coins: *BMC* IV *MA & LV*, nos. 155 ff.; 949 ff.

10 *HA Marc.* 8.1.

11 Fronto, *Ad Ant. Imp.* 4.2.3 (vdH 11) = Haines I 302 ff. (date conjectural).

12 *Ad Verum Imp.* 1.2–3 (vdH 111 ff.) = Haines I 294 ff.

13 *Ad Verum Imp.* 1.3.2 (vdH 113) = Haines I 298 ff. I see no reason to date this to 162 rather than 161, as does Schwendemann 143; cf. E. Champlin, *JRS* 64 (1974) 146 f.

14 *Ad Verum Imp.* 1.1 (vdH 111) = Haines I 305 (date uncertain, cf. E. Champlin, *JRS* 64 (1974) 147); *Ad Ant. Imp.* 4.1 (vdH 109) = Haines I 300 ff.

15 *HA Marc.* 8.3–4; Dio 71.1.2. A sophist called Lucius mocked him for attending Sextus' lectures 'at his age': Philost., *VS* 2.1.9. 'stepmother': *Med.* 6.12. *felicitas*: *BMC* IV *MA & LV*, nos. 841, 845.

16 *HA Marc.* 8.4–5; 11.3; Pliny, *Epp.* 5.14.2 (cf. 3.6.6); *ILS* 2927; cf. R. Syme, *Tacitus* (1958) 79 f. Nepos: *ILS* 5932 (already in office early in 161). Priscus: *ILS* 1092.

17 A.R. Birley, *The Fasti of Roman Britain* (1981) 123 ff.

18 *HA Pius* 12.7; *Marc.* 8.6; Dio 71.2.1; cf. *PIR²* A 1341 for Cornelianus – who must be the tiresomely petty *praeses Syriae* who made Pertinax, newly appointed prefect of a cohort c. 160, walk from Antioch to his posting because he had travelled by the *cursus publicus* without a permit: *HA Pert.* 1.6.

19 Severianus: Lucian, *Alexander* 27 (hardly a Galatian, as suggested by G.W. Bowersock, *Greek Sophists in the Roman Empire* (1969) 86 f., who identifies him with 'Sedatus' of Nicaea, a friend of Aristides. Cf. H. Halfmann, *Die Senatoren aus dem östlichen Teil des Imp. Rom.* (1979) 164, reporting an unpublished inscription from Poitiers honouring Severianus as patron); *quom. hist. conscr.* 21; 24; 25. Cf. G. Alföldy, *Konsulat und Senatorenstand* (1977) 220; 245. Rutilianus: Lucian, *Alexander* 4; 30 ff.; cf. A.R. Birley, *The Fasti of Roman Britain* (1981) 248 ff. The legion destroyed was perhaps IX Hispana, transferred from Britain to the east some years earlier, cf. Birley, op. cit. 220 ff.

20 *HA Marc.* 8.7.
21 Cf. *CP* nos. 142; 156; E. Birley, *Roman Britain and the Roman Army* (1953) 142 ff.; 151 ff.
22 *CP* no. 141.
23 Priscus: A.R. Birley, *The* Fasti *of Roman Britain* (1981) 123 ff. Agricola, Victorinus: *HA Marc.* 8.8; W. Eck, *Die Statthalter der germ. Provinzen* (1985) 65 ff.
24 Marcianus: *CIL* VIII 7050–1. V Macedonica: *ILS* 2311. II Adiutrix: *ILS* 1091; I Minervia: *ILS* 1097–8. Cf. *RE* 12.1 (1924) 1298 ff. Northern threat: *HA Marc.* 12.13; cf. Zwikker 35 ff. Cornelianus: *HA Marc.* 8.6 (perhaps not defeated until 162, as he was still governor in that year – *CIL* III 129 = 6658).
25 Dio 71.1.3; *HA Marc.* 8.9; *Verus* 5.8.
26 Victorinus: *CP* no. 139. Laelianus: *ILS* 1094 + 1100; Fronto, *Ad Verum Imp.* 2.1.22 (vdH 122) = Haines II 148 ('vir gravis et veteris disciplinae Laelianus Pontius'); cf. *RE* 22.1 (1953) 39 ff.; A.R. Birley, *The* Fasti *of Roman Britain* (1981) 273 f. *Comites*: cf. the list in H.-G. Pflaum, *Bayer. Vorg. Bl.* 27 (1962) 90 f.
27 Bassus: *PIR²* I 4. Libo: *HA Verus* 9.2, cf. *PIR²* A 668; *RE Supp.* 14 (1974) 48; his consular date is known from *AE* 1972. 657. Freedmen: *HA Verus* 9.3–5; cf. 8.6. Nicomedes: *CP* no. 163. Fleet: C.G. Starr, *The Roman Imperial Navy* (1941) 188 ff.
28 *BMC* IV *MA* & *LV*, nos. 200 ff.; 1029 ff.; *HA Verus* 6.7–9; Fronto, *Ad Verum Imp.* 2.6 (vdH 126) = Haines II 84 ff. Eleusis: *SIG³* I 869; 872; *HA Had.* 13.1. Shooting star: Cassiodorus senator *s.a.* 162. Fronto later took the chance to tell Lucius he was on the best of terms with Herodes: *Ad Verum Imp.* 2.9.1 (vdH 130) = Haines II 232 ff. For the date of departure (summer not spring), cf. E. Champlin, *JRS* 64 (1974) 147.
29 Lucian, *Quom. hist. conscr.* 20 (a joke); *HA Verus* 7.1; Dio 71.3.1.
30 *De feriis Als.* 1; 3; 4 (vdH 212 ff.) = Haines II 2; 4 ff.
31 *De bello Parthico*, esp. 10 (vdH 210) = Haines II 20 ff. (esp. 30).
32 *Ad Ant. Imp.* 1.1 (vdH 80) = Haines II 30 ff.; 1.2.2 f. (vdH 89) = Haines II 34 ff. Cyzicus: 1.2.6, 9 (vdH 91, 92) = Haines II 38 ff. E. Champlin, *JRS* 64 (1974) 145 f. assigns this speech to August 13, 161, but that dating depends on the mistaken placing, in 160–1, of the Asian proconsulship of L. Antonius Albus, cf. R. Syme, *ZPE* 51 (1983) 276 f. = *RP* IV (forthcoming).
33 *De eloq.* 2.14, 19 (vdH 138, 141 f.) = Haines II 62 ff., 70.
34 *Ad Ant. Imp.* 1.1.3 (vdH 88) = Haines II 32; 1.3 (vdH 93 f.) = Haines II 118 ff.; 1.4 (vdH 94) = Haines II 120 ff. 'another son': *HA Marc.* 21.3, cf. App. 2.
35 *BMC* IV *MA* & *LV*, nos. 233 ff.; *HA Marc.* 9.1; *Verus* 4.6 ff.; 6.1–5; 7.1–6; Fronto, *Princ. hist.* 18 (vdH 199 f.) = Haines II 216.
36 *HA Verus* 7.10; Lucian, *Imagines*; *Pro imaginibus*.
37 *Ad Verum Imp.* 2.1, esp. 22–3 (vdH 122 f.) = Haines II 128 ff.; 2.2 (vdH 123 f.) = Haines II 116 ff.; *Princ. hist.* 13 ff. (vdH 196 f.) = Haines II 208 ff.; 14 (vdH 189) = Haines II 212; *Pan. Lat.* 4 (10). 24. 6–7.
38 Mannus: *PIR²* M 169; replaced by a Parthian nominee from 163–165. Dausara and Nicephorium: Fronto, *Ad Verum Imp.* 2.1.5 (vdH 115) = Haines II 132. The letter dates to 164, cf. Champlin, *JRS* 64 (1974) 147, but the victories belong to 163, as argued by M.L. Astarita, *Avidio Cassio* (1983) 41. However, Astarita is misled over Dausara's location by Stephanus of Byzantium, *s.v.*

Dausara, described as 'near Edessa'. It was actually on the Euphrates, as was Nicephorium, also mistakenly located near Edessa by Stephanus, *s.v.* Cf. L. Dillemann, *Haute Mésopotamiae Orientale et pays adjacents* (1962) 109. The battle at Sura is known only from Lucian, *Quom. hist. conscr.* 29.

39 Fronto: *PIR²* C 874. Verus: M 348. Cassius: A 1402 f.; 1405; M.L. Astarita, op. cit.; R. Syme, *HAC* 1984 (forthcoming) = *RP* IV (forthcoming). Anthemusia: cf. p. 281 n. 2, below.

40 *HA Verus* 4.2–3; *CIL* III 199 (Julius Verus); *Digest* 23.2.16.

41 *HA Marc.* 9.4–6; *Verus* 7.7. Barbarus: *AE* 1958. 15. 'his sister': an alternative is to suppose that the text of *HA Marc.* 9.4 is faulty and originally read *sororis suae filio* rather than *sorori suae*. This would refer to M. Ummidius Quadratus, son of Cornificia, and Lucilla's first cousin, now in his twenties (App. 2). 'Augusta': *BMC* IV, *MA & LV*, nos. 303 ff. The date of the wedding is uncertain, cf. T.D. Barnes, *JRS* 57 (1967) 72. The *Vita Abercii*, which he cites, makes Lucilla still only betrothed to Lucius when she was sixteen (3.20 = 44 ff.), i.e. in 166; this conflicts with *HA Marc.* 9.4 (*medio belli tempore*). 164 seems the likeliest year (cf. App. 2 on Lucilla's age; App. 4 on the *Vita Abercii*).

42 Dio 71.3.1. Sohaemus: *RE* 3A.1 (1927) 798 ff.; *BMC* IV, *MA & LV*, nos. 261 ff.; 300 ff. The ceremony need not have taken place in Armenia.

43 *Ad Verum Imp.* 2.1.5–6, 18 (vdH 115 f., 120) = Haines II 130 ff., 144.

44 *Ad Ant. Imp.* 2.1–2 (vdH 98) = Haines II 94 ff.; cf. *Ad am.* 1.14.1 (vdH 173) = Haines II 98. Matidia was still alive in 161: *Ad Ant. Imp.* 4.1.1 (vdH 109) = Haines I 301.

45 *Ad am.* 1.12 (vdH 171) = Haines II 172; *De nepote amisso* 2 (vdH 220 ff.) = Haines II 222; *Ad Verum Imp.* 2.9–10 (vdH 129 f.) = Haines II 232 ff. Cf. E. Champlin, *JRS* 64 (1974) 155 f. on Victorinus' sons: the one born in Germany died young, but another, Victorinus, was probably born c. 165–6. 'Germans': H. Schönberger, *JRS* 59 (1969) 171. 'legate': Dio 72.11.3–4.

46 Cf. G. Alföldy, *Konsulat und Senatorenstand* (1977) 232 f. (Moesia Inferior); 234 f. (Moesia Superior); 236 f. (Pannonia Superior); 245 f. (Dacia); 251 (Pannonia Inferior). I take a different view of the Moesian governorships of Servilius Fabianus.

47 *CJ* 7.2.6; *Digest* 31.67.10 (cf. *CJ* 6.35.11); Victor, *De Caes.* 16.11. In general, cf. P. Noyen, *RIDA* 1 (1952) 349 ff.; id., *Ant. Class.* 24 (1955) 372 ff.; and comments in App. 1.

48 *HA Marc.* 9.7–12.6, discussed in detail by Schwendemann 28–51. Maecianus: *CP* no. 141. Arrius Antoninus: *PIR²* A 1088. iuridici: W. Eck, *Die Organisation Italiens* (1979) 249 ff. alimenta: ibid. 151. Lollianus: *PIR²* H 40. Scaevola: *PIR²* C 681; *CP* no. 168a.

49 *Digest* 23.2.57a; 25.4.1.*pr.*

50 Priscianus: he might be the son of the homonymous disturber of the peace condemned in 145 (p. 91 f. above); *Digest* 28.4.3.

51 *Digest* 48.18.1.27; 48.19.33.

52 *CJ* 6.27.2; *Inst.* 3.11.1; *Digest* 40.5.37; 4.2.13.

53 *Digest* 48.18.1.*pr.* Class-distinctions: cf. esp. P.D.A. Garnsey, *Social Status and Legal Privilege in the Roman Empire* (1970), who places the beginnings of this development much earlier. Titles: O. Hirschfeld, *Sitzb. Berlin* 1901, 579 ff., esp. 584 ff. = *Kleine Schriften* (1913) 646 ff., esp. 652 ff. is still valuable. Cf. also

R.J.A. Talbert, *The Senate of Imperial Rome* (1984) 193.

54 W. Williams, *JRS* 66 (1976) 67 ff., esp. 74; 78 ff.

7 Triumph and Crisis *(pages 140–158)*

1 Mannus: *PIR²* M 169. Nisibis, Chosrhoes: Lucian, *Quom. hist. conscr.* 15; 19. Dura: ibid. 20; 28. Dio 71.2 (from the *Suda*) describes an opposed river crossing achieved by Cassius, involving the construction of a bridge of boats. Probably not the Euphrates, cf. M.L. Astarita, *Avidio Cassio* (1983) 48 n. 124, and n. 11, below. Seleucia, Ctesiphon: *HA Verus* 7.1; 8.1–4. Cf. generally D. Magie, *Roman Rule in Asia Minor* (1950) I 661 f.; II 1532 f.; M.L. Astarita, op. cit. 43 ff.

2 R.H. McDowell, *Coins from Seleucia on the Tigris* (1935) 124 ff. gives the date (the end of the year 165). For the history, size and wealth of the city, cf. *RE* 2 A.1 (1921) 1149 ff., esp. 1183 f. (its destruction). The city's prosperity had already been affected by Parthian creation of a rival trading centre, cf. *RE*, loc. cit. 1181 f. 'Roman version': *HA Verus* 8.3–4. 'Imp. III': *BMC* IV, *MA & LV*, nos. 384 ff.; 1248 ff.; 1271 ff. Claudius Fronto may at this stage, in 165 – if not in 164 – have occupied Osrhoene and Anthemusia, with his task force (*ILS* 1098); his consulship may have been held *in absentia* (G. Alföldy, *Konsulat und Senatorenstand* (1977) 179).

3 Avitus: *PIR²* H 46. Maximianus: *AE* 1956. 124. Spain: G. Alföldy, *Fasti Hispanienses* (1969) 32 ff. Changes in status: *HA Marc.* 22.9. Titianus: *AE* 1947. 146, cf. Lucian, *Quom. hist. conscr.* 21 (there are alternatives: *PIR²* C 1043–4; *CIL* III 537).

4 Fronto, *Ad Verum Imp.* 2.3 (vdH 125) = Haines II 194 ff.

5 G. Alföldy and H. Halfmann, *ZPE* 35 (1979) 195 ff. analysed and explained this remarkable inscription. Fronto, *Ad am.* 1.6 (vdH 168 f.) = Haines II 190 ff.

6 G. Alföldy, *Konsulat und Senatorenstand* (1977) 179 ff. On Cassius' age, R. Syme, *HAC* 1984 (forthcoming) = *RP* IV (forthcoming).

7 New legions: cf. J.C. Mann, *Hermes* 91 (1963) 483 ff., and App. 3. Bassus: *PIR²* I 4; G. Alföldy, *Konsulat und Senatorenstand* (1977) 237. Pompeianus: *PIR²* C 973; Alföldy 251. Fronto: *PIR²* C 874. Verus: *AE* 1956. 123; cf. further Alföldy 179 n. 167.

8 twins: *HA Comm.* 1.4. Faustina in the east: Fronto, *Ad Verum Imp.* 2.4 (vdH 126) = Haines II 236 (*socrum et liberos vestros saluta*).

9 *De nepote amisso* 1; 2; 4 (vdH 220 ff.) = Haines II 220 ff.

10 *Ad Verum Imp.* 2.9 (vdH 129 f.) = Haines II 232 ff.

11 M.L. Astarita, *Avidio Cassio* (1983) 48 ff. (as she suggests, 48 n. 124, the river-bridging by Cassius described in Dio 71.2 may belong in this campaign). Titles: *BMC* IV, *MA & LV*, nos. 401 ff. *Medicus* is not on the coinage but common on inscriptions: cf. P. Kneissl, *Die Siegestitulatur der römischen Kaiser* (1969) 99 ff. India: Lucian, *Quom. hist. conscr.* 31. China: J.O. Thomson, *A History of Ancient Geography* (1948) 312.

12 *Ad Verum Imp.* 2.4 (vdH 126) = Haines II 236; cf. App. 2.

13 fleet: C.G. Starr, *The Roman Imperial Navy* (1941) 188 ff. Ostia: *CIL* XIV 106. Garrisons, etc.: M.G. Angeli Bertinelli, *ANRW* 2.9 (1978) 30 f.; A.R. Birley, in R. Klein (ed.), *Marc Aurel* (1979) 480 f.

14 Damianus, Vedius: D. Magie, *Roman Rule in A. Minor* (1950) I 662; II 1532 n. 6. Vedii: cf. further *RE* 8 A.1 (1955) 563 ff.; *AE* 1959. 13, with *REG* 72 (1959) 241.

15 *RE* 12.1 (1924) 1297 ff.; G. Alföldy, *Konsulat und Senatorenstand* (1977) 222 f.

16 *HA Verus* 7.8–9. Cassius, Verus: G. Alföldy, *Konsulat* 24; 221; M.L. Astarita, *Avidio Cassio*.(1983) 56 ff.; R. Syme, *HAC 1984* (forthcoming) = *RP* IV (forthcoming).

17 *ILS* 366, cf. App. 2.

18 *Ad Verum Imp.* 2.5 (vdH 126) = Haines II 236; 2.8 (vdH 128 f.) = Haines II 238 ff.

19 *Ad am.* 1.9; 10; 20; 27 (vdH 170i 178) = Haines II 240 ff. But the dating of these is very uncertain, cf. E. Champlin, *JRS* (1974) 151 ff. On Fronto's death, cf. id., *Fronto and Antonine Rome* (1980) 139 ff.

20 *Med.* 1.11; *ILS* 1129; cf. E. Champlin, *JRS* 64 (1974) 157.

21 *HA Marc.* 12.7–10; 12.8, with *Comm.* 11.13 gives the date. Victorinus: *PIR²* F 584. Laelianus: *ILS* 1094 + 1100. Claudius Fronto: *PIR²* C 874.

22 *HA Had.* 6.3; cf. T. Mommsen, *Römisches Staatsrecht* I³ (1887) 426 f.

23 *HA Marc.* 12.9–12 (note 15.1: jokes about his dealing with documents at the games); Dio 71.29.4.

24 Dio 71.3.1a (cf. *ILS* 1107). *Imp. V*: *CIL* XVI 123 (AD 167); *BMC* IV, *MA & LV*, nos. 458, etc. (AD 168). Cf. Zwikker 35 ff.; P. Oliva, *Pannonia and the Onset of Crisis* (1962) 259 ff.; A. Mócsy, *Pannonia and Upper Moesia* (1974) 185 f.

25 *HA Marc.* 13.3–6; 17.2; 21.7–7; *Verus* 8.1–4; Lucian, *Alexander* 36; Ammianus 31.6.24; Orosius 7.15.5–6; 7.27.7. Cf. J.F. Gilliam, *AJP* 82 (1961) 225 ff., who believes that its effects were somewhat exaggerated; but F. Millar, *A Study of Cassius Dio* (1964) 13 n. 4 undermines one of his arguments.

26 R.J. and M.L. Littmann, *AJP* 94 (1973) 243 ff. discuss Galen's evidence. Marcus on the plague: *Med.* 9.2 (cf. *HA Marc.* 28.4).

27 *HA Marc.* 13.3–6; *Digest* 47.12.3.4; 11.7.39; 11.7.14.14; 11.7.6.1 (cf. 1.8.6.5; 1.8.7); 2.4.3.

28 *HA Marc.* 13.1–2; cf. Zwikker 63 ff.

29 Gold mines: *CIL* III, pp. 921–60. V Mac.: *ILS* 2311. Pompeianus: *CIL* XVI 123. roads: *CIL* III 10615; 10632; 10638 (the road from Sirmium to Aquincum, useful preparation for an offensive). I find it impossible to accept the view, expressed e.g. by A. Mócsy, *Pannonia and Upper Moesia* (1974) 187, that 'the logic of the – admittedly little known – events supports the dating' of the invasion of Italy to the year 167; cf. App. 3.

30 *HA Verus* 8.6–11; cf. H.G. Pflaum, *HAC* 1972/74 (1976) 182 f.

31 All three versions are printed by H. Musurillo, *The Acts of the Christian Martyrs* (1972) 42 ff. G. Lazzati, *Gli sviluppi della letteratura sui martiri* (1956) 119 ff. shows that the short version is the earliest.

32 Eusebius, *HE* 4.16.1–9. 'deeply imbued with Greek philosophy': H. Chadwick, *The Early Church* (1967) 79.

33 *Med.* 11.3; 1.7; Epictetus, *Disc.* 4.7.6. Cf. App. 4.

34 G. Alföldy, *Konsulat und Senatorenstand* (1977) 161 (but *CIL* VI 253 probably refers to an ancestor, cf. R. Syme, *RP* I 328 n. 5); *RE* Supp. 6 (1935) 818. Paphos, etc.: *Acts* 13. 6 ff. Galen, *On Prognosis* 2. 24; 5. 17 ff. = Nutton 80; 98 ff. Annia Faustina: App. 2.

35 *Frag. Vat.* 195.

36 *HA Marc.* 14.1–4. Furius: *CP* no. 139. Aufidius: G. Alföldy, *Fasti Hispanienses* (1969) 38 ff. Pollio: *ILS* 1112–3. Laelianus: *ILS* 1094 + 1100. Tuscus: *ILS* 1081. Fronto: *ILS* 1098. Cf. App. 3.

37 *HA Marc.* 14.5; cf. Zwikker 66; Eutropius 8.12; Jerome, *Chron.* pp. 206 f. Helm; cf. Orosius 7.15.5–6; *HA Marc.* 17.2.

38 Rufus: *CP* no. 162 + *add.* Vindex: *CP* no. 161.

39 'crossed Alps': *HA Marc.* 14.5–6; Verus 9.7–8. 'shrine': *AE* 1982. 777, correctly rendered 'consis[t]ent(ium)'. This inscription appears to render doubtful the theory of G. Barta, *ACD* 7 (1971) 67 ff. (based on a slightly forced interpretation of *ILS* 1098) that Lucius was active in Moesia and Dacia while Marcus was in Pannonia. Adventus: *PIR²* A 754; cf. App. 3.

40 Fabianus: G. Alföldy, *Konsulat und Senatorenstand* (1977) 232; 234 f. takes a different view of his career. Fronto: *ILS* 1098. doctor: *IGR* I 482. Galen 19.18 K = *scr. min.* 2.98 f.; *On prognosis* 9.6 = Nutton 118. Harnouphis (the correct spelling): *AE* 1934. 245, as brilliantly elucidated by J. Guey, *RPh* 22 (1948) 19 ff.

41 Arrius: *PIR²* A 1088. Pertinax: *CP* no. 179; *AE* 1963. 52. Julianus: *CP* no. 180.

42 Galen, 19.18 K = *scr. min.* 2. 98 f.; *On prognosis* 9.6 = Nutton 118; *HA Marc.* 14.7–8; *Verus* 9.10–11. Cf. T.D. Barnes, *JRS* 57 (1967) 73.

43 *HA Verus* 10.1–5, 11.2–3; *Marc.* 15.5–6; Dio 71.3.1.

44 P. Lambrechts, *Ant. Class.* 3 (1934) 173 ff. offered a rehabilitation; cf. T.D. Barnes, *JRS* 57 (1967) 65 ff. *HA Marc.* 20.3–4 claims that Marcus promised a fresh start now that Lucius was gone, and took the credit for planning the Parthian war. Not discussed by Schwendemann; but not necessarily fiction – perhaps from Marius Maximus (and perhaps true).

8 The Northern Wars *(pages 159–183)*

1 *HA Marc.* 15.3–4; 20.1–5. The priests: cf. H.G. Pflaum, *Les sodales Antoniniani de l'époque de Marc-Aurèle* (1966). Consecration: *BMC* IV, *MA & LV*, nos. 503 ff.; 1359 ff.

2 *CIL* III 14507; *HA Marc.* 21.6–8; cf. Zwikker 105 ff.

3 *HA Marc.* 21.9; 17. 4–5.

4 Sabinianus: *AE* 1920. 45. council of Gallic states: I owe this interpretation to the late H.G. Pflaum. Debasement: cf. esp. D.R. Walker, *The Metrology of the Roman Silver Coinage* III (1978) 125 f., who finds that there was debasement from 161–6; an improvement from 166–70; then debasement from 170–80.

5 Agricola, Fronto: G. Alföldy, *Konsulat und Senatorenstand* (1977) 222 f. Macrinius: *PIR²* M 22. Pertinax: *CP* no. 179; *AE* 1963. 52. Cf. generally *HA Marc.* 22.9.

6 *HA Marc.* 20.6–7; cf. *RE* 13.2 (1927) 1700. Pompeianus: *PIR²* C 973. Cassius: A 1402, cf. 1405 (Heliodorus).

7 *HA Marc.* 21.3–5; cf. *RE* Supp. 5 (1931) 617 ff. The death of this child forms an important episode in Walter Pater, *Marius the Epicurean.*

8 App. 2.

9 Galen, *On Prognosis* 9.6–7 = Nutton 118.

10 Laelianus: *ILS* 1094 + 1100. Tuscus: *ILS* 1081. Priscus: *CIL* VI 31753, cf. Zwikker 182. Verus: *ILS* 1057 + 8794, cf. *AE* 1956. 123.

11 The chronology is discussed in App. 3.

12 *BMC* IV, *MA & LV*, nos. 1371 ff.; 531 ff.; Lucian, *Alexander* 48.

13 Ammianus 29.6.1. Adventus: *PIR²* A 754; cf. App. 3.

14 Fronto: *PIR²* C 874. Clemens: ibid. 1340. Caerellius: ibid. 160; cf. A.R. Birley, *The* Fasti *of Roman Britain* (1981) 132 ff.

15 Pausanias 10.34.4; Aristides, *Or.* 22. 31 (dated by the proconsulship of Nonius

Macrinus, AD 170–1); *ILS* 8830; *AE* 1964. 252 (a decurion of Tropaeum Traiani, 'deceptus a Castobocas' (sic)). Cf. Zwikker 167 ff.; S. Follet, *Athènes au IIe et IIIe siècle* (1976) 258; M.L. Astarita, *Avidio Cassio* (1983) 62 ff.

16 Dio 71.3.1–2; *HA Pert.* 2.4; *ILS* 1327; *AE* 1956. 124.

17 Salona: *ILS* 2287. Four newly raised cohorts of Dalmatae played an even larger part in building; cf. J.J. Wilkes, *Dalmatia* (1969) 116 ff.

18 *Digest* 50.10.6; *CIL* III 6121 = 7409.

19 Eutropius 8.13.1; *HA Marc.* 21.10; *BMC* IV, *MA*, nos. 540 f.; 1388 etc. (IMP. VI); 1394 ff. Carnuntum: *AE* 1982. 778, cf. *CIL* III 3347 (Aquincum), explained otherwise by W. Jobst, *Öst. Ak. Wiss. Sb.* 335 (1978); cf. App. 3.

20 G. Alföldy, *Fasti Hispanienses* (1969) 38 ff.; cf. *CP* no. 180; A.R. Birley, *Septimius Severus* (1971) 84 f.

21 Dio 71.3.2; *HA Marc.* 14.1; 22.1.

22 *BMC* IV, *MA*, no. 540; cf. 541; 1388 (VIC GER); Dio 71.3.3–4; *HA Marc.* 22.3–8.

23 Dio 71.11.1–5.

24 Dio 71.12.1–3; cf. 11.6. Paternus: *CP* no. 172; cf. *AE* 1971. 534 (for the spelling of his *gentilicium*).

25 *BMC* IV, *MA*, nos. 1425–7; Dio 71.3.5; *HA Pert.* 2.6, 9. Statianus: *CP* no. 166. Rufus: *CP* no. 162.

26 *HA Marc.* 24.4; *BMC* IV, *MA*, nos. 566–7. Cf. App. 3.

27 Dio 71.8–10; *BMC* IV, *MA*, nos. 609 ff.; 1483 ff. Cf. App. 3.

28 J. Guey, *RPh* 22 (1948) 16 ff. Julianus: *PIR²* J 91.

29 Orosius 7.15.10; Eusebius-Jerome, *Chron. ad 2189* (= AD 173); forged letter: a convenient text with translation in Haines' edition of Fronto, II 300 ff.; Dio 71.13.2. Cf. further App. 3, accepting J. Guey's arguments for dating the episode to 172.

30 *HA Comm.* 11.14; Dio 71.3.5; *BMC* IV, *MA*, nos. 566 f.; cf. 1412 f.

31 Carnuntum: *AE* 1982. 778 (cf. App 3); Lilybaeum: *AE* 1964. 181.

32 Dio 71.4; cf. 71.3.1; Philostratus, *VS* 2.1.13. J. Winkler, *JHS* 100 (1980) 175 ff. gives reason to believe that Dio's story about the Bucoli contains a large element of myth. The date of Cassius' special powers is uncertain: hardly 166, when he became governor of Syria; possibly 169 (death of Lucius); 170 (invasion of Italy and Greece); or 172 (to permit him to enter Egypt). Cf. A. Baldini, *Latomus* 37 (1984) 641; M.L. Astarita, *Avidio Cassio* (1983) 56 ff.

33 Dio 71.3.1¹. Martius: *PIR²* M 348. M.L. Astarita, *Avidio Cassio* (1983) 47 n. 121 prefers to separate the restoration of Sohaemus (placed in the 160s) and the punishment of Tiridates (after 169).

34 Medallion: Gnecchi II p. 27, *M. Aur.* no. 2; cf. Zwikker 135 ff. Maximianus: *AE* 1956. 124; *CP* no. 181 bis + add. L. Rossi, *Quad. tic.* 6 (1977) 223 ff. argues plausibly that this action is depicted on the Column (scene 43). Avitus: *PIR²* M 22.

35 Sabinianus: *AE* 1920. 45. Piso: *ILS* 1111, cf. *PIR²* J 477; G. Alföldy, *Konsulat und Senatorenstand* (1977) 297 n. 81 (who dates this command c. 175–6). Note also the career of Macrinius Avitus: G. Alföldy 371 ff.

36 Dio 71.13.1–14.2. Captives: cf. E. Levy, *CP* 38 (1943) 159 ff.

37 Dio 71.7.1.

38 Dio 71.15–16.

39 IMP. VIII, *mater castrorum*: Dio 71.10.5; *BMC* IV, *MA*, nos. 609 ff.; 1483 ff. two incidents: Dio 71.5.1–2.

40 Cf. esp. P.G. Hamberg, *Studies in Roman Imperial Art* (1945).

41 Dio 71.6; Galen, *De antidotis*, 14.3–4 K. Cf. R. Dailly and H. van Effenterre, *REA* 56 (1954) 347 ff.; T.W. Africa, *JHI* 22 (1961) 97 ff.; E.C. Witke, *CP* 60 (1965) 23 f.

42 *HA Marc.* 10.4–5. Maecianus: *CP* no. 141. Pertinax: see esp. G. Alföldy, *Situla* 14/15 (1974) 199 ff. Avitus: id., *Konsulat und Senatorenstand* (1977) 371 ff. Priscus: A.R. Birley, *The Fasti of Roman Britain* (1981) 124 ff.

43 *Digest* 36.1.23 (22). *pr.*

44 Philostratus, *VS* 2.1.11–12; cf. W. Ameling, *Herodes Atticus* (1983) I 136 ff. Quintilii: G. Alföldy, *Konsulat und Senatorenstand* (1977) 260 ff. Sabina: App. 2.

45 *HA Marc.* 23.4–7.

46 App. 2.

47 Galen, *On prognosis* 10. 22, 12.1–12 = Nutton 126; 130 ff. Condianus: ibid. 9.10–10.21 = Nutton 120 ff.

48 *HA Marc.* 23.8–24.3, cf. Schwendemann 51 ff. On settlement, the most comprehensive treatment is by G.E.M. de Ste Croix, *The Class Struggle in the Ancient Greek World* (1981) 511 ff.

49 Dio 71.16.1; *HA Marc.* 24.5–6; *ILS* 2747, cf. *CP* no. 198; 1111, cf. G. Alföldy, *Konsulat und Senatorenstand* (1977) 297 n. 81. On the plan to create new provinces, cf. App. 3.

9 The Last Years *(pages 184–210)*

1 Dio 71.17; 71.23.3. Alexander: *PIR²* A 503; *Med.* 1.12 (probably not a former teacher, as maintained by Schwendemann 11 ff.). Clemens: *CP* no. 156. Paternus: *CP* no. 172 (cf. *AE* 1971. 534 for his first name). Tertullus: *CP* no. 252 + *add.* Sanctus: *CP* no. 178 *bis*.

2 *HA Marc.* 24.6 (reproduced in *Av. Cass.* 7.1); Dio 71.22.3. Bogus letters: *HA Av. Cass.* 9.5–11.8; cf. App. 1. Cf. the discussion by M.L. Astarita, *Avidio Cassio* (1983) 91 ff.; R. Syme, *HAC* 1984 (forthcoming) = *RP* IV (forthcoming).

3 Unwell: Dio 71.1.2; 71.6.3–4; 71.24.4; 71.36.2–3. Death: *Med.* 2.2; 2.11; 2.17 (among the Quadi). Nero: *PIR²* D 129. Faustina and Cassius: cf. esp. R. Syme, *HAC 1984* (forthcoming) = *RP* IV (forthcoming).

4 *HA Marc.* 24.4; *Av. Cass.* 7.6–7. Dryantianus: *PIR²* C 879. The family is registered in *IGR* III 500 (omitting Cassius). M.L. Astarita, *Avidio Cassio* (1983) supplies a stemma opposite p. 32; parts are speculative, especially regarding Cassius' wife, who is unknown (perhaps called Maecia). Calvisii: *CP* nos. 166, 177; Fronto, *Ad am.* 1.52 (vdH 168) = Haines I 290 ff. Statianus' prefecture in Egypt ran unbroken from 172 to 175 (confirmed by *SB* 9393).

5 *SB* 10295, convincingly attributed to Cassius by A.K. Bowman, *JRS* 60 (1970) 20 ff.; cf. R. Syme, *HAC 1984* (forthcoming) = *RP* IV (forthcoming).

6 Philostratus, *VS* 2.1.13.

7 *HA Marc.* 25.2; *Av. Cass.* 7.7; *AE* 1920. 45 (Sabinianus); Dio 71.22.2.

8 *HA Comm.* 1.10; 2.1; 12.1–3; *BMC* IV, *MA* & *C*, nos. 1517 ff.; 1495 ff.; cf. 625. Pollio: named as prefect only in the forged letter tacked onto Justin's *Apology* (convenient text in Haines' ed. of Fronto, II 300 ff.), but his *cursus* inscription, *ILS* 1112, could well have recorded the post.

9 Dio 71.23.3.

10 Dio 71.24.1–4; 71.25–71.27.1. Peace-party: cf. *HA Marc.* 22.8, J. Morris, *JWI* 15 (1952) 37.

11 *HA Av. Cass.* 7.1–3; cf. 1.1–7; 14.2–8.

12 *HA Comm.* 1.11; 2.2; 12.2–3.

13 Dio 71.27.1a; 71.27.2–28.1; *HA Av. Cass.* 8.1. Verus: Dio 71.29.2.

14 Dio 71.27. 2; cf. R. Rémondon, *CE* 26 (1951) 364 ff. Titles: *BMC* IV, *MA* & *C*, nos. 1513; 1523. Peace: Dio 71.17.

15 Dio 71.16.

16 Adventus, Caerellius: A.R. Birley, *The* Fasti *of Roman Britain* (1981) 131 ff. Victorinus: G. Alföldy, *Fasti Hispanienses* (1969) 38 ff. Julianus: *CP* no. 180. Later troubles: *CP* no. 221 + add.; *HA Marc.* 22.11; cf. p. 000, below.

17 *HA Did.* 1.7–8; *Marc.* 22.10. On Didius: *PIR²* D 77. Pertinax: *HA Pert.* 1.1–2.10; Dio 71.22.1 (Euripides, *Supp.* 119); cf. G. Alföldy, *Situla* 14–15 (1974) 199 ff.

18 *AE* 1956. 124; *CP* no. 181 *bis* + add.; G. Alföldy, *Situla*, loc. cit.

19 Date and route: M.L. Astarita, *Avidio Cassio* (1983) 155 ff. Elder Quintilii: Philostratus, *VS* 2.9.2. Their sons: Dio 71.33.1, cf. G. Alföldy, *Konsulat und Senatorenstand* (1977) 237 f. Arrius: ibid. 221 f. Rufus: *PIR²* B 69; *CP* no. 161. Pompeianus: this is the hypothesis of N. Gostar, *Hommages Renard* II (1969) 290 ff.

20 *HA Marc.* 26.4–9; Dio 71.29.1; 31.1–2; *Med.* 9.3.1; cf. 9.42 (also p. 286, below, and App. 1). Route: M.L. Astarita, *Avidio Cassio* (1983) 156 ff. Faustinopolis: ibid. 114. Coins: *BMC* IV, *MA* & *C*, nos. 698 ff.; 1550 ff. Philostratus, *VS* 2.1.12, quoted below, shows that Faustina died in winter 175, not in 176: cf. the persuasive arguments of Astarita, op. cit. 137 ff.; 151 ff.

21 *HA Marc.* 25.4–7; 26.10–13; Dio 71.30.1–31.2; cf. Astarita, op. cit. 23 ff.; 105 ff. Oath: cf. the speculations by A.R. Birley, *CR* 12 (1962) 197 ff.

22 Philostratus, *VS* 2.1.12. The vow was perhaps made when Marcus heard the news of the Costobocan ravaging of Eleusis.

23 Hermogenes: Philostratus, *VS* 2.7.1. Antioch, Cyrrhus: *HA Marc.* 25.11–12. Exclamation: Ammianus 22.5.5; cf. Astarita, op. cit. 118 f.

24 For documentation and full discussion cf. Astarita, op. cit. 119 ff.

25 Dio 71.28.2–4; *HA Marc.* 25.4 ff.; 26.1–3, 10 ff.

26 Daughter: *HA Marc.* 26.3. Route: *HA Marc.* 26.1 ('postea tamen Antiochiam vidit') seems best explained by a visit to Syria in 176, in spite of Astarita, op. cit. 159 ff. (who does not discuss this passage); cf. Schwendemann 112. Aristides at Smyrna: Philostratus, *VS* 2.9.2. Cf. also App. 4 of Melito.

27 *HA Marc.* 27.1. Memmius: *SIG* I³ 872; cf. Astarita, op. cit. 142 f.

28 Cf. T.D. Barnes, *JTS* 26 (1975) 111 ff; and App. 4.

29 J.H. Oliver, *Hesperia*, Supp. 13 (1970) 3 ff.; cf. C.P. Jones, *ZPE* 8 (1971) 161 ff.; W. Williams, *ZPE* 17 (1975) 37 ff.

30 Dio 71.31.3; Philostratus, *VS* 2.2.1. Severus: *PIR²* C 1024. Adrianus: *PIR²* H 4. Galen, *On Prognosis* 5. 16 ff. = Nutton 98.

31 *HA Marc.* 27.2–3.

32 Dio 71.32.1; *HA Marc.* 27.5; 29.10; *Comm.* 2.3–5; 12.5. Fadilla: App. 2.

33 *HA Marc.* 29.10. Children, and Lucilla's children: App. 2.

34 Galen, *On Prognosis* 11.1–8 = Nutton 126 ff.

35 *HA Marc.* 16.2; *Comm.* 2.4; *ILS* 374. Coins: *BMC* IV, *MA* & *C*, nos. 736 ff.; 740 ff., etc. Rufus: *ILS* 1326. Laelianus: *ILS* 1094 + 1100. Verus: the missing part of his *cursus* inscription, in the gap between *ILS* 8974 and 1057, may be assumed to have supplied details. Priscus: *CIL* VI 31753, cf. Zwikker 182. Pertinax: *HA Pert.* 2.10, a compressed passage; G. Alföldy, *Situla* 14–15 (1974) 208 ff. argues that he was assigned to Lower Moesia in 176. Maximianus: *AE* 1956. 124; he was made procurator of Lower Moesia just when Pertinax became governor there, cf. Alföldy, loc. cit.

36 *HA Comm.* 27.5; cf. F. Grosso, *La lotta politica al tempo di Commodo* (1964) 124 f.

37 *HA Comm.* 1.6. Sanctus: *AE* 1961. 280; cf. *CP* no. 178 *bis* (with a slightly different dating).

38 *HA Comm.* 1.7–9; *Marc.* 2.6; Dio 72.1.1.

39 Dio 71.33.1; IMP. IX: *BMC* IV, *MA* & *C*, nos. 1632 ff. Maximianus: *AE* 1956. 124. Didius: *HA Did.* 1.9. Sabinianus: *AE* 1920. 45. Cf. G. Alföldy, *Konsulat und Senatorenstand* (1977) 190; 226.

40 *Digest* 1.18.14. Scapula: *PIR²* J 556; G. Alföldy, *Konsulat* 195 f.: he was probably proconsul of Africa at the time, either for 178–9 or 179–80.

41 *Digest* 48.5.53(32).*pr.*; 48.5.39(38).8.

42 *Digest* 11.4.1.2–4; 29.5.2.

43 *CJ* 4.57.2; cf. *Digest* 44.11.1; 26.4.3.2; 40.1.20.*pr.* G. Alföldy, *Fasti Hispanienses* (1969) 38 ff. argues that Victorinus was governor of Syria 178–9 and then prefect of the city from 179.

44 Cf. esp. J.H. Oliver and R.E.A. Palmer, *Hesperia* 24 (1955) 320 ff. for the best text, with commentary. *trinqui*: A. Piganiol, *REA* 20 (1922) 283.

45 Cf. however T.D. Barnes, *JTS* 19 (1968) 518 and in *Les martyrs de Lyon* (1978) 137 ff., expressing serious doubt whether Eusebius really knew the exact date, or indeed whether the emperor in whose reign the persecution at Lyon took place was necessarily Marcus at all; cf. App. 4.

46 Thus Oliver and Palmer, *Hesp.* 24 (1955) 320 ff., followed e.g. by W.H.C. Frend, *Martyrdom and Persecution in the Early Church* (1965) 5 ff. Others, notably T.D. Barnes, *JTS* 19 (1968) 518 f., reject any connection between *SC* and persecution. Cf. App. 4.

47 Eusebius, *HE* 5. praef. and 1.1–63. Cf. further App. 4.

48 App. 4.

49 Cf. now G. Alföldy, *Chiron* 15 (1985) 91 ff., esp. 103 ff. Italica, Singilia Barba: *ILS* 1354, 1354a. Vallius: *CP* no. 221 + *add.*

50 *AE* 1971. 534; cf. esp. W. Williams, *ZPE* 17 (1975) 50 ff.

51 *Digest* 38.17; *Inst.* 3.4; *CJ* 6.57; 9.8.6.*pr.*, cf. S. Jameson, *AS* 16 (1966) 126.

52 Dio 71.32.2.

53 Dio 71.32.3; Philostratus, *VS* 2.9.2.

54 *BMC* IV, pp. cxxx; cxliii; Dio 71.33.1.

55 Dio 71.33.1; *HA Marc.* 27.8. Praesens; Crispina: *PIR²* B 165, 170. Martius: G. Alföldy, *Konsulat und Senatorenstand* (1977) 240. Julius Verus: *PIR²* J 618. Pollux: Philostratus, *VS* 2.12.2; *PIR²* J 474.

56 *HA Marc.* 29.4; Victor, *De Caes.* 16.9–10 (the statement about Commodus may be a confused version of his elevation in 177; he had of course been Caesar since 166).

57 Dio 71.33.2–3.

58 *HA Comm.* 12.6 gives the date. Pompeianus: *PIR²* C 973. Pollio: *ILS* 1112.
Paternus and Perennis are named eighth and ninth among the signatories of the
tabula Banasitana (*AE* 1971. 534). Cf also *CP* no. 172; *RE* 6 A.1 (1936) 952 ff.
Victorinus: G. Alföldy, *Fasti Hispanienses* (1969) 42 ff.

59 *AE* 1956. 124; Dio 71.34.4.

60 *AE* 1962. 183; cf. F. Millar, *The Emperor in the Roman World* (1977) 288.

61 Dio 71.33.3–4; *BMC* IV, *MA* & *C*, nos. 1695 ff.

62 Dio 71.18–19.

63 Dio 71.20–1; cf. App. 3.

64 *CIL* III 13439; *AE* 1956. 124. Verus: *PIR²* J 618.

65 *HA Marc.* 27.11–12; Dio 71.33.4–71.34; *Epit. de Caes.* 17.2 Victor, *De Caes.*
16.4 and the *Epit. de Caes.* 16.12 give Vindobona, Tertullian, Apol. 25 gives
Sirmium. H. Bannert, *Festschrift Hanslik* (1977) 9 ff. argues convincingly in
favour of Bononia, the Danube port of Sirmium. I omit Herodian's death-
scene, which is riddled with inaccuracies (I.3–4): cf. G. Alföldy, *Latomus* 32
(1973) 345 ff.

10 **Marcus to Himself** *(pages 211–223)*

1 *HA Marc.* 27.7 (Plato, *Rep.* 473 D); cf. Victor, *De Caes.* 16.9–10; *Med.* 9.18;
9.27; 10.36; cf. also 11.13.

2 Haines, in the introduction to his translation of the *Med.*, xiv., suggests
Victorinus and Pompeianus, Cornificia (citing Dio 77.16.6a) and Chryseros
(*PIR²* C 724); doubted by Farquharson I xiii, who suggests instead the Greek
secretary Alexander. Clement: Farquharson II 548 f. Dio: cf. 71.24.2 and *Med.*
5.33. P.A. Brunt, *JRS* 64 (1974) 1 ff. warns against the notion of 'publication' as
opposed to gradual transmission.

3 Herodian 1.2.3; Themistius, *Or.* 6. 81 C; *HA Av. Cass.* 3.6–7. Arethas: *Cod.
Mosc.* 315 f. 115 r., ed. Sonny, *Philologus* 54 182, quoted from Farquharson I
xvii.

4 Cf. App. 1 for some further comments on the *Meditations*. Date of Book 1: thus
H. Schenkl, *WS* 34 (1912) 86, followed by Haines and many others. Tributes to
Pius: 1.16 and 6.30.2–4. Farquharson I lxxiii; 346, and J. Dalfen, *Form-
geschichtliche Untersuchungen zu den Selbstbetrachtungen Marc Aurels* (1966) 4,
doubt Schenkl's argument. Tributes: 1.7 (Rusticus); 1.8 (Apollonius); 1.9
(Sextus); 1.15 (Maximus); cf. 1.17.5, singling out Apollonius, Rusticus,
Maximus (in that order).

5 'At Carnuntum': cf. *AE* 1982. 778, Carnuntum (AD 172: Marcus and
Commodus 'cons(sistentium) cas[tris]; Eutropius 8.13; Orosius 7.15.6). 'Some
passages': cf. Farquharson I lviii ff. J. Dalfen, op. cit., esp. 204 ff., regards the
Med. as Marcus' attempt to recollect the teachings of all those he had admired
(in particular those named in Book 1. Farquharson I lxvii concludes: 'that the
larger bulk has a decided literary aim appears to be indisputable'. Brunt, *JRS* 64
(1974) 1 ff. prefers the view that Marcus wrote for himself alone. 'What are you
thinking . . .': *Med.* 3.4.2; cf. 11.15.

6 3.10; 4.3.3; 4.19; 7.21; 4.32–3 (cf. 8.31); 7.19; 7.47–9.

7 'no echo': P. Oliva, *Pannonia and the Onset of Crisis* (1962) 22. 'put away . .':
2.2–3. 'Deeds': 3.14.

8 10.10. Cf. P.G. Hamberg, *Studies in Roman Imperial Art* (1945).

9 2.2 (cf. 8.37); 3.8; 3.13; 4.39; 8.34.

10 3.3; 4.21; Lucian, *Alexander* 48; *HA Marc.* 13.5.

11 Dio 71.6.4; *Med.* 7.64; 7.33; 6.33.

12 Galen, *De Antidotis* 14. 3 f. K.; *Med.* 5.1; 8.12; 6.2; 6.31. The inferences drawn by T.W. Africa, *JHI* 22 (1961) 97 ff. seem extreme; cf. Nutton 218.

13 2.5; 3.5; 7.7; 7.45 (cf. Plato, *Apol.* 28 E).

14 2.7; 11.9; 4.51; 2.17.

15 4.43; 5.10.2; 5.23; 9.29. P.A. Brunt, *JRS* 64 (1974) 19 pours scorn on the notion that his choice of imagery 'has anything to do with Marcus' experience of warfare or impressions of the Danube!' But cf. Farquharson II 810 on 9.29: 'There is, I think, no parallel to the expression here, which treats the principle of reality as itself a torrent.'

16 9.2; 9.9.2; 9.42.4; 9.38; Dio 71.27.1. Faustina: this is suggested by Brunt, *JRS* 64 (1974) 13 n. 80. Loss: 10.35.1. Commodus (?): 9.11; 10.4; 11.18.9.

17 10.25; cf. *Digest* 11.4.1.2–4; *Med.* 10.28.

18 2.4; 2.5 (cf. 7.69); 2.3; 4.34.

19 4.26 (cf. 6.30.1); 4.47; 7.56; 3.8 (cf. 11.1.1); 11.3; 9.3.1 (cf. 7.69: 'live each day as if the last').

20 4.5 (cf. 2.12); 4.44; 3.3; 4.48; 6.24; 8.5; 7.35; 7.44–46 (Plato); 7.50–1 (Euripides); 8.31; 8.25; 8.37.

21 6.10; 7.32 (cf. 4.14; 4.21; 5.13; 6.4; 6.10; 7.19; 7.25; 7.32; 8.5; 8.18); 12.5; 12.14 (more fully in 2.11); 12.36.

22 6.28; 5.4; 5.31; 2.1; 5.10; 6.48; *HA Marc.* 22.4; *Med.* 6.21; 10.12 (cf. 8.16).

23 4.3; 8.9; 8.1; 11.7; 6.12.

24 4.4; 2.16; 3.11; 4.29; 5.22; 6.54; 4.23.

25 8.1; 10.1; 10.16.

26 4.23; 3.4.4; 4.3.4; 10.38; 8.51; 8.48; 5.33 (cf. Epictetus, frag. 10 and *Discourses* 4.8.20). Cf. Brunt, *JRS* 64 (1974) 11 ff.; 19 f., discussing 11.18 and related passages that deal with anger; and ibid. 8 ff., on truth. He cites (p. 9) Fronto, *Ad MC* 3.13 (vdH 45) = Haines I 16 (but *Ad Verum Imp.* 2.2.1 (vdH 124) = Haines II 118 to which he also refers reads '*verumque amorem*' not '*verique amorem*').

27 6.38; 4.3.2 and 10.55 (world-city); 5.7; 9.40. On his attitude to religion, cf. the instructive comments of Brunt, *JRS* 64 (1974) 14 ff.

28 3.12; 3.2; 4.20; 5.6; 5.33; 1.7; 2.3.

29 6.36; 6.44; 9.29; 1.14; Ammianus 31.5.14; Dio 71.36.3.

11 Epilogue *(pages 224–225)*

1 Dio on Commodus: 72.15.1. 'royalest': *ILS* 398.

2 Severus: cf. A.R. Birley, *Septimius Severus* (1971). 'dowry': *HA Marc.* 19. 8–9.

3 *HA Marc.* 19; 23.7; 26.5; 29.1–3; *Comm.* 1.3–9; 8.1; *Med.* 6.13; 1.17.8.

4 Severus on Marcus and Commodus: Dio 76.14.7. On two controversial aspects of Marcus' principate, his frontier policy and the treatment of and attitude to Christians, cf. App. 3 and 4.

Select Bibliography

Abbreviations for appendices, notes and bibliography:
Titles of periodicals are mostly abbreviated as in *L'Année Philologique*. The works of ancient writers are given in an easily recognisable form. Note that Fronto is cited by the pagination of van den Hout (vdH) and of Haines as well as by the original book divisions. The *Historia Augusta* is abbreviated *HA* (not *SHA*), followed by the particular *vita*. Cassius Dio is cited by the book numbering of Boissevain. A few modern works are cited by author's name alone; or with an abbreviated title.

Other special abbreviations:

AE   *L'Année épigraphique* (Paris, 1888 ff.)

ANRW   H. Temporini & W. Haase, eds., *Aufstieg und Niedergang der römischen Welt* (Berlin & New York, 1972 ff.)

BMC IV   H. Mattingly, *Coins of the Roman Empire in the British Museum* IV. Antoninus Pius to Commodus (London, 1940): the individual sections are abbreviated: *AP* (Antoninus Pius); *MA & LV* (Marcus Aurelius & Lucius Verus); *MA* (Marcus alone); *MA & C* (Marcus & Commodus)

CIL   *Corpus Inscriptionum Latinarum* (Berlin 1863 ff.)

CP; Supp.   H.G. Pflaum, *Les carrières procuratoriennes équestres sous le Haut-Empire romain* I–III (Paris, 1960–1); *Supplément* (Paris, 1982)

HAC   *Historia-Augusta-Colloquium Bonn* (the year of the Colloquium is given as well as the year of publication; first Colloquium 1963, published 1964)

IGR   *Inscriptiones Graecae ad Res Romanas pertinentes*

ILS   H. Dessau, *Inscriptiones Latinae Selectae* (Berlin, 1892–1916)

Inscr. It. XIII.1 A. Degrassi, *Inscriptiones Italiae XIII* 1 (Rome, 1947)

ODCC²   F.L. Cross & E.A. Livingstone, *The Oxford Dictionary of the Christian Church* (2nd ed., Oxford, 1974; revised ed., 1983)

PIR²   E. Groag, A. Stein, L. Petersen, eds., *Prosopographia Imperii Romani* (Berlin & Leipzig, 1933 ff.)

POxy   B.P. Grenfel et al., eds., *The Oxyrhyncus Papyri* (London, 1989 ff.)

RE   Paulys *Real-Encyclopädie der classischen Altertumswissenschaft*, ed. G. Wissowa et al. (Stuttgart, 1893–1978)

SB   *Sammelbuch griechischer Urkunden aus Ägypten* (Berlin & Leipzig, 1926 ff.)

Abbreviations used in captions:

HCC II   A.S. Robertson, *Roman Imperial Coins in the Hunter Coin*

Cabinet, University of Glasgow. II. Trajan to Commodus (Oxford 1971)

Petersen   E. Petersen, A. v. Domaszewski, G. Calderini, *Die Marcus-Säule auf Piazza Colonna in Rom* (Munich 1896)

RIC II, III, IV.1   H. Mattingly & E.A. Sydenham, eds., *The Roman Imperial Coinage* (London 1926, 1930, 1936)

Africa, T.W. 'The opium addiction of Marcus Aurelius', *JHI* 22 (1961) 97 (repr. in German in R. Klein, 133)

Alföldy, G. *Fasti Hispanienses. Senatorische Reichesbeamte und Offiziere in den spanischen Provinzen des römischen Reiches von Augustus bis Diokletian* (Wiesbaden, 1969)

'Der Friedenschluss des Kaisers Commodus mit den Germanen', *Historia* 20 (1971) 84 (repr. in R. Klein, 389, with addenda)

'Herodian über den Tod Mark Aurels', *Latomus* 32 (1973) 345

'P. Helvius Pertinax und M. Valerius Maximianus', *Situla* (Ljubljana) 14/15 (1974) 199

Konsulat und Senatorenstand unter den Antoninen. Prosopographische Untersuchungen zur senatorischen Führungsschicht (Bonn, 1977)

'Bellum Mauricum', *Chiron* 15 (1985) 91

—, and H. Halfmann 'Iunius Maximus und die Victoria Parthica', *ZPE* 35 (1979) 195

Ameling, W. *Herodes Atticus. I. Biographie. II. Inschriftenkatalog* (Subsidia Epigraphica 11, Hildesheim, 1983)

Astarita, M.L. *Avidio Cassio* (Rome, 1983)

Bannert, H. 'Der Tod des Kaisers Marcus', in *Latinität und alte Kirche. Festschrift R. Hanslik* (Wiener Studien, Beih. 8, Vienna, 1977) 9 (repr. in R. Klein, 459, with addenda)

Barnes, T.D. 'Hadrian and Lucius Verus', *JRS* 57 (1967) 65

'A note on Polycarp', *JTS* 18 (1967) 433

'Legislation against the Christians', *JRS* 58 (1968) 32

'Pre-Decian *Acta Martyrum*', *JTS* 19 (1968) 509

'The chronology of Montanism', *JTS* 21 (1970) 403

'The embassy of Athenagoras', *JTS* 26 (1975) 111

The Sources of the Historia Augusta (Coll. Latomus 155, Brussels, 1978)

'Eusebius and the date of the martyrdoms', in: *Les martyrs de Lyon* (1978) 137

Constantine and Eusebius (Cambridge, Mass. & London, 1981)

Barta, G. 'Lucius Verus and the Marcomannic wars', *ACD* 7 (1971) 67

Béranger, J. 'L'hérédité du Principat', *REL* 17 (1939) 171

Birley, A.R. 'Two names in the *Historia Augusta*', *Historia* 15 (1966) 249

'The invasion of Italy in the reign of Marcus Aurelius', in *Provincialia. Festschrift R. Laur-Belart* (Basel, 1968) 214

'Some teachers of Marcus Aurelius', *HAC 1966/67* (1968) 39

Septimius Severus the African Emperor (London, 1971)

'Roman frontier policy under Marcus Aurelius', *Roman Frontier Studies 1967* (Tel Aviv, 1971) 7

'Roman frontiers and Roman frontier policy: some reflections on Roman imperialism', *Trans. Architectural & Archaeological Soc. of Durham & Northumberland* 3 (1974) 13

'Die Aussen- und Grenzpolitik unter der Regierung Marc Aurels', R. Klein, ed., *Marc Aurel* (1979) 473

The Fasti *of Roman Britain* (Oxford, 1981)

Birley, E. 'A note on Cornelius Repentinus', *HAC 1982/83* (1985) 69

Böhme, H.W. 'Archäologische Zeugnisse zur Geschichte der Markomannenkriege (166–180 n. Chr.)', *JRGZ Mainz* 22 (1975) 153

Bol, R. *Das Statuenprogramm des Herodes-Atticus-Nymphäums* (Olympische Forschungen 15, Berlin, 1984)

Bowersock, G.W. *Greek Sophists in the Roman Empire* (Oxford, 1969)

Bowman, A.K. 'A letter of Avidius Cassius?', *JRS* 60 (1970) 20

Brunt, P.A. 'Marcus Aurelius in his *Meditations*', *JRS* 64 (1974) 1

'Marcus Aurelius and the Christians', in C. Deroux, ed., *Studies in Latin Literature and Roman History* I (Collection Latomus 154, Brussels, 1979) 483

Caprino, C., et al. *La colonna di Marco Aurelio* (Rome, 1955)

Carcopino, J. 'L'hérèdité dynastique chez les Antonins', *REA* 51 (1949) 262

'Encore la succession d'Hadrien', *REA* 67 (1965) 67

Chadwick, H. *Origenes* Contra Celsum (Cambridge, 1953)

Champlin, E. 'The chronology of Fronto', *JRS* 64 (1974) 136

'Hadrian's heir', *ZPE* 21 (1976) 78

Fronto and Antonine Rome (Cambridge, Mass. & London, 1980)

'The glass ball game', *ZPE* 60 (1985) 159

Dailly, R. and M.H. van Effenterre 'Le cas Marc-Aurèle: essai de psychosomatique historique', *REA* 56 (1954) 347

Dalfen, J. *Formgeschichtliche Untersuchungen zu den Selbstbetrachtungen Marc Aurels* (Diss. Munich, 1967)

Dobiáš, J. 'Rom und die Völker jenseits der mittleren Donau', in *Corolla Memoriae E. Swoboda Dedicata* (Graz & Cologne, 1966) 115

Eck, W. *Die staatliche Organisation Italiens in der hohen Kaiserzeit* (Munich, 1979)

Die Statthalter der germanischen Provinzen vom 1.–3. Jahrhundert (Epigraphische Studien 14, Cologne & Bonn, 1985)

Farquharson, A.S.L. *The* Meditations *of Marcus Antoninus*, I–II (Oxford, 1944)

Fittschen, K. *Die Bildnistypen der Faustina minor und die Fecunditas Augustae* (Abhandlungen Akad. Göttingen, ph.-hist. Kl., 3rd ser., 126, 1982)

Fitz, J. 'Der markomannische-quadische Angriff gegen Aquileia und Opitergium', *Historia* 15 (1966) 81

'Claudius Pompeianus, *gener Marci*', *Alba Regia* 19 (1981) 289

'Ti. Claudius Pompeianus und die geplante Provinz Sarmatia', *Lebendige Altertumswissenschaft. Festgabe H. Vetters* (Vienna, 1985) 123

Gilliam, J.F. 'The plague under Marcus Aurelius', *AJP* 82 (1961) 225 (repr. in German in R. Klein, 144)

Gnecchi, F. *I Medaglioni Romani descritti e illustrati* I–III (Milan, 1912)

Grenade, P. 'Le réglement successoral d'Hadrien', *REA* 52 (1950) 258

Grosso, F. *La lotta politica al tempo di Commodo* (Mem. Accademia Scienze Torino, cl. sci. mor. stor. fil., ser. 4, 7, Turin, 1964)

Guey, J. 'La date de la "pluie miraculeuse" (172 après J–C) et la Colonne Aurélienne', *MEFR* 60 (1948) 105; 61 (1949) 93
'Encore la "pluie miraculeuse": mage et dieu', *RPh* 22 (1948) 16

Haines, C.R. 'The composition of the *Thoughts* of Marcus Aurelius', *Journ. Philol.* 33 (1914) 278
The Communings with Himself of Marcus Aurelius Antoninus Emperor of Rome (Loeb ed., London & New York, 1916)
The Correspondence of Marcus Cornelius Fronto I–II (Loeb ed., London & New York, 1919–20)

Halfmann, H. *Die Senatoren aus dem östlichen Teil des Imperium Romanum bis zum Ende des 2. Jh. n. Chr.* (Hypomnemata 58, Göttingen, 1979)

Hamberg, P.G. *Studies in Roman Imperial Art, with special reference to the State Reliefs of the Second Century* (Copenhagen & Uppsala, 1945)

Hampl, F. 'Kaiser Marc Aurel und die Völker jenseits der Donaugrenze. Eine quellenkritische Studie', in *Festschrift R. Heuberger* (Innsbruck, 1960) 33

Hout, M.P.J. van den *M. Cornelii Frontonis Epistulae*, I: *Prolegomena, text, index* (Leyden, 1954)

Hüttl, W. *Antoninus Pius*. I. *Historisch-politische Darstellung* (Prague, 1936); II. *Römische Reichsbeamte und Offiziere unter Antoninus Pius. Antoninus Pius in den Inschriften seiner Zeit* (Prague, 1933)

Jobst, W. *11. Juni 172 n. Chr. Der Tag des Blitz- und Regenwunders im Quadenlande* (Sb. Akademie Wien 335, Vienna, 1978)

Jones, C.P. 'A new letter of Marcus Aurelius to the Athenians', *ZPE* 8 (1971) 161
'Aelius Aristides, EIS BASILEA', *JRS* 62 (1972) 134
'The EIS BASILEA again', *CQ* 31 (1981) 224

Kerler, G. *Die Aussenpolitik in der Historia Augusta* (Habelts Dissertationsdrucke, Reihe Alte Geschichte 10, Bonn, 1970)

Klein, R., ed. *Marc Aurel* (Wege der Forschung 50, Darmstadt, 1979)

Lambrechts, P. 'L'Empereur Lucius Verus: essai de réhabilitation', *AC* 3 (1934) 173 (repr. in German in R. Klein, 25)

Langmann, G. *Die Markomannenkriege 166/167 bis 180* (Militärhistorische Schriftenreihe 43, Vienna, 1981)

Littmann, R.J. and M.L. 'Galen and the Antonine plague', *AJP* 94 (1973) 243

Magie, D. *Roman Rule in Asia Minor* I–II (Princeton, 1950)

Mann, J.C. 'The raising of new legions under the principate', *Hermes* 91 (1963) 483

Martyrs de Lyon, Les (Colloques Internationaux du CNRS, 575, Lyon 20–23 septembre 1977, Paris, 1978)

Millar, F. *A Study of Cassius Dio* (Oxford, 1964)
The Emperor in the Roman World 31 BC–AD 337 (London, 1977)

Mócsy, A. 'Das Gerücht von neuen Donauprovinzen unter Marcus Aurelius',
 ACD 7 (1971) 63
 Pannonia and Upper Moesia (London, 1974)
Morris, J. 'The dating of the Column of Marcus Aurelius', *JWI* 15 (1952) 33 (repr.
 in German in R. Klein, 67)
Musurillo, H. *The Acts of the Christian Martyrs* (Oxford, 1972)

Nesselhauf, H. 'Hadrians Reskript an Minicius Fundanus', *Hermes* 104 (1976) 348
Noyen, P. 'Divus Marcus princeps prudentissimus et iuris religiosissimus', *RIDA* 1
 (1954) 349
 'Marcus Aurelius the greatest practician of Stoicism', *AC* 24 (1955) 372 (repr. in
 German in R. Klein, 105)
Nutton, V. *Galen on Prognosis. Edition, Translation, and Commentary* (Corpus
 Medicorum Graecorum 5.8.1, Berlin, 1979)

Oliva, P. *Pannonia and the Onset of Crisis in the Roman Empire* (Prague, 1962)
Oliver, J.H. 'The Ruling Power. A study of the Roman empire in the second
 century after Christ through the *Roman Oration* of Aelius Aristides' *Trans.
 Amer. Philosoph. Ass.* 43 (1953) 869
 Marcus Aurelius: Aspects of Civic and Cultural Policy (Hesperia, supp. 13,
 Princeton, 1970)
—, and R.E.A. Palmer 'Minutes of an Act of the Roman Senate', *Hesperia* 24
 (1955) 320

Petzl, G. 'T. Statilius Maximus Prokonsul von Asia', *Chiron* 13 (1983) 33
Pflaum, H.G. *Les procurateurs équestres sous le Haut-Empire romain* (Paris, 1950)
 Les carrières procuratoriennes équestres sous le Haut-Empire romain I–III (Paris,
 1960–1) (abbr. *CP*)
 'Les gendres de Marc-Aurèle', *JS* 1961, 28
 'Le réglement successoral d'Hadrien', *HAC 1963* (1964) 95
 Les sodales Antoniniani de l'époque de Marc-Aurèle (Mémoires prés. par. divers
 savants à l'Acad. des Inscr., 15, Paris, 1966)
 'La valeur de la source inspiratrice de la Vita Hadriani et de la Vita Marci
 Antonini à la lumière des personnalités contemporaines nommément citées',
 HAC 1968/9 (1970) 173

Rist, J.M. *Stoic Philosophy* (Cambridge, 1969)
 'Are you a Stoic? The case of Marcus Aurelius', in B.F. Meyer & E.P. Sanders,
 eds., *Jewish and Christian Self-Definition*, III: *Self-Definition in the Graeco-
 Roman World* (London, 1982) 23
Rossi, L. 'Sull' iconografia e storiografia celebrativa di Marco Aurelio dall'
 epigrafe di M. Valerio Massimiano', *Quaderni ticinesi di numismatica e antichità
 class.* 6 (1977) 223

Šašel, J. 'Über Umfang und Dauer der Militärzone *Praetentura Italiae et Alpium* zur
 Zeit Marc Aurels', *MH* 31 (1974) 225
Schenkl, H. 'Zum ersten Buche der Selbstbetrachtungen des Kaisers Marcus
 Antoninus', *WS* 34 (1912) 82

Schmid, W. 'Ein Inversionsphänomen und seine Bedeutung im Text der Apologie des Justin', in: *Forma Futuri. Studi in onore di Card. M. Pellegrino* (Turin, 1975) 253

Schumacher, L. *Prosopographische Untersuchungen zur Besetzung der vier hohen römischen Priesterkollegien im Zeitalter der Antoninen und Severer (96–235 n. Chr.)* (Diss. Mainz, 1973)

Schwendemann, J. *Der historische Wert der Vita Marci bei den Scriptores Historiae Augustae* (Heidelberg, 1923)

Sordi, M. 'I "nuovi decreti" di Marco Aurelio contro i Cristiani', *Studi Romani* 9 (1961) 365 (repr. in German in R. Klein, 176)

Stanton, G.R. 'Marcus Aurelius, emperor and philosopher', *Historia* 18 (1969) 570 (repr. in German in R. Klein, 359, with addenda)
'Marcus Aurelius, Lucius Verus, and Commodus: 1962–1972', *ANRW* 2.2 (1975) 478

Swoboda, E. *Carnuntum. Seine Geschichte und seine Denkmäler* (4th ed., Graz & Cologne, 1964))

Syme, R. 'Antonine relatives: Ceionii and Vettuleni', *Ath.* 35 (1957) 306 = *RP* 325
Tacitus I–II (Oxford, 1958)
'Pliny's less successful friends', *Historia* 9 (1960) 362 = *RP* 477
'Hadrian the intellectual', in *Les Empereurs romains d'Espagne* (Colloques du CNRS, Paris, 1965) 243
'The Ummidii', *Historia* 17 (1968) 72 = *RP* 659
Roman Papers I–II (Oxford, 1979) (abbrev. *RP*)
'Ummidius Quadratus, *capax imperii*', *HSCP* 83 (1979) 287 = *RP* 1158
'The proconsuls of Asia under Antoninus Pius', *ZPE* 51 (1983) 271 = *RP* IV (forthcoming)
Roman Papers III (Oxford, 1984) (abbrev. *RP*)
'P. Calvisius Ruso, one person or two?', *ZPE* 56 (1984) 173 = *RP* IV (forthcoming)
'The *Testamentum Dasumii*: some novelties', *Chiron* 15 (1985) 41 = *RP* IV (forthcoming)
'Avidius Cassius. His rank, age and quality', *HAC 1984* (forthcoming) = *RP* IV (forthcoming)
Roman Papers IV–V (Oxford, forthcoming) (abbrev. *RP* IV)

Thomas, J.D. 'An imperial *constitutio* on papyrus', *BICS* 19 (1982) 103

Vidman, L. *Fasti Ostienses* (2nd ed., Prague, 1982)

Williams, W. 'Formal and historical aspects of two new documents of Marcus Aurelius', *ZPE* 17 (1975) 37
'Individuality in the imperial constitutions. Hadrian and the Antonines', *JRS* 66 (1976) 67

Witke, E.C. 'Marcus Aurelius and mandragora', *CP* 60 (1965) 23

Zwikker, W. *Studien zur Markussäule.* I (Allard Pierson Stichting, Arch.-hist. Bydragen 8, Amsterdam, 1941)

Addenda to Bibliography

Alföldy, G. 'Die Führungselite des Imperium Romanum unter Marcus Aurelius', in: W. Eck, ed., *Prosopographie und Sozial-geschichte der Kaiserzeit* (Cologne 1993)

Ameling, W. 'Der Archon Dionysios. Zur Datierung einiger attischer Portraits der mittleren Kaiserzeit', *Boreas* 11 (1988) 62–70

'Die Kinder des Marc Aurel und die Bildnistypen der Faustina Minor', *ZPE* 90 (1992) 147–66

Daniels, C.M. 'The Antonine abandonment of Scotland', in: V.A. Maxfield and M.J. Dobson, eds., *Roman Frontier Studies 1989* (Exeter 1991) 48–51

Dietz, K. 'Zur Verwaltungsgeschichte Obergermaniens und Rätiens unter Mark Aurel', *Chiron* 19 (1989) 407–47

Di Vita-Evrard, G. 'De la date du procès d'Hérode Atticus à l'ère d'Hadrien et à l'association au pouvoir de L. Septimius Géta', in: *Praktika tou 8. synedriou ellenikes kai latinikes epigraphikes* II (Athens 1987)

'Des Calvisii Rusones à Licinius Sura', *MEFRA* 99 (1987) 281–338

Görgemanns, H. 'Der Bekehrungsbrief Marc Aurels', *RhM* 134 (1991) 96–109

Holford-Strevens, L.A. *Aulus Gellius* (London 1988)

Hout, M.P.J. van den *M. Cornelius Fronto. Epistulae* (Leipzig 1988)

Kaiser-Raiss, M.R. *Die Stadtrömische Münzprägung während der Alleinherrschaft des Commodus* (Frankfurt 1980)

Piso, I. 'Die Inschriften vom Pfaffenberg und der Bereich der canabae legionis', *Tyche* 6 (1991) 131–69

Raepsaet-Charlier, M.T. *Prosopographie des femmes de l'ordre sénatorial* (Louvain 1987)

Rutherford, R.B. *The Meditations of Marcus Aurelius: a Study* (Oxford 1989)

A Selection from the Letters of Marcus and Fronto (Oxford 1989)

Scheidel, W. 'Der Germaneneinfall in Oberitalien und die Emissionsabfolge der kaiserlichen Reichsprägung, *Chiron* 20 (1990) 1–18

'Probleme der Datierung des Costoboceneinfalls in Balkanraum unter Marcus Aurelius', *Historia* 39 (1990) 493–8

Stahl, M. 'Zwischen Abgrenzung und Integration: Die Verträge der Kaiser Mark Aurel und Commodus mit den Völkern jenseits der Donau', *Chiron* 19 (1989) 289–317

Syme, R. *Roman Papers* IV–V (Oxford 1988); VI–VII (Oxford 1991)

Wachtel, K. 'L. Lamia Silvanus, Suffektkonsul im Jahre 145 n.Chr.', *Klio* 74 (1992) 246–9

Wolff, H. 'Welchen Zeitraum stellt der Bilderfries der Marcus-Säule dar?', *Ostbairische Grenzmarken. Passauer Jahrbuch* 32 (1990) 9–29

The relevance of some of the above items is apparent from their titles: the new edition of Fronto by van den Hout replacing that of 1954; Holford-Strevens' study of A. Gellius, important for the intellectual background; Rutherford on the *Meditations*. Görgemanns disputes Champlin's interpretation of Fronto, *Ad MC* 4.13 (cf. pp. 93 ff., 226, above). Di Vita-Evrard (*MEFRA*) offers radically new ideas on the Calvisii, Marcus' kinsmen, about which I have some doubts; she has not yet published a further study designed to show that Marcus was closely related to Hadrian. Her paper on Athenian chronology – published only in a summary (*Praktika*), but of which she kindly showed me the full version in typescript – has important implications, if correct: a. that Marcus' youngest daughter, Vibia Aurelia Sabina, was born *c.* 166 (not 170, as p. 248 and elsewhere, above); b. that the trial of Herodes at Sirmium took place in 169, not 174 (as p. 180 f., above). Meanwhile Ameling (who accepts my dating of the youngest daughter's birth) casts doubt on the existence of some of the other children. Wachtel identifies the *cos.suff.* 145 in a new diploma as Antoninus Pius' son-in-law; I prefer to suppose the consul was the son-in-law's father, *cos.*116, *cos.II suff.* 145 – his colleague could have been Lollius Urbicus (cf. p. 275 n.9 above). Piso has demonstrated that *AE* 1982, 777–8 have been wrongly restored to show Marcus and Lucius (in 168) and Marcus and Commodus (in 172) at Carnuntum (cf. 156 f., 174, 228, 249, above); further that 11 June 172 had no special significance. Scheidel offers support for the dating of the invasion of Italy by the Marcomanni to 170 (*Chiron*) but prefers 171 for the Costobocan invasion of Greece (*Historia*), plausibly enough. Daniels provides a plausible redating (*c.* 167) and explanation of the withdrawal from Scotland under Marcus. Stahl discusses Marcus' plans for the territories beyond the Danube again, without adding much of substance. Kaiser-Raiss (pp. 16, 75, 82 n. 72) interprets the medallion PROPAGATORIBVS IMPERII on the same lines as here (cf. p 253 f., above), evidently unaware of my articles cited p. 292 above. Dietz has interesting ideas on the state of the northern frontier at the time of Marcus' death. I am not convinced by Wolff's interpretation of the Column.

Index

I PERSONS

299

2 GEOGRAPHICAL

3 GENERAL